THE MAKING OF
PEAK PRACTICE

THE MAKING OF **PEAK PRACTICE**

GEOFF TIBBALLS

BOXTREE

First published in Great Britain in 1995
by Boxtree Limited

1 2 3 4 5 6 7 8 9 10

Cover and text designed by Millions Design
Photography by Sven Arnstein, Tim Biller, John Brown,
Rod Ebdon, Stephen Morley, Tony Nutley, John Rogers,
Tony Smith and Chris Wedgbury

Printed in Great Britain by Bath Press Colourbooks, Glasgow
for
Boxtree Limited
Broadwall House
21 Broadwall
London SE1 9PL

A CIP catalogue entry for this book is available
from the British Library.

ISBN 1 85283 938 4

CONTENTS

1

Early Symptoms 7

2

From Script to Screen 23

3

Filming in the Peak District 32

4

House Calls 51

5

Case Histories 75

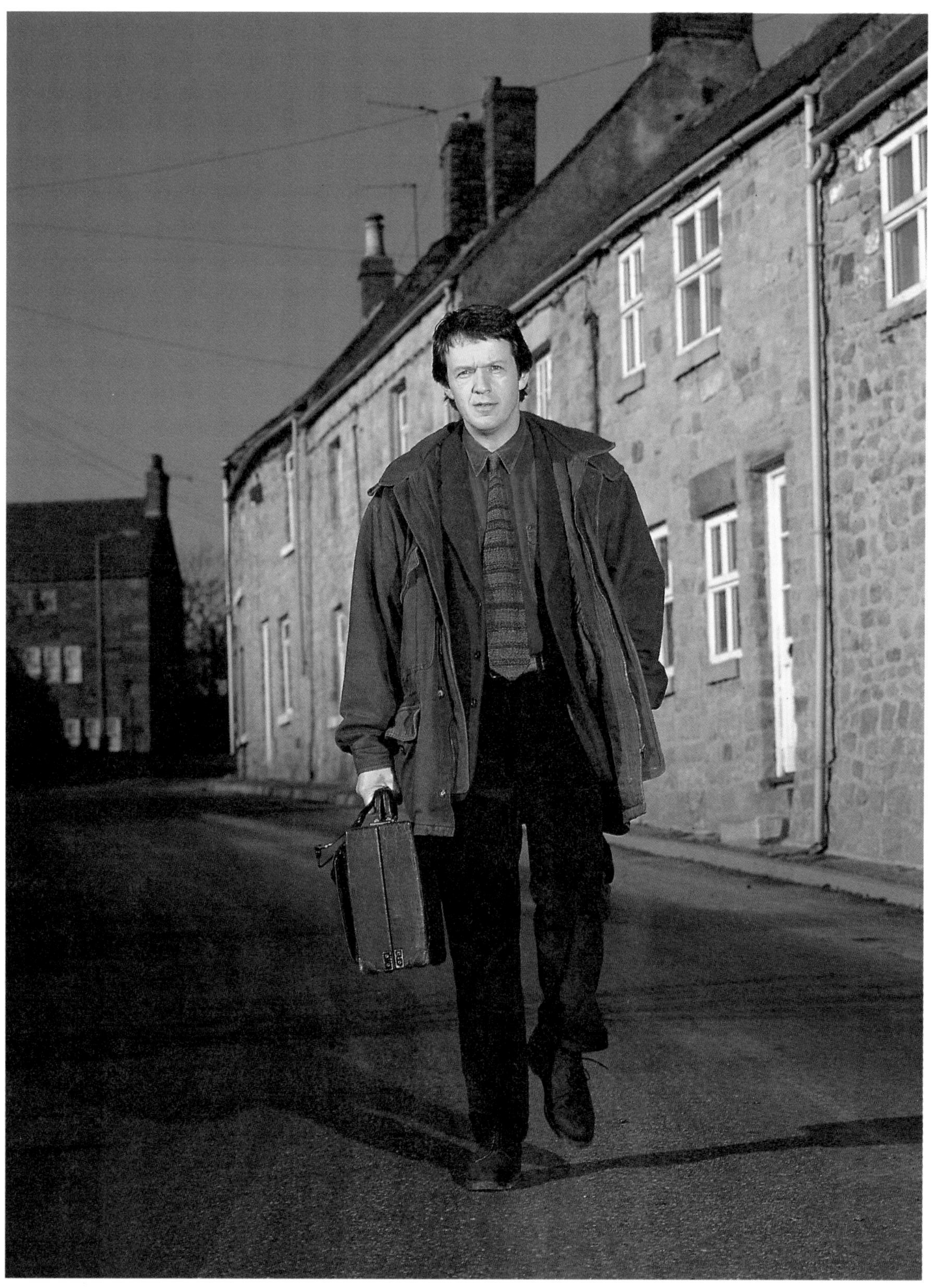

Kevin Whately as Dr Jack Kerruish, on call at Cardale

1

EARLY SYMPTOMS

Inspector Morse was about to tackle his last case. Ken Boon was finally riding off into the sunset. And so the cry went out from Central Films: 'Is there a doctor series in the house?'

Managing Director of Central Films, Ted Childs, knew the very person to approach — Lucy Gannon, award-winning writer of the company's hugely successful 'Soldier, Soldier' and, by a happy coincidence, a nurse for some 20 years before she devoted her energies to writing.

GENESIS OF THE SERIES

'"Boon" was made from Central's Nottingham studios,' says Lucy, 'but with that series reaching a natural end, Ted wanted to continue using Nottingham as a drama base. So he said to me: "How about a medical series based in that area?" He didn't specify any particular branch of medical series but as I began to think about the idea, I became drawn to the potential of rural GPs. Where I live, just outside Church Broughton, a village some eight miles west of Derby, the rural GPs have a mixed bag of patients — not only farmers and villagers but also factory workers from the various plants which exist in the locality. This diversity of patients struck me as particularly interesting.'

The other key factor in the development of the new programme was the impending demise of 'Inspector Morse'. Ted Childs was keen to make further use of the talents of actor Kevin Whately, who had played Morse's faithful sidekick Sergeant Lewis, and so Lucy Gannon wrote the part of Jack Kerruish in 'Peak Practice' specifically for Kevin.

'I knew Lucy's stage work,' says Kevin, 'so when Ted said he was thinking of using her for this new medical drama, I thoroughly approved. I wanted a complete change from Lewis and was delighted to find myself playing someone who is not so permanently nice as Lewis! I wanted to play a character who does things for himself — rather than simply reacting to someone else, as Lewis did. Jack Kerruish is a much more pro-active character. He's full of energy and ideas but he can also seem selfish and uncaring. He is a passionate man and quite obsessive about his work — and this tends to mess up his private life. He's got a lot of sides to his character to explore which makes him interesting.'

THE AUTHOR

Lucy Gannon's background is almost worthy of a screenplay in its own right. Born in Londonderry, her father was in the Army, as a result of which the family regularly moved. Lucy's was a nomadic existence as she found herself trying to settle in such far-flung locations as Colchester, Scarborough, Cyprus and Egypt. It was this life as an Army 'brat' (as soldiers' children are known) and a spell in the Military Police on leaving school which inspired her to write 'Soldier, Soldier'.

'I thought being in the Army would give me the opportunity to travel,' says Lucy, 'but I never got further than Catterick in my two years with the Military Police. It was great fun — there were very few girls and the men spoilt us rotten — but I was stunningly unsuccessful. The trouble was I thought it would be a form of social work whereas in reality it was more like traffic patrol.'

Lucy preferred turning a blind eye to transgressors rather than arresting them, a tactic which ultimately led to her being hauled in before her Commanding Officer. 'He told me: "You've been with us for two years but you have yet to arrest a single person. I suggest you either get into social work or nursing." '

She took the hint and spent the next twenty years working in the health service as a nurse for the mentally handicapped. By 1987, she was in her late thirties, living in a council house at Chaddesden on the outskirts of Derby, working a sixty-hour week, bringing up her daughter and helping husband George to look for a job.

'I was fairly hard up and used to do word competitions for cash prizes. One day, my dad sent me an entry form for the Richard Burton Award. I had been good at writing when I was at school but that was all. I hadn't written a thing since — not even for pleasure. Anyway, my dad said to me: "You're good at writing letters, try this..."

'So I entered the Richard Burton Award, which was offering a £2,000 prize, while I was working nights at the hospital. I used to take my portable typewriter in with me. The other staff thought I was barmy. I actually had to go down to the library and get a play out because I had no idea how they were set out. I know it sounds corny but I'd actually forgotten about it when I heard that I'd won the £2,000 prize. It was a lovely surprise.'

Drawing on her own experiences, the subject for Lucy's winning play, Keeping Tom Nice, was the health service. It was so successful that it was later adapted for television, starring Gwen Taylor and John Alderton. As part of her prize, Lucy was also offered a six-month writing residency with the Royal Shakespeare Company but had to turn it down simply because she could not afford to give up her nursing job. However, Richard Burton's widow Sally, who had been deeply impressed by the play, intervened and offered to fund Lucy through the six months so that she was able to accept the residency.

Lucy's writing career has since gone from strength to strength, and has seen her pick up a host of awards. She believes that finding her vocation comparatively late in life has probably contributed to her success. 'I've got a head full of ideas and characters. If I was 21, it would be a very different matter. I wouldn't have done enough in my life to be able to draw on. I think I'm also a bit more rational and realistic than I would have been twenty years ago. I'm very fortunate in that I find writing easy and love every minute of it. I know I'm very privileged, especially when I look at the number of people who are out of jobs or working in grotty jobs earning two quid an hour. I think writers who sit and say it's all torture are ridiculous and pathetic. Let's face it, if I hadn't won that prize, I would still be doing the bed pans.'

DRAMATIS PERSONÆ

When devising 'Peak Practice', Lucy decided to opt for a small core of main characters. 'I didn't want a gang show like "Soldier, Soldier" so I settled for just the three principals. I was particularly keen to include a strong female character. Some people don't realize that strong women can also be warm and sexy — they think strong means cold. I think the good public reaction to Beth Glover vindicated my decision.

'Having placed a female character alongside two men, it was essential to build sexual tension, not only between Jack and Beth, but also between Will and Beth. That was very deliberate.'

At the start of 'Peak Practice', Dr Jack Kerruish was just finishing a three-year stint setting up and running a mobile clinic in Africa. Prior to that, he had worked for ten

Amanda Burton as Dr Beth Glover

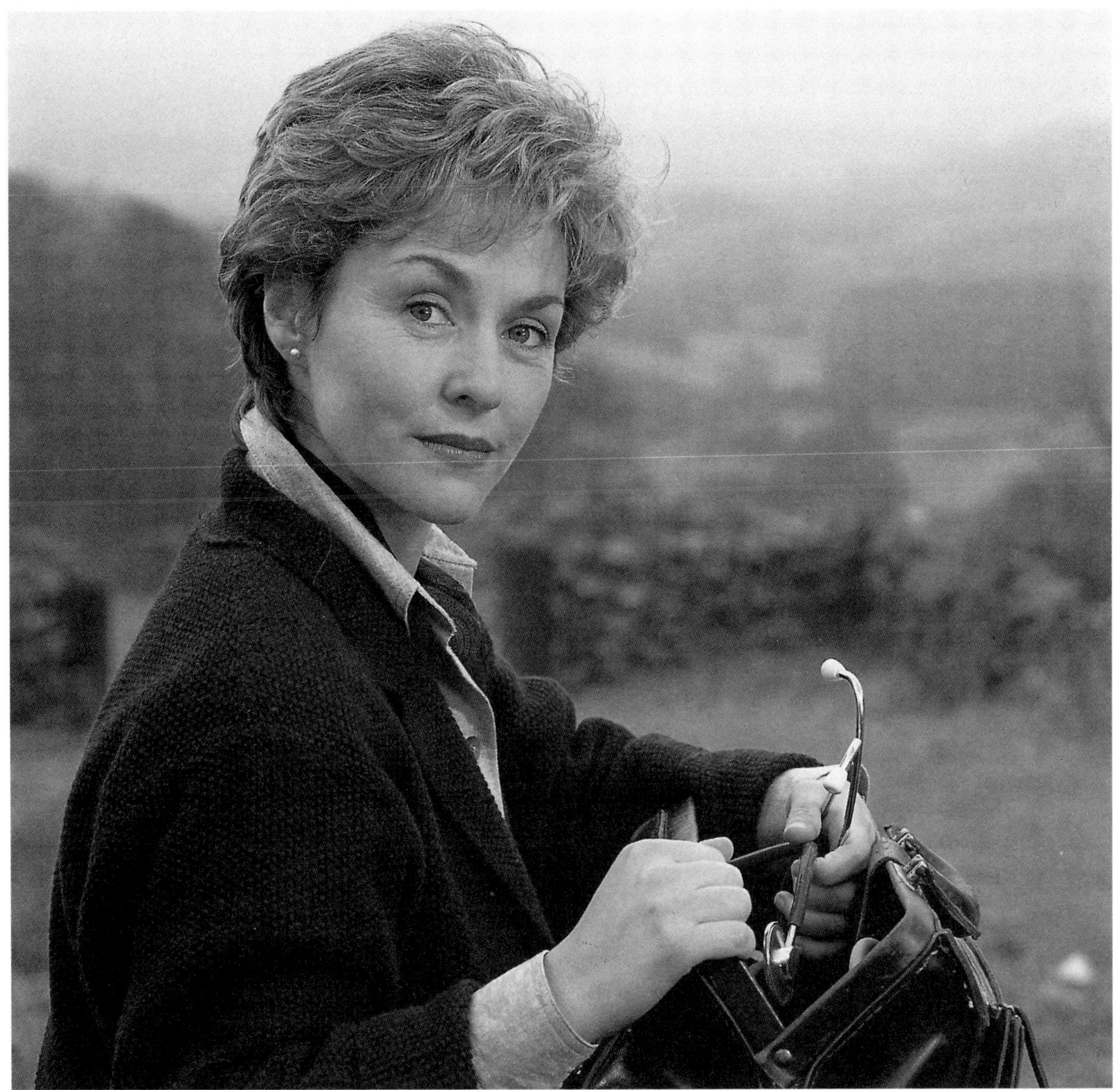

years in an inner-city area. Working as a GP in a country practice offers Jack a fresh challenge in life — and life for Jack is all about challenges. He is very professional and disciplined about his work but his time in Africa, where he is sorely missed by the locals, has given him a dislike for formality. His long hair is testimony to that. A charismatic, dynamic figure, who drives around in a distinctive 1955 Bristol, he can also be stubborn and headstrong with an alarming tendency to behave like a bull in a china shop. But his unswerving belief in what is right and his genuine concern for his patients make him an excellent doctor. Even those colleagues who dislike him cannot help but afford him a grudging respect. Will Preston used to sneeringly refer to him as 'Superman' and once said of Kerruish. 'That man is so honest and above board, it hurts.' Jack is something of a ladies' man but, with one failed marriage behind him (it lasted 11 years), he is frightened of commitment, much to the dismay of his long-term girlfriend Sandy. He also has a selfish and thoughtless side to his nature, but he would never intentionally hurt those close to him: it's just that he doesn't always think before he acts.

Dr Beth Glover took over The Beeches surgery in Cardale from her father and is the senior partner in the practice. She is an extremely good doctor but a hopeless businesswoman. Her fiery nature brings her into frequent conflict with Jack, with neither being prepared to back down. She is independent and enjoys being in charge of her own destiny but does have a niggling suspicion that she would be even happier with a man in her life. When Jack sweeps into Cardale, her well-organised routine is thrown into chaos. She becomes torn between the tantalising prospect of settling down with him and that of keeping her independence and freedom. She finds herself on a roller-coaster of emotion and inevitably Jack is the first casualty of her mood swings. Where work is concerned, Beth is a true professional and would never permit the turmoil of her private life to spill over into her patient care. Consequently, she is regarded by all who know her as a fine doctor.

Public school-educated Dr Will Preston is less committed to the practice than Beth. He likes the medical side of the job and can be very caring but at the end of surgery, he is happy to leave any problems behind and enjoy a game of squash or a round of golf. For Will, life doesn't begin and end at The Beeches which leads to early conflict with the dedicated Jack. Will's wife Sarah, keen to shake off her working-class background, is the ambitious member of the family. They married when he was a handsome, young doctor with the world at his feet but now she can see her dreams turning sour. She would like Will to be more assertive, to realise his potential. She wants him to be a pit-bull terrier whereas he is happy being a labrador. They have two children, Tony and Julian, both at public school, and both adored by Will but their marriage is shaky as a result of Sarah's constant demands. They are constantly in debt because they enjoy a luxurious lifestyle beyond their means. And debts, like diseases, have a nasty habit of not going away unless properly treated.

Lucy Gannon wanted to create a real community for Cardale and so she introduced a number of peripheral characters, each of whom cropped up on a semi-regular basis.

Widow Isabel de Gines is a JP and is well respected in Cardale, having lived there all her life. A bright, independent woman, she is an

The Prestons in happier times. Jacqueline Leonard as Sarah and Simon Shepherd as Dr Will Preston

Sylvia Syms as Beth Glover's confidante, Isabel de Gines

old friend of Beth's family and someone in whom Beth can confide. Before Jack's arrival, she was the one person who would stand up to Beth. Her natural good humour means she is much in demand to serve on committees but, although her life is full, she is searching for something more. A little romance perhaps?

James and Chloe White are the jovial landlords of the village pub, The Manor Hotel, but behind the merry banter lies an element of sadness. For they are desperate to start a family and have been trying for many years without success. They are patients of Beth Glover.

Dr John Reginald is the senior partner in the rival new health centre. He has ploughed a great deal of his own money into the project and views it first and foremost as a business. He is ruthlessly determined to make it succeed and would happily see The Beeches go under in order to increase his patient list. Away from the health centre, he also runs a private clinic.

Dr Daniel Acres used to be the third partner at The Beeches before he was poached by Dr Reginald to join his health centre. Single and flash, the extra money being offered proved too tempting for him to turn down although, on a personal level, he enjoyed working alongside Beth.

Trevor Sharp is the part-time village bank manager, a man very much in the pocket of Drs Reginald and Acres who are pressuring him to foreclose on a bank loan which Beth

The staff at The Beeches (left to right): Dr Jack Kerruish, receptionist Kim Beardsmore (Esther Coles), Dr Beth Glover, former nurse Ellie Ndebala (Sharon Hinds) and Dr Will Preston

has taken out. He is having a wildly passionate relationship with Leanda, a local hairdresser.

Kim Beardsmore is the receptionist at The Beeches. A loyal employee, she appears to be somewhat disorganised but is extremely popular with the patients who find her very approachable.

Ellie Ndebala has been the nurse at The Beeches for four years. Not as outwardly friendly as Kim, she can be very touchy and she and Jack get off on the wrong foot when he criticises her over a dressing she is applying. She has old-fashioned ideas about nursing and finds Jack too flippant. At the start of 'Peak Practice', the health centre is trying to woo her away.

Douglas Hart is a war veteran and retired solicitor. A proud man, he will not admit to ailing health and relies heavily on the support of his cantankerous companion Alice North, a woman feared throughout Cardale.

GETTING UNDER WAY

It was in June 1992 that producer Tony Virgo, who has also produced 'EastEnders', 'The Bill' and 'Perfect Scoundrels' and directed such popular series as 'All Creatures Great and Small' and the Australian soap 'A Country Practice', and script editor Julian Murphy, sat down with Lucy Gannon's draft script.

'It was set in the Peak District,' recalls Tony Virgo, 'but the series itself was earmarked to be made from Nottingham. We wanted to film up in Derbyshire but were told stories of doom and gloom about how we would never be able to film through the winter, how our entire crew would be cut off. It was strongly suggest-

Kevin Whately filming in Zimbabwe for the first episode of 'Peak Practice'

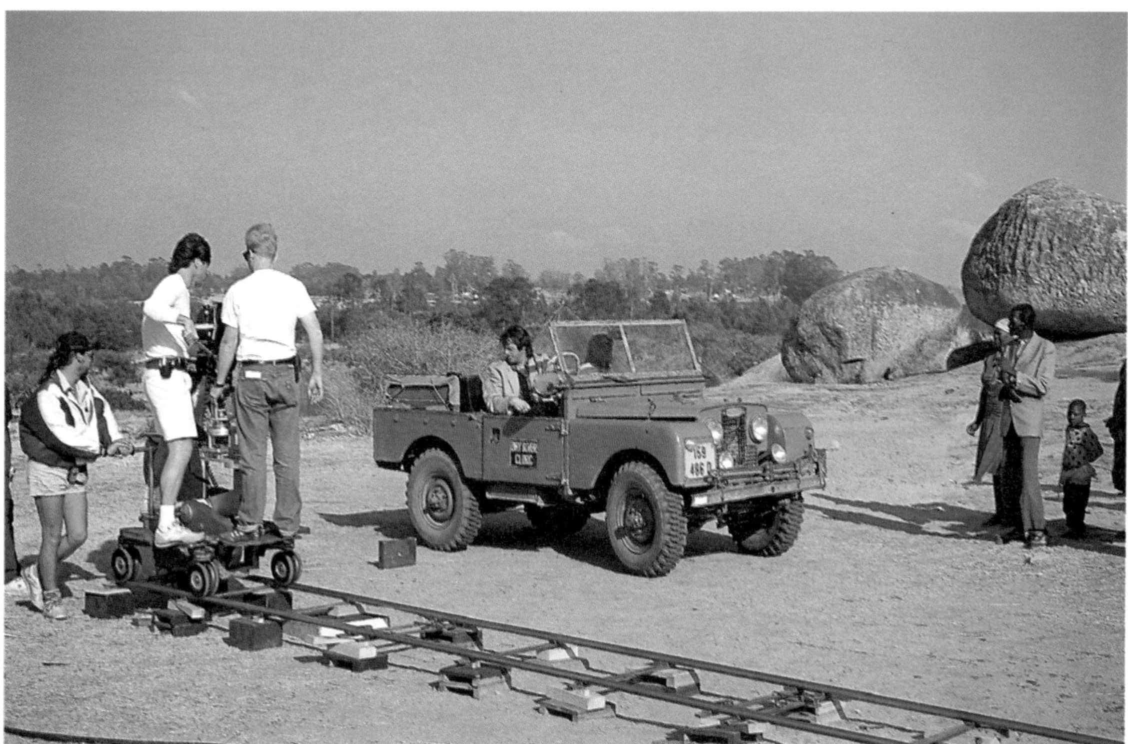

ed to us that we should set the series in the Belvoir Valley instead, but Lucy and I didn't fancy that at all. It looked no different from the Thames Valley — it had no individual identity. So we stuck to our guns and Derbyshire it was.'

Lucy Gannon wanted Jack Kerruish's background to be revealed in episode one and, rather than put it in the type of contrived introductory speech so loved by American mini-series ('You've been in Africa for three years, haven't you, Jack? Did it help you get over the break-up of your 11-year marriage from which there were no children?'), she proposed showing Jack's farewell in Africa.

'We didn't know precisely where in Africa we wanted to film,' says Tony Virgo. 'We couldn't afford to do a recce so all the arrangements were made over the phone or by letter. We considered South Africa but eventually settled on Harare in Zimbabwe. The great thing about Harare was that it was used to having film crews around. There were a couple of American films being made out there, a French crew had just left, so it was like a mini Hollywood. It was a big advantage because it meant we didn't have to educate people as to our needs. Everybody was wonderful and the four days' filming out there only cost £27,000 which is pretty reasonable.'

Gordon Flemyng had been hired to direct that first episode. A vastly experienced director, his television career dates back to 'The Army Game' and has encompassed 'Philby, Burgess and McLean' plus the new ITV series 'Ellington', not to mention Hollywood movies and home-produced films such as *Dr Who and the Daleks* and *The Last Grenade*. 'Gordon is a

Gordon Flemyng directs operations in the evening light of Zimbabwe

great character,' says Tony Virgo, 'and did really well with our hastily assembled crew. I remember though that we had a boom operator out in Zimbabwe who wasn't quite up to scratch. In the middle of shouting instructions to this guy, Gordon marched over and lifted him three feet in the air and turned him to the left — otherwise nobody would have heard any of the actors' dialogue!'

Gordon Flemyng remembers an even more alarming moment. 'The African light can be very harsh. Between 11.30 in the morning and about 2.30 in the afternoon, it casts heavy shadows over the face. So I decided that rather than adopt the standard filming hours of 8am to 5pm, we would start early, at 6.30am, break off at 11.00 and then resume at 3pm and carry on through till 7.00. That way, we would be filming in a much gentler light.

'The first three days worked perfectly and all went well on the morning of the fourth. We broke off at 11.00 and returned to our hotel in Harare, ready to pick up the threads in the afternoon. But while we were lounging in the hotel pool, we suddenly noticed it was clouding over — fast. We began to panic. We still had half a scene to shoot and it was our final day. What's more, we had told Tony Virgo that everything was under control so he had gone off sightseeing to the Victoria Falls. So while the producer was away, we were in danger of mucking everything up!

'We raced back out to the location, which was a good hour from Harare, beneath a sky which was getting darker by the second. Hundreds of miles away in the distance, we could see that it was pouring with rain — and heading our way. To complicate matters, the actress in the remaining scene was inexperienced and so not used to hurrying.

'Somehow we managed to get the shot by the skin of our teeth before it went completely dark. It was just as well because they'd have killed us back in the UK for taking a break in the middle of the day...'

Kevin Whately thoroughly enjoyed the African experience. 'Filming in Africa was terrific,' he says. 'The scenery was absolutely stunning and I loved the people out there. I'd been to North Africa before but never Zimbabwe. I think if I'd have been Jack Kerruish, I'd have stayed.'

CASTING

One of the first considerations on 'Peak Practice' was casting. Julian Murphy says: 'After Kevin had accepted, Amanda Burton was the second to be cast. We had worked together on "Boon" but really she was Gordon's choice.'

Gordon Flemyng says: 'I had just done an episode of "Minder" in which Amanda played a solicitor who was prosecuting Arthur Daley. She was very good so when I moved on to "Peak Practice", I thought she would be ideal for the female doctor. Not everybody was convinced — some people thought she was too glamorous for the part. So I persuaded her to dress down for the auditions. Eventually, they came round to my way of thinking. And I think it's fair to say they haven't regretted it.'

Simon Shepherd had made a big impact as Lord Piers in the Central series 'Chancer'. Julian Murphy says: 'We always wanted Simon to play Will after his performance in "Chancer". But Will didn't have a particularly big part in that opening episode and so Simon was a little reluctant at first. We had to assure him that the role would grow. In the end, I know Simon was glad he signed up and he was absolutely superb when Will was having his breakdown.

'When it came to casting Isabel, somebody threw in the name of Sylvia Syms. Hers is one of those names that is always suggested for a part — rather like Meryl Streep or Mel Gibson — but you're very rarely lucky enough to get her. We were lucky.'

Looking back, Tony Virgo says: 'We must have seen about thirty actresses for the part of Beth. When we decided on Amanda, I thought I'd better buy her lunch to get to know her since we had never worked together before. I took her to a spaghetti house in London but when it came to paying the bill, I realised I had lost my Barclaycard. So Amanda had to pay. What a great start!

'We nearly lost Simon, simply because the final stages of the contract were being drawn up while I was out in Africa. It was simply a question of logistics. It was touch and go but we got him in the end. I think what appealed to Simon was that Will was a bit of a failure in life and was therefore a complete contrast to Piers. In fact, although our three leading actors were all well known to TV audiences, their characters in "Peak Practice" were quite different to those they had played before.

'I had worked with Sylvia on Nancy Astor for the BBC. She was very keen to do "Peak Practice". She admired Lucy's writing and also liked the fact that the show was written by a

Have car, will travel: Jack Kerruish in the heart of the Peak District

woman with strong female characters.

'An early problem on the series was deciding what sort of car Jack Kerruish should drive. The production buyer at Central showed me lots of books but it was so difficult to find something which hadn't been done somewhere before. Kevin fancied a Volvo while I had thought about an Alfa Romeo — if only because I like Alfa Romeos. Then, on the Friday before the first readthrough, I spotted a 1955 Bristol in a street just around the corner from Central's London offices at Portman Square. It looked old and seedy, absolutely perfect for Kerruish.

'I lay awake thinking about it all that night and, so convinced was I that it would be gone by the Monday, that I drove up to London from my home in Berkshire over the weekend to take some photos of it. I thought that at least if I had the registration number, I would be able to trace the car if it wasn't there on Monday.

'Anyway, come the Monday it was still there. When Kevin walked into the readthrough, he immediately said he'd just seen the very car for Kerruish — a 1955 Bristol — just around the corner. So I went straight round there and put a note on the windscreen. The owner of the car phoned me that night and I bought it the next day for £8,000. It has been just right for "Peak Practice" — an English car in an English setting.'

STORYLINES

While casting director Julia Lisney filled in the supporting roles, additional writers were brought in to supplement Lucy Gannon's five episodes — Andy de la Tour (brother of actress Frances), who had worked with Julian Murphy on 'Boon', contributed two and Tony Etchells, who has written for 'Casualty', 'The Bill', 'EastEnders' and 'Medics', provided one.

'I had worked with Tony Etchells on "The Bill",' says Tony Virgo, 'where his scripts were usually about dilemmas — the sort of thing we face in everyday life. That was the sort of input I wanted for "Peak Practice".'

'We were determined to maintain the quality of the scripts,' adds Julian Murphy. 'If a script wasn't good enough, we simply would not shoot it. We'd use a different one instead. We wanted to ensure that artistic standards prevailed in the face of logistic pressure. Occasionally, scripts were held over. The story "Long Weekend", about Jack's schizophrenic ex-girlfriend Karen, which eventually went out as number six of the second series, was originally written for series one!

'The stories came from various sources — sometimes from the cast themselves. The idea that Beth should be assaulted was actually suggested by Amanda Burton. The episode with the car crash in series two was inspired by the film *Wild at Heart*; the AIDS story was developed from a euthanasia episode which we eventually binned and re-wrote; and the epilepsy story came from Gordon Flemyng. He knew a director in the United States who was sacked because he was an epileptic.'

That last-mentioned episode was one which stood out for Kevin Whately. 'I had a lot of feedback from that story,' he remembers. 'In the village where I live, a young girl had an epileptic fit only two days after the episode went out and her boyfriend knew what to do because he'd watched the programme. It's important for us to feature that sort of illness because people can feel very isolated if they're not aware just how many others are in the same boat.'

Another dramatic storyline was based on a personal experience of Tony Virgo. 'My wife was taken ill at home one day. She was writhing on the floor in agony — I think it was probably food poisoning — so I phoned the local health centre and said: "Can you get a doctor out — quick!" They said they would but nobody arrived. So I had to phone up again. The receptionist repeated her promise but still there was no sign of a doctor. In the end, I had to get really angry and when the doctor did finally show up, the first thing she said was: "We've been really busy. I've had to give up my lunch break to come out." I said: "Never mind your lunch! What about my wife?"

'And that saga formed the basis for "Enemy Within", the episode where Beth was too busy to get out to see a young boy, and the boy's father ended up hitting her.

'The AIDS story was particularly sensitive. AIDS in a rural community is a difficult subject and we had a responsibility not to put people off going to their doctor's surgery.'

For the second series, medical advisor Dr Derek Cooke also became an important source of ideas and, in addition, a researcher was hired to scour newspapers for likely material.

Following the success of the first series, which attracted some 13 million viewers, the number of episodes was increased from eight to 13.

'We decided to make the second series a bit

Beth Glover and Lisa (Elizabeth Chadwick) feel the cold in 'Chance Encounter'

harder,' says Julian Murphy. 'Tony Virgo had been influenced by "thirtysomething" and wanted to include longer, more emotional speeches. For the first run, we had been based at Central's Nottingham studios but now we took the plunge and moved the production office to Belper in Derbyshire. Since we were that much nearer to our locations, we were able to go further and see more of the Peak District. Visually, it was very exciting.

'The only problem was that whereas in the first year, the weather had been quite reasonable, for the second series, it threw everything at us. It was often brutally cold, dropping to minus 12 at night. And snow sent our continuity right up the spout!'

Tony Virgo points out: 'We deliberately chose to film "Peak Practice" in winter because we wanted that winter look. We wanted the cold, moorland exteriors to contrast with the warm interiors of the cottages. We wanted to show that living in the country can be just as difficult as living in an inner-city area.

'Having established the characterisations of the three main doctors in the first series, we were able to move on and explore some serious issues — topics which appear in the newspapers every day — although we still maintained a quota of more light-hearted stories. "Peak Practice" is not just about doctors, but about the whole community of Cardale, and the 13 episodes of the second series gave us the opportunity to find out more about the people living in the village as well as those in the practice. Above all, we were able to tackle more adventurous storylines. If anything, I felt that the first series was sometimes a bit too slow. So we speeded things up.'

The result was further critical acclaim and even higher audience figures, with almost 15 million viewers tuning in to see whether Beth and Jack would ever get their act together.

'The producers did consider marrying off Beth and Jack at the start of the second series,' says Kevin Whately, 'but decided against it. They thought it would have made the story too boring. Besides, it was better to keep the audience on tenterhooks for a while longer.'

The decision paid off handsomely. So what is the reason for the show's success?

Kevin Whately says: 'When I finished "Morse", I fully expected never to be in anything as successful as that again. So I was really delighted and amazed when the first run of "Peak Practice" attracted more viewers than the first series of "Morse". I put its success down to good scripts, nice locations, chemistry between the actors and a lot of luck!'

Lucy Gannon thinks the strength is that so many people can identify with the situations. 'We have all played doctors and nurses,' she says. '"Peak Practice" is just an extension of that.

'All human life is found in a general practice and it's something that we all have some experience of, whether good, bad or indifferent. I would love a doctor like Will Preston, Jack Kerruish or Beth Glover, but only in the same way that I'd like the local policeman to be like Jack Warner!

'The characters all have their own problems and shortfalls but I don't think it does any harm at all to show that doctors are human and that they can make mistakes. If "Peak Practice" enables people to feel brave enough to go to a doctor and ask questions, then I think it's doing some good.

'My main priority has always been to make "Peak Practice" entertaining drama. I don't particularly want to educate people but I do feel it is important to have a strong social awareness about those who are watching. After all, we're not dealing with made-up illnesses and diseases. There are going to be people watching who are suffering from them. You have to tackle them in a sensible and sensitive way — I wouldn't want to upset people.'

Whilst Lucy has helped with the storylines for the third series, she is not writing any of the scripts. 'I quit "Soldier, Soldier" after two series as well,' she reflects. 'I feel that my strength is in setting up series. I have devoted two and a half years to "Peak Practice" and now I want to move on to other things.'

The third series, in which Laura (played by Veronica Roberts) replaces Ellie as practice nurse, sees a further increase in the number of episodes, to 15 — testament to the show's growing popularity. There is also a new producer, Michele Buck, responsible for such hit series as 'Gone to the Dogs' and two series of 'Boon'. But arguably her finest hour was the axeing of the woolly-hatted, woolly-brained Benny from 'Crossroads': 'We sent him up to the top of the Christmas tree one year and he never came down again. For all I know, he's still up there!

'The new series begins on Beth and Jack's first wedding anniversary and, in that intervening year, we learn that Isabel has developed pancreatic cancer. She does not recover. The reason we're killing her off is because her role

James and Chloe White (Richard Platt and Hazel Ellerby), mine hosts at the Manor

was almost that of Beth's surrogate mother, acting as a buffer between Beth and Jack. Now they're married, it's different. Married people don't confide in others, so Isabel is a bit of a spare part.

'The ramifications of her death on Beth are huge which enables us to explore Beth and Jack's relationship even more deeply than before. For the first time, we see Beth in a vulnerable light and Jack doesn't like what he sees. So he goes back to Africa to rediscover his roots.

'For Beth and Jack, it's very much a question of will they or won't they start a family and even will they or won't they stay married. Their situation is similar to that of many married couples — "now we're married, is that all there is? What happens next?"

'I think this series will be a bit grittier than before although we're still aiming to keep that balance between drama and entertainment. In my opinion, the strength of "Peak Practice" is two-fold: there is the ongoing element of Beth and Jack and also the free-standing medical stories which people are either curious about, know of, or want to know more about.'

Among the subjects tackled in the new series are plastic surgery, carbon monoxide poisoning, alcoholism, measles, kidney dialysis and donation, and Weil's Disease where rats' urine finds its way into the water supply.

Perhaps the most remarkable aspect of 'Peak Practice' was that it ever got written at all. For no sooner had Lucy Gannon started work on moulding the series than her husband George dropped dead of a heart attack in the kitchen of their home at the age of 58.

She reflects: 'After the first script, Kevin Whately was landed with a writer whose husband had suddenly died. I remember Kevin turning up on my doorstep with a bunch of flowers which was really sweet.

'I used "Peak Practice" to get through George's death and it saved my sanity. I told my agent that I was taking three weeks off, then picked up where I'd left off and got on with it. I said I'd meet all my deadlines, and I did.'

Lucy feels that had her husband's heart condition been detected earlier, his life might have been saved. So she was anxious not to portray the doctors in 'Peak Practice' as superheroes.

'I made sure from the start of "Peak Practice" that I've shown people questioning their doctors. The more pedestals that are knocked away from under these professional people, the better. We, the patients, need to be aware. That's why the character of Jack Kerruish is so important. If he was a sleazeball who made mistakes, people would say: "My doctor's not like that." But they *are* like Jack — credible doctors with feet of clay. He is not incompetent, but there are instances in everyone's life of incompetence. Doctors are just like everyone else in that respect. Kerruish is capable of being arrogant, foolish, clumsy and of following his own prejudices. He is not by any means a hero.'

Lucy wrote her own tribute to George in the episode 'Act of Remembrance' where war veteran Douglas Hart attends a fly-past of Spitfires. 'George was mad on Spitfires,' says Lucy. 'So that was my secret salute to him.

'I went up to Ladybower Reservoir in North Derbyshire for the filming but snow prevented the planes from taking off from Lincolnshire. After hanging around for three hours, we had to do it the following day. It was worth waiting for though. As the Spitfires flew past, I thought to myself: "That was for George. He should have been here."

2

FROM SCRIPT TO SCREEN

Each episode of 'Peak Practice' takes ten days to shoot which averages out at around five minutes of actual screen time per day. It may not sound much but there are usually in the region of 60 scenes per episode and switching from one to another can be a time-consuming business.

Yet the production process actually begins nearly a year before the series is transmitted. That is when the producer, the script editor and the writer get together to discuss future storylines.

'We aim for a story first rather than a particular topic,' says Julian Murphy who served as script editor on the first two series. 'My belief is that if you base drama solely around issues, the result is not realistic. To us, the story was always more important than the issue.

'Each script has a main plot, a sub-plot and running stories. Although it was certainly not conceived as a serial, "Peak Practice" has become more of a serial as it has gone on. This can make life difficult since we shoot episodes out of sequence. We therefore rely a great deal on the continuity people.

'From the original idea to the finished script usually takes between six and eight weeks. Some writers are faster than others. Lucy Gannon is very quick and can complete a 52-minute script in a couple of weeks.

'Time was particularly tight on the second series where we had under two months to prepare 13 hours of television. And at the end of that two months, we had to be ready to start shooting. It was hectic to say the least.'

The finished script goes to the various heads of department. The casting director and the episode director cast the supporting roles, the production designer plans the look of the episode and the location managers seek out likely filming venues. Once these are approved, there is a technical recce attended by the location manager, the director, his production assistant, the director of photography, the designer, the lighting director and property master at which the director explains how he wants to shoot that particular scene. This usually takes place about a week before filming.

By the time filming comes around, the production staff will have sorted out precisely what camera and lighting equipment is required for the shoot. Each day, a call sheet, written by the second assistant director, is issued to check that everything and everybody

Kevin Whately and Sylvia Syms on location in Derbyshire

will be in the right place at the right time. This includes transport to and from the location and, arguably most important of all, location catering without which no film crew can survive — particularly in the depths of a Derbyshire winter.

At the end of each day's filming, the laboratory picks up the rushes and processes them overnight. The sound tapes are also transferred and everything comes under the eagle eye of the editor who puts together a rough cut of the finished article. The director then views it and makes appropriate suggestions. He might ask for certain shots to be put back or suggest that others be taken out. They may feel that a certain section is a little flat for sound, in which case the dubbing editor, who works on sound only, may be asked for something like the bark of a dog, moo of a cow or sound of a tractor to be inserted, just to make sure there is something going on in the background. Finally, the titles and any incidental music are added.

'Each episode is around six weeks in post-production,' says Julian Murphy. 'Overall, there can be as many as eight different episodes at various stages of production at any one time, ranging from storyline to editing.'

It all sounds like a well-oiled machine, but spanners do creep into the works from time to time.

'One of the problems with having a regular supporting cast,' admits Julian Murphy, 'is that it's not always easy to get actors back when we want them. They do their episode of "Peak Practice" and then go off and do other things which means they might not be available. So we've had to re-jig things from time to time.

'At the end of the episode "Old Habits", we had a shot featuring actor Peter Armitage which didn't work. We needed a close-up of him and tried to get him back for another day. But when we got in touch with him, we found that he had shaved off his beard! We had no option other than to re-cut the end and live with it...'

THE CORRECT DIAGNOSIS

'Body language is one of the most important attributes of being a good doctor.' So says Dr Derek Cooke, the Belper GP who serves as medical advisor on 'Peak Practice'. It is his job to ensure that the series is medically accurate and that Kevin Whately, Amanda Burton, Simon Shepherd and any other actors playing doctors appear as much like the real thing as possible.

'That is where body language comes in,' says Dr Cooke. 'It is such an essential part of a doctor's equipment. When we did the consultation scene in the episode "Love Thy Neighbour" where Jack told Chloe and James White that her scan had revealed Stage 4 Hodgkins Disease, I went to a lot of trouble to make sure that the atmosphere was right. I talked to Kevin about how he would break such bad news, how he would speak and, indeed, how he would sit. I got him to sit diagonally opposite the patient — I hate directly opposite because that is too much like going to see your bank manager — and the scene worked beautifully. When the director, Moira Armstrong, said, "Cut!", there was absolute silence. There was hardly a dry eye in the crew. It was very moving.

'On other occasions, I might suggest that Kevin uses a different sort of body language, by sitting on the edge of his desk. It all helps to put the patient at ease. And I would also advise on what body language a GP would use in dealing with a consultant.'

Dr Cooke has been a GP in Belper for 17 years and has called upon his wealth of experience to inject added realism into 'Peak Practice'. 'The medical advisor on the first series came from Nottingham but when the production base moved to Belper for the second series, it was too far for him to travel. So Central began scouting round for local practices. I am a partner in a five-man practice and when Central phoned up, I met the producer,

Dr Derek Cooke, medical advisor on 'Peak Practice'

'The secret of good blood is Camp coffee.' So says make-up supervisor C.J. Wills, who is responsible for creating the wounds and scars on 'Peak Practice'. 'I buy proprietary blood — which comes in different shades — but to make it darker still, particularly for that dried-up look, I add some coffee. It not only looks good, it tastes better too!

'For most wounds, like Will's black eye, Beth's bruised face and the leg wound in the car crash episode, I use Geleffects, which is a mix of gelatine. We tend not to have lots of blood and gore with bones protruding. It's not like "The Bill", where I once had to give a guy who was supposed to have been slashed with a carpet knife, 29 stitches on his face. "Peak Practice" is a gentler series than that.

'For instance, on the episode where the two boys were electrocuted, I did a lot of research, including looking at London Fire Brigade photographs. I knew that after such a horrific accident, the boys' bodies would be badly charred. But in the end, my research wasn't needed because we decided not to go into graphic detail on screen. I think it might have upset too many viewers.'

The make-up department add a touch more blood to actress Samantha Morton, who played the wayward Abbey

One of the make-up deparment's most challenging tasks was the bloody, bruised face of Elizabeth Chadwick in 'Chance Encounter'

Martin Keel (George Irving) takes out his frustrations on Beth in the episode 'Enemy Within'

Tony Virgo, and the script editor, Julian Murphy, and quickly found that we were on the same wavelength. I ended up taking a six-month part-time sabbatical, so I was working three days a week for Central and two at the practice.

'I had never previously had anything to do with television so I had to start from scratch, learning to work with directors and actors. I had a couple of ideas of my own and sometimes they have been taken on board. I have come up with stories that have happened to me and they have been able to use them as secondary storylines in particular episodes, although obviously the main ideas came from Lucy Gannon. When Beth was assaulted by a patient in the episode "Enemy Within", it represented a situation which most doctors have some experience of. The man misinterpreted the situation because of his anxiety and just snapped in anger. I know of a colleague who was threatened with a shotgun by a patient and I have been threatened with a knife. We've also had times when we've had to call out the police to deal with abusive patients. Thankfully, most of the people who come to see me are very pleasant!'

Dr Cooke's advisory role begins right at the start of the production process. 'I talk to the writers at the idea stage and give out notes at script level. For example, when we did the AIDS episode, I was closely involved in the discussions for that. It was so important to get it right.

'Sometimes the production team will ask me to come up with a disease to fit certain criteria. With Chloe White, they wanted a cancer with a good chance of recovery for a young person. So I chose Hodgkin's Disease which very much fitted the bill.

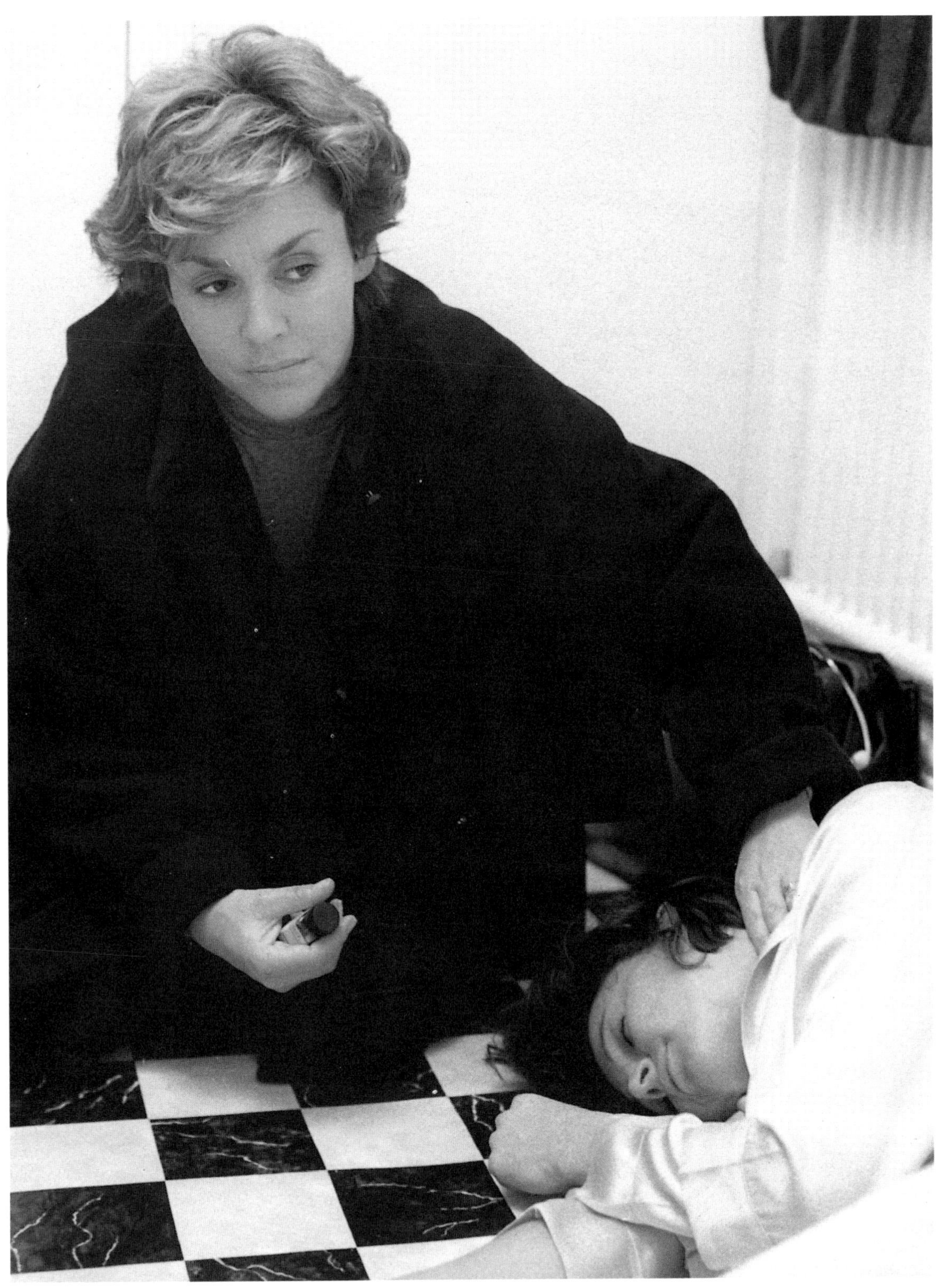

Amanda Burton looks the part, tending the stricken Angie Wilkes (Donna King) in 'Life Changes'

Dr Kerruish dashes to the rescue — with his bag firmly closed!

'We also wanted to do a diabetic story, hence the episode about Abbey the teenage girl. We wanted to portray the misunderstanding of diabetics — how we see a needle and immediately jump to the erroneous conclusion that they're drug addicts. Unfortunately, we received a few complaints from some medical people who thought that the episode didn't give young diabetics much hope, but they were missing the point which was how young diabetics are so mistreated. I hope the episode did a lot of good. The health education message in "Peak Practice" is all important.

'Of necessity, the programme is a fine balancing act between drama and total accuracy. We do have to cheat on timing occasionally but not much else. I have to remember that it is a drama and not a medical documentary. The practice in which I am a senior partner is a fundholding practice — in other words, we are responsible for our own finances, we buy our own services — but if we devoted an entire episode to the issue of fundholding, it would bore everyone to tears. It would be like watching paint dry. So I have to summarise fundholding in a few lines so that we can speed up the action.

'I did actually do a seminar for the cast on fundholding so that they knew a little more about it and so that they could see how their characters would react to the prospect of The Beeches becoming a fundholding practice.

'I think Kevin, Amanda and Simon all look very much at home as doctors. They carry themselves as doctors — they look the part. They're very disciplined. One of my aims is to allow them to concentrate primarily on their acting without worrying about me picking

Manure. It's all part of 'Peak Practice's promise to make sure that the Derbyshire countryside doesn't only look right, but smells right too. It also presents an occupational hazard for dresser Stevie Groves.

'We did one scene where Kevin Whately had to walk through a farmyard. And he had to do it four times which meant that after each "take", it was my job to clean all the cow's mess off his boots. I was really pleased when we moved on to the next scene.

'In the episode "Love Thy Neighbour", the script called for actor Alan David to have his face, hair and clothes covered in pig manure. We got a bag of fake stuff — a mix of peat, straw and water — but, because we didn't think it looked very authentic, we also collected some real manure. Alan David thought we were going to use the peat-based material and got the shock of his life when I plastered him in genuine, 24-carat pig manure! For some reason, nobody seemed too keen to get near him afterwards...'

Jack Kerruish has a talk with pork in 'Love thy Neighbour'

them up on things. Obviously, I have to help them out with some of the tricky pronunciations of diseases from time to time but that's only to be expected. And I've helped them do injections. Even now, Kevin will look over at me to make sure he's holding the syringe correctly. In the episode "Act of Remembrance" when old Mr Hart had to be injected in his knee for arthritis, it was actually my hand, rather than Kevin's, which appeared on screen in close-up doing the injection. And the knee was that of the director, Colin Gregg!

'I also advise the actors on the contents of their medical bags — stethoscopes, ampoules of drugs, prescription pads and so on — although perhaps I should have warned Kevin that they can have a nasty habit of flying open at the most inopportune moment. On more than one occasion, he's grabbed his bag, ready to hare off on a dramatic mission, only for the contents to spill all over the floor. Luckily, he's very philosophical about it.

'I like to go out on location as much as possible. I am still fascinated by the separate stages of production — the different layers of television which make it rather like a painting. Some of my patients and colleagues have tried quizzing me about what's happening in the new series but, like any good GP, I know confidentiality is everything.'

One aspect of television which has particularly impressed Dr Cooke is the teamwork involved in putting together a series.

'Last year,' he says, 'the location manager picked my brains looking for suitable filming sites in Derbyshire. I went out on the "recce" and we were introduced to householders as the location manager, the script editor, the producer and the doctor. Everyone we met must have thought the producer was pretty unhealthy if he needed his own doctor travelling with him!'

Apart from ensuring that everything is accurate on location, Dr Cooke is also on hand in case of accidents on set. 'Fortunately, I've never had to treat anything more than the odd minor cut,' he says, 'although I was a little apprehensive when we filmed last year at the old Devil's Mill at Monsal Dale for the episode "Old Habits". The two young actors playing Tony Preston and Harry Clulow had to sit high up on the fifth storey of this dangerous-looking building but happily all was well.

'In fact, I find that most of my time on location is spent dispensing medical advice to the crew! It's amazing how often one of them will come up to me and say: "Doc, I've had this bad back for years. Can you help?" They are all keen to make the most of a free consultation...'

3

FILMING IN THE PEAK DISTRICT

Amanda Burton still shivers at the recollection. 'I don't think I've ever been so cold in my life!'

The cause of her misery was a night shoot in December up on bleak, barren Beeley Moor, high above the lush green pastures of Chatsworth.

'It was a horrible shoot,' remembers producer Tony Virgo. 'Andy de la Tour had written this episode, "Chance Encounter", set almost entirely at night, where Beth became stranded on the moors after attending to a car crash. It was a real risk even to do the episode with so much night filming at that time of the year. The location was so exposed — it was too windy to put the lights up at first.

'We spent two nights up there, wondering whether we could do it, and eventually we had to make a decision. After all, we had deadlines to meet. We decided to go for it, hoping against hope that it wouldn't rain all the time because filming in the rain is so uncomfortable. In the event, it didn't rain. It snowed instead...'

The cast and crew spent two weeks up on Beeley Moor with Amanda the centre of the action. 'It was well below freezing,' she recalls. 'I was wearing an insulated water-skiing wet suit under my clothes for extra protection but after a few hours standing around on a windswept moor with snow on the ground in the middle of the night, the cold starts to get to you. Our medical advisor, Dr Derek Cooke, was on standby in case anybody got hypothermia.

'It was terrible having to try to act through the blizzard. You're not thinking about what you are there for. Instead you're thinking about the cold. It's not easy. But at least we were able to get some dramatic effect from the snow.

'At one point in the story, I had to fall into a river — and I had to film it three times to get it right. I was absolutely amazed how quickly my hands started to swell from the intense cold. They puffed up like huge sausages.

'There was a stuntwoman available but I decided I wanted to do the scene myself. I'm a tomboy in that respect. Even though I thought I was never going to thaw out, I don't regret doing it. I think it made the whole thing very realistic.'

Everything was not quite as it seemed, however. Having made the decision to film with the snow which fell on the first night, continuity dictated that snow had to be seen for the remainder of the shoot. Since the real snow soon began to melt during daylight, artificial snow had to be brought in.

Filming in the snow, real or otherwise, was a painful experience for Elizabeth Chadwick and Amanda Burton

(Below) Jack Kerruish finds the crashed car in 'Chance Encounter'

The usual type of artificial snow used on filming is a weak dilution of fire-fighting foam but here Tony Virgo went for the de luxe version. 'I imported special artificial snow from Hollywood — six or seven bags in all. It's crunchy, a bit like bath salts, and although it's fairly expensive, it's really effective and gives a good sensation underfoot.'

For Amanda, that particular shoot was a curious one in other ways. 'Beeley Moor had a spiritual atmosphere which I can't explain,' she says. 'A slightly unearthly sensation. But I had a very strange mystical feeling about the spot we were filming — as if I was being drawn down to it — and, oddly enough, the director did too. The whole place had a very eerie silence to it.'

The Peak District has, until comparatively recently, been one of Britain's secret gems.

Kevin Whately filming against the beautiful backdrop of the Peak District

People knew about the Lake District, the Scottish Highlands, Snowdonia, Dartmoor, the Norfolk Broads, the Cotswolds and the Yorkshire Dales but the Peak District remained relatively untouched by human hand. All that has changed. Any summer weekend sees a flood of tourists spread out across the 542 square miles that is the Peak District National Park.

The reason for its newfound popularity is simple — nowhere in Britain does any one area boast such a diversity of scenery. To the north are the wild moors around High Peak and the caves of Castleton; to the west, the spectacular rocks of the Roaches; to the south, lie the gorges of beautiful Dovedale; and to the east, the hills and dales around the Derwent valley. Dotted throughout the region are attractive small towns such as Bakewell, Buxton and Hathersage plus picturesque villages including Hartington, Tissington and Ashford in the Water with the River Wye running through its heart. And all around are walls and cottages of Derbyshire stone — dark and sombre in winter, bright and welcoming in the summer sunlight.

The Peak District is steeped in history. Richard Arkwright, one of the key figures in the Industrial Revolution, built three mills at Cromford, the Bronze Age remains of Nine Ladies Stone Circle sit on Stanton Moor, while well dressing is a popular ceremony throughout Derbyshire. On a more sinister note, Eyam is best remembered for being virtually wiped out by the Great Plague of 1665 which claimed the lives of 259 villagers.

Peregrine falcons and hen harriers soar above the moors, red grouse roam among the heather, sparrowhawks inhabit the dense pine forests and slowworms slither along the warm southern slopes. Little wonder then that, despite the winter weather, the cast of 'Peak Practice' fell in love with the Peak District.

In fact, the colder and wetter it is, the more Kevin Whately likes it. 'It's my sort of countryside — my sort of weather,' he smiles. 'There's a stark, rugged beauty about the Peak District which I never tire of. On its wettest days, it reminds me of Northumberland where I grew up, so I feel very much at home here.

'The only problem with the cold is one of continuity. I remember we did a scene inside a special care baby unit where it was stiflingly hot. My red face had to be toned down so that it matched up with the next scene, which had been shot earlier, where I was outside in the cold and my face was white. Otherwise, my face would have been seen to change colour completely just by walking through a door!

'For me, the country beats the town every time. I'm definitely a country boy at heart. Any time off that I'm given I explore the area and enjoy long walks around the villages and some of the more remote spots. There's nothing like a good walk over the hills to clear your head. And, fortunately, there aren't too many tourists out of season.'When filming started, I stayed in Nottingham but I soon shifted up into the Peaks so that I could take advantage of actually living in the countryside.

'But we didn't want to show the country as an idyllic place. It's harder to be ill here and with the car not working, than it is in the city. It's not "All Creatures Great and Small" and dappled sunlight.'

Amanda Burton is also the outdoor type. 'I already knew the Peak District quite well because during my time on "Brookside", I lived in

Beth Glover takes in the scenery, suitably dressed

Frank Windsor (as Ken Alton) and Sylvia Syms wrap up against the Peak District winter

Manchester and used to pop over to Derbyshire as often as I could. I used to have a jeep in those days and I loved jumping in it and endlessly roaming around the area.

'Recently, I've started going on long walks in the Peaks — serious hiking. It's a great feeling. I managed 16 miles in one go ... but I was shaking when I got back to the car. My aim is to do 30 miles.

'The Peak District is an amazing place. When we start filming, in September, it is like a velvet glove — nothing like the place it will become in a few months' time. The trees are like big ball gowns, hiding the bleakness. That's what I find fascinating about this landscape. It changes so dramatically with the onset of winter.

'I've always loved the countryside because I was brought up in Derry in Ireland. Consequently, I've tended to seek out the wilder parts of England. I live in London because of work commitments but my idea of heaven would be to live somewhere like the Peak District.

'Mind you, I have to wear a huge amount of thermal underwear under my clothes to get through some of the scenes. It's very hard to stand in the middle of a field at 8am with the wind biting, and act in those conditions. It's difficult to look jolly and animated when your nose is blue and you can't feel your toes.'

Amanda is prepared to put up with the cold because she knows that the landscape plays an important part in the series. 'We spend about 12 hours a day for six months filming in whatever the Derbyshire weather can throw at us. It's made me realise that it's a good job human beings are waterproof. The series would lose a lot of character if we filmed it in summer, though. It's not one of those easy, pretty countryside programmes. All that sleet gives it an edge.'

As if the weather wasn't bad enough anyway, producer Tony Virgo ordered extra rainfall for the second series. 'When we began filming,' he says, 'there was hardly any sun. Everywhere looked grey and depressing. So before each scene, we sprayed the roads, houses and walls with water. That way, they reflected the sky and provided a glistening effect and if there was a bit of light, it caught the water and made things look more exciting. If you look closely, you can often see blue skies on screen but the roads are always wet! The water company must have made a lot of money out of us ... '

Finding quiet locations, away from the public gaze, is the domain of location managers Charles Hubbard and Josh Dynevor. 'Crich, which plays our fictional Cardale, is mostly stone,' says Charles Hubbard, 'so when we venture outside Crich for locations, we go for stone buildings rather than brick. We find that when we knock on homeowners' doors saying we're from "Peak Practice", we get a very good reaction. People say it's their favourite programme which obviously helps us since it makes them more willing to allow us to use their homes.

'Touring the area makes you realise what a close-knit community it is around Crich. For the third series, we filmed in a woman's shop in Crich. It turned out that in the first series we had filmed on her father's farm; in the second, at her brother's cottage; and now not only were we filming in her shop but also at her uncle's farm!

'The scripts throw up all sorts of location requirements. It might say two houses with a stream running across the back, in which case I simply follow the bits of blue on the Ordnance Survey map. One of the trickiest has been finding somewhere to film the potholing rescue at the start of the third series. It had to be somewhere which was accessible to a crew of 50 people.'

Some of the potholing scenes were eventually filmed at the underground caves at the Heights of Abraham, Matlock Bath. But the underwater scenes were shot in a new swimming pool.

Producer Michele Buck explains: 'The tanks which are usually used for underwater filming are too shallow. We managed to find a swimming pool that had yet to be tiled and, by building some rocks on top, we were able to create our own underwater cave.'

Another trick of the trade was employed in the episode "Abbey", part of which was filmed on a knoll above a quarry near Wirksworth. Josh Dynevor says: 'We wanted a nice big moon to illuminate the scene. Obviously, you can't guarantee weather conditions and cloud cover on any particular night so, after filming it at night without a moon, we had one added on later at the laboratories. That way, you can insert any size of moon. We used one from somewhere like Hawaii...'

A squat scene for the same episode, supposedly at a large warehouse, was filmed at an old railway shed in Derby. 'Because it snowed,' recalls Nic Brown, the associate producer on the second series, 'we had to provide artificial snow for the next scenes. This meant covering the whole of Crich Square with fake snow.

'It took about an hour to do in all. We try to keep the amount of disruption to a minimum and the locals are usually very understanding, even when we have to ask them to stop hammering or whatever while we're filming.'

Simon Shepherd confirms: 'In the shops and pubs around where we film, people are always telling us how much they love "Peak Practice".

Simon Shepherd as Dr Will Preston, ready for anything in his green wellies

Because it's set in their backyard, they seem to have adopted it as their own series. When the show is on, families and friends like to crowd round and watch it together, even though they've all got TV sets in their own homes. It's like the war all over again!'

One of the most ambitious exterior shoots was for the dramatic mountain rescue at the end of the first series. This was filmed at Curbar Gap, a rocky area, popular with climbers and hikers alike, high above the pretty village of Baslow. The highest point is some 1200 feet above sea level and affords magnificent views over Chatsworth and the Derwent valley.

But one man's view is another man's nightmare. Nic Brown explains: 'Trying to get all our filming equipment up the steep, winding lane was a horror story. Even the Land Rovers struggled. We actually broke the axle of the generator trying to get it up there on the Land Rover. In the end, we resorted to three-wheeled motorbikes to haul up essential items such as hot chilli for lunch.

'The climax of the scenes at Curbar Gap was to be a helicopter rescue. We didn't want sunshine since that would have taken the edge off the drama but we weren't prepared for what we did get — mist and low cloud. Consequently, the helicopter was stuck for a day and a half on the lawn of the Cavendish Hotel at Baslow while the pilot waited for the mist to lift.

'Happily, it did and we were able to shoot the rescue. And the murky atmosphere which still prevailed certainly made it look good on screen.'

Delays are all part and parcel of filming... but some could be avoided. Julian Murphy remembers an awkward afternoon on the episode "Life Changes". 'We arrived in Derby with 22 dancers

Jack and the mountain rescue team descend from the peaks in 'Giddy Heights'

For a particularly tricky scene, doubles are used to stand in for the actors. The canoeing scene in the episode 'Giddy Heights' was filmed at the National Watersports' Centre at Holme Pierrepont, near Nottingham. 'None of the cast could canoe,' says Nic Brown, 'and although we gave them lessons, they were still pretty useless. So we had to use doubles.' In 'Roses Around the Door', actor Wayne Foskett was replaced by a stunt double when he crashed his tractor. The scene, filmed at a farm near Riber, with the sinister black walls of Riber Castle in the background, necessitated the introduction of a small crane to lift the tractor and place it upside down to give the impression of a crash.

Stunt doubles at work in 'Roses around the Door' (above) and 'Giddy Heights' (below)

but couldn't get into the location hall because the guy with the key had disappeared. We all had to wait two and a half hours on the street in the freezing cold.

'The weather is not the only problem with filming in Derbyshire. It is certainly difficult to get transport up to some of the more remote spots and a lack of large hotels in the area means that it's not always easy to get rooms for cast and crew. But the fact that the Peak District looks so spectacular on screen makes all these hassles worthwhile.'

One of the most beautiful spots in the Peak District is Monsal Head which overlooks the Wye valley and the Monsal Dale viaduct which once carried the railway line between Bakewell and Buxton. This stretch of line used to be known as 'Little Switzerland'. It is now popular with walkers. The episode 'Old Habits' required a derelict mill and the location managers came up with the Devil's Mill at Monsal Head.

'Its name derives from its days as a child labour mill,' says Nic Brown, 'but whilst it has a wonderful facade, the interior is in a terrible state. There are holes in the floor and, with a dozen kids running around for the gang-fight scene, we had to cordon off large areas. It was all pretty hairy. I think we were all glad when we finished there without mishap.

'Wisely, we've steered clear of too many scenes with animals although we did use a number of pigs in the episode "Love Thy Neighbour". The trouble with pigs is that they don't possess the herd instinct of sheep. They won't automatically follow the leader. So to try and persuade six of them to follow actor Alan David [who played their owner] down the main street in Crich posed something of a problem. Alan was armed with a bucket of feed which was supposed to prove irresistible to the pigs but they seemed more interested in nosing in the gutter. Eventually, they did move into some kind of formation and we were able to get what we wanted.

'We also had to do a scene where one of the pigs, Alberta, went to the front door of Jack's cottage. Unfortunately, the pig in question was highly strung and we had to cajole it very gently. There were people with boards to channel it up the path and then, to keep it at the front door, we fed it lumps of sugar. No wonder it looked as if it had a smile on its face!'

If there's one thing certain about a wedding day, particularly a television wedding day, it's that something will go wrong. The history of television is littered with marital mishaps — bride jilted at altar; groom's car breaking down on the way to church; best man running off with the vicar, etc., etc. But Beth and Jack's wedding was different. The problems were not on screen, but behind the scenes.

Filmed in the Derbyshire village of Kirk Ireton, it should have been a joyous occasion. It was very much a local affair. The choir came from the village school, the organist was a local magistrate and one of the bellringers was a farmer's wife who lived nearby. There were even a couple of local doctors in the adult section of the choir.

As Kevin Whately recalls: 'The day started really well. A lot of the actors who had been in previous episodes came back as wedding guests so there was a genuine party atmosphere. To take advantage of the best natural light, we filmed all the exterior shots first and then moved into the church to film the actual wedding.'

Then things started to go wrong. Midway through the morning, the generator for the lighting equipment developed a fault so a replacement was ordered from Manchester. Guests, choir, vicar, organist, bellringers, bridesmaids, best man, bride and groom waited patiently. The replacement generator eventually arrived at 3pm but no sooner had everything been set up again, than that too packed in. Finally, at 6pm, with no hope of salvation in sight, the wedding was postponed until another day.

Kevin Whately says: 'So we had Beth and Jack on film arriving at the church and leaving after the ceremony in a horsedrawn carriage, but we hadn't actually said, "I do"!

'We went back a week later and — apart from one of the guests not being able to make it — Beth and Jack's wedding went off very smoothly the second time around.'

Nic Brown laments: 'To have one generator pack up is bad luck, to have two break down is almost unheard of. I think we must have been on some ancient burial ground...'

There's definitely no chance of Beth Glover ever forgetting her wedding day.

A TOURIST'S GUIDE TO CARDALE

The pretty village of Crich stands on a hill above the Derwent Valley, 11 miles north of Derby and four miles west of Wirksworth. It is by nature a quiet little spot, off the beaten track except for traffic visiting the nearby National Tramway Museum, but for eight months a year it is transformed into Cardale, the fictional setting for 'Peak Practice'.

Lucy Gannon, the creator of 'Peak Practice',

The event of the year in Cardale — Beth and Jack's wedding

Is this the start of a bumpy road for Beth and Jack?

Jack comes to the rescue of the diabetic Abbey, a scene filmed in Crich market place

says: 'I wrote Cardale with the soft end of the Peak District in mind. I didn't want filming to end up out in the wilds of Buxton where we could be cut off for half of the winter! Producer Tony Virgo and I spent an afternoon touring suitable sites to play our fictional village. First, we tried the Vale of Belvoir — on the Leicestershire/Nottinghamshire border — if only to confirm our reservations about using it. Neither of us thought it was right for the series. It was too pastoral, too pretty, too prosperous — it could have been anywhere. So we decided that it would have to be the area north of Derby and, after a bit of driving around, we alighted on Crich which is almost a small town rather than a village. Crich is perfect. It is readily accessible for the crew, doesn't become too isolated in winter and — with some lovely stone buildings and mills — it looks good on screen.'

Gordon Flemyng, who directed the first two episodes of 'Peak Practice', had no doubts about choosing Crich. 'People kept telling me there would be a problem with snow in the winter but I said they were worrying unduly. The weather was OK while I was filming there although I gather conditions were much worse for the second series. But by then, I was long gone,' he laughs, 'so it wasn't my problem!

'I saw Cardale as being roughly half the size of Crich so I deliberately avoided shooting all of the shops and houses. I had to be careful with angles and backgrounds so as not to make Cardale look too big.'

Crich certainly boasts some fine structures, among them a three-storey framework knitter's cottage dating from the eighteenth century and a multiple horse trough which once served the needs of the packhorses with their loads of lead and stone. Its famous attraction, however, is the National Tramway Museum, situated in a former limestone quarry owned by George Stephenson. The quarry ceased working in 1957 and the museum opened two years later. It now boasts some 50 trams, dating from 1874, running along a mile-long section of track. Another well-known landmark is Crich Stand, a memorial dedicated to the soldiers of the Sherwood Foresters who perished in the two World Wars. It stands at 950 feet and the views are said to extend from Lincoln Cathedral in the east to the Wrekin in the west.

Crich market place has been the setting for many scenes in the series, notably when young diabetic Abbey was bundled into Jack's car by Dr Kerruish and James White. In the story, the two men had walked a matter of yards from the Manor Hotel but in reality the Manor is two miles away in the neighbouring village of South Wingfield.

James and Chloe White outside the Manor Hotel

'The real Manor Hotel is closed most lunchtimes,' says location manager Charles Hubbard, 'and that is when we do our filming there. It would be impossible to film during normal opening hours. Apart from the crush of fitting in all the crew, people can get rather the worse for drink...'

Beth Glover's old house was situated in Crich next to the Black Swan public house while Crich Foodmarket doubled up as the village bank, run by Trevor Sharp. A few doors along, enterprising owners even renamed their shop the Cardale Fish and Chip Shop. Jack Kerruish's cottage was played by Melkridge House which lies just out of the village centre, a quarter of a mile down Dimple Lane.

The Beeches is also a short distance from Crich, down a road called Bobbin Mill Hill in the village of Fritchley. Gordon Flemyng immediately spotted its potential. 'Filming in a real surgery was obviously impossible because of the time restrictions on our access, but this place looked ideal.'

The house's real name is Chestnut Bank and it is believed to date from 1704. In its time, it has served as a farmhouse and then in the nineteenth century as a Quaker school. When Central first took out a lease on it for use in 'Peak Practice', it was divided into three flats. Over a period of some seven weeks, with careful attention to detail, Central converted it back into one house as a doctor's surgery.

The programme's medical advisor, Dr Derek Cooke, recalls: 'When I saw The Beeches all

The Beeches as it is today

done up, it really could have passed as a typical doctor's surgery. It was so authentic I almost wanted to shout: "Next!" '

Chestnut Bank is owned by the Hudson family. John Hudson, a hand-made furniture manufacturer with a business in nearby Ambergate, says: 'I was very pleased when I saw what Central had done to it. It was nice to see it back as one house, which was something which I had always intended. It has become something of a tourist attraction now, of course, and we get busloads of visitors pulling up outside to take a look at the house which plays The Beeches.'

For the third series, the house serves a double purpose. Since his separation from Sarah, Will Preston has moved out of his old house (which was located in Matlock) and into a flat. The interior of his flat is in a previously unused part of the house above The Beeches although the front door is in the centre of Crich. Such are the wonders of television!

The other new property for the latest series is Jack and Beth's new married home. 'We were really lucky,' says Charles Hubbard. 'On the first day of our search, we saw the perfect place in an estate agent's window. It was a seventeenth century cottage in Old Matlock which used to be a pub called the Wheatsheaf. Anyway we went to see the family who live there to see whether they would be willing to let us use it and happily they agreed. On average, we film there two days per fortnight.

'One of the first things we did was to redecorate it to Jack and Beth's taste. Our production

Chestnut Bank, the house that 'plays' The Beeches, back in the days before television was invented

Nineteenth-century Fritchley, with Chestnut Bank at the top of the picture

designer, Jeff Tessler, showed the family what he wanted to do and they went along with it. So for eight months, they have had to live with Jack and Beth's decorations. But they do have the option of changing the decor again at the end of filming.'

The Prestons' old house in Matlock, a four-storey Victorian building, was owned by teachers Angela and David Moore who were paid the standard rate of £500 per filming day plus expenses by Central.

'We didn't mind relinquishing our privacy,' says Angela Moore. 'We liked the programme and thought it would be interesting to see how it was filmed. And I must admit the money was very useful too, especially with a new baby. In fact, our friends and neighbours were so intrigued that afterwards they all wanted to offer their homes to TV companies.

'Having said that, the first day was such a shock. We came home from work to find our living room redecorated, our furniture replaced with hired items, and more than 100 people in our house and garden filming a house-warming scene. But it's amazing how quickly you get used to things. Soon we just looked on it as being "Peak Practice" day.'

In return for their fee, the Moores agreed to keep their house available throughout the series for a minimum of six days' filming and to allow rooms to be redecorated and refurbished while their belongings were put into storage. For their part, Central promised to leave the home as they found it and to repair any damage caused during filming.

'Since we moved in, we had been trying to decide how to decorate it,' adds Angela Moore. 'Having the film crew in solved the problem without us having to lift a paintbrush.

'We were never barred from the house during filming. I used to potter about in my dressing gown in the kitchen while rehearsals were going on. I've been pinging on the microwave, warming baby Daniel's breakfast, while Simon Shepherd and Jacqueline Leonard were practising their lines.

'The only drawbacks were that we missed our books and videos which were packed away in storage and because there wasn't enough room to move about, we had to put tables in the hallway in the evening. And there was always a queue to get to the toilets. We got through a lot of loo rolls when they were here.'

4

HOUSE CALLS

DR JACK KERRUISH

The dynamic, buccaneering Dr Jack Kerruish has a confession to make — for years he has been scared of needles. Indeed, actor Kevin Whately can remember the precise moment that the fear took hold.

'I was playing a doctor in an episode of "Hazell" and I had to give an injection to another character. The actual injection was off camera. I was playing to the camera and looking her in the face but when I glanced down afterwards, I got the shock of my life. I had stabbed the poor girl with the needle and drawn blood!

'Since then, the sight of a needle going in has made me go weak at the knees. But I think things may be getting better. Back in September, when I had my jab to go to Africa, it didn't bother me at all. So perhaps I've finally overcome my fear of needles.'

What makes Kevin's dread of the jab more surprising is that he once harboured ambitions of becoming a doctor.

'After I finished my "O" levels, I fancied being a doctor. It was something that I had wanted to do for several years. My best subject at school was biology but unfortunately my chemistry was appalling. In the end, I was put off by the thought of having to wait another eleven years till I was a fully qualified doctor. I didn't like the thought of that much studying so it was a combination of that and my inability at chemistry which turned my head away from medicine to acting.'

Raised near Hexham in Northumberland, 44-year-old Kevin says it was his sister Alison who first got him interested in acting. 'When she was young, she used to write little plays and persuade me, my other sister Hilary and my brother Frank to perform them in an old garage. Our parents, the neighbours and anyone else who was mad enough, came to watch us.'

Kevin Whately outside The Beeches

Playing the doctor: Jack treats the injured leg of Wayne (David Harrison) in 'Old Habits'

It was a happy childhood but Kevin's world was torn apart when he was 17 by the death of his father. 'Dad had been in the Navy and came back from sea when I was just a youngster. He had a couple of heart attacks not long after and even though he had to take things easy, I wasn't really aware that he was in any particular danger.

'Then suddenly he was gone. It was a big loss. I was just getting to know him really well. When you're approaching manhood, I think you need a role model.

'Our family doctor was around a lot when Dad died and he was tremendous — always cheerful and kind. I remember that whenever he looked at us youngsters to give us flu jabs or whatever, he would hum quietly. In his job, he used to drive miles all around the countryside but he always came out whenever you needed him. I had great respect for him and I think this contributed towards my desire at that time to become a doctor myself.'

Kevin left school at 18 with nine 'O' levels and three 'A' levels. He teamed up with a pal, Andy McKay, to form a folk duo, playing guitar and banjo. They spent a year touring pubs and clubs in Ireland and, on their return, won a talent competition in Carlisle. This led to an appearance on the local television programme, 'Look North'. 'After that, whenever they were short of a news item, they just rang us up and we went on.'

While Andy was persuaded to take on a sensible career, Kevin set about purusing his growing interest in acting.

'My maternal grandmother had been a music-hall singer, but otherwise nobody in our family had thought of working in the theatre. I'd never considered it either until a talent-spotter had seen me in a school play and suggested that I might consider it as a career.'

However, the careers advisor in Newcastle dismissed such pretensions and arranged for Kevin to join a firm of accountants instead. Kevin surrendered quietly.

'I was with the accountants for three years and it was pretty awful. Then I joined the People's Theatre in Newcastle and did acting at night. That was great, such a contrast to my day job. With growing up in the Northumberland countryside, I had spent more time with dogs than with other people. So it was a great release being able to get up and act. As time went on, I realised that I was living for my nights.'

Despite the fact that he had passed all his accountancy exams and was held in high regard by the firm he worked for, Kevin was determined that it would be an actor's life for him. He said goodbye to the world of accountancy and won a place at London's Central School of Speech and Drama. He rented a spartan bedsit in Swiss Cottage and paid his way through drama school by busking.

'I used to sing in Tube stations but the police were always after me and I was arrested twice. The first time, I was fined £2. The second time, I read out a speech in court about how buskers made commuters feel happier on Monday mornings. The magistrate took pity on me and only fined me £1.'

On leaving drama school, one of Kevin's first TV roles was that of a miner in the popular BBC series 'When The Boat Comes In' which starred James Bolam as Jack Ford. Playing the part of Ford's girlfriend, Dolly, was Madelaine Newton.

In 1981, Kevin and Madelaine appeared at Newcastle together in a play entitled *And A Nightingale Sings*. 'Madelaine was a big star at the time and had the lead in the play. I had a very small role. As soon as I met her, I liked her. There was an instant affinity. Within a week or so, we got together and have been ever since.

'The most remarkable thing was that we hadn't met before. Madelaine was born in Hexham, only five miles from where I grew up, and just a week after I was born! All I know is that when our paths did finally cross, it was the luckiest thing that ever happened to me. It may sound corny, but as well as being my wife, Madelaine is my best friend.'

Still in 1981, Kevin appeared in a couple of episodes of 'Coronation Street' as a Geordie lorry driver. 'Although I'd had some good parts in the theatre by then, I hadn't done much TV so this was a good break for me. I had to chat up a waitress in Elsie Tanner's cafe before driving my lorry out of Weatherfield for good!'

Little did Kevin know it at the time, but his big break was just around the corner.

Franc Roddam dreamed up the idea for a series about a gang of British building-site workers who escaped native unemployment by joining the exodus to Germany. It was taken up by writers Dick Clement and Ian La Frenais, the men responsible for 'The Likely Lads' and 'Porridge', and given the title 'Auf Wiedersehen, Pet'.

Clement and La Frenais created a motley crew of seven, at the core of which were three Geordies. The producers were looking for relative unknowns and Kevin landed the role of the naive Neville, a fresh-faced chippie, recently-married and desperately homesick, an innocent abroad.

They were an odd bunch. Apart from Neville, there was the leader of the gang, the philosophical Dennis (played by Tim Healy); Oz, a trainee psychopath (played by Jimmy Nail); Barry, the boring Brummie electrician with a face like a potato (played by Timothy Spall); womanising Wayne, the Cockney carpenter (played by Gary

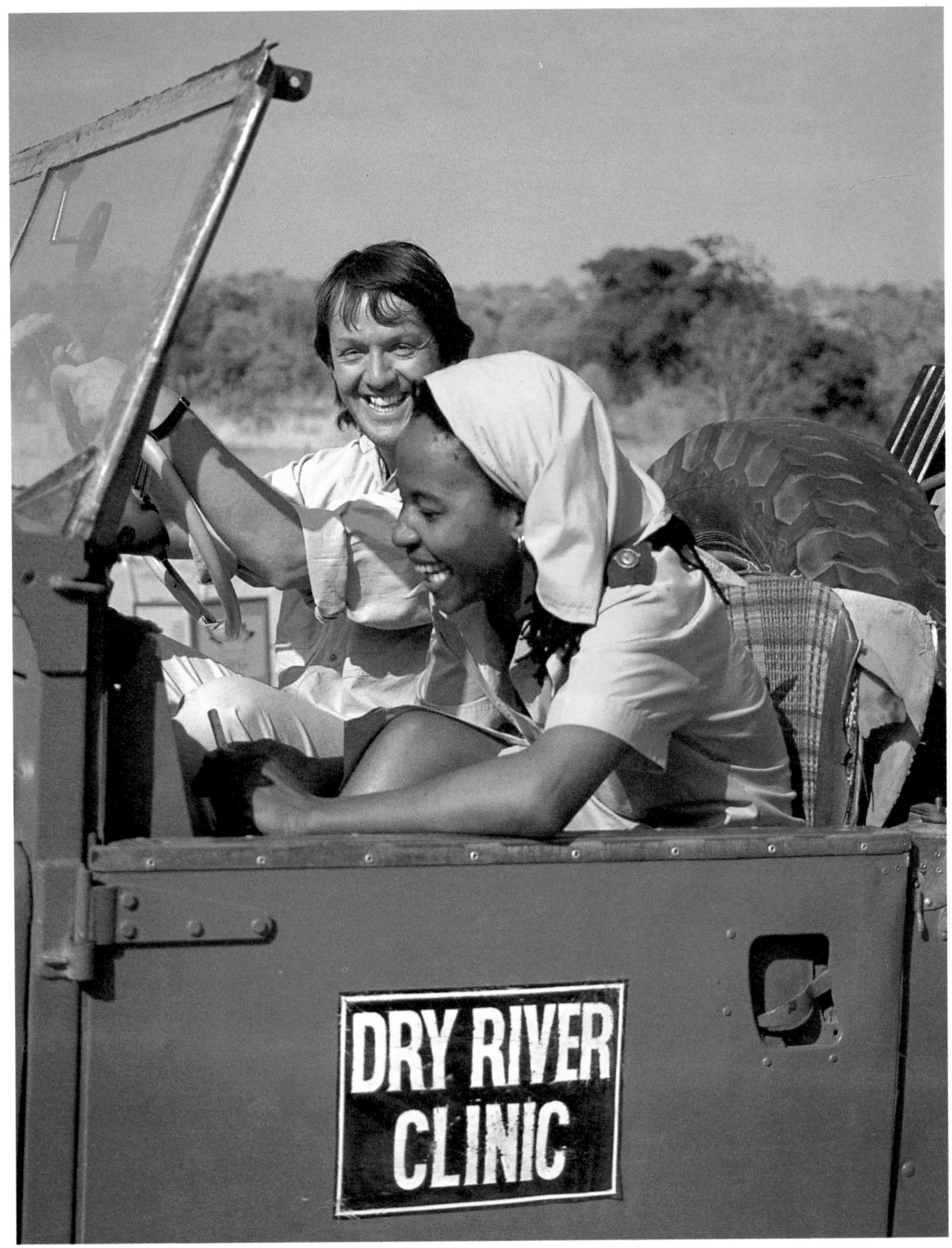

Out in Africa: Jack Kerruish with Sisu Walanda (Agatha Husle)

Holton, who died during the making of the second series); former west country wrestler Bomber (Pat Roach); and Moxey, a Scouser and part-time arsonist (Christopher Fairbank). Compared with the rest, Neville was an absolute saint.

Produced by Central, 'Auf Wiedersehen, Pet' became a runaway success. The magnificent seven captured the hearts of the nation, even those needing sub-titles to decipher some of the regional accents. The cast were plunged into the limelight. It was Kevin's first taste of fame and he relied heavily on Madelaine who also had a part in the series as the girlfriend of Dennis. The show turned into a real family affair for in the second series, which was set in Spain, Kevin's two-year-old daughter Catherine appeared as Neville's daughter.

'Madelaine was fantastic at helping me cope with the recognition on "Auf Wiedersehen, Pet". I'm terribly shy and I grew a beard in the hope of remaining anonymous. I stayed at home a lot while Madelaine did everything for me. She was marvellous.

'I still keep in touch with most of the guys from the show. We were a pretty undisciplined lot but the anarchy in the group was somehow captured on TV. The producers and directors had to put up with a hell of a lot from us but the end result made it all worthwhile.'

The stars of 'Auf Wiedersehen, Pet' were immediately in demand for other projects and Central wasted no time in snapping up Kevin to play Sergeant Lewis alongside John Thaw's Inspector Morse in the television adaptations of Colin Dexter's novels.

Neville's tousled hair, jeans and T-shirts were replaced by Lewis's sober suits and slicked-back hair. Overnight, Kevin aged ten years.

It was by no means Kevin's first foray into the force. He had played an equally downtrodden sergeant in the Miss Marple story, 'A Murder Is Announced', and had also appeared as a constable in an episode of 'Juliet Bravo'. 'The thing which first attracted me to "Inspector Morse",' says Kevin, 'was that it wasn't a conventional, action-packed cops and robbers drama. It also had the advantage of being filmed in Oxford which meant that I could get home to Bedfordshire after each day's shooting.'

It was an added bonus for Kevin when Madelaine was cast in the 'Morse' episode, 'Masonic Mysteries', as the Inspector's lady friend, Beryl Newsome. 'Since we've both got similar accents and are about the same age, it's inevitable that we've often been cast in the same productions. What is odd is that my wife seems to play other people's girlfriends when we've been on television together,' laughs Kevin. 'Not that we actually worked together as such on "Morse" since Madelaine's character was fatally stabbed before Lewis arrived on the scene!'

Kevin played Lewis for six years. 'I think it was good to end when we did. In fact, if anything, I think we should have called it a day a year earlier. There's something discouraging about going back to the same part year after year.'

Although they knew they would have to lose 'Morse', Central did not want to lose Kevin and discussions were held to design a new vehicle for him. The result was 'Peak Practice'.

'From the start, we wanted Jack to look quite different from Lewis,' says Kevin. 'Obviously, it's still my face but at first he had quite a scruffy appearance with long hair. This was because he had been in Africa for three years and had turned into an ageing hippie.

'It was one thing wanting a complete change from Lewis but in a way, it was quite unnerving. In "Auf Wiedersehen, Pet", there was a big crowd of us and with "Inspector Morse", John Thaw always felt like a safety net. He carried the weight of the series. If there was any flak, it would fly in his direction. But when we started "Peak Practice", I felt very exposed because, for the first time, there was nobody for me to hide behind.'

The unassuming actor had more cause for concern when, shortly before the first series of 'Peak Practice' was screened, John Thaw's successor to 'Morse', the much-vaunted 'A Year In Provence', was roundly panned by critics and public alike.

'John and I had talked about "A Year In Provence" while we were filming the final series of "Morse". He thought it was excellent and was full of optimism. It just shows, you never know what the reaction will be.

'Being in a show as successful as "Morse" doesn't guarantee anything. It doesn't matter how famous or popular you are, if the story isn't right and the ingredients don't mix, you've had it. John was unfortunate in that the first episode of "A Year In Provence" went out the day after "Morse" finished. People had no time to change gear in their brain and see him differently. I had a three-month gap which gave people a bit of a rest from me. Nor was I as high profile in "Morse" as John was. The higher profile you have, the more difficult it becomes to do something new.

'There was something very comfortable about doing "Morse" because you knew that it was always going to be good and once it was established, it had a built-in success factor. With "Peak Practice", I was starting from scratch.'

Chloe White (Hazel Ellerby) and daughter Sarah Jane (Kendal Wood) visit their friendly GP

As it transpired, Kevin had nothing to worry about. 'Peak Practice' has furthered his reputation as one of our finest and most popular actors. 'I was gobsmacked by the size of the audience,' he says. 'People just seem to love it. My elder sister, who is a doctor's receptionist in Surrey, tells me she really enjoys "Peak Practice". And she hated "Morse"!

'Jack's character is closer to mine than Neville's or Sergeant Lewis's were. He's more like me emotionally and idealistically, and he's also in a similar position in his life. He's worked in various aspects of his profession and found his niche. I feel I've done that too. I like him a great deal but I suspect if I was playing Hitler, I'd find something in him that I could empathise with!'

Kevin talked to his own local GP to learn more about the behaviour of a country doctor but declined the offer to sit in on surgery. 'I didn't really want to know too much, because I wanted to create the character myself. The one thing I did find interesting about doctors is the way they can sound sympathetic, but at the same time keep slightly at arm's length so that they don't get involved with their patients.

'Our medical advisor was always on hand to spot any slip-ups, like the time I held the stethoscope the wrong way round!

'First and foremost, "Peak Practice" is entertainment but I'm glad it educates at the same time. One of the problems with our health service is that people don't question their doctors — partly because medicine is such a mystery — so they treat what doctors say as gospel. But it's not a particularly healthy attitude and that's why, in "Peak Practice", all three doctors are flawed.

'Having said that, I suppose a part of you has to believe that your doctor is God or Superman, that he'll always be able to sort you out whatever the problem. We tend to believe that doctors have a magical quality about them and I think that must be part of their appeal on television. Humans in crisis always make good drama.'

Playing Jack Kerruish has certainly rekindled Kevin's interest in medicine. 'I find myself reading all the medical articles in newspapers and absorbing all manner of mindless statistics. I'm pleased that a lot of the stories we have covered are subjects which subsequently hit the headlines. I think it gives the series a very realistic feel.

'Doctors do a really marvellous job and working on "Peak Practice" has shown me just how important they are in the community. I have a lot of admiration for them — it must be awful knowing that if you make a mistake at work, someone could die. I could never handle that. I met my own GP out walking one Sunday morning. I noticed she had her mobile phone with her, on call ready to dash off at a moment's notice. She couldn't relax properly, knowing she was only one call away from an emergency. I hope we manage to capture some of that tension on "Peak Practice".

'I think my favourite episode to date has been the one where Jack had to tell Chloe White that she had Hodgkins Disease. That was a particularly strong story.'

In 'Good Faith', the story of young asthma sufferer Penny revived painful memories of Kevin's own childhood. 'When I was about five, I started having dreadful attacks and found myself fighting for breath and falling over in a wheezing heap. Watching actress Sara Cragg, I was reminded of my own pain when I used to feel my air passages tightening and my chest heaving. Fortunately, it never got so bad that I was hospitalised and the condition started to clear up when I was 11. Now asthma hasn't troubled me for many, many years.'

Kevin is unsure as to what the future holds for Beth and Jack. 'He really loves her and was desperate to get married but he's the sort of person who, once he's got what he wants, moves on to something else. The only thing that is certain is that with two such forceful characters, it's bound to be a volatile marriage!'

Kevin's own home life contains no such doubts. He is devoted to Madelaine and children Kitty, now 12, and Keiran, 10. 'I try to spend as much time with my family as I can. I hate being away from home for too long but unfortunately that's an occupational hazard with acting. And with Madelaine sometimes away working too, our lives take a bit of juggling.

'I was delighted when Madelaine was cast in the "Peak Practice" episode "Giddy Heights". She played a mountain rescue ranger who had the job of trying to lick Jack into shape when he volunteered to join the group as their medical expert. We shot the scenes in one of the most beautiful areas of the Peak District. It was nice to share with Madelaine some of what had been keeping me away from her and the kids.

'I don't think the kids are too impressed with seeing me on television, particularly when they see me kissing Amanda. It must be strange for them watching me kiss another woman but I think they realise it isn't for real. Even so, if there is a romantic scene, they want to switch off. Their reaction is simply: "Yuk!" '

Kevin remains very much a reluctant star. 'Fame changes your life a lot. Some actors handle it well but I find it overwhelming. John Thaw's the same as me. We both put ourselves in a public situation as little as possible. Sometimes it can be

Kevin Whately's wife Madelaine Newton joined him for the episode 'Giddy Heights'

quite difficult when you're trying to make a quick dash around the supermarket or you're out with the family, and you suddenly start getting pestered for autographs. I do get asked to do lots of after-dinner speaking but that would be my idea of hell.'

He knows the ideal place for getting away from it all — his childhood home of Northumberland. 'We usually stay with Madelaine's sister who is married to a farmer and lives in a remote area of the Cheviot hills. It's a hard life, working the land, but for us, as visitors, it's an idyllic world with lots of animals for the kids to enjoy, and good food and talk around the big kitchen table. It's just the kind of life I love.

'I could never have got so far without Madelaine's support. She's kept the home together while I've been working. She has been absolutely invaluable. That's why I really am happiest at home with my family.'

Are you listening, Jack Kerruish?

DR BETH GLOVER

For four years, Amanda Burton played everyone's favourite accountant, Heather Haversham, in 'Brookside'. Grown men were reduced to tears as the beautiful Heather proved to be desperately unlucky in love. Twice, she was cheated on from a great height. First husband, Roger Huntington, had an affair and second husband, Nicholas Black, was a secret drug addict, a condition which led to his untimely death. The nation mourned — not for Nick, but for poor Heather.

Now the public are enduring similar agonies over Amanda's latest character, Beth Glover. Will her turbulent relationship with Jack Kerruish calm down now that they are married? Will their

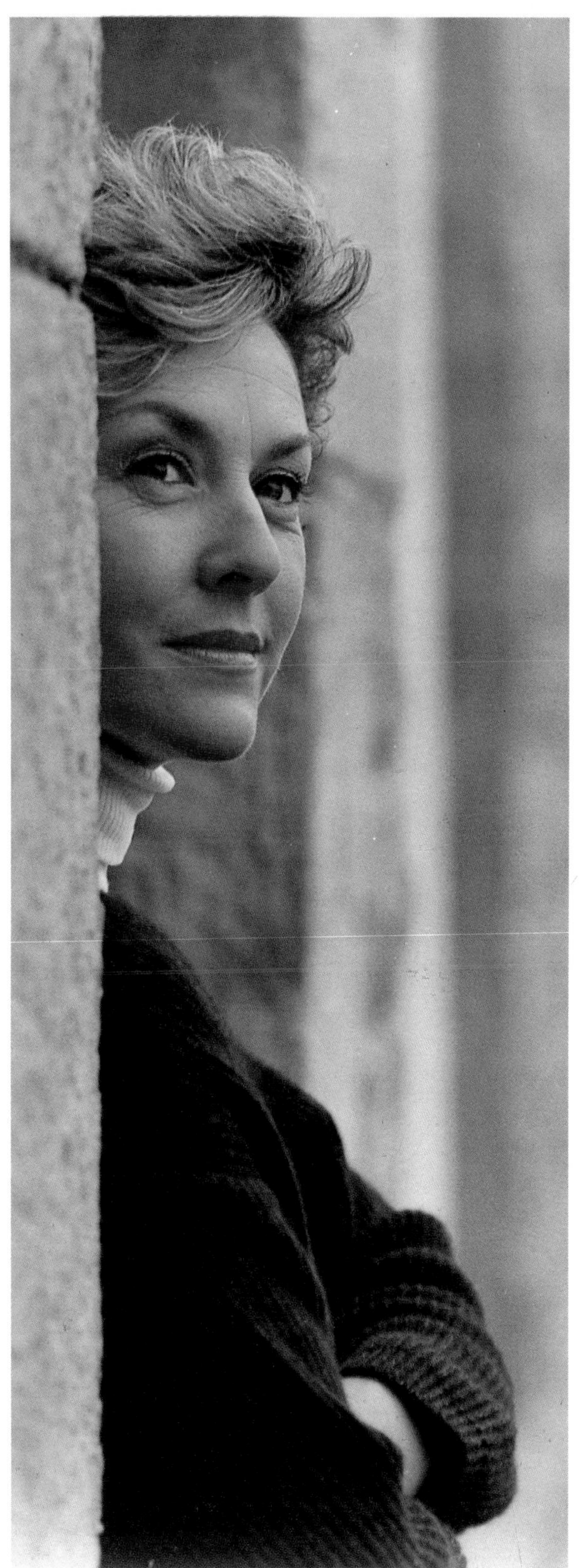

Beth Glover considers her future

They make a lovely couple — when they're not fighting

marriage even survive? And if it does, will there be the patter of tiny feet? The nation waits.

'They're both strong personalities,' admits Amanda, 'so it wouldn't exactly be a union made in heaven. Beth's no Sindy homemaker. There are things which they have to address a year on into marriage. For example, the matter of Beth's age comes up when the question is raised about starting a family. If they do stay together, there'll be a lot of in-house fighting. I think relationships at work can be extremely inadvisable.

'Having said that, I think their relationship is no more rocky than any which addresses big life changes. For Beth, it's an interesting journey since she has never been a particularly maternal woman.'

Amanda is full of admiration for Beth. 'She's very honest, hard-working and very straight. She doesn't mess people around. And she's a first-class doctor. She's got a dry sense of humour but she can also be very cutting. She's a stubborn and independent woman who doesn't suffer fools gladly.

'She is a much earthier and more mature character than Heather who wouldn't have been seen dead in the countryside. Heather was a real townie and was happiest jumping in and out of sports cars!

'The thing which first attracted me to the role of Beth was her strength of character. I like the fact that she is very much her own woman. I like her independence. It's something I have. My mother brought me up — brought us all up, I've got three sisters — to think there was nothing we couldn't do.

'I could never imagine playing a character who isn't strong — after all, Heather was no shrinking violet. A lot of series are fronted by men. They are given the push and drive in a series and the women are the romantic interludes. I'm lucky with Beth. She's a character who knows her own mind and isn't afraid to speak it. She was a well-defined character right from the beginning and has lost none of her rough edges.

'At the same time, Beth can also be quite vulnerable and has a very sensitive side, so she has a whole range of emotions to explore. She's a great character to play.

'I'll admit that I was always worried how Beth and Jack got together quite quickly — that jarred with me — but I think there's a more normal timespan now. They'll never be completely in harmony. They'll always spar — but that's what makes the drama. I'm pleased that there is still a lot of tension in their relationship. It's much more interesting to play out this sort of relationship than to portray an easy-going partnership. Watching a happy couple is like watching paint dry.'

Amanda was raised near Derry, Northern Ireland, one of four daughters. Her father was a headmaster and her grandfather, W.A. Burton, a well-known artist whose speciality was architectural drawings. Her parents were also keen amateur actors and this interest was passed on to the young Amanda who envisaged the stage as her future career right from an early age.

She enjoyed a delightful childhood in rural County Derry. 'I had a wonderful godmother called Ivy Moore who lived in a grand house on a huge estate. Every year, she gave a birthday party for her daughter and I'd be invited. I can remember at one such party wearing a blue dress which had been made by one of my aunts in England for her daughter and had been passed on to me. It was absolutely lovely — even the underskirt had forget-me-nots embroidered on it. I can still remember sitting in my fairytale dress feeling absolutely beautiful. There was a huge feast of marble cake and meringues as big as a fist. It was a wonderful day. And I've still got the dress...'

At 18, Amanda left home to study drama at the Manchester Polytechnic School of Theatre. Although it took her a step nearer her chosen goal, at the time it was quite a wrench. 'I was very homesick — a blubbing wreck,' she admits.

Having completed her studies, she joined the Octagon Theatre, Bolton, as assistant stage manager. 'I'll never forget the excitement of my first wage packet. I spent it all on a pair of Italian designer boots. They cost £50 in 1976 which was a small fortune in those days. I've still got them too — and they're still looking good!'

Further theatre work brought Amanda to the attention of those casting for the new Channel 4 serial 'Brookside'. She stayed with Brookside for four years and when she eventually quit in 1986, she says it was rather like leaving school. 'I emptied my locker and drove off into the future with my car loaded with flowers. I never once looked back.'

As the sexy but intellectual Heather, she won a sizeable following of male admirers and was described at the time as the actress who brought glamour to the earthy world of Brookside Close.

'If people see me like that, then that's their view,' says Amanda. 'I've certainly never tried to promote myself as a sex symbol. In fact, I'm not terribly interested in myself. I think it's much more interesting to slip into other people's shoes, which is why I like acting so much. I like being other people.

'I have very happy memories of my time on "Brookside". It was very exciting being in right from the outset but I knew that once I'd made the decision to leave, I would never go back. I'm not the sort of person who ever goes back. Also, soaps on TV have now become sensational in the extreme — I think there has been a dramatic decline in their standard. It seems to me that they're now in the business of making controversial statements just to get viewers. It makes me very cross.'

It is not without irony that while 'Brookside' was providing such marital misery for Heather, it resulted in Amanda meeting her future husband. One day, top photographer Sven Arnstein arrived on set to take publicity pictures for Brookside. He and Amanda clicked almost immediately.

'There was a strong attraction,' she recalls, 'but shortly after we met, he went off to work in Russia for four months. I thought to myself: "I don't want to get involved with someone who has this kind of life." Finally, though, it proved irresistible.' They married in 1989.

Amanda went on to become a regular in 'Boon' as Margaret Daly before landing the role of Beth Glover. It was the first time she and Kevin Whately had worked together although they had a 'near miss' on one of the 'Inspector Morse' films. 'I played an undercover agent in a "Morse" story but all of my scenes were with John Thaw and Robert Stephens so I never actually met Kevin — apart from on the location bus at lunchtime. However we hit it off really well at the start of shooting "Peak Practice" and both share a real love of being out and about in the beautiful Derbyshire countryside. It reminds me so much of where I was brought up in Ireland.'

The subject matter of 'Peak Practice' is also very dear to Amanda's heart. 'I've always been interested in medicine since I was little. I did an odd combination for "A" levels — Literature and Biology.'

Now that she has children — daughters Phoebe, aged six, and Brid, aged four — Amanda is even more aware of the need for a basic grasp of medicine.

'I think it's vital if you have children. They're always picking up little ailments so it's important to have some knowledge. But even before I had my children, I found the subject fascinating, particularly alternative medicine. I've studied reflexology, aromatherapy and massage. I find the aromatherapy oils totally relaxing. Even back in my schooldays, I was wearing patchouli oil.'

As part of her research for the part of Beth, Amanda sought help from her own GP in London. 'I sat in on a few of his surgeries and that gave me a really valuable insight into doctor–patient care. Being able to experience first-hand what GPs face each day was great. I saw about 18 patients who all had vastly different problems. He dealt with each one quite differently and showed a very good personal touch. That's the type of doctor I've tried to make Beth.

'One of my sisters is a nurse but being a GP is such a different branch of medicine. I think it's an extraordinarily demanding job. To be responsible for the welfare of so many people and also to make sure that your practice is well run is challenging, as well as rewarding.

'There's an awful lot of counselling goes into being a GP — a lot to do with communicating with people. Again, that's very dear to my own heart and one of the reasons I was immediately attracted to the role. You can sit in a doctor's surgery for the morning and the amount of prescriptions he writes out are very few. A lot of people just need someone to talk to.

Crawford (David Credell) leads Beth to the spot where the two boys were electrocuted in 'Sharp Practice'

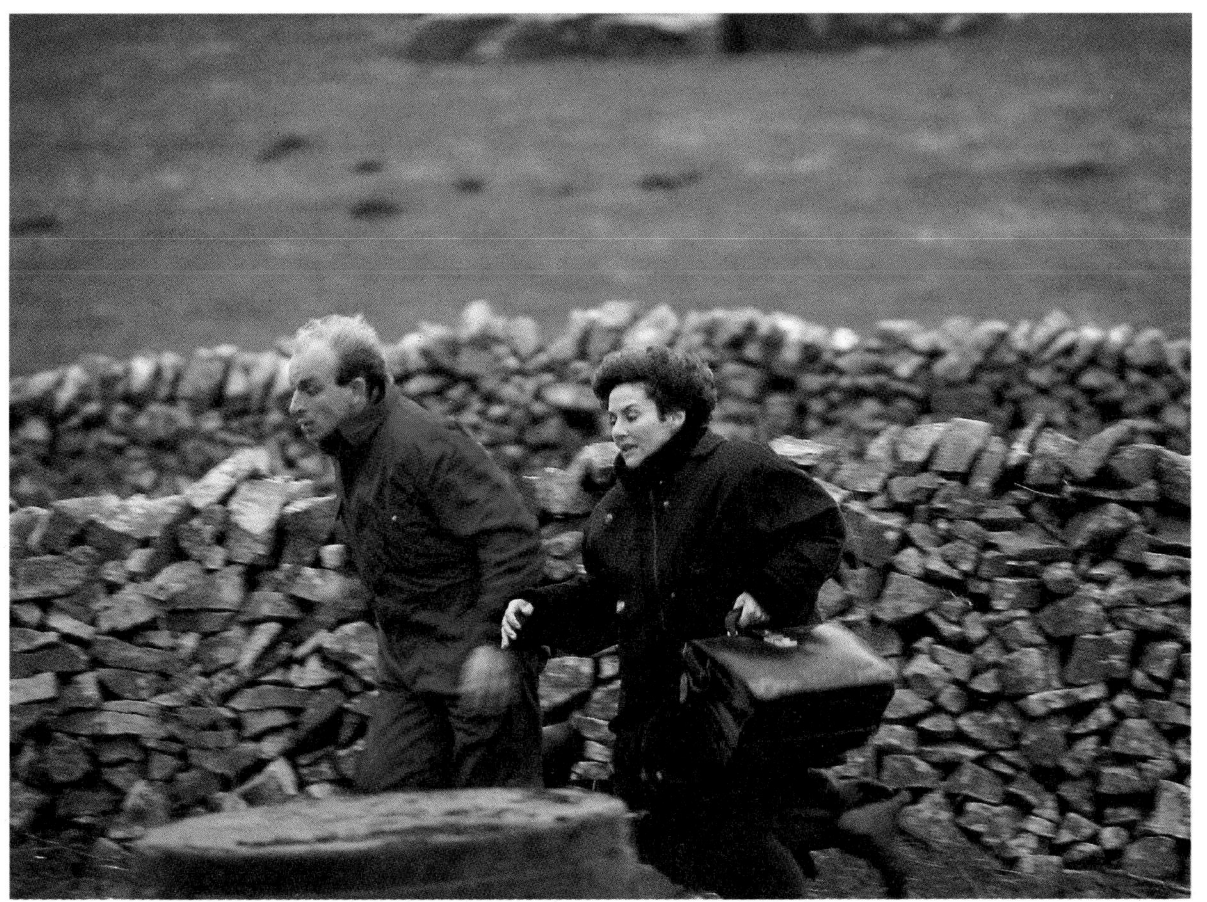

'As people have become more isolated in life from their families and friends, their GP plays a vital part. As people's expectations of life are so high, there are an awful lot of depressed people because they can't ultimately reach their goals. There is enormous pressure, as a result of which people get so distraught that they have to talk to their GP. They don't want pills, they just want to talk.

'I am pleased if "Peak Practice" is able to help in some way. I don't get sanctimonious about it — I don't believe we're providing a public service. We just do a programme, but it's a bonus if people receive help from it.'

It is one thing knowing what makes a good doctor but another actually putting it into practice. Amanda knows her place. 'I think I'm probably better at playing a doctor than being a genuine one,' she confesses, 'because I'm sure I would take everyone's problems home with me if it were for real. As it is, I find it quite easy to switch off from playing a character at the end of the day, but then I've got a lot going on in my life to absorb me. As soon as I get home, I throw myself into my family life.'

'With the family home being in West London, people are always asking me whether it's hard working so far away from home. Of course it is. But if you want to have a career as well as a good family life, you just have to work at it and make it happen.

'I've been lucky in being able to combine my work with family life. I was pregnant towards the end of "Boon" and I returned to work when Phoebe was eight weeks old to do a Freddie Forsyth thriller for TV. I think if you have the right attitude and don't make life too complicated, you can combine the two. I have some wonderful help which means I can relax about the children when I'm working.

'We talk about a lot of things on the phone and the children come up to Derbyshire quite a lot, which they enjoy. I discuss with them what I'm doing and how long I'm going to be away and, by understanding what's going on, they're not fazed by it. You have to trust yourself that you're doing the right thing and also be prepared to make some compromises. Doing a series probably makes things a little easier because you can plan ahead. I love my work and I love my independence but I always feel so excited when I'm going home to see Sven and the children, even though I have to drive 140 miles through the night. I have intimate knowledge of the roadworks on the M1!

'Since having the children, I've developed a huge amount of energy which I put to good use. I feel that having had a break to have my children, I've come into a different stage of acting. When I came back to work, I had to feel my way in for a while. I now feel a lot more confident and, ironically, more ambitious than when I was younger.

'People talk about my "career" now and I'm astonished. All I wanted was to act a bit! Luckily, the parts have got progressively bigger. Although I did a fair bit of theatre even before "Brookside", I must say I do enjoy television. I like the idea of playing a different scene every day.'

Inevitably, increased recognition can lead to a loss of privacy. Like Kevin Whately, 39-year-old Amanda is uneasy in the public eye. 'I just like doing my job and getting on with it. I do get spotted to a certain extent but I try to make quite sure that I'm not easily recognisable. Last year, I had to power-walk through Dovedale for about four miles at speed because hordes of people were looking at me saying: "Is it? Isn't it?" I was in shorts and I thought to myself: "This is not a day I want to be recognised really..." '

Simon Shepherd as Will Preston, a very human doctor

DR WILL PRESTON

The six-year-old boy in the blue fur jacket with immaculate stand-up ears looked every inch the budding thespian. The popular consensus of opinion among the audience at Hurst House School, Henley-in-Arden, was that they had not seen a finer Peter Rabbit. For young Simon Shepherd, Beatrix Potter's fluffy-tailed hero was to be the first step in an illustrious acting career.

Simon was raised in Stratford-upon-Avon where his father ran a pub, the Dirty Duck, opposite the Shakespeare Memorial Theatre, as the Royal Shakespeare Theatre was then known. Situated barely more than a loud prompt from the theatre, it was a popular watering-hole for actors. The association was put to good use for Simon's stage debut.

'I'm sure everyone else in the school play was in tea towels,' he says, 'but I had this fantastic outfit made by the wardrobe department at the Shakespeare Theatre who were friends of my parents. I've still got a photo of it. But I'm afraid that after Peter Rabbit, it has been downhill all the way!'

Simon and his family lived above the pub for six years, between 1959 and 1965, and the theatrical atmosphere inspired him to consider acting as a career. He joined the National Youth Theatre before training at the Bristol Old Vic.

'A lot of my early film and television roles were floppy-haired artistic types in period pieces, such as Lord Alfred Douglas in 'Lillie', and Rupert Brooke in the BBC play *Sweet Wine of Youth*.' Thereafter, Simon played a succession of upper-class cads, most notably the floppy-haired, scheming Piers Garfield Ward in two series of 'Chancer'. That in turn led to Will Preston in 'Peak Practice'.

'Will is still public school,' says Simon, 'but he's far less self-assured than Piers. I find that I get a very positive public reaction to Will. People's interest in his plot-line — his failed marriage and his financial plight — seems to be very detailed. I think maybe Will's appeal to the audience is that he has so many problems and foibles. He's a very flawed, human character. Although he is a doctor, nobody is in awe of him.'

The extent to which members of the public sympathise with Will was illustrated when he had his breakdown. 'The breakdown episode was the last one we recorded in the first series. Coming right at the end of seven months' filming, I was very tired anyway. So no make-up was required to make me look haggard!

'Beforehand, I talked to a few friends who'd been through breakdowns and did quite a bit of reading on the subject. What made the whole thing complicated was that it was not shot in order. Episode eight was filmed before episode seven so I had to do the post-breakdown scenes before the breakdown itself. Therefore I had to know exactly what sort of breakdown it was, to determine what Will's reaction, if any, would be. What I did was chart the actual graph of the breakdown, breaking the script up so that I knew at any given time where I was — what stage of the breakdown I was at.

'I don't take my characters home with me but you do have to reach into parts of yourself as an actor for occasions that can be unnerving. This was one such occasion.

'It was certainly the biggest response I've had to any character I've played before. I think it took people aback because we showed Will's breakdown quite graphically rather than just skirting around it. It shocked some people because they don't expect to see doctors cracking up before their eyes. I had hundreds of sympathetic letters

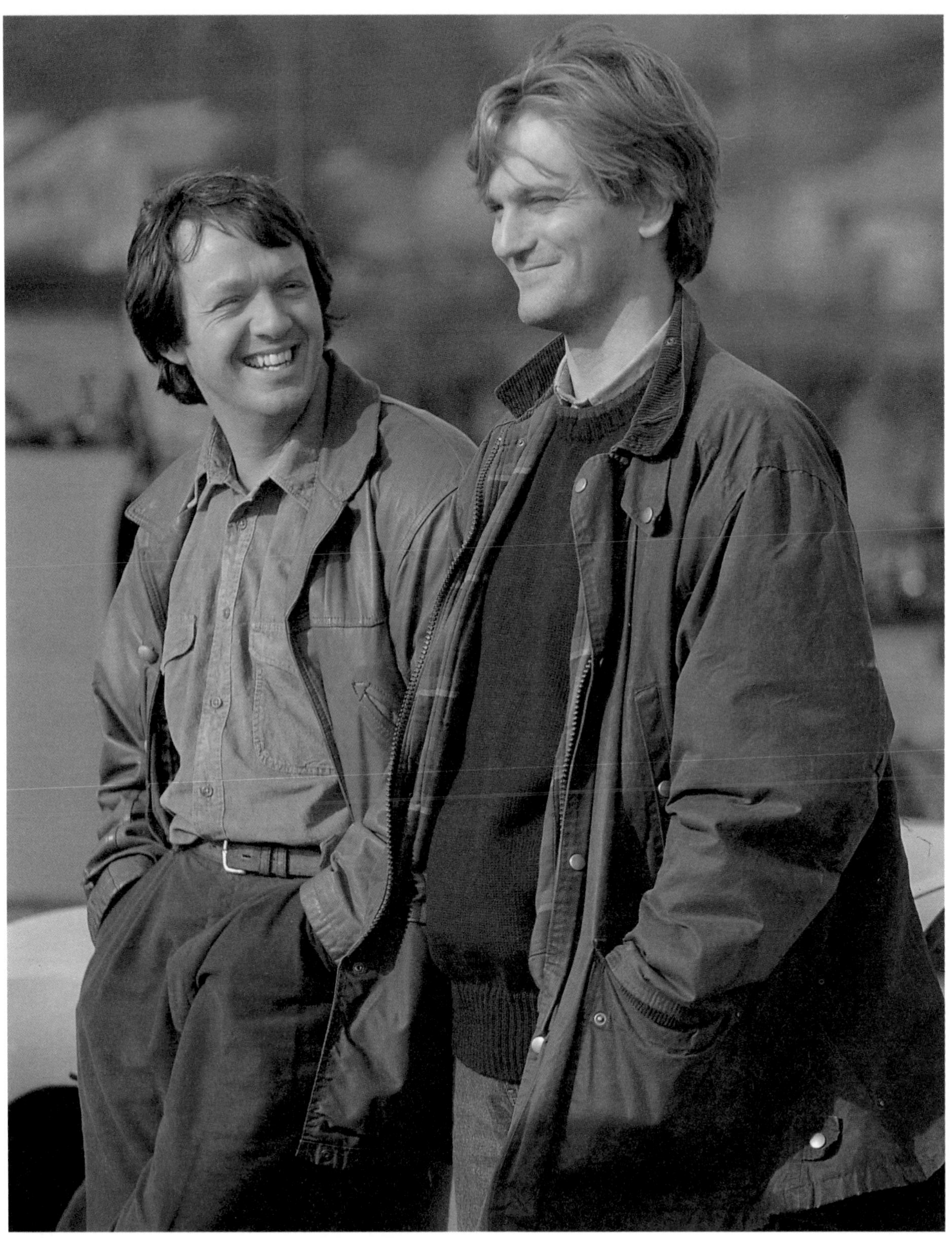

Doctors at large — Jack Kerruish and Will Preston

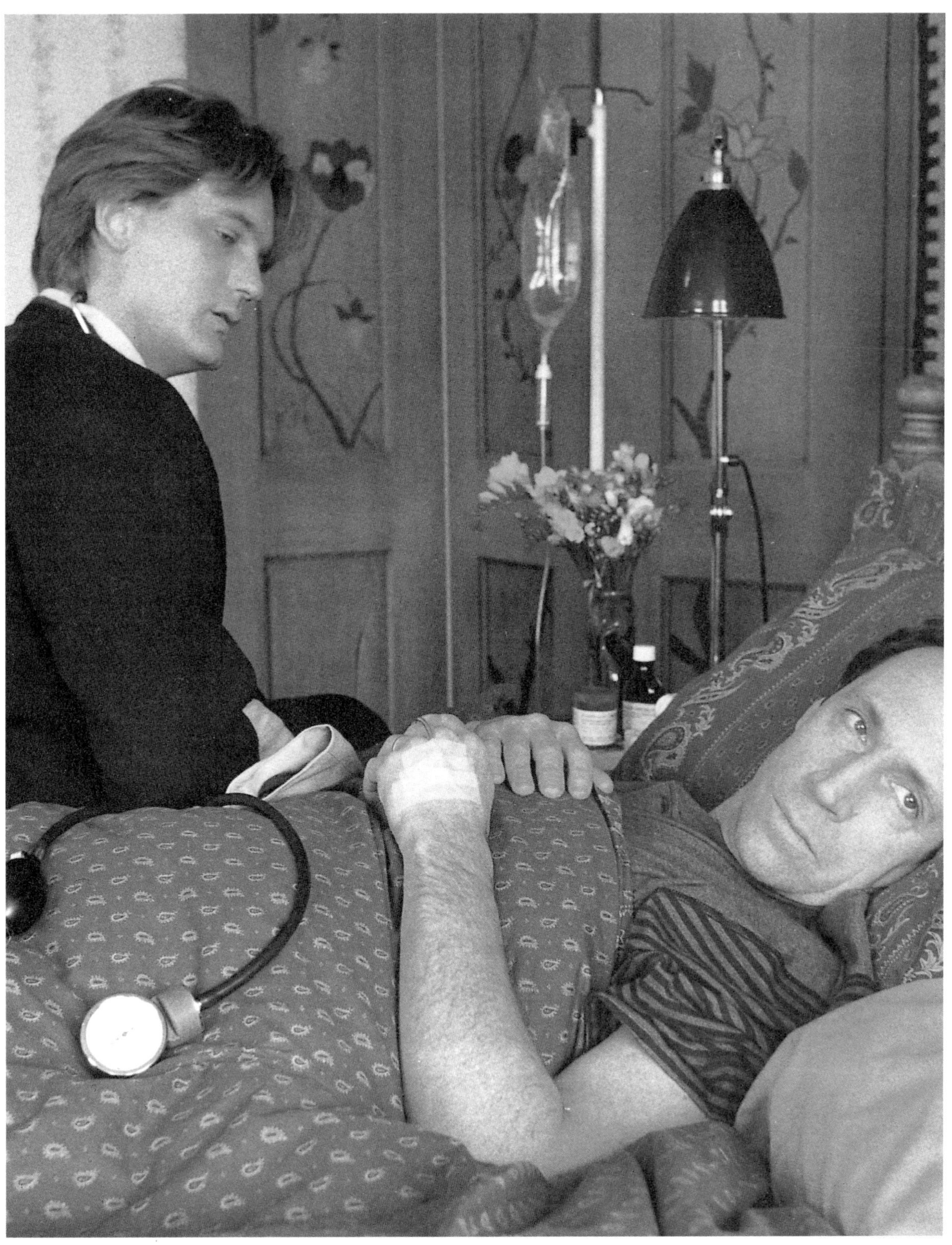

Will agonises over his old friend Stuart Mosely (Jonathan Hyde), who has been diagnosed HIV positive

from viewers and I also experienced a few people coming up to me while I was shopping in Sainsbury's to tell me I was looking better! One woman asked me if I was up to pushing my trolley!

'Fortunately, no one has asked me to take their pulse yet. I'd be hopeless.'

Simon is not only interrogated about Will's health but also about the state of Dr Preston's love life.

'If they're not commenting that I'm looking a little happier these days, they want to know: "Is the bitch coming back?" They're referring to Will's wife, Sarah. People love to hate Sarah and are very upset that Will is married to someone like that.'

When Simon and Jacqueline Leonard were originally cast as husband and wife, both were surprised at the 'mixed marriage' the scriptwriters had in mind. Simon says: 'We thought it was rather odd to put Will, who is an educated middle-class character, with Sarah who is very much from a working-class background. But once the marriage headed into trouble, our different backgrounds gave us more scope. I think there's a lot more pressure and tension between them because they were brought up differently and have a different set of values. The nub of their problem is that they married young and started to grow apart. Sarah began to realise that the man she married is not the dynamic person she thought he was, and Will started to feel that Sarah was very materialistic.'

Simon has had no shortage of advice on medical matters to help him prepare for Will's various traumas. 'Because we film episodes back to back, there is no time for detailed research but I have been able to call upon my mother-in-law, Jill Byrne, who was manager of a practice in Warwickshire, not dissimilar to The Beeches. And for each specific requirement in an episode, the researchers find us an expert to talk to.

'So when I did the AIDS episode, one of the researchers and I talked to Body Positive in Derby which is an AIDS support group for HIV sufferers. We talked to four men and one woman and everyone was really helpful. I was surprised at how positive they all were and we spent a lot of time laughing. I think they were pleased that a prime-time TV programme like "Peak Practice" was tackling the subject.

'I also talked to friends who'd known people with AIDS and read as much as possible.

'After his marriage turning sour and then his mental breakdown, the devastating news that his best friend Stuart had contracted AIDS was just one more emotional hurdle for Will. A lot of real GP practices are dealing with AIDS at their surgeries for the first time so we decided to reflect that in "Peak Practice" and explore the different ways Will, Beth and Jack handle it. Will's initial reaction is a mixture of anger and great sympathy. As an actor, you couldn't really ask for a better part. Both series have given me interesting and emotional storylines to explore, which is very rewarding. I've been around in the business for 15 years but Will is without doubt the best part I've been given. Playing Piers in "Chancer" brought me recognition and it was a very clever script to work with. But "Peak Practice" has given me the chance to be more emotional on screen.

'Like a lot of people, I had a fuzzy knowledge of the HIV virus and AIDS. In my professional life, I have known a few people who have died from AIDS. It's a disease which makes you feel so helpless because you know there's no cure. I wasn't ignorant about AIDS in general terms but I certainly know a lot more about how it really affects people now. I hope that our story helped people understand the disease a little more and

Taking the pressure — Will lends an ear to old Mr Hart (Maurice Denham)

will stop them being judgmental.'

One of the things which pleases Simon most about 'Peak Practice' is its educational side. 'I think it's great that people aren't only interested in the characters' storylines but also in the medical aspect. The health care company which sponsored the second series received no fewer than 72,000 calls for leaflets relating to the various diseases and illnesses we covered. Osteoporosis — which we dealt with in the episode "Life Changes" — attracted the biggest response with about 15,000 callers. Interestingly, AIDS was comparatively low down which hopefully means that people are already well aware of it.

'Doctors certainly seem to be impressed by "Peak Practice" and often say how much they like it. If there is a criticism of the programme from the medical establishments, it's that it's too leisurely — we have far too much time to be involved with patients' problems in depth.

'It's definitely changed my view of the medical profession. I didn't realise how hard they worked. It has made me very aware of the pressure on doctors and also everybody in the surgery. I've got three young children so we spend quite a lot of time at the doctors but, for my part, I now keep a long way away unless there's something really wrong.

'People enjoy the fact that the series is humanising doctors. You tend to go to the doctors when you're feeling rotten, and you often forget that they're human beings. The doctor is the same as you. He breathes in and out, has family pressures like everyone else, and his own problems. Yet everyone treats doctors like saints.'

Simon says that he has no inclination whatsoever to be a doctor. 'I have to close my eyes when I go to the dentist!' he laughs. 'And whenever I see needles on TV or at the cinema, I close my eyes. I can't look at any bloody scenes in case I faint, but at the same time I can't really look away. I keep telling myself that it's only actors covered in fake blood and surrounded by cameras. I'm fine with real blood — I just hate seeing gore on screen.

'The only time I've had a lot of blood on "Peak Practice" was when I had to take glass out of Isabel's foot. I managed to get through that without too much discomfort.'

So what is the worst thing that Simon has had to do on 'Peak Practice'? 'I hate doing blood pressures because you know that feeling — you know it's uncomfortable — and you have a poor actor coming in for that episode, thinking: "Oh my God!" And you can see them going red in the face...

'I haven't had to do any injections yet. I always manage to get my injections done at the end of scenes where I'm just taking the syringe out. I think if I did have to do a full injection, I'd hold up filming for ages!'

Now 38, Simon has been married to costume designer Alex Byrne for 14 years. The couple have three-year-old twins, Arthur and Billie, and a seven-year-old son, Simon.

'Although my situation and character is quite different from Will's, I can identify with some of his problems. Having a career which is not nine to five can be quite difficult with a young family. My wife's work takes her away as well so you have to do a lot of juggling and be very organised. Where possible, we split the school runs, the shopping and chores between us. It's the only way to stay on top of things. However, we've got three great kids who have changed our lives dramatically. When you collapse with a bottle of wine at the end of a day, it's worth the hard work.

'Playing Will certainly makes me thankful for my home life. He's experienced so much unhappiness. When the camera stops rolling, I think: "Thank God, that's not really me." '

Having been present at the birth of his own children, Simon had no qualms when asked to 'deliver' Chloe's baby in 'Peak Practice'. 'Being a spectator at the birth of any baby, let alone twins, is an amazing and unforgettable experience, so I had no problems with the scene. It was a bit of a shock when we learned that we were expecting twins, and their birth was quite an ordeal. We really wanted a daughter, but when Arthur was born first, I was convinced that the next one would be a boy too. When the nurse handed me Billie and said, "You've got a little girl," I was completely overwhelmed.'

Simon went to boarding school but has no plans to pack his children off to a similar establishment. 'I like seeing them every day when I'm not away working,' he says. 'I would miss them too much. Before I know it, they'll be grown up. I want to make the most of these years.'

Above all, he doesn't want to miss that first school play. You never know, it could be a revival of Peter Rabbit...

ISABEL DE GINES

Sylvia Syms was playing a teenager when the word had only just come into everyday usage. It was back in 1956 that she made her film debut alongside Anna Neagle, Kenneth Haigh and Wilfrid Hyde White in *My Teenage Daughter*, playing a wayward 17-year-old in a British answer to *Rebel Without a Cause*. She has been described as 'a sex kitten who fired up a million fevered fantasies in the Fifties.' It is all a

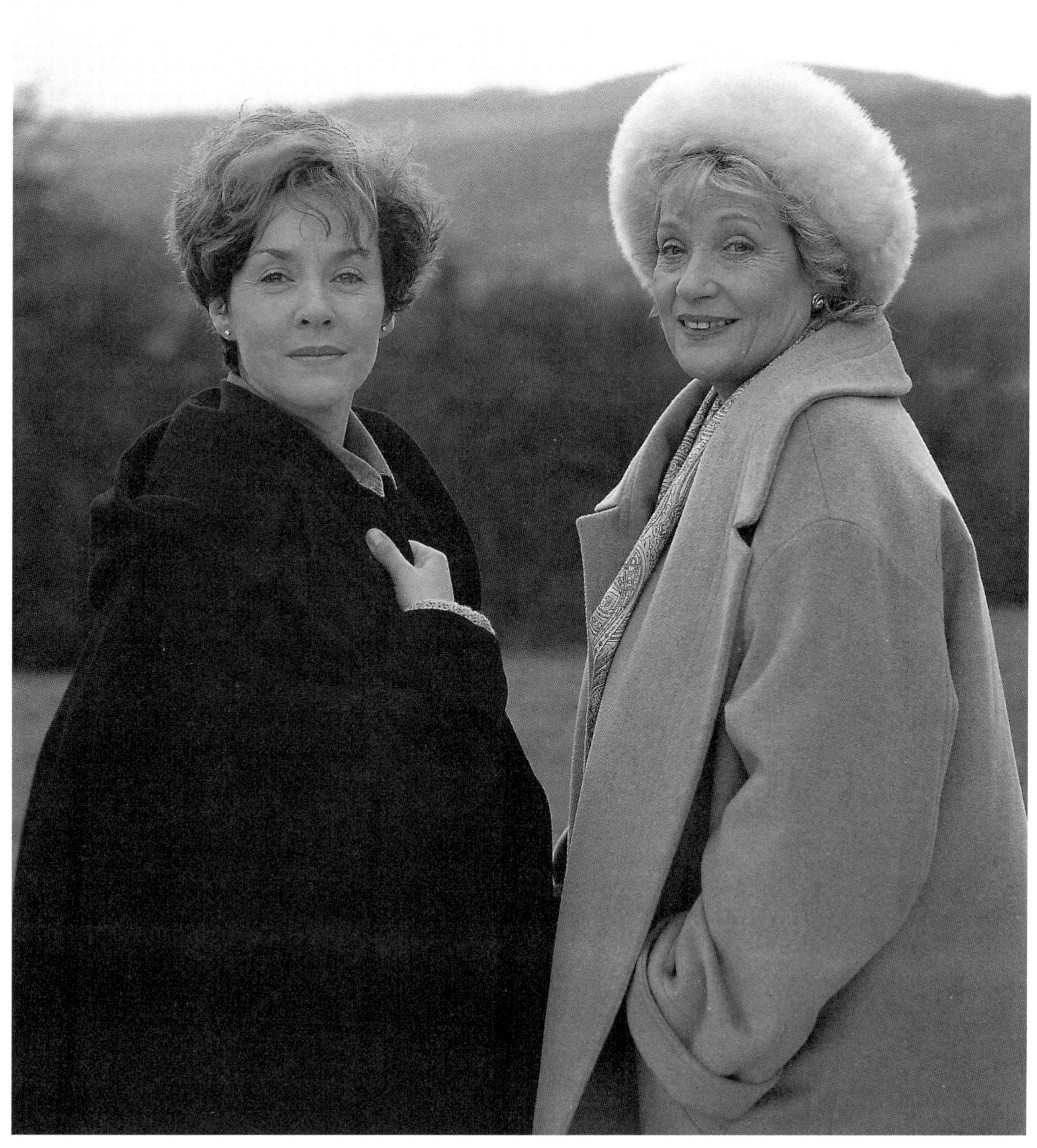

Best friends — Beth and Isabel de Gines

far cry from the ill-fated Isabel de Gines, JP, pillar of the Cardale community.

Sylvia is pleased that her career has encompassed such varying roles. 'I've really enjoyed playing Isabel in "Peak Practice" because she's such a vigorous character. She has always been a lot of fun. She is young at heart and that's what matters. In the same way, I don't think of myself as a woman who has turned 60. In fact, I don't really know what it feels like to be 60 because I have so many young friends who don't treat me as some sort of Crimplene geriatric!

'I went on holiday to France last year with a young actress and her boyfriend, but I didn't worry about them finding me boring because I'm 60 and they are in their thirties. My son Ben and daughter Beattie (actress Beattie Edney) are in their thirties. I've been away on holiday with Ben and his girlfriend and not felt out of place. As for my daughter, she's infinitely older than me — she is so knowledgeable and experienced.'

To play Isabel, Sylvia drew on the experience of her own friendships. 'I liked the idea of being an older woman who is Beth's friend. A friendship between two women of different ages happens in real life but it is not often explored on television. Close friendships between the generations are not at all unusual. When I was about 13, I met a woman on a bus, who was then about 30 and had two young children. That woman became my best friend and was a profound influence on me.

'Even with my own doctor, who is a woman, I have a more intimate friendship than the usual doctor–patient relationship, because I have known her for a long time and can remember her graduating.

'Beattie has friends who are older women with whom she enjoys a different relationship than the one she has with me. And, as I say, I have lots of younger friends other than my daughter.

'I suppose Jean and Leslie Crowther are among my closest friends. Our two families grew up together and have spent a lot of time with each other. I probably have a similar relationship with their children, especially Charlotte, as Isabel has with Beth.'

Sylvia looks back philosophically on her long, distinguished career. 'I wish I had known how beautiful I was when I *was* beautiful. I always saw other people as being much more glamorous than me. I was never very good at the glamour — it didn't really interest me. In fact, I was turned down for my screen test with Rank because they didn't think I was glamorous enough.

'I had been spotted on stage and I thought they were interested in me for my acting talent. Later on, I realised it was my salvation as an actress that I didn't get into the Rank charm school because I was able to do a lot more interesting work with very interesting people.

'I was even offered a contract to go to Hollywood but I didn't take it. I didn't think I could keep up the pace. Imagine having to look good all the time. I would never have been as disciplined as Joan Collins. I couldn't have stayed as beautiful. She works very hard at it.'

Sylvia's career certainly did not suffer from the Rank rejection. In 1958, she starred with John Mills, Anthony Quayle and Harry Andrews in the classic war film, *Ice Cold in Alex*, and through the Sixties became a leading light of the British film industry, appearing in the likes of *Victim* (with Dirk Bogarde), *The Quare Fellow* (with Patrick McGoohan), *East of Sudan* (with Anthony Quayle), *Operation Crossbow* (with a cast of thousands), *Hostile Witness* (directed by and starring Ray Milland) and *Run Wild, Run Free* (with John Mills).

The 1970s brought little respite and in 1974

Sylvia earned a BAFTA nomination for the spy romance, *The Tamarind Seed*, in which she starred with Julie Andrews, Omar Sharif and Anthony Quayle. Simultaneously on the small screen, she was demonstrating her comic talents as Leslie Crowther's wife in the long-running ATV sitcom 'My Good Woman'.

More recently, she received widespread critical acclaim for her formidable portrayal of the Iron Lady in the BBC production 'Margaret Thatcher — The Final Days'.

'I enjoy keeping busy although sometimes it's a case of having to. I'm not married now (she was divorced from businessman Alan Edney six years ago) so I still need to work hard to earn a living. People think if you've made a few films, you're rolling in money, but that's absurd.'

Nevertheless, she admits to being choosy about which roles to accept. 'I was asked to do a super part in the movies a couple of years ago, but I had to turn it down because of an unbelievable nude scene! The American producers were very funny because they wined and dined me and were very polite but they wouldn't send me the script. When they finally explained, I said I had no objection to nudity but I didn't think I could quite manage that, thank you!'

Sylvia is justifiably proud of daughter Beattie who is rapidly carving out a name for herself in the acting profession. Among her recent credits is the controversial film *In the Name of the Father*.

'I didn't encourage her to go into acting,' says Sylvia, 'because Beatrice was not the kind of child you encouraged or discouraged from doing anything. In fact, I was surprised when she took it up. But I'm absolutely gutted with admiration for her because she's a wonderful actress and she's also lovely and very clever.

'My son Ben works in the restaurant business. He did act as a little boy — he was with me when he played Sophia Loren's son in a remake of *Brief Encounter* — but when he grew up, he lost interest.'

One of the things Sylvia enjoys most about 'Peak Practice' is the spectacular Derbyshire countryside.

'I know the area well because I have some friends who live there and I used to have a cottage just a bit further north of Crich, where we film. It was in a similar village to our fictional one, overlooking Chatsworth. I think the Derbyshire countryside is fabulous. I love the outdoor life. Unfortunately, I don't ride anymore but I walk a lot. I don't like sitting down too long — I like to explore.

'I've had walking holidays in Derbyshire and really love the beauty of the place. For me, Derbyshire is one of the stars of "Peak Practice". I find the space and the way people have time such a relief after the hustle and bustle of London. I don't even mind the weather...'

5

CASE HISTORIES

SERIES ONE

SHARP PRACTICE

TRANSMISSION DATE: 10 MAY 1993
WRITER: LUCY GANNON
DIRECTOR: GORDON FLEMYNG

Jack Kerruish needed a fresh challenge after Africa. He found it in Cardale.

For the past three years, Dr Jack Kerruish has thrown himself into the task of setting up the Dry River Clinic in a remote part of Africa. The mobile clinic has been a lifesaver to villagers and Jack has been training local doctors to carry on the good work. Now his job is done, the go-getting Kerruish is looking for a fresh challenge and a change of scenery. He has spotted an advertisement in a medical journal for a doctor to join a

The kite rescue turns to tragedy in 'Sharp Practice'

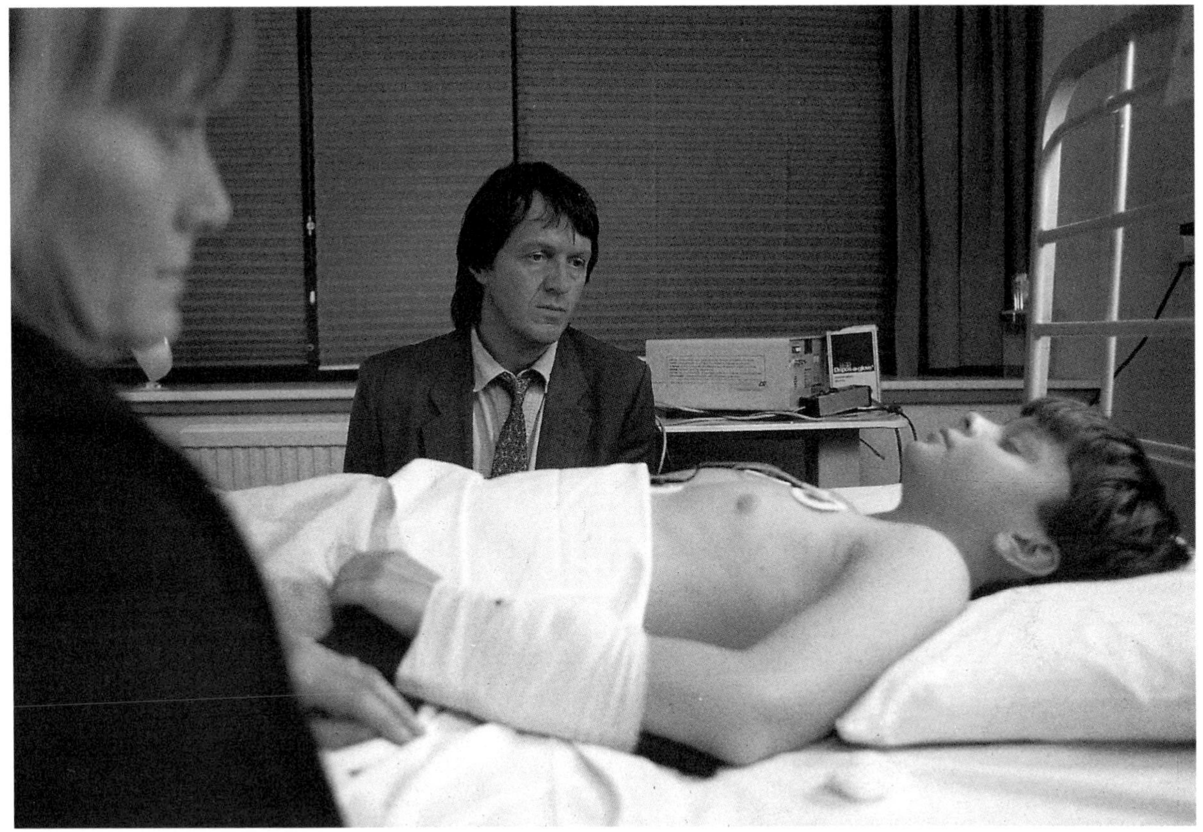

Only moments to live for young Rob Barnes (Christopher Brown)

'picturesque and unsuitable' surgery. It could be exactly what Jack is looking for.

The surgery in question is The Beeches in the small Derbyshire Peak District village of Cardale. The vacancy has been caused by the departure of Dr Daniel Acres who has left the practice to join Dr John Reginald at the new hi-tech Brompton Health Centre, the rival clinic in the village. Dr Acres is also trying to entice away The Beeches' senior partner, Dr Beth Glover, but she politely declines, as does the other partner at The Beeches, Dr Will Preston. Over a leisurely game of golf, Will tells Dr Acres that he fully intends staying with Beth, if only because he is lazy.

Jack is divorced. His long-standing girlfriend Sandy has a successful career, a flat and friends in London. On his return from Africa, he stays with her for two weeks before setting off for his interview in Cardale. He steps straight into a drama. For two ten-year-old boys, Paul Elliott and Rob Barnes, both playing truant from school, have been electrocuted after their kite became entangled in a pylon. Beth arrives on the scene to find both boys lying face down on the ground. Jack, his car having broken down on the way to Derbyshire, spots the commotion and pulls up. The current is cut off. Jack pulls Rob clear and Beth starts cardiac massage. But Paul is already dead. As Beth cradles Paul in her arms, she roundly chastises Jack for being late.

At the interview, Jack tells Beth and Will that he went to Africa to escape a failed marriage and a relationship that wasn't going anywhere. Before that, he had spent 15 years working in inner cities. Beth, having seemingly decided that Jack is unsuitable, says that they are looking for someone who is good at management and the administrative side. Indignant, Jack responds by reminding her that he set up a complete practice in Africa from scratch. Beth will not be dissuaded. She also says Jack is too scruffy.

Jack leaves but on his way back to London, he visits Rob in hospital. There he bumps into the boy's parents, Ted and Sue, who both blame Paul for the accident. Soon afterwards, Rob too dies. By the time of the inquest, Jack has smartened himself up considerably, to the extent that Beth, under pressure from her best friend Isabel de Gines who thinks that Jack could be ideal for the practice, offers him the job. Jack's delight is interrupted by Ted Barnes who rebukes Jack and Beth for laughing. Ted also has words with the Elliott family which results in the headstrong Jazz smashing the windows of Ted's car. For good measure, Ted thumps Jack who is staying at the village pub, the Manor Hotel. Jack begins to wonder what he has let himself in for.

At Paul's funeral, his parents, Jan and Dave Elliott, are reconciled with Ted but the latter returns home to find his house wrecked by Jazz. In the heat of the moment, Ted's wife Sue tells the errant teenager that Ted is her real father. Stunned by the news, Jazz hurls a knife at him. Finally, with a little help from Jack, Jazz buries

Breaking up was hard to do for Sandy (Melanie Thaw) and Jack

the hatchet — and not in the head of her new-found father.

Jack has relationship problems of his own. He and Sandy have fallen out over his acceptance of the job at The Beeches. They clearly have different goals in life. She wants to stay in London, he wants to move to the Peak District. Furthermore, she is fed up with conducting a long-distance love affair — she has had that for the past three years. She accuses Jack of wanting everything but of offering nothing in return.

At the Manor, Drs Acres and Reginald have a conspiratorial word with Trevor Sharp, the local bank manager. Knowing how hard it will hit The Beeches' practice, they want Trevor to foreclose on Beth's loan because of her known overdraft. Trevor has other things on his mind at first. He too is staying at the Manor where he uses his room as the setting for clandestine, adventurous frolics with his hairdresser girlfriend, Leanda. Being a bank manager, Trevor is none too keen on the withdrawal method.

Downstairs, the pub landlords, James and Chloe White, are eager to start a family. They think that Chloe might be pregnant and Dr Acres diagnoses that she has an ectopic pregnancy. Jack and Beth think it is appendicitis. Jack asks Beth out to dinner.

Trevor has frozen Beth's overdraft and when Jack goes to see him about obtaining a bank loan in order to make improvements to the practice, Trevor gives him a hard time and announces his intention to call in the surgery's debts. Jack relates the bad news to Beth.

Meanwhile Trevor is otherwise tied up — or at least Leanda is. She is handcuffed to the bed, wearing an Annie Oakley costume. He is wearing nothing more than a posing pouch, a holster and a hat. He is preparing to draw his six-shooter. For a dramatic entrance, he climbs on top of the wardrobe but, as he is about to jump off, the wardrobe collapses beneath him. His anguished screams for help alert Jack and James. When Jack witnesses a scene which owes more to *Playboy* than *Banking World*, he has little trouble in blackmailing not-so-clever Trevor into agreeing to the loan after all.

CAST

Dr Jack Kerruish	Kevin Whately
Dr Beth Glover	Amanda Burton
Dr Will Preston	Simon Shepherd
Isabel de Gines	Sylvia Syms
Sandy	Melanie Thaw
Trevor Sharp	Shaun Prendergast
Leanda	Beth Goddard
James White	Richard Platt
Chloe White	Hazel Ellerby
Kim Beardsmore	Esther Coles
Ellie Ndebala	Sharon Hinds
Dr Daniel Acres	Tom Beard
Dr John Reginald	Andrew Ray
Ted Barnes	Andrew Wilde
Sue Barnes	Amelda Brown
Rob Barnes	Christopher Brown
Jazz Elliott	Rebecca Callard
Paul Elliott	Ross Holland
Dave Elliott	Paul Broughton
Jan Elliott	Kate Lock
Sisu Walanda	Agatha Husle
Jacob	Walter Mupasutsa
Alice North	Margery Mason
Crawford	David Credell
Doctor	Stuart MacKenzie
Coroner	John Pennington
Samson	Desmond Stokes
Digger	Craster Pringle
Shop Assistant	Gail Kemp
George Cuthbert	Iain Mitchell
Vicar	Vass Anderson

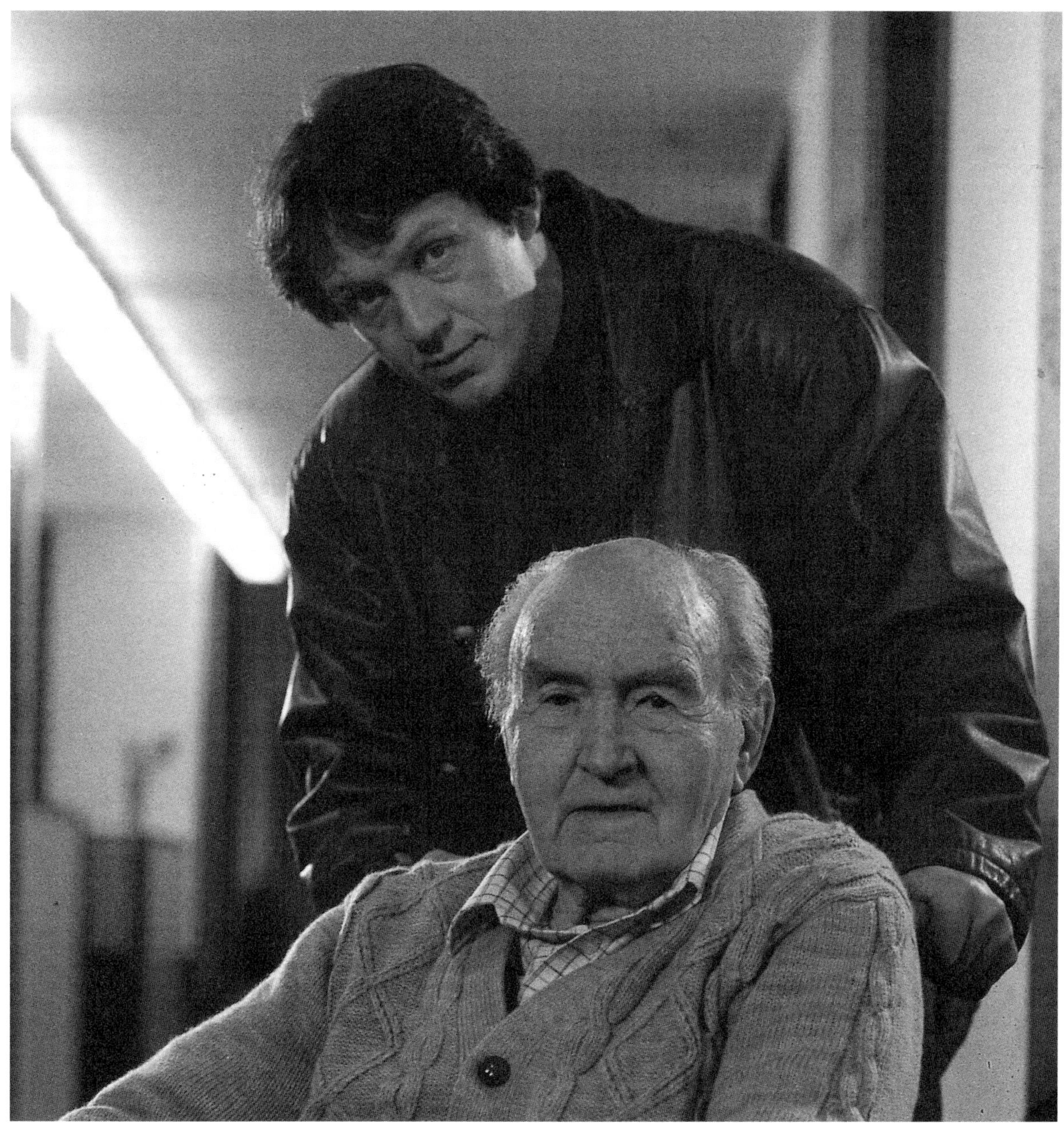

Douglas Hart's eye trouble causes concern in 'Outsiders'

OUTSIDERS

TRANSMISSION DATE: 17 MAY 1993
WRITER: LUCY GANNON
DIRECTOR: GORDON FLEMYNG

Douglas Hart, war veteran and retired solicitor, has been having problems with cataracts. A dignified, frail man, he hates to make a fuss but when Ellie Ndebala, the nurse at The Beeches, visits him for his annual assessment, his companion, Alice North, reports that his eye trouble caused him to scald his hands recently. She says something must be done.

Everyone at The Beeches is in a dilemma. While Dr Acres, Dr Reginald and the staff at the health centre celebrate their new fundholding status, Beth says she disagrees with fundholding, that it creates a two-tier system. Jack refuses to commit himself. Will's glamorous wife Sarah, an ambitious woman, is worried that Jack's arrival might push Will out into the cold, particularly if Jack and Beth should ever become more than just business partners. Certainly after Beth's initial hostility, their relationship seems to be heading that way. Beth invites Jack round for dinner and the evening ends in a kiss.

Ellie quizzes Beth about how much progress she has made regarding Mr Hart's appointment with the eye clinic. Beth and Jack discuss long waiting lists and organise a meeting at the surgery to pinpoint how many patients have left the practice for the new health centre. Jack suggests that they make receptionist Kim practice manager to follow up on appointments. Hungover from his evening at Beth's, he also privately agrees to no more socialising. Beth chats to Isabel about Jack. Isabel says that simply because the great love of her life was a doctor and a bastard, it doesn't mean all doctors are like that.

Jack has also been attending to Menzies Wilson, a 55-year-old head waiter at a local hotel restaurant. Wilson, who has fallen out with the hotel manager Mr Hobbs, is told by Jack that his high blood pressure is down to too much drinking and smoking. It is not what Wilson wishes to hear and he storms out. When the newlywed Derek falls to the floor unconscious after dining in the restaurant, Beth diagnoses dodgy oysters. Wilson tries to hide the evidence and is sacked for his — and everyone else's — pains.

Following a sudden collapse, old Mr Hart is in hospital. Jack goes to see Neil Archer, unit manager of the eye clinic. Desk-bound and unimaginative, Archer is accused by Jack of sucking up to fundholding practices. On leaving, Jack is appalled to see Mr Hart being sent home and offers him a lift. He puts him to bed and tells him to stay there until the nurse arrives. But, at the end of his tether, Mr Hart takes an overdose.

Luckily, Jack and Ellie find him in time and call an ambulance. Back at the hospital, Mr Hart's son Ian argues with staff about his father's need for an operation. Getting nowhere fast, he storms into the eye clinic looking for the consultant, Mr Kelley. Later, Jack and Kelley argue about whose fault the situation is and finally Kelley agrees to operate on one eye in four weeks' time. Despite Will's fears and objections, Beth decides to offer Jack a partnership.

SUPPORTING CAST

Isabel de Gines	Sylvia Syms
Menzies Wilson	Tim Wylton
Mr Hart	Maurice Denham
Alice North	Margery Mason
Ian Hart	Michael Cadman
Sarah Preston	Jacqueline Leonard
Ellie Ndebala	Sharon Hinds
Kim Beardsmore	Esther Coles
Dr John Reginald	Andrew Ray
Dr Daniel Acres	Tom Beard
Mr Hobbs	Julian Gartside
Neil Archer	John Hudson
Mr David Kelley	Kevin Costello
Chef	Glen Davies
Mr Naughton	James Noble
Derek	Oliver Young
Rachel	Annie Cowan
Staff Nurse Smythe	Kate Doherty
Driver	Martin Rattler

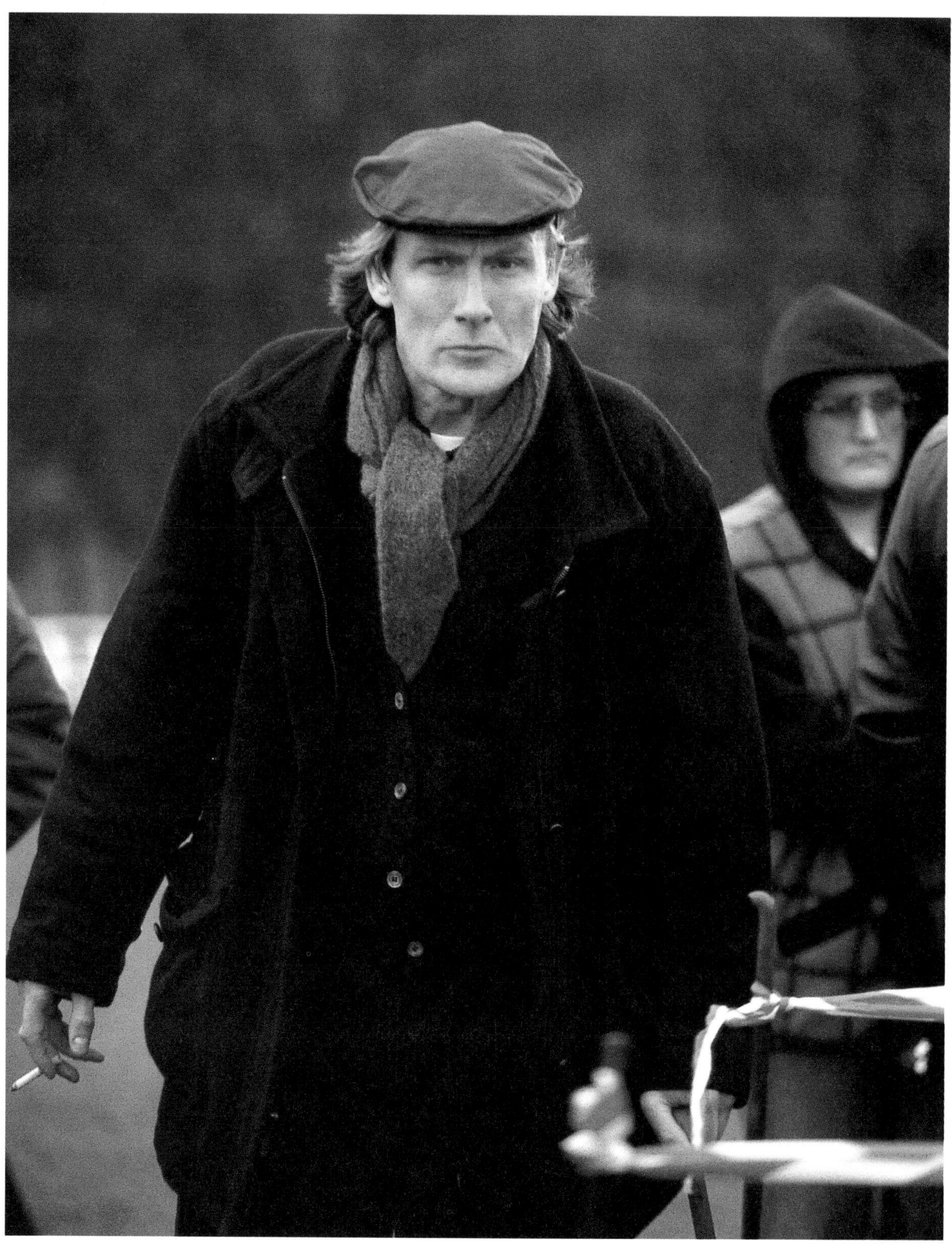

Alan Sinclair (Bill Nighy) disapproved of his daughter's friendship with Jack

GROWING PAINS

TRANSMISSION DATE: 24 MAY 1993
WRITER: ANDY DE LA TOUR
DIRECTOR: ANTONIA BIRD

Sixteen-year-old Gemma Sinclair is training for a forthcoming cross-country championship under the watchful eye of her father Alan. Himself a former athlete but now reduced to walking with the aid of a stick as a result of the onset of arthritis, Alan is a hard taskmaster, desperate for his daughter to succeed. So when Gemma sprains her knee, he is anxious to dismiss the injury as trivial. However, his wife Maureen is concerned that Gemma may be following in her father's footsteps in more ways than one and that the injury may be a sign of arthritis. She calls Jack.

Sarah Preston is having an affair with Dr Daniel Acres. She uses their lovemaking as an opportunity to persuade Acres to have Will taken on as a third partner at the health centre. Sarah's motives are basic enough — she wants Will to earn enough money to pay for a promised skiing holiday. At a musical recital in the village, she blatantly pushes Will's case with Dr John Reginald.

Gemma is clearly smitten with Jack. When she arrives at The Beeches for a blood test, she is offered the services of Ellie but insists on seeing Dr Kerruish. Noticing that her hand is swollen, he prescribes pain killers. On leaving the surgery that night, he finds a jiffy bag under the windscreen wipers of his car. It contains a cassette tape on which Gemma declares her love for him.

Politely declining Gemma's overtures, Jack attacks her father for pushing her too hard. He

Gemma Sinclair (Natalie Morse) wanted more than a doctor/patient relationship with Jack

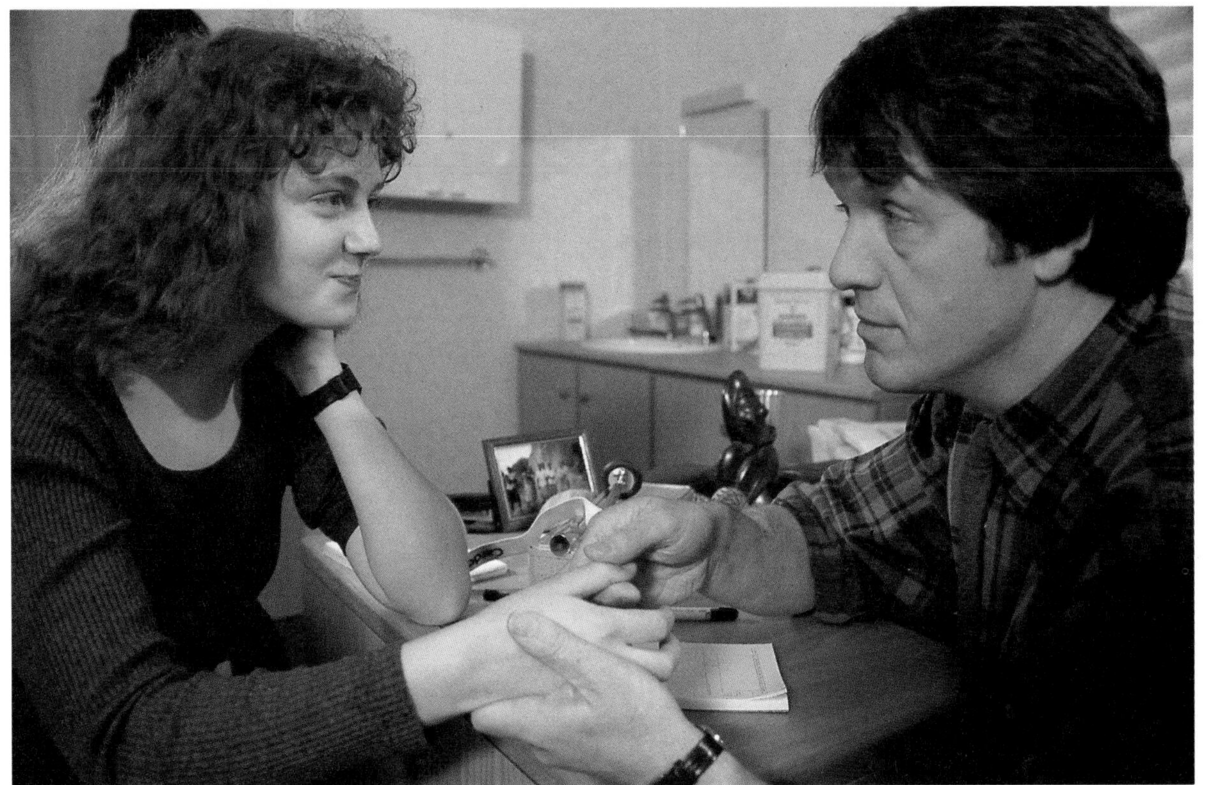

As rumours spread through Cardale, Jack had to be brutally frank with young Gemma

warns Sinclair that Gemma is displaying the first signs of rheumatoid arthritis and adds that she could be in a wheelchair before she is twenty. Gemma remains besotted and takes to waiting for Jack at the Manor. He drives her home, telling her that a relationship is out of the question — that it's just a teenage crush. Gemma is adamant, however. 'I want you to make love to me,' she declares and plants a lingering kiss on Jack's lips, a scene witnessed by the passing Sarah.

Gemma compounds the felony by telling her father that Jack has told her he loves her and also that she will never run again. More worried about his daughter's athletic than her emotional future, Sinclair confronts Jack and threatens to have him struck off.

By now the gossip is all over Cardale. Beth gives Jack a dressing-down and says the rumours must be scotched for the sake of the practice. She tells him: 'You're one of life's charmers, Jack, and now it's landed you in trouble.'

Will discovers the origin of the gossip. Sinclair

tells him that Dan Acres' girlfriend had seen Jack and Gemma kissing. The girlfriend's name is Sarah. Will begins to put two and two together.

Beth tries to defuse the situation but Sinclair puts in a formal complaint about Jack. It looks as if Jack will be driven out of Cardale.

Although warned to stay away from Gemma, Jack passes on the results of the blood tests. She hasn't got rheumatoid arthritis — the hand swelling was a legacy of German measles — and she can race on Saturday. Realising the trouble she has caused, she apologises and, to the delight of her father, resumes training.

Sinclair withdraws the complaint after Gemma tells him the truth and, as Gemma celebrates victory in the cross-country championships, Will warns Acres off Sarah. He has no intention of accepting Dr Reginald's job offer, one made to undermine The Beeches. Sarah's plans are scuppered.

SUPPORTING CAST

Alan Sinclair	Bill Nighy
Gemma Sinclair	Natalie Morse
Sarah Preston	Jacqueline Leonard
Dr Daniel Acres	Tom Beard
Maureen Sinclair	Frances Low
Kim Beardsmore	Esther Coles
Ellie Ndebala	Sharon Hinds
Dr John Reginald	Andrew Ray
James White	Richard Platt
Chloe White	Hazel Ellerby
Eve	Kitty Scopes
Hargreaves	James Warrior
Singer	Grace Kinirons
Pianist	Crispin Harris
Girl 1	Lisa Twigger
Girl 2	Emma Leyland

ROSES AROUND THE DOOR

TRANSMISSION DATE: 31 MAY 1993
WRITER: LUCY GANNON
DIRECTOR: CHRIS LOVETT

Chloe White's sister, Val Mason, has been trying for years to have a baby. She has undergone numerous tests but is prepared to do absolutely anything which will increase her chances. So when Will informs her that her ovaries are becoming cystic and that the only possible solution is IVF, she jumps at the prospect. He points out that it will cost £800 for one attempt at an IVF done privately and that she may need two or more tries. Val unhesitatingly agrees to go on the private list.

Her husband Ray is a farm labourer, riddled with a disease which causes poor circulation in the hands, giving him a vast amount of pain and a loss of feeling. There is no known cure but it can be eased with drugs. Ray has kept his illness a secret from both Val and his boss, Ken Waight, fearing that he may lose his job (it is becoming increasingly painful to drive the machinery) and also the cottage which is owned by Ken and comes with the job.

There is a strained atmosphere at The Beeches where the three doctors are struggling against the odds to provide 24-hour cover for 5,000 patients. Beth's suggestion to share cover with the health centre has been thwarted by Will who refuses to work with Daniel Acres following the discovery of Sarah's affair. Will is also adamant that he will not devote Monday afternoons to performing minor operations — it will interfere with his golf. Jack bullies him into a change of heart about the operations, threatening to make a formal issue of his inactivity. This, plus the arrival of Dr Rhiann Lewis, a vocational trainee doing six months at the health centre, increases the number of potential doctors in the area and eases Beth's worries.

Ray Mason's health is deteriorating. Barely able to operate the gear lever, he crashes his tractor and is trapped beneath it. He is taken to hospital with a broken collarbone and reluctantly tells Val and Ken about his illness. Whilst sympathetic, Ken says that a permanently incapacitated farmhand is of no use to him.

Meanwhile Isabel de Gines has been seeing a lot of Gerard, a handsome widower. He escorts her on a shopping spree to Derby, at the end of which she reveals that she wants some excitement in her life, a romantic fling. Gerard backs away, later explaining that he has no wish to become a geriatric joke, the subject of Cardale gossip. They stay friends and set off for a country walk. As they reach a spot known as Lovers' Gate, Isabel treads on a broken bottle, badly gashing her foot. Gerard drives her to the surgery. While Will is treating Isabel, receptionist Kim teases Gerard about the accident happening at Lovers' Gate. This serves to confirm Gerard's worst fears and he leaves in a hurry without waiting to take Isabel home. In conversation with Kim, she realises the reason for his sudden vanishing act.

The Masons are faced with eviction as Ken Waight brings a new family to look at the house. Beth is furious to learn that Jack had blackmailed Will and calls him an 'arrogant bastard'. It is not meant as a term of endearment. She has a quiet chat with Will and gently persuades him to agree to share cover with the health centre. Will voices the belief that it was his long working hours which pushed Sarah into the affair with Acres.

At that, Will heads off for the golf club. This time he is not skiving — he asks the secretary to give Ray work as an odd job man, a post which comes complete with its own cottage. While the Masons inspect their new home, Jack shows off the cottage which he has just bought.

SUPPORTING CAST

Isabel de Gines	Sylvia Syms
Ray Mason	Wayne Foskett
Val Mason	Elizabeth Edmonds
James White	Richard Platt
Chloe White	Hazel Ellerby
Kim Beardsmore	Esther Coles
Ellie Ndebala	Sharon Hinds
Ken Waight	George Raistrick
Gerard	Patrick O'Connell
Dr Rhiann Lewis	Jaye Griffiths

IMPULSIVE BEHAVIOUR

TRANSMISSION DATE: 7 JUNE 1993
WRITER: ANDY DE LA TOUR
DIRECTOR: ANTONIA BIRD

Father Mel Daley is a Catholic priest and local youth leader. While preparing dinner, he badly cuts himself and Jack is called out to stitch up the wound. He learns that it is Mel's third accident in the space of a few weeks.

Later, at the small Catholic church in Cardale, Mel receives a visit from Bishop Stirland who is questioning him closely regarding his youth work. The Bishop says there have been a few complaints, particularly about joyriders. At the end of their discussion, Mel steps out into the road and is hit by a tractor.

Jack tends to Mel's leg, which is badly bruised but not broken, and asks him to come to the surgery the next day. At confession beforehand, Mel tells his colleague, Father Clement Jennings, that he is angry because he doesn't know what is wrong with him. Clement suggests that he talk to Jack.

Jack arranges for Mel to see a neurologist for tests. The tests reveal that Mel is epileptic. He suddenly has a fit at morning mass and drops the

Before sorting out the boys of Sun Hill in 'The Bill', Jaye Griffiths played easy-rider Dr Rhiann Lewis in 'Peak Practice'

wine, causing Father Clement to take over. He later has a full convulsive fit at the youth club dance.

In anguish, Mel seeks solitude in the wilds of the Peak District. Jack manages to track him down and tries to talk him round. Mel admits that he can no longer face people because of his condition but Jack says that if a priest can't cope, how can other epilepsy sufferers hope to? As blunt as usual, Jack scolds Mel for running away from his problems. The truth may hurt Mel but it has the desired effect and he returns to the church to deliver a heart-warming sermon as proof that he has come to terms with his illness.

Dr Rhiann Lewis, the new recruit at the health centre, seems to be making a beeline for Jack. They flirt during a tedious hospital lecture, at the end of which she asks him out. She is not backward in coming forward. Their date is a trip to the City Ground, Nottingham, on the back of Rhiann's motorbike, to see Forest play Newcastle. For Jack, sitting on the pillion behind the glamorous Rhiann brings a whole new meaning to fantasy football...

Beth's time is spent dealing with 82-year-old farmer Hilda Lyons who enjoys nothing more than ploughing the fields on her small tractor. Fiercely independent, she has been a farmer all her life and has never married. She has been suffering from pleurisy but prefers to resist medical advice. To be on the safe side, Beth calls on her neighbouring farmers, the Barbers, a couple in their mid-forties, and asks them to keep a diplomatic eye on Hilda. Shortly afterwards, Hilda is

Beth Glover and Rhiann Lewis — two of the many women in Jack's tangled love life

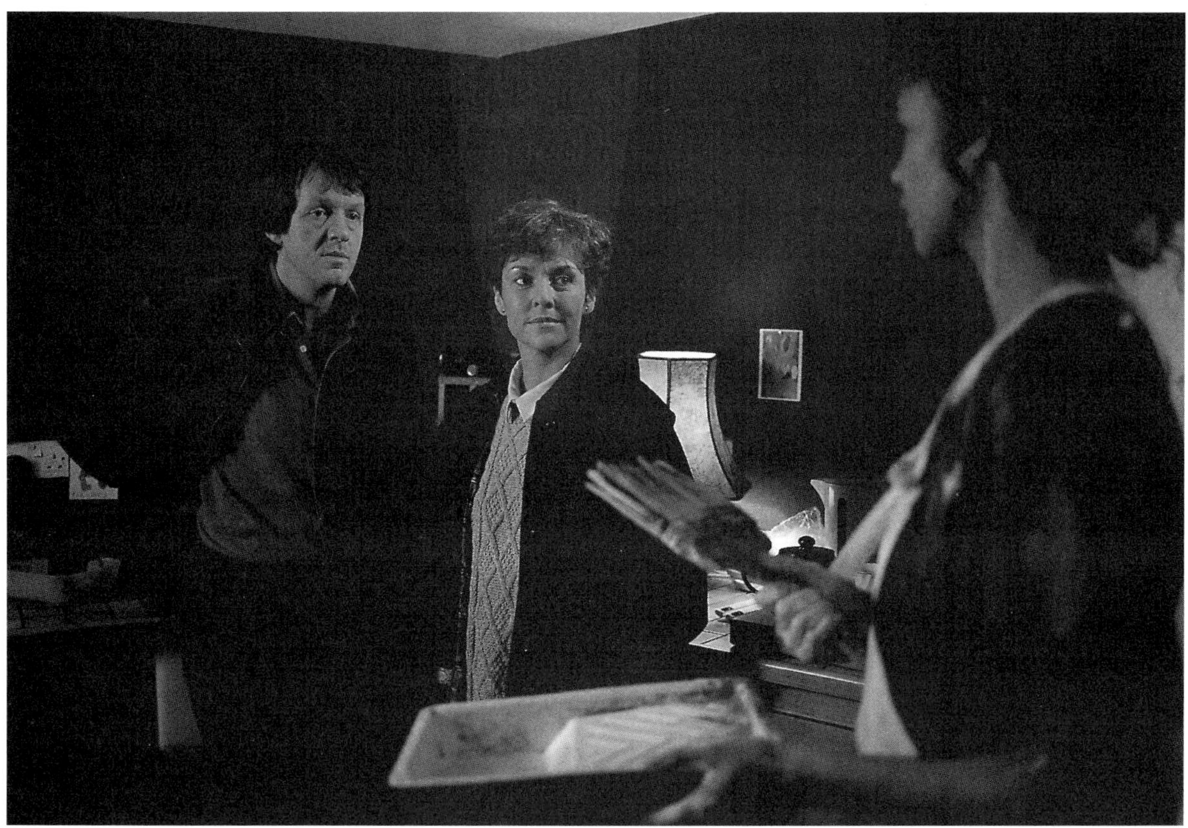

repairing a dry-stone wall with the help of a quarter bottle of whisky when she slips and scratches her face against the rough stone. Liz Barber summons Beth who puts a sling on Hilda and tells her to stay in bed for a couple of days. Beth says that if Hilda doesn't obey her instructions, she'll put her in a home. Although she is joking, the point is serious.

Back at The Beeches, Beth, Jack and Will are arguing about the merits of using patients as guinea pigs for testing new drugs. Beth is against the idea but Will is in favour. He needs the money and can collect £100 for each patient who agrees.

As a result of the shared cover arrangements with the health centre, it is Rhiann who is next called out by the Barbers to attend Hilda. She takes Hilda's temperature and, seeing that her neck hurts, rings for an ambulance. When Beth visits and finds an empty house, she traces Rhiann and Jack to the pub. Beth tells Rhiann that her diagnosis of meningitis is wrong and that she should not have made the old lady go back to hospital. Rhiann thinks Beth is simply trying to have a dig at her because of her involvement with Jack. When Rhiann falls out with her landlady and is asked to leave, she turns up at Jack's cottage in the middle of a meeting with Beth and Will. To Beth's disgust, she asks if she can stay. An embarrassed Jack shows her to the spare room and makes it clear that he doesn't want her creeping across the landing in the night. But when the coast is clear, that is precisely what she does do, going into Jack's room and asking for a cuddle. He is unable — or unwilling — to resist. The next day, Beth apologises to Rhiann for her behaviour. Jack assures Beth that Rhiann is nothing more than his lodger but Beth doesn't believe him. So he tells Rhiann that he doesn't think they should sleep together again.

Supporting Cast

Isabel de Gines	Sylvia Syms
Father Mel Daley	John Lynch
Dr Rhiann Lewis	Jaye Griffiths
Hilda Lyons	Margery Withers
John Barber	Bernard Strother
Liz Barber	Elaine Donnelly
Kim Beardsmore	Esther Coles
Ellie Ndebala	Sharon Hinds
Eve	Kitty Scopes
Chloe White	Hazel Ellerby
Dr Daniel Acres	Tom Beard
Dr John Reginald	Andrew Ray
Father Clement Jennings	Bruce Alexander
Bishop Alexander Stirland	Rio Fanning
Marjorie	Tilly Vosburgh
Kevin	Richard Brinkmann
Candy O'Neill	Nadia Sparham
GP	James Snell
Tina	Ladene Hall
Patient	Roger Bingham
Mrs Haines	Eileen O'Brien
Sylvia O'Neill	Kate Percival

HOPE TO DIE

TRANSMISSION DATE: 14 JUNE 1993
WRITER: TONY ETCHELLS
DIRECTOR: ALAN GRINT

When his best friend, young ex-miner Francis Barrat, is taken ill and a pile-up on the M1 delays the ambulance, Danny Jackson drives him to hospital with Jack as passenger. En route, Francis stops breathing. Jack tries cardiac massage and mouth-to-mouth resuscitation but has elicited no response by the time they reach casualty. The staff manage to stabilise him but Jack's relief is tempered by the news that Francis has had heart trouble for eighteen months but nobody has done anything about it.

Francis is Beth's patient and the cardiologist, Dr Reeve, resents Jack's interference. In turn, Jack demands to know why Francis is not even down for surgery to treat his hereditary heart condition. Reeve replies that it's a question of resources — there are many other patients who are equally ill but who would have a better chance of survival. Reeve is happy keeping Francis on drugs.

In the wake of Reeve's reluctance, Jack proposes to Danny that Francis could have the operation done privately. It would cost at least £5,000, a sum which Danny contemplates getting from the miners' social fund, formed when the pit closed down. A major stumbling block is that Francis has previously refused permission to be operated on. As Jack leaves the miners' social club, he sees that the wheels on his car have been replaced by four piles of bricks.

Against Beth's wishes, Jack continues to press for a second opinion. He convinces Francis's mum Rita of the need to go private. Beth is hurt

The day of the fun run, with Chris Walker as Bernie Clifton-impersonator Danny Jackson

that Rita had not discussed the matter with her first. With the money available, Jack fixes a consultation for Francis at the Fairlane Centre. Beth bridles at the fact that Jack has gone out on a limb and accuses him of acting like God. 'You've got a whole community hanging on your every word,' she tells him. 'They're expecting a miracle. Let's hope you can deliver.'

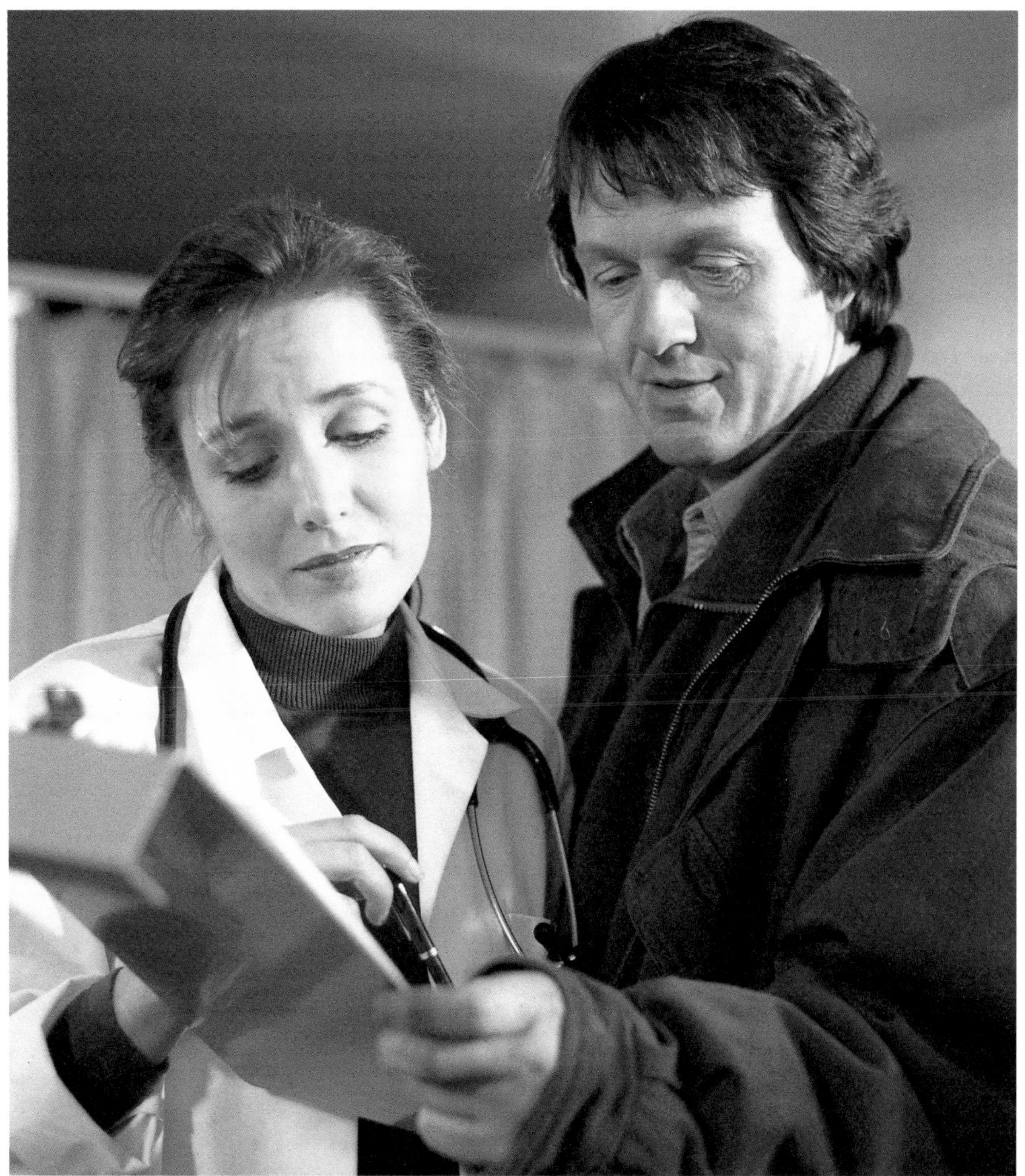

Jack compares notes with Dr Susan Lees (Caroline Langrishe)

Will and Sarah's marital problems are worsening — he is reduced to sleeping on the sofa. Jack tries to take his mind off it by dragging him along to the social club for a pint or five. In spite of his ongoing financial crisis, when Will wins £60 on the horses, he puts it into a collection box for Francis.

The social club arranges a fun run to raise money for Francis. Danny is dressed as a chicken. Jack and Will take part too. Moved by everyone's efforts, Francis finally agrees to have the operation.

Unable to concentrate on his other patients, Jack anxiously awaits news of the outcome of the operation. The phone rings. Jack puts it down, stunned. Francis is dead. He never regained consciousness after surgery.

Having raised everyone's hopes, Jack fears a backlash but Rita, for one, is very understanding. She knows that Jack did what he thought was right. He had explained to Francis that there was a risk involved. Jack finds comfort in Beth's arms.

SUPPORTING CAST

Isabel de Gines	Sylvia Syms
Francis Barrat	Sean Pertwee
Danny Jackson	Christopher Walker
Sarah Preston	Jacqueline Leonard
Rita Barrat	Anne Reid
Dr Laurence Reeve	Benjamin Whitrow
Dr Susan Lees	Caroline Langrishe
Kim Beardsmore	Esther Coles
Ellie Ndebala	Sharon Hinds
Casualty Officer	Leonard Preston
Susan Davey	Danielle Tilley
Colliery Band	Thoresby Colliery (DOSCO) Band

LISTENING SKILLS

TRANSMISSION DATE: 21 JUNE 1993
WRITER: LUCY GANNON
DIRECTOR: CHRIS LOVETT

Times are hard in the Preston household. Sarah is embarrassed when a cheque to the village grocer bounces. It emerges that Tony's school fees haven't been paid either and that Will has been ignoring letters from the bank. His answer has been to indulge in a spot of extra-curricular activity, conducting patient trials for a drug company. The company rep, Peter Thorn, pays him handsomely but is concerned because Will is behind schedule with the results. Will tells him not to worry. Will has deliberately kept his involvement in the trials a secret from Jack and Beth — he knows that Beth strongly disapproves of using patients as guinea pigs.

One of Will's patients for testing, old Alice North, is taken ill while playing bowls. Jack thinks her diet is to blame. She is jaundiced — 'so yellow she almost glows' — and probably has a gall bladder infection. Alice has been seeing Will every week of late but Beth is puzzled when she can find no trace of Alice's records.

By now, Will is in a panic. He is a week late with the test results and some of his patients, who had initially agreed to help, are letting him down. He needs the money. He decides to fake the results.

Alice spills the beans about Will's drug trials, forcing him to reveal the truth to Jack. Kerruish is livid. Alice's husband died of stomach cancer and Will's testing made Alice think she was going the same way. And his failure to record Alice's visits put the patient's health at risk.

Will has to face Beth. He confesses that 25 patients were listed as taking part in the trials but half hadn't turned up. So he had made up the

Jack tries to help Will sort out his problems

results, including putting Alice down as 'no reaction' even though she had been ill. Beth tells Will he has committed fraud and wants him out of the practice. Jack is more sympathetic, suggesting that Will needs help.

Will cracks up and stays off work. Sarah shows no mercy, announcing that if he leaves the practice, it is the end of their marriage. She blames him for the financial mess in which they find themselves. 'You always wanted to be the great middle-class GP,' she rages. 'You've got the looks, the accent, but none of the backbone.'

Alice recovers in hospital which at least lets Will off the hook in that direction. Sarah returns the new car Will bought her and buys back her old one. They argue again and Will snaps, hurling things at Sarah and smashing up the house. When the dust settles, Beth calls round. Sitting on the floor amidst the carnage, he tells her: 'I want to die.' Beth realises that Jack is right — Will needs help not the sack.

SUPPORTING CAST

Alice North	Margery Mason
Mr Hart	Maurice Denham
Sarah Preston	Jacqueline Leonard
Chloe White	Hazel Ellerby
James White	Richard Platt
Kim Beardsmore	Esther Coles
Ellie Ndebala	Sharon Hinds
Derek	Chris Sanders
Peter Thorn	Michael Thomas
1st Footballer	Tim Stanley
2nd Footballer	James Hooton
Referee	Edward Clayton
Ambulanceman	Paul Butterworth
Man	Steven Brough
Woman	Jackie Montem

GIDDY HEIGHTS

TRANSMISSION DATE: 28 JUNE 1993
WRITER: LUCY GANNON
DIRECTOR: ALAN GRINT

After spending the night together, Beth drops Jack off a short distance from the surgery so as not to give everybody the right impression. Jack is planning to go mountain climbing in the Peak District, a goal shared by Ian Hilliard, his girlfriend Marie and mate Paul who are sampling an adventure holiday in the area. One of the holiday activities is whitewater canoeing during which Ian rolls over into the raging waters and has to be pulled to safety. It transpires that Ian had a kidney transplant five years earlier. He and his friends fear that should this be a recurrence of kidney trouble, it would put an end to their holiday. They would certainly not be able to go on the eagerly anticipated expedition without a fitness certificate.

Ian goes to see Beth with the intention of obtaining the necessary certificate but, once she is aware of his history, she refers him to a renal unit. Ian disregards her fears for his health and pretends to Marie and Paul that everything is OK. He and Paul set off hill-walking to Curbar Gap, a bleak, windswept outcrop north of Baslow.

Back in Cardale, Chloe White is in the latter stages of pregnancy. She is due to give birth in a month's time. Husband James rebukes her for doing too much around the pub and gets Jack to have a word with her about washing the cellar. Soon James decides to remove temptation by packing Chloe off to a quiet cottage, far away from barrels and optics.

Will remains off work, suffering from reactive depression. Relations are strained with Sarah who tells him he's letting the family fall to pieces.

She cannot come to terms with the fact that he is so submissive. In an attempt to help her understand, Jack recalls how his father used to hit his mother and how, as a boy, he was frustrated by her refusal to fight back. Eventually, when Jack was 14, the mother walked out and never returned. Sarah is grateful for Jack's interest.

High on the Peaks, the weather is closing in. Ian and Paul pitch their tents overnight but the following morning, Paul finds that his friend is unconscious. In his haste to fetch help, he tumbles down a rock face and breaks his leg. The mountain rescue team receive a call that two men are lost near Curbar Gap. Jack sets off with them and they quickly find the injured Paul. He says that Ian is higher up, in a green tent, although he is unable to be more specific about the location. They discover Ian who is airlifted by helicopter to hospital. With the weather deteriorating by the minute, there is no time for Jack to rest on his laurels. He must begin the descent to civilisation.

As a storm brews in Cardale, Chloe goes into labour. Beth and a midwife hurry to the cottage, only to discover that the road is blocked. Not fancying a mile walk, Beth tries to summon the assistance of Jack who lives much nearer to the cottage. Exhausted after his exploits at altitude, Jack doesn't answer the phone. Salvation arrives in the unlikely form of Will who, learning of Chloe's plight, pulls himself together and volun-

The mountain rescue team find the injured Paul (Thomas Craig)

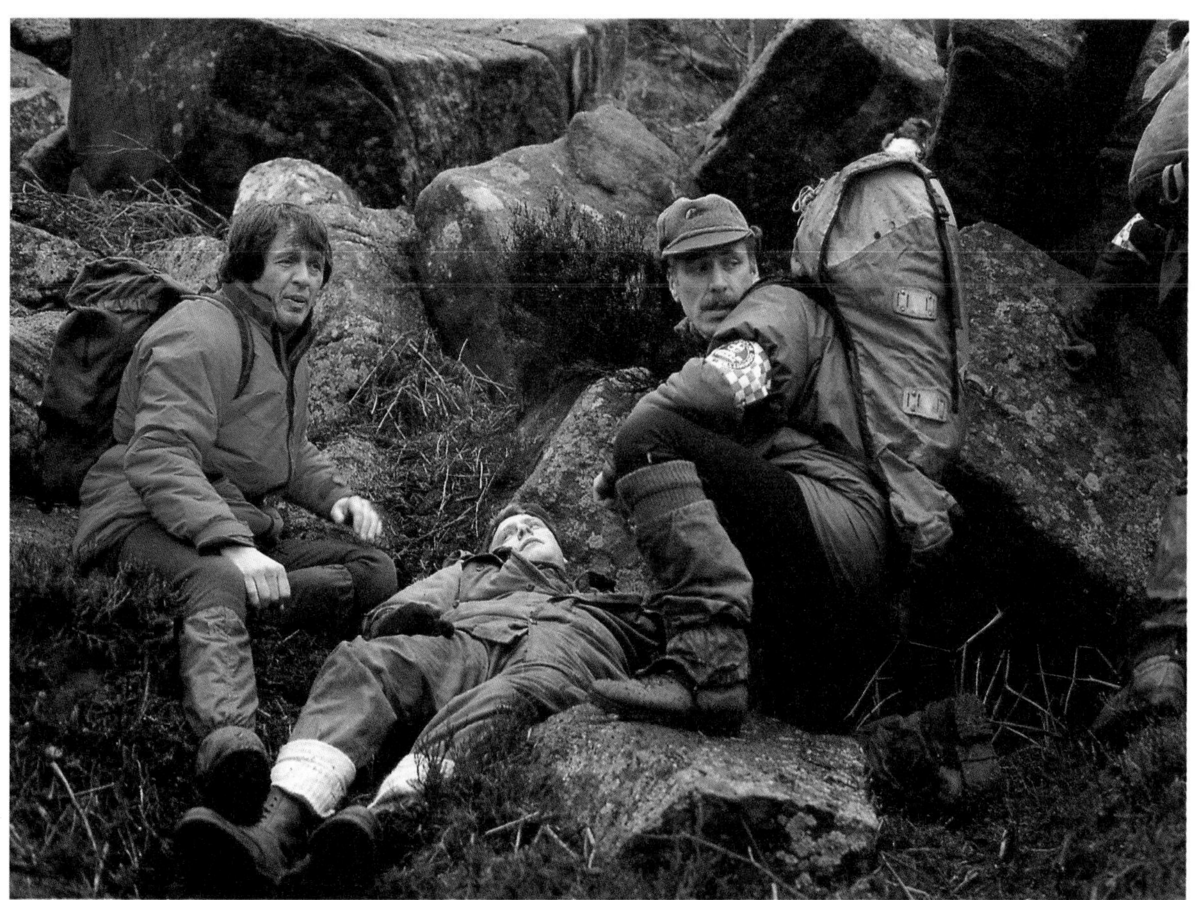

teers to take the four-wheel drive over to the cottage. Together, Will and Beth deliver Chloe's baby, a girl to be named Sarah Jane. As the baby emerges into the world, James promptly faints. Clearly the publican is in need of a stiff drink.

As Ian accepts the verdict that his kidney has packed in, Will and Sarah seem reconciled. She even invites him back into the marital bed. And Beth, coming in from the cold, decides that the best way to warm herself up is to wrap herself around Jack. He offers minimal resistance.

SUPPORTING CAST

Isabel de Gines	Sylvia Syms
Ian Hilliard	Sean Gallagher
Sarah Preston	Jacqueline Leonard
Chloe White	Hazel Ellerby
James White	Richard Platt
Kim Beardsmore	Esther Coles
Ellie Ndebala	Sharon Hinds
Marie	Jayne Ashbourne
Paul	Thomas Craig
Graham	Phil Smeeton
John Crier	James Masters
Irene	Madelaine Newton
Policeman	Dave Roberts

Will and Beth bask in the afterglow of delivering Chloe White's baby

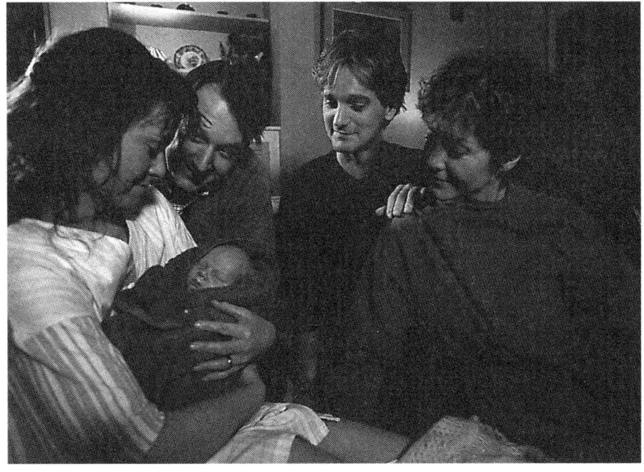

SERIES TWO

IN GOOD FAITH

TRANSMISSION DATE: 1 MARCH 1994
WRITER: LUCY GANNON
DIRECTOR: MOIRA ARMSTRONG

Anne Meadows has lost faith in conventional medicines. So she takes her young daughter Penny, an asthma sufferer, along to a British Evangelical Youth Service conducted by the charismatic John Adams, a man who promises healing to those who believe. Anne Meadows is greatly impressed and later asks Beth Glover her opinion on faith healing. But Anne's husband, Colin, and the local pastor, the Rev. Neil Winters, remain sceptical.

Mrs Meadows presses on regardless and proceeds to hide all of Penny's puffers. When Penny has an attack, John Adams is summoned to pray for her, to the disgust of Colin. Slowly, Penny's heaving subsides. Mrs Meadows feels utterly vindicated and joyously gives testament in church of how her daughter has been 'cured'.

Her celebration proves a trifle premature. At school, Penny has a fierce attack. Jack arrives and calls an ambulance but Mrs Meadows indignantly snatches her daughter away and flatly refuses to listen to his warnings. Increasingly concerned about Penny's health, Jack visits the Meadows' house but Anne leaves him standing on the doorstep. In frustration, Jack threatens to get an emergency order.

Once again, the mother's answer to her daughter's illness is to solicit the help of John Adams. However, he becomes terrified as Penny's condition worsens and he begins to realise he is out of his depth. Jack returns, this time with Ellie, the practice nurse, and John Adams agrees to let them in. By now, Anne

Meadows is hysterical as Jack sweeps Penny into his arms and rushes her off to hospital where the youngster is immediately put into an intensive care unit. Mrs Meadows realises that any further delay could have been disastrous. She has good reason to be grateful to Jack.

Another of Jack's patients also has a delicate problem. Bank manager Trevor Sharp's adventurous fling with vivacious local hairdresser Leanda has been going a little limp of late. He tells Jack that he feels listless and can't sleep at night. Leanda doesn't want him to sleep at night but nevertheless feels rejected when he shows a distinct lack of enthusiasm at the prospect of hours of unbridled passion. Jack examines him but can find nothing amiss.

Over the next few days, Trevor spends almost as much time at The Beeches as the staff. But he is remarkably coy about the exact nature of his complaint until Jack finally drags it out of him. Sure enough, Trevor's worries are sexually related. He can no longer manage it twice a day, as a result of which he is starting to feel demoralised at work. Jack tells him not to demand so much of himself, to lower his expectations. After all, it's not a sperm bank he's running. Trevor takes his advice and is relieved when Leanda tells him she loves him just the way he is. They agree to marry in August.

If only the course of true love were as smooth for Will and Sarah who, following his six months' rehabilitation, are currently in the throes of moving to a smaller house in a bid to reduce their debts and rekindle their marriage. Sarah takes up

Jack resorts to drastic measures to save young asthma sufferer Penny Meadows (Sara Cragg)

Trevor Sharp (Shaun Prendergast), the bank manager that likes to say 'yes' to hairdresser Leanda (Beth Goddard)

a new job as school secretary but receives a cool reception from the other mothers.

Jack's pursuit of Beth is also going through an unsteady phase. She decides that she needs some space, some time to be alone with her thoughts. On her day off, she takes a solitary hike and begins spending evenings alone. Her behaviour serves to make Jack confused but keener than ever. Finally, he plucks up courage to propose. His timing is bad. Beth is on edge and is not ready for such a conversation. She tells him that she's not ready to 'bow out'. Jack feels hurt and misunderstood.

SUPPORTING CAST

Sarah Preston	Jacqueline Leonard
Anne Meadows	Elizabeth Rider
Penny Meadows	Sara Cragg
Colin Meadows	Philip Martin Brown
John Adams	Colin Wells
Ellie Ndebala	Sharon Hinds
Trevor Sharp	Shaun Prendergast
Leanda	Beth Goddard
Rev. Neil Winters	David Hargreaves
Kim Beardsmore	Esther Coles
Tony Preston	Adam Berman
Julian Preston	Laurie Billson
Melanie	Michelle Chadwick
Mum 1	Sue Taylor
Mum 2	Elizabeth Hetherington
Head Teacher	Judy Liebert
Ambulanceman	Graeme Green
Dr David Ashmore	Chris Stanton
Choir	Viva Voce

OLD HABITS

TRANSMISSION DATE: 8 MARCH 1994
WRITER: LUCY GANNON
DIRECTOR: ALAN GRINT

Villager Rob Clulow has raised his three children single-handedly since his wife left him for another man. Now daughter Amanda is getting married, leaving Rob to look after 17-year-old David and 11-year-old Harry. The latter is finding life particularly difficult and is frequently bullied by a gang of local louts headed by Wayne and Terry.

Rob is very much the life and soul of any party but he is clearly not in mint condition. He has already undergone heart surgery and now needs a bypass, admitting to Beth that he has been unable to stop smoking. Despite this, she has a soft spot for him and recommends that he put in for light duties at the quarry where he works. Fearing redundancy, he backs out at the last minute.

The other members of the practice are decidedly gloomy. Jack is feeling insecure since Beth turned down his marriage proposal while a new house has brought little respite for Will. The boys, particularly Tony, have not adjusted well to the move. And Sarah is annoyed at Will's reluctance to sell his car which was to be a crucial factor towards the solution of their financial plight.

One day, young Harry gets into a fight and Rob takes him to see Jack who comes to the conclusion that it must be the Village boys versus the North End boys feud rearing its ugly head again. Rob's next port of call is to Mr Jenkins the consultant about the possibility of having a bypass. Jenkins bluntly informs him that it's a waste of time having the operation unless he gives up smoking. He gives Rob two years to live if he doesn't stop. Rob departs in a distressed state and later collapses in pursuit of Harry. Beth rushes to the scene, leaving Jack to cope with a soggy barbecue. Back at The Beeches, the three partners debate Rob Clulow's dilemma. Will is unsympathetic while Jack is morally outraged. Beth is so angry that she goes to see Jenkins. But he refuses to back down.

Tony Preston and Harry Clulow are perched high up in a derelict mill contemplating the meaning of life when they are suddenly set upon by Wayne's gang. A chase culminates in Tony, cornered, outnumbered and desperate, hurling a fire extinguisher which crashes through a glass roof below, badly injuring Wayne's leg. Tony summons help and Jack arrives with the police. To Sarah's intense embarrassment, the police turn up in the middle of the Golf Club Dinner to break the news to her and Will.

Tony is ticked off by the police and Will comforts him, obviously handling the matter better than Sarah who is so mortified that she cannot bring herself to speak to her son. Will firmly tells her to lighten up.

Having seen Rob in considerable pain, Jack visits Jenkins to try and persuade him to operate on humane grounds. But the consultant stands firm. Meanwhile Will has had a change of heart about the whole business and uses a round of golf with Jenkins as an opportunity to make him see reason. Will contends that Rob is in a life-threatening situation and recounts his own anxi-

Will Preston deals with his son Tony (Adam Berman)

ety over the incident involving his son and Harry Clulow. He adds that Rob must be under enormous stress. Impressed by the arguments, Jenkins finally gives in.

At last, Rob has the operation. All is well until daughter Amanda suddenly bursts in with the news that she has left her husband and wants to come home. What's more, she's pregnant. Rob's hopes of a quiet life are receding fast. No wonder he feels the need for a furtive fag on the hospital fire escape.

SUPPORTING CAST

Amanda Clulow	Kate Reynolds
Rob Clulow	Peter Armitage
David Clulow	Francis Lee
Harry Clulow	Shaun Tunaley
Terry	Peter Dalton
Wayne	David Harrison
Chloe White	Hazel Ellerby
James White	Richard Platt
Sarah Preston	Jacqueline Leonard
Dominic Jenkins	Miles Anderson
Sue Jenkins	Eve White
Tony Preston	Adam Berman
Julian Preston	Laurie Billson
Kim Beardsmore	Esther Coles
Dr John Reginald	Andrew Ray
Ginge	Gavin Abbott
Policeman 1	Dave Roberts
Policeman 2	Paul Gladwin
Inspector	Robert Hudson

LOVE THY NEIGHBOUR

TRANSMISSION DATE: 15 MARCH 1994
WRITER: ANDY DE LA TOUR
DIRECTOR: MOIRA ARMSTRONG

Jack's new neighbour Richard has a penchant for pigs. Jack has nothing against them but is none too pleased when one of their number, Alberta, wakes him in the middle of the night by squealing on his doorstep. Worse is to come. A night of passion with Beth is wrecked when Richard starts banging around outside. Frustrated, Jack tells Beth he feels used. The next morning, he discovers that Richard's master-plan is to generate his own power from the methane gas in pig shit. Jack is finding it increasingly difficult to love his neighbour.

On one of his regular trips to the pub, Jack mentions to landlord James White that his wife Chloe looks very tired and despondent. Jack later examines Chloe and finds a swelling under her chin. He expresses concern about her depressed state of mind and suggests that she attend counselling for young mothers. Chloe politely declines the offer.

Leafing through Chloe's medical records, Jack notices that she has been losing weight and decides to do a biopsy to rule out cancer. He is angry with himself for not spotting the danger signs earlier. The results reveal that Chloe has Hodgkins Disease — cancer of the lymphatic system. As Jack breaks the news to her, he tells her that it is treatable with drugs and radiation therapy. Naturally distressed, she says she doesn't want her husband to know.

Jack and Beth talk about commitment. Beth doesn't want marriage because she is afraid of losing her identity. Jack feels rejected and suggests a break. In the pub, Beth comforts Chloe who still refuses to tell James. He discovers that

Chloe has concealed a visit to The Beeches but when he confronts her about it, she walks off. James storms into the surgery demanding an explanation but Jack refuses to break confidentiality. He later meets Chloe from her scan appointment. They talk about fighting the disease and she reluctantly accepts that James will have to be told. The results of the scan do nothing to ease the burden. In the most difficult consultation of his career, Jack has to tell the Whites that the scan has revealed Stage Four Hodgkins when he had only anticipated Stage Two. James is devastated. Chloe is shocked and angry. Later Beth takes Chloe to her father's grave and tells her that she must not give up, if only for the sake of her daughter. Beth's verbal remedy works and Chloe adopts a more positive attitude.

On the home front, Beth seeks out Isabel's advice. Isabel bluntly tells Beth that she has been stringing Jack along. Beth prepares for a momentous announcement and, fighting the overpowering stench from Richard's pigs, tells Jack that their affair is over.

Jack soon has a willing replacement — although not exactly the girl of his dreams. For as Richard's money-making scheme ends in an almighty explosion, Jack finds Alberta gazing longingly into his eyes. Yes, love can be a pig.

SUPPORTING CAST

Richard Morris	Alan David
Chloe White	Hazel Ellerby
James White	Richard Platt
Sarah Preston	Jacqueline Leonard
Greg Miller	Jon Glover
Dr John Reginald	Andrew Ray
Brian Drake	Roland Oliver
Kim Beardsmore	Esther Coles
Customer	Desmond Stokes
Ellie Ndebala	Sharon Hinds

Beth threatens to give Jack the cold shoulder

ACT OF REMEMBRANCE

TRANSMISSION DATE: 22 MARCH 1994
WRITER: LUCY GANNON
DIRECTOR: COLIN GREGG

When ex-RAF Squadron Leader Douglas Hart learns of a forthcoming 'fly past' to commemorate the Battle of Britain, he is determined to attend despite his ailing health. However, the site of the fly past, a reservoir, is a few hours' drive from Cardale and an inhospitable place during the bleak Derbyshire winter. Since Mr Hart's son Ian is going overseas on business, the old man's close companion, Alice, agrees to accompany him to the event.

Isabel de Gines is attending a counselling course at which she has met a potential suitor, Ken Alton, the boss of a local dye works where Beth is employed as medical advisor.

Meanwhile Mr Hart begins to suffer momentary lapses of memory. Alice calls on him one morning and is horrified to find a blazing pan on the stove with him fast asleep in an armchair. After extinguishing the flames, she offers to move in with him so that she can keep an eye on his welfare. She decides that he is not well enough to attend the fly past but he stubbornly refuses to listen. When Alice refuses to join him, Isabel and Ken step in. Alice leaves in a huff.

Mr Hart thoroughly enjoys himself at the fly past. As the other onlookers disperse, he remains for a moment, gazing at the sky, remembering. Suddenly he feels dizzy and collapses. Ken and Isabel sit in a warm car nearby, unaware that their charge has suffered a stroke and is in a coma. Mr Hart dies. Alice is at his house waiting for him, having prepared a special tea as a peace offering. Anxious when he fails to return, she calls on Will who breaks the sad news to her.

Beth and Jack are finding it difficult to work together following the break-up of their relationship. Carol Dart, a workaholic office employee from the dye works, visits Jack at the surgery. She has repetitive strain injury in her wrists and is told to stay away from her computer keyboard for at least a week. When her condition fails to improve, Jack cursorily informs Beth and suggests that she take action in her capacity as medical advisor. Jack is convinced that Carol has continued to type as a result of pressure exerted by her employer but has to eat humble pie when Carol confesses that she has been sneaking back to work out of hours. Ken Alton has been totally unaware of this.

Jack realises he has been unfair to Beth and apologises. The frostiness between them begins to thaw...slowly.

SUPPORTING CAST

Mr Hart	Maurice Denham
Alice North	Margery Mason
Isabel de Gines	Sylvia Syms
Ken Alton	Frank Windsor
Ian Hart	Michael Cadman
Carol Dart	Caroline Catz
Ellie Ndebala	Sharon Hinds
Sarah Preston	Jacqueline Leonard
Tony Preston	Adam Berman
Julian Preston	Laurie Billson
Secretary	Peter Stockbridge
Security Guard	Stan Nelson
Tutor	Max Mason
Jake	Dominic Tandy
Veteran	George Malpas
Organiser	Colin Bower
Casualty Officer	Tim Briggs

Dye works boss Ken Alton put the colour back into Isabel's cheeks!

ENEMY WITHIN

TRANSMISSION DATE: 29 MARCH 1994
WRITER: TOM ANTHONY
DIRECTOR: ALAN GRINT

Arriving at the milk depot where he works, Martin Keel is informed that he is to be made redundant. The news comes as a devastating blow. His young son Matthew is on the milk float with him and father and son drive out into the countryside to release Martin's beloved homing pigeons. While they are out, Matthew becomes unwell. Martin panics and speeds through the lanes to The Beeches. His wife Sue, the cleaner at The Beeches, reprimands him for over-reacting when Jack diagnoses nothing more than a minor virus.

Later Matthew has a febrile convulsion. Martin, by now a time bomb waiting to explode, summons Beth but, to his dismay and disgust, she is busy on another call. By the time she does eventually reach the Keel household, she finds Sue and Matthew leaving in an ambulance called by Martin. Increasingly agitated, Martin overhears that meningitis is the suspected cause of his son's fit and, in a combination of frustration and rage, he lashes out at the unsuspecting Beth.

The following morning, Beth turns up for work with a split lip. She knows that she must report the attack to the police and a furious Jack demands that Martin be removed from the Beeches' patient list. But when Sue calls the surgery because her husband has injured himself, Jack agrees to make the visit. He finds that Martin is suffering from depression and has lacerated himself deliberately. Jack sends him to the hospital and, realising that Martin needs psychiatric help, makes the necessary referral. Beth decides to drop the legal proceedings although Martin will still be required to find a new GP. There is relief all round when Matthew makes a steady recovery.

Beth tries to compose herself after being attacked by Martin Keel

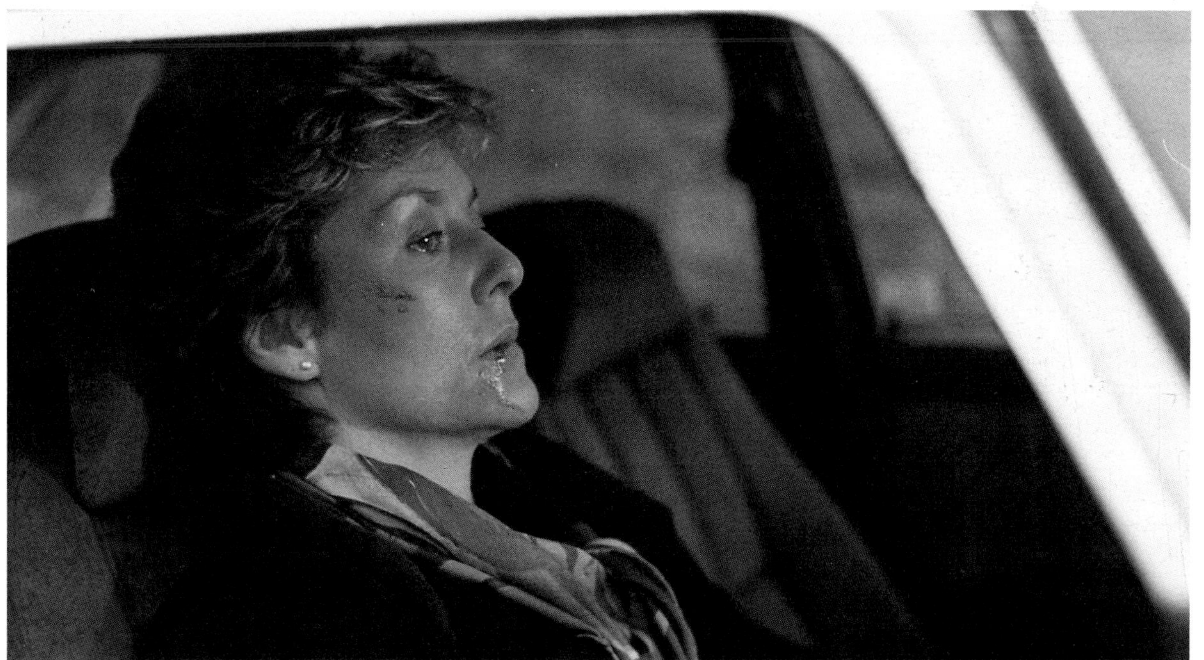

Chloe White's chemotherapy has not been working and a new protocol is to be introduced. She is apprehensive about her next hospital visit, fearing that once she goes in she will never come out, but husband James promises her that she will not have to stay in. However, in the wake of her chemotherapy session, Chloe is very ill. She and James concede that she must go into hospital for a short period. A few days later, she is sent home, having responded well to treatment.

Sarah Preston is bored with her job as a school secretary but Will expresses a concern that the children will suffer if she gets a more demanding job. Nevertheless when Peter Doland, a smarmy drug rep, suggests that he may be able to help her make a career move, she jumps at the opportunity. She boldly informs Will that she has got a new job but omits to mention that Doland has fixed it — a wise move since the two men do not see eye to eye. It appears that Doland has an ulterior motive in assisting Sarah but when she fails to offer him any encouragement, the job offer suddenly falls through. Sarah is back to square one.

SUPPORTING CAST

Martin Keel	George Irving
Sue Keel	Minnie Driver
Matthew Keel	James Peachey
Kim Beardsmore	Esther Coles
Sarah Preston	Jacqueline Leonard
Chloe White	Hazel Ellerby
James White	Richard Platt
Peter Doland	Vincent Regan
Ellie Ndebala	Sharon Hinds
Ogden	Ian Keith
Anne Howell	Anita J. Altinbas
Ambulance Driver	Rebecca Jackson
Senior House Officer	Leonard Preston
Senior Registrar	Gabrielle Reidy
Casualty Officer	Claire Walters

LONG WEEKEND

TRANSMISSION DATE: 5 APRIL 1994
WRITER: LUCY GANNON
DIRECTOR: ALAN GRINT

When Jack was at medical school, he was engaged to a fellow student named Karen Eastman. But then Karen developed schizophrenia and the pair went their separate ways. So it comes as a shock when Jack receives a call from Karen, begging him to come and see her. She is in a London phone box in a highly agitated state, convinced that 'they' are trying to kill her by putting poison in her medication.

The next day, Jack takes a call from a London psychiatric hospital. Karen has been brought in by the police who found her wandering the streets in search of her missing purse. Jack's name was the only one she would give to the hospital staff. Jack immediately takes off for the capital, leaving Beth and Will to speculate as to the reason for his hasty departure.

At first, the trip is a disaster with Karen flatly refusing to see Jack. But before he returns to Cardale, she relents and they have a friendly meeting which ends with him promising to visit her again, very soon.

Back at The Beeches, Kim is sent home from work with a heavy cold, thus putting a halt to the horse-riding lessons she has been having with Beth. Jack asks for a few more days off. Beth and Will are not thrilled with the situation but have little option but to agree. Before departing for London, Jack is called out to see Kim whose condition has deteriorated. He suspects that she has a virus and doesn't prescribe any medication for it.

Karen seems to be becoming obsessed with Jack. Her elderly mother is worried to learn that Karen will have to leave the hospital in a few days. Her anxiety is heightened when Karen absconds from the hospital in a bid to reach Jack in Derbyshire.

Meanwhile Beth decides to admit Kim to hospital as an emergency. Her temperature is alarmingly high and her throat is almost closed. Initially, everyone is mystified by her illness until Beth remembers their riding lessons. It transpires that Kim has picked up a rare infection (Streptococcus Zoo Epidemicus) from the horses. After a few days in hospital and the correct treatment, Kim is fine.

Having hitched up to Cardale, Karen turns up at The Beeches. She demands to speak to Jack. Ellie thinks she is a vagrant. In Jack's absence, Beth comes out to talk to Karen but finds that Karen has suddenly disappeared. After surgery, Beth is alone at The Beeches when she is disturbed by what she believes to be a burglar. Her heart pounding, she has the presence of mind to slip out into the car park and call the police. Jack arrives on the scene before the police and instinctively knows that it is Karen in the surgery. He finds her toying with the medical equipment in the consulting rooms. They talk but he doesn't like what he's hearing. For Karen has got it into her head that she is to be Jack's partner in the practice. Sensing the awkward atmosphere, Beth suggests that they both spend the night at her house.

Later, Jack explains to Beth about his past relationship with Karen. It's a tender moment between the two, repairing the rift that has been growing since Beth turned down his marriage proposal. The peace is shattered when, on her way to bed, Beth discovers that Karen has mutilated herself in a moment of self-realisation and lucidity — she knows that she is ill and will never be a doctor. Beth and Jack manage to calm her

Jack's ex-fiancée Karen (Dearbhla Molloy) caused him no end of headaches over a 'Long Weekend'

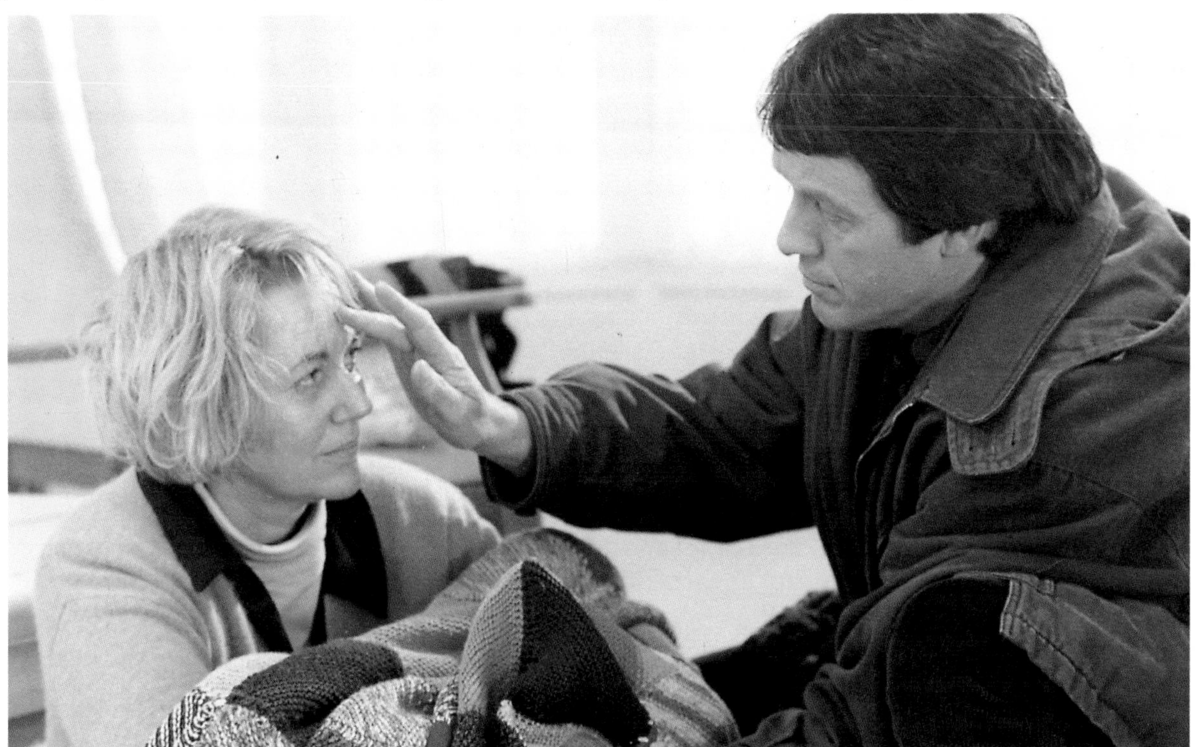

down and patch her up. At their last meeting, Karen tells Jack that she never wants to see him again, no matter how much she begs for his attention when she is sick.

SUPPORTING CAST

Karen Eastman	Dearbhla Molloy
Kim Beardsmore	Esther Coles
Ellie Ndebala	Sharon Hinds
Gavin	Kieron Forsyth
Chloe White	Hazel Ellerby
Mary Eastman	Doreen Mantle
David Eastman	Tenniel Evans
Woman Driver	Dorothy Atkinson
Liz	Catherine Terris
Keith	Geoff Lawson
Riding Instructor	Michael Greatorex
Sam Beardsmore	Andrew Chisholm
Bus Driver	Larrington Walker
Nurse	Pinkey Devaz
Eve	Kitty Scopes
Lorry Driver	Brian Southwood
Lorry Driver's Girlfriend	Patti Lamar

Beth takes to the saddle

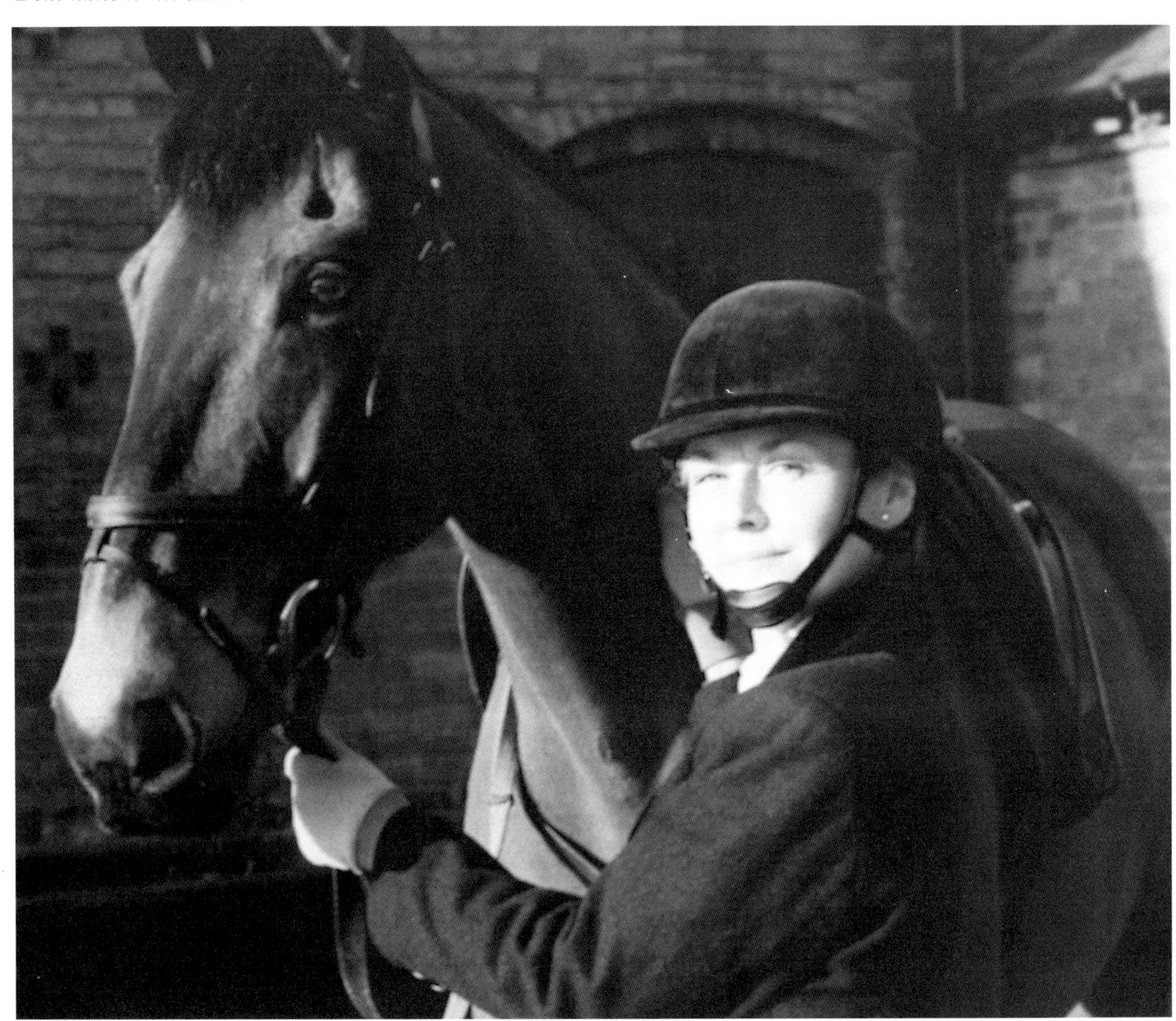

CHANCE ENCOUNTER

TRANSMISSION DATE: 12 APRIL 1994
WRITER: ANDY DE LA TOUR
DIRECTOR: ALAN GRINT

Jack is planning to attend a 'men only' lunch, staged to celebrate Cardale's football team winning a trophy. Will is going too but is none too pleased about being on call. So he asks Beth to cover for him but she declines, saying she has arranged to visit an old school friend.

In truth, Beth has gone off to meet Michael, an ex-lover, at a country hotel. Arriving late, Michael tells her that he hopes to rekindle their old romance. After a good deal of wavering, Beth eventually decides against this and speeds back towards Cardale through driving rain.

After the lunch, Jack, suitably mellow, made a semi-conscious decision to go and declare his undying love to Beth and went to her house to await her return. He has a long wait. For, her visibility impaired by the atrocious conditions, Beth takes a wrong turning and ends up in an isolated spot on High Peak. As she is driving along, trying to regain her bearings, her car is flagged down by a young man, Sean, whose car has veered off the road and rolled down a steep slope. His girlfriend, Lisa, is still in the wreckage and bleeding heavily from a leg wound. To her horror, Beth finds that her mobile phone will not work in the area and so she sends Sean off in her car to find a phone box and call an ambulance. In the meantime, Beth drags Lisa clear of the crashed car and comforts her on a nearby wooded hillside which affords some shelter from the elements.

Little does Beth know that the crashed car is stolen. Consequently, to avoid involving the police, Sean does not call the emergency services. Instead he dumps Beth's car in a lay-by near Cardale and returns home to his brother Damien's house.

By now, Jack is beginning to fret about Beth.

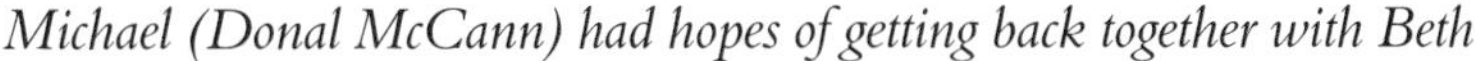

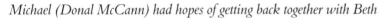

Michael (Donal McCann) had hopes of getting back together with Beth

He calls the police but no accidents have been reported. He calls Isabel. She knows about Beth's secret rendezvous and cannot cover for her when Jack discovers a message from Michael on Beth's answerphone. Jack presumes that Beth is safely tucked up in a hotel room with another man. The thought doesn't exactly please him but he is no longer concerned for her safety.

The warmth of a hotel room is a far cry from the conditions being experienced by Beth out on High Peak. She realises that Sean is not going to raise the alarm and, despite her attempts to wrap Lisa up in an effort to stem the onset of hypothermia, she is aware that Lisa has only a matter of hours to live unless help can be summoned. In desperation, Beth tells the barely conscious Lisa that she is going to fetch assistance. With no passing traffic, it is a futile mission and Beth soon returns in despair to the scene of the crash.

Damien has come to the conclusion that Sean is suffering from concussion. Knowing his brother only too well, he guesses about the crash. Believing that Sean was alone in the car, he does not contact the police. However, he does call Will.

Jack and Will arrive in the nick of time to save Beth, after she has spent a night on the frozen moors

Showing very early signs of hypothermia herself, Beth struggles to make a beacon out of twigs. But she is very weak. Lisa, with whom she has formed a real bond, knows that she is going to die.

The police at last find Beth's abandoned car and inform Will who calls round at Beth's house to find Jack alone. Knowing what he does about Beth's mystery assignation with Michael, Jack remains unconcerned and when Damien calls Will out again, Jack goes along for the ride. This time, Susie, Damien's girlfriend, tells them how Sean really sustained his injuries. In his delirium, Sean utters Lisa's name. Alarm bells start ringing in the doctors' heads. They alert the emergency services and set out together to scour the unforgiving landscape in search of the scene of the accident.

Certain that Beth is involved and is out there somewhere, they find the crashed car. Then Jack spots the remains of the makeshift beacon and finds Beth unconscious. Nearby, Lisa is dead. Partially revived by the warmth of Will's car, Beth summons up just enough strength to ask Jack to marry her.

SUPPORTING CAST

Michael	Donal McCann
Isabel de Gines	Sylvia Syms
Sean	Matthew Wait
Lisa	Elizabeth Chadwick
Damien	Daniel Ryan
Susie	Louise Delamere
James White	Richard Platt
Chloe White	Hazel Ellerby
Alan	Nicholas Caunter
Man 1	Kemal Sylvester
Man 2	Alan Westaway
Stunt Double	Abbi Collins

Safe at last: a relieved Jack cradles Beth in his arms

LIFE CHANGES

TRANSMISSION DATE: 19 APRIL 1994
WRITER: ANDY DE LA TOUR
DIRECTOR: COLIN GREGG

Beth and Jack have dinner with Beth's talented dancer friend Angie Wilkes and her husband Drew, a South African lecturer at Nottingham University. Beth has been prescribing painkillers to Angie for backache but, telling her that she needs to eat more, books her in for an exploratory x-ray.

After teaching an energetic jazz routine to a class of young dancers, Angie helps Ben, a promising black dancer, to go through his routine for a forthcoming audition. Later, she is clearly in pain but hides her discomfort from Drew.

The x-ray reveals nothing untoward but Beth wants to do a blood test and a scan. She asks Angie about her diet and whether in the past she has gone without periods for any length of time. Angie guesses that Beth is concerned about osteoporosis, which makes the bones brittle. In an emotional outburst, she says she would rather die than give up dancing.

A distraught Angie cancels her classes and sadly tells Ben that he's on his own from now on. Drew is worried about her taking so many painkillers but agrees to pick up some more from The Beeches the next morning. He sees Jack and tells him that they are for Angie's back. Beth breaks the news to Angie that she has osteoporosis which is treatable with hormone replacement therapy and that she will be able to dance under controlled conditions. Angie is devastated. Drugged up, she goes to the studios and goes through Ben's routine with him, then dances on silently in her own world. Later, Drew finds her on the bathroom floor having overdosed. It appears that she has carried out her threat until Beth races over and realises that Angie has been prescribed the wrong pills by Jack who didn't know that she had a history of acute dyspepsia. Angie is taken to hospital.

Will and Sarah's marriage is irretrievably breaking down. They live separate lives under the same roof, coming and going like strangers. Will has been sleeping in the boys' bedroom. When their son Tony is involved in a fight at school, Sarah acts the disciplinarian. She lays down the law to Tony who responds by screaming that Will hates her. In a furious rage, she lashes out at her son who tumbles, cutting his face on the door. Meanwhile Will and Kim are working late on fundholding business and are becoming quite close. He finds himself able to talk to her in a way he cannot with his wife and ends up confiding in her that he doesn't think his marriage will survive much longer.

In a conciliatory mood, Will tells Sarah that Tony is angry with them arguing all the time. He says he wants her to start investing in their family and marriage but she coldly dismisses his ultimatum.

When the fundholding meeting takes place, it results in Beth storming out. She is still distressed about Angie and loses her temper with talk of budgets rather than patient care. Jack visits Angie in hospital to apologise for his error. She tells him that she has no intention of trying to top herself and that she has told Drew about her condition. A tearful Sarah calls on Jack and confesses that she is not cut out for the role of wife and mother and that she doesn't have a real friendship with Will. She makes Jack promise to be her friend if the village turns against her.

Trying to clear the air, Kim has a chat with Beth about fundholding and how it need not interfere with the patients. She explains how she will take on the bulk of the work and how proud she is of her own admin systems. Beth is impressed with Kim's commitment and later tells Jack that she has seen her in a new light. She had underestimated Kim in the past.

Jack, who has been trying to sell his cottage, receives an offer and hurries off to meet the prospective buyers. In the middle of the discussion, Beth suddenly appears to announce that the cottage is no longer for sale as she and Jack are going to live there. Delighted, Jack asks the couple whether they would be interested in a lovely town house — Beth's!

A hesitant Angie goes to watch Ben at his audition. He dances brilliantly and sees how proud she is of him. At Sunday lunch, Angie and Drew announce that they are returning to South Africa. Beth and Jack excitedly consider the prospect of an African honeymoon.

SUPPORTING CAST

Angie Wilkes	Donna King
Drew Wilkes	Jack Klaff
Kim Beardsmore	Esther Coles
Sarah Preston	Jacqueline Leonard
Ben	Nicholas Pinnock
Greg Miller	Jon Glover
Sam	Andrew Chisholm
Julia	Jacqueline Beatty
Steve	Philip Mulhaire
Ellie Ndebala	Sharon Hinds
Tony Preston	Adam Berman
Julian Preston	Laurie Billson
Prospective Buyer	Janet Crawford
Choreographer	Arlene Phillips

A BRAVE FACE

TRANSMISSION DATE: 26 APRIL 1994
WRITER: LUCY GANNON
DIRECTOR: DANNY HILLER

Will is pleasantly surprised to receive a phone call from Stuart Mosely, an old colleague and close friend with whom he had lost touch. Stuart was best man at Will and Sarah's wedding — a happy occasion far removed from the daily domestic warfare which the couple are now enduring. Stuart left a glowing career as a GP to work in an executive position for a charity.

However, Will's delight at seeing his old friend is cut short when Stuart visits him at the surgery and reveals that he is HIV positive and is now exhibiting signs of full-blown AIDS. Stuart is determined that the eye disease, retinitis, which he is suffering from and his overall condition be kept a secret from the medical profession, the general public and indeed everyone except his wife Zoe. The stunned Will cannot come to terms with the fact that his friend has not informed the Health Authority under which he practised of his predicament. Nevertheless, he agrees to treat Stuart at home. Stuart loses his sight.

Zoe is as determined as her husband to put on a brave face to mask the pain which they both feel over Stuart's illness. She does not enquire, or know, how he contracted HIV. When Will informs them that he will have to contact the Director of Public Health for advice on whether or not to disclose Stuart's medical status, the couple close ranks on him. Stuart is worried that should the news leak out, his family will be hounded by the media. He also fears that the future of his daughter, Sally, will be placed in jeopardy after she leaves medical school.

In an attempt to die before it becomes obvious

to outsiders that he has AIDS and to prevent any scandal affecting his family, Stuart tries to commit suicide. Although he has asked Jack to take over the case, Will stills feels personally responsible and rushes over to the Mosely household when Zoe calls him. He summons an ambulance for the unconscious Stuart and then telephones the casualty officer at the hospital, alerting him to the HIV status of the incoming patient. Sally overhears this conversation and, although deeply shocked, does not let on that she knows her dad is HIV positive. Preoccupied with the events of the morning, Will misses a lunch appointment with Sarah who has been trying to have meaningful talks with her husband.

At home, Stuart tells Sally how he contracted HIV via a long-term sexual relationship with a man named Alan. To help her father, Sally supplies him with the necessary drugs to commit suicide. This time Stuart is successful. Sally is not implicated in the death.

While Will is preoccupied by the Mosely case, Beth and Jack try to sort out the problems of the Clarke family. Lou and her husband, affectionately known as Clarkey, take their two young daughters to see Jack with minor colds brought on by the damp caravan in which they are living. Lou is in the late stages of pregnancy but has not been attending ante-natal classes. When Jack offers to send Ellie out to see her, Lou quickly promises to make the long journey to The Beeches. She is clearly ashamed of her living conditions.

At a routine ante-natal check-up, Beth is concerned that Lou's high blood pressure is attributable to the hard work involved in living in a caravan. Beth admits Lou to hospital because she fears that she will develop pre-eclampsia. Later, Beth suggests that Jack let his cottage to the Clarkes now that the doctors have decided, after all, to live at Beth's once they are married. Jack is initially reluctant but eventually backs down.

As the necessary forms are signed at The Beeches to make them fundholders, Will returns home after the missed lunch to find that Sarah has left him, taking the boys and most of the furniture with her.

SUPPORTING CAST

Stuart Mosely	Jonathan Hyde
Zoe Mosely	Jenny Quayle
Sally Mosely	Paula Hunt
Sarah Preston	Jacqueline Leonard
Tony Preston	Adam Berman
Julian Preston	Laurie Billson
Lou Clarke	Tracy Brabin
Clarkey	Ian Mercer
Kim Beardsmore	Esther Coles
Swan	Oliver Smith
Mayor	Richard Evans

ABBEY

TRANSMISSION DATE: 3 MAY 1994
WRITER: ANDY DE LA TOUR
DIRECTOR: COLIN GREGG

WPC Benson and Inspector Rossiter oversee the grim night-time scene of a dead, abandoned baby being loaded into an ambulance high on a lonely moor just outside Cardale. Jack is visiting Chloe when a report about the baby appears on the local television news. Chloe, who is nearing the end of her courses of chemotherapy, faints. Jack warns her that she has been overdoing it. Downstairs in the Manor, Beth tells Will to keep her informed of any developments regarding the placement of hospital contracts, now that The Beeches is a fundholding practice.

Ellie is driving Kim home when they spot an unkempt, teenage girl walking alone across the moor. Her name is Abbey. Kim shouts across to offer her a lift but Abbey ignores her and instead makes her own way to the church in Cardale. Looking pale and ill, she breaks in and settles down for the night. The following morning, she is disturbed by the pastor but runs off before he can speak to her.

James sees Abbey stealing milk from his doorstep and dashes out just as Jack is arriving with Chloe's anti-emetics. The fleeing Abbey is nearly mown down by Jack's car but, before he can remonstrate with her, she has disappeared. She is becoming as elusive as the Surrey Puma.

WPC Benson visits the surgery, asking the staff to keep an eye open for the abandoned baby's mother who may try to seek medical attention. Beth is angered when Murdoch, a hospital consultant and an old friend, reveals that Will is negotiating contracts with private hospitals. Will is trying to put a brave face on things and cope with his situation since Sarah left him.

Abbey resurfaces and is moved on when caught begging in the Square. She also has a run-in with Steve, a local teenager, who later spots her crouched down in an alleyway injecting herself. Wrongly presuming her to be a drug addict, Steve destroys her hypodermics and kicks her in the stomach. The following day, Abbey turns up at The Beeches. She meets Jack but, unwilling to fill in a registration card, leaves before having a proper consultation. Jack suspects that she may be the mother the police are looking for.

Abbey next pops up in the mini-mart, stealing chocolate. Chloe clocks her, as does the shopkeeper. When he approaches her, Abbey goes mad and starts screaming. She cuts her head on a shelf and runs out into the Square. Chloe fetches Jack who's in the Manor with James. Jack recognises that Abbey is having a hypoglycaemic attack, caused by badly managed diabetes. He and James bundle her into the Bristol and take her to The Beeches where Jack administers a glucose injection to prevent her from falling into a coma. Further examination shows that she is also suffering from retinitis and Jack is determined to get her the laser treatment which will save her sight, even if she is evasive about revealing details of her past. Going out on a limb, he refuses to tell WPC Benson of Abbey's whereabouts when the policewoman asks to see her regarding the shoplifting incident. Jack has changed his mind about Abbey. He now has a gut feeling that she is not the mother of the dead baby and allows her to stay the night at Beth's house. Beth is less convinced.

Abbey is seen by a consultant at the hospital but Jack is disappointed to be told that the laser treatment cannot be done for at least another three weeks. He is worried that Abbey will be long gone before then. Will makes himself unpopular with Beth by suggesting that he 'buy in' Abbey's operation at a private hospital. Jack agrees.

Kim calls on Will, offering him the opportunity to chat through his problems. They get a little drunk and she expresses interest in his bedside manner. Embarrassed, he spurns her advances and then tells her that he doesn't think she is suitable for the post of Practice Manager. Kim appears to have blown it in a big way.

Inspector Rossiter informs Jack that the mother of the dead baby has been traced. It is not Abbey. But he has linked Abbey to a description of a runaway. Her real name is Pauline Jones. She is only 15 and has absconded from a children's home. Jack realises that she is too young to be operated upon without the consent of her legal guardians. He returns home to find that Abbey has gone, taking Beth's cheque book with her. He finally manages to track her down at a squat but she is reluctant to speak to him and refuses to go back into care. Jack leaves but later decides to notify the social services of her whereabouts. Abbey is soon picked up by the police and social services. She may not think it but she should be grateful to Jack. For without the appropriate treatment, which she can now get, she would soon go blind.

SUPPORTING CAST

Abbey	Samantha Morton
Kim Beardsmore	Esther Coles
Sam Beardsmore	Andrew Chisholm
WPC Benson	Gaynor Faye
Inspector Rossiter	Eamon Boland
Ellie Ndebala	Sharon Hinds
Chloe White	Hazel Ellerby
James White	Richard Platt
Pastor	Peter Meakin
Alice North	Margery Mason
Murdoch	George Little
Steve	Danny Cunningham
Alf	Bill Gavin
Stevens	Christopher Baines
Customer 1	Bob Gilligan
Customer 2	Mike Chapman
Drinker 1	Nik Hedges
Drinker 2	Howard Grace
Girl 1	Emma Leyland
Girl 2	Fiona Johnson

PERFECT LOVE

TRANSMISSION DATE: 10 MAY 1994
WRITER: LUCY GANNON
DIRECTOR: JENNY KILLICK

As the day of Beth and Jack's wedding approaches, the happy couple are distracted by a tricky abortion case. Beth and Jack are visiting Dominic and Annie Kent, an affluent couple who are old friends of Beth's. The Kents have a two-year-old daughter, Victoria, who is entrusted to the care of Sarah, a young nanny. Annie has problems relating to Victoria and admits to Dominic that she feels no love for her daughter. Jack senses this. Dominic confides in Beth that Annie is expecting a second child.

Annie is a private patient of John Reginald's. She calls on him to request an abortion but Reginald refuses to arrange a termination, as a result of which Annie leaves his surgery in an extremely distressed state. Ten hours later, Dominic phones Beth and asks her to come and see him. Annie has not returned home yet — and Victoria is with her. Dominic fears the worst and tells Beth about his wife's rejection of their daughter. Shocked, Beth suggests that Annie may need counselling.

With Dominic out of his mind with worry and a storm raging outside, Annie finally comes home, soaked to the skin. She explains that she ran out of petrol some distance away. Unable to see Victoria, Dominic assumes that she has been abandoned along with the Range Rover. He dashes out to look for her but returns in a state of panic without her. Beth calmly explains that Victoria is safely tucked up in her bed. Annie had brought her home with her but had put her in the nursery before seeing Dominic.

Annie tells Dominic that she wants an abortion, an idea to which he is firmly opposed. The next day, Annie visits Jack in an attempt to obtain a referral for an abortion. Jack agrees to grant this on condition that she take a one-week 'thinking' period, during which she should try and talk to Dominic about her decision. Beth is angry about this and Dr Reginald remains tight-lipped. When Beth calls on Dominic to inform him of Jack's decision, he says that he no longer wants Annie. Reluctantly, she leaves him.

But Dominic still loves her and asks Jack where she is staying. He is worried because Annie is scared of hospitals and, although he doesn't condone what she is doing, he cannot bear to think of her going through the operation alone. It emerges that Annie suffered a long and arduous birth with Victoria which may have contributed to the lack of feeling she now has for her daughter. When Annie learns that Dominic wants to see her, she rings him. They meet and decide to try and save their marriage. Annie has the abortion.

Alice North is mending her ramshackle chicken coop when her foot is pierced by what she presumes to be a nail. She hobbles in to see Will who dresses the wound and gives her a tetanus booster jab. Meanwhile Chloe has been told by Jack that she has responded well to the chemotherapy course. She can now stop the treatment and just have regular tests to monitor her condition. Hopefully, the Hodgkin's disease has been eradicated. Chloe calls on Alice the day after her foot injury and finds her looking decidedly weary. She and James take Alice to see Will again. Now that the swelling on her foot has subsided, Will can see that Alice has been bitten by a rat. She has become infected with Streptobacillus Moniliformis and is given antibiotics. But she draws the line at having the pest control van outside her house. What would the neighbours think?

Beth and Jack make a lovely couple in a horse-drawn carriage for two

Will has problems looking after the boys, who visit him at weekends, whilst he is on call and has to concede that they can stay with Sarah when he is working. One extracurricular activity is for he, Jack and James to destroy Alice's rat. But the trio are too squeamish and the task falls to the redoubtable Isabel who kills the offending creature with no qualms whatsoever!

The happy day finally arrives. Beth and Jack are married.

Supporting Cast

Annie Kent	Tam Hoskyns
Dominic Kent	Richard Bonneville
Isabel de Gines	Sylvia Sims
Ken	Frank Windsor
Kim Beardsmore	Esther Coles
Ellie Ndebala	Sharon Hinds
Chloe White	Hazel Ellerby
James White	Richard Platt
Dr John Reginald	Andrew Ray
Alice North	Margery Mason
Trevor Sharp	Shaun Prendergast
Leanda	Beth Goddard
Sarah	Hilary Lyon
Victoria Kent	Nicola Wyatt
Tony Preston	Adam Berman
Julian Preston	Laurie Billson
Eve	Kitty Scopes
Vicar	Philip Childs

POWER GAMES

Transmission date: 17 May 1994
Writer: Emily Brigdon
Director: Jon Scoffield

Fifty-six-year-old Bob Massey owns and runs a textile factory in Cardale. He is a self-made man who has built his business up from scratch with the help of his wife Sheila. Bob regards Sheila as his 'right hand man' whereas she feels she has often been nothing more than a glorified secretary and would like to take a more 'hands on' role in the business before she is too old. Their son, Michael, who is 28, also works for the family firm, in a managerial position.

One night, Bob is kept awake by indigestion. He hears a gang of youths trying to steal statues from his garden and angrily fires a gun over their heads to frighten them away. In doing so, he over-exerts himself and suffers a minor heart attack. Sheila calls Beth who is her friend as well as being the doctor on call. Despite Bob's protestations, Beth sends him to hospital.

In Bob's absence, Sheila decides that she will run the factory. She calls a meeting with the factory foremen and approves some overtime, much to the annoyance of Michael who says it is unnecessary. He eventually backs down but Sheila is not pleased that he has questioned her authority. Then one of the foremen, John, complains about Joe Wilson, an electrician who has been with the company for 30 years but is perplexed by modern, computerised machinery. His inability to adapt often holds up production but Sheila, appreciating the value of loyalty, defends him to the hilt. Both Sheila and Joe Wilson call on Bob in hospital, visits which leave him less concerned about his own health than that of the business. He promptly discharges himself so that he can keep an eye on Sheila, Michael and the

Looking as worried as he ever did in the Rovers Return, Roy Barraclough had plenty on his mind as electrician Joe Wilson

factory. Beth goes to see Bob after receiving a call from an angry hospital consultant and warns Sheila and Michael to work together in harmony for the sake of Bob's health.

However, the power struggle between Sheila and Michael continues to rage until Bob decides to return to work against Beth's advice. While Bob takes a couple of hours off work to have some tests done at the hospital, Joe Wilson clashes with Michael, resulting in the former leaving Massey Textiles. When Bob is told of Wilson's departure, he is furious. Whilst talking to Wilson, he has a cardiac arrest. Wilson attempts to resuscitate Bob until Beth and Will arrive. Bob is rushed to hospital, leaving Sheila and Michael feeling responsible for the second attack. Sheila thinks it best if she stands down and allows her son to run the factory. Bob survives and peace is restored to the Massey household.

Frank Hooley, a local handyman with the ability to take on just about any given task, has dislocated his shoulder. He calls on Jack at morning surgery. Jack snaps the shoulder back into its socket and gives him a sick note, signing him off work for one week. But his injury doesn't stop him working and soon he is building a wall for Isabel. He returns to the surgery and asks to see Will, complaining that his other shoulder is now dislocated. Will returns it to its rightful position with some relish.

There is tension between Beth and the male partners because she is, unfairly, being allocated the heavy workload entailed in taking all of the women's clinics that The Beeches operates. The disquiet is temporarily forgotten when Hooley returns to The Beeches with his usual complaint.

(Above) Joe Wilson comes to the aid of factory boss Bob Massey (Tony Doyle)

(Below) Sheila Massey (Judy Loe, left) comforts husband Bob

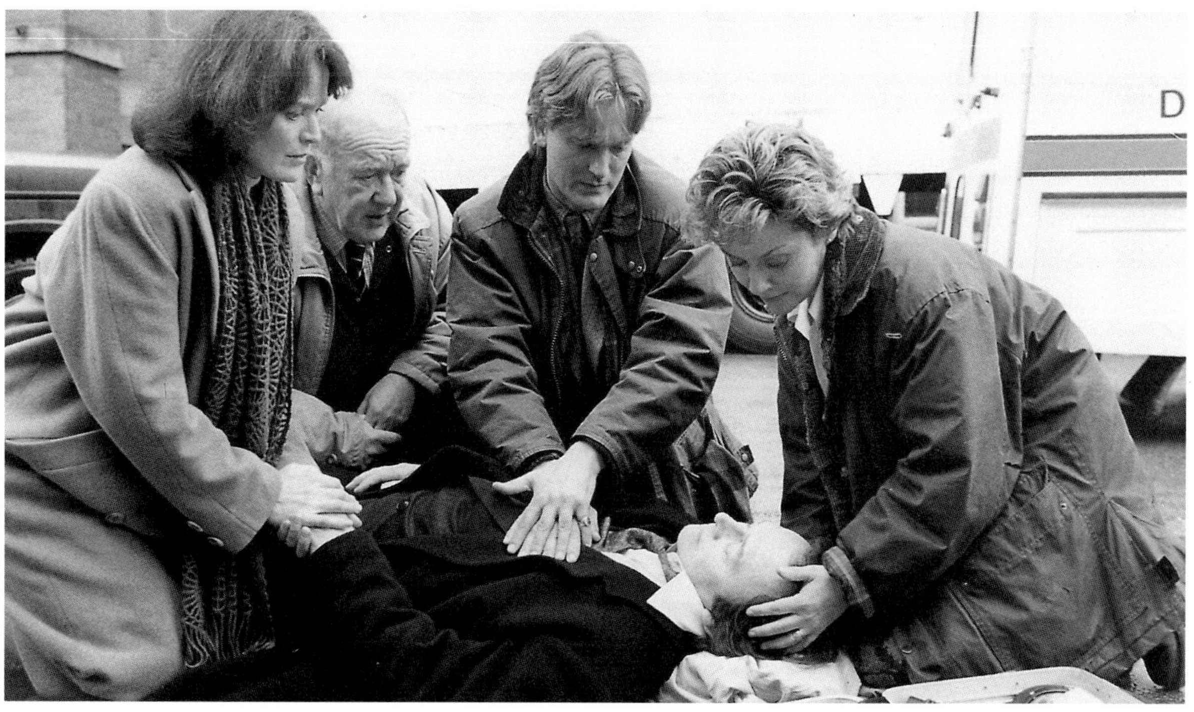

This time it is Beth who tends to his shoulder. Later, an insurance inspector arrives at the surgery. He explains to Will how Hooley was previously a circus contortionist and how he currently makes a living moving around the country, assuming numerous aliases and putting in bogus sick leave claims with various insurance companies. Will and Kim have no intention of shouldering the burden and turn Hooley in.

SUPPORTING CAST

Isabel de Gines	Sylvia Syms
Sheila Massey	Judy Loe
Joe Wilson	Roy Barraclough
Bob Massey	Tony Doyle
Michael Massey	Valentine Pelka
Frank Hooley	Robert Demeger
Kim Beardsmore	Esther Coles
Ellie Ndebala	Sharon Hinds
John	Simon Corris
Annabel	Annabel Hampson
Nurse	Tessa Harrison
Doctor	Stuart MacKenzie
Worker	Paul Waring

HAPPY EVER AFTER

TRANSMISSION DATE: 24 MAY 1994
WRITER: LUCY GANNON
DIRECTOR: COLIN GREGG

After failing to appear in court to face charges of non-payment of her Council Tax, Alice North is visited at home by two uniformed police officers. They explain that they will not take her into custody if she pays a 'doorstep' bail, amounting to the outstanding balance of Council Tax. She either cannot or will not hand the money over and so the police have no option but to arrest her.

Meanwhile Jack receives a visit from 19-year-old Carl Clarke, brother of Clarkey, the tenant at Jack's cottage. Unbeknown to Jack, Carl has also been living temporarily at the cottage. Carl requests tranquillisers, saying that he hasn't been sleeping well of late. He admits to having a minor drink problem and to being on police bail for breaking and entering. Jack presumes that the reason for Carl's inability to sleep is that he hasn't had a drink for a few days and so he prescribes some tranquillisers which will ease the symptoms of alcohol withdrawal.

A bewildered Alice is led into the dock to find Isabel sitting on the bench. Isabel immediately stands down because she knows the defendant but takes the unusual step of phoning Beth to ask whether she can pop by and check Alice over. Isabel does not, however, reveal the nature of Alice's case. Alice is told that she may go. Beth escorts her home since the old lady nearly collapses in jail. They talk in the safety of Alice's home but, although Beth knows that something is amiss, she cannot quite pinpoint what it is.

Carl Clarke is the next person in the dock. He faces Isabel who renews his bail but is puzzled to see that he is residing at Jack's cottage.

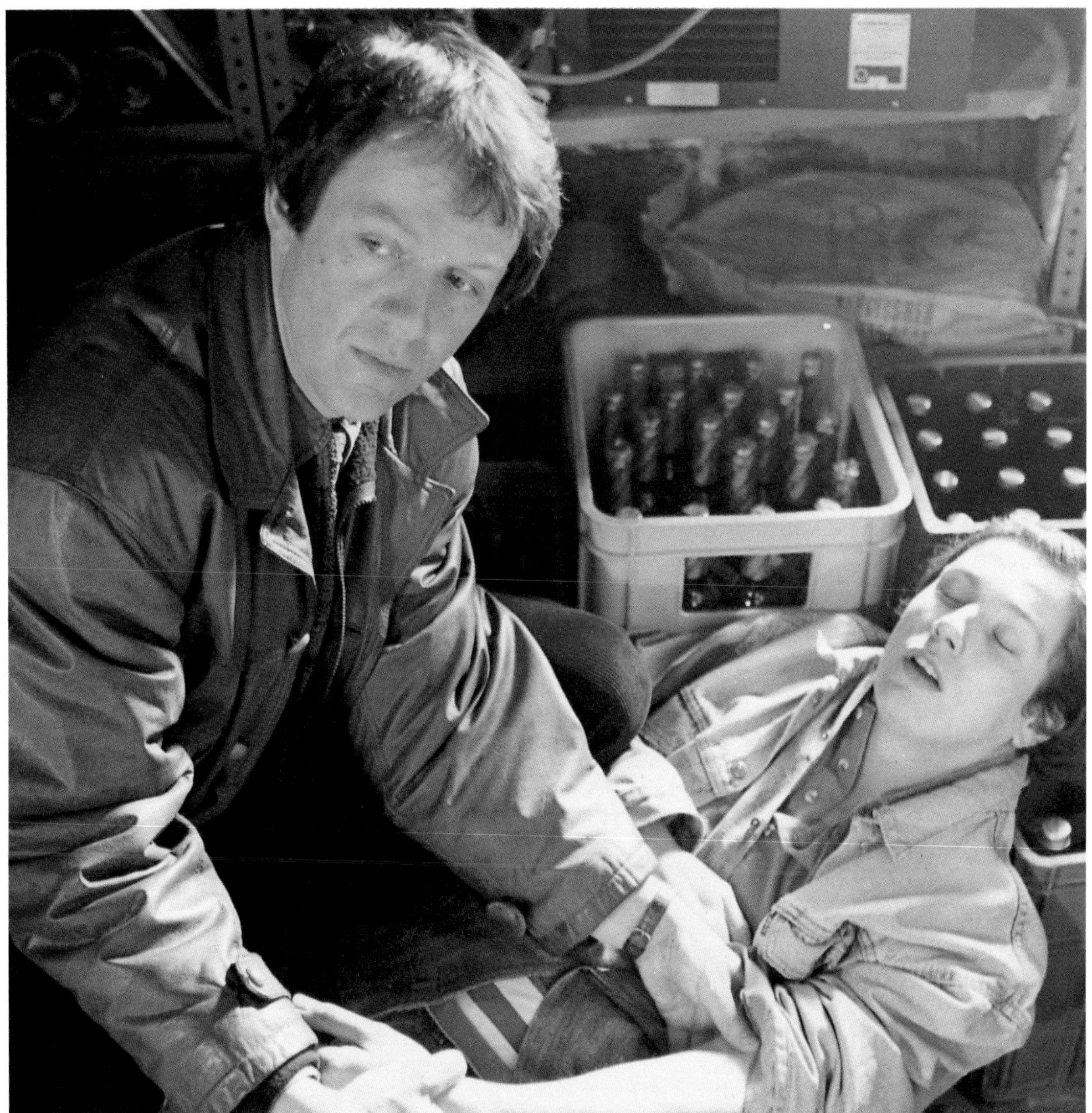

Jack discovers Carl Clarke (David Kitchener) drunk in the cellar of the Manor

Back at the cottage, it emerges that Carl's upbringing has been anything but stable. As a result, he is a bitter young man. Now that he has run out of pills, he becomes agitated and desperately searches for something to calm him down. He even asks his two young nieces 'where mummy keeps her medicine'. The promise of a few days' work with Clarkey soothes him for a short period but he soon becomes restless and irritable and goes out. He breaks into the cellar at the Manor and gets well and truly drunk.

Beth and Jack have invited Isabel and Will over to dinner. The subject of Alice is raised and soon turns into a critique of the magistrate's role.

Isabel is offended and leaves. The warmth and comfort of Beth's house are in stark contrast to the circumstances experienced by Alice North. Afraid to leave her house to collect coal, she suffers a cold, sleepless night.

The following morning, James calls Jack to the Manor, having discovered the drunken Carl in the cellar. Before taking Carl back to the cottage, Jack looks at the lad's arms. He has obviously been injecting drugs. Jack tackles Carl who admits to injecting Tamazepam, a prescribed tranquilliser. Carl is angry with himself for missing his first day at work.

Beth is surprised to see Alice conducting a conversation with the milkman through the letter box. Furthermore, she learns at the post office that Alice has been sending a neighbour to pick up her pension. It dawns on Beth that what Will believes to be a case of slight depression could in fact be the first outward signs of agoraphobia. Will and Beth call on Alice who manages to talk through her problems and finally agrees to take a short course of very mild tranquillisers to set her on an even keel.

Back at the cottage, Carl walks out after a row with Clarkey. He plans to hitch and stay with a friend who tells him to bring 'something' with him. In order to obtain the necessary 'something', Carl breaks into The Beeches but the alarm rings through to the police station and a car hurries to the scene. Carl escapes with only a box of syringes and breaks into Isabel's garage for shelter. Isabel finds him the next morning and calls Jack. Then she calls the police. When Carl realises who she is, he threatens her with a knife but Isabel bravely stands her ground and he backs down. Jack rings round the drug rehabilitation centres but is unable to find a place for Carl. In court, he reiterates Carl's need for help but Benn, the top magistrate, refuses to listen to any pleas for clemency and remands Carl to prison. Isabel is so saddened by this that she decides to resign from the bench.

Against this dramatic backdrop, interviews for the position of Fund Manager have been held at The Beeches. The final candidate of the day is Trevor Sharp, the local bank manager. Thirsting for revenge, Jack and Will can hardly wait to grill him and so it is much to Trevor's surprise when he proves to be the successful candidate. Kim is pleased about his appointment but Ellie is less enamoured. Following the announcement, Beth attends a bogus call at the Manor, finding instead a surprise birthday party arranged for her by Jack.

SUPPORTING CAST

Alice North	Margery Mason
Isabel de Gines	Sylvia Syms
Carl Clarke	David Kitchener
Clarkey	Ian Mercer
Trevor Sharp	Shaun Prendergast
Lou Clarke	Tracy Brabin
Leanda	Beth Goddard
Chloe White	Hazel Ellerby
James White	Richard Platt
Kim Beardsmore	Esther Coles
Ellie Ndebala	Sharon Hinds
PC Warren	Paul Gladwin
WPC Benson	Gaynor Faye
Abigail	Elizabeth Hickling
Pasco	David Warwick
Geraldine	Karen Gledhill
Clarkey's Girls	Alice Betterton
	Katie Whiting
Clerk of the Court	Tim Meats
Mr Benn	Henry Moxon
Eve	Kitty Scopes
Milkman	Bunny May
Pal 1	Tim Stanley

ACKNOWLEDGEMENTS

The author would like to thank the following for their invaluable help in the preparation of this book:

Nic Brown,
Michele Buck,
Amanda Burton,
Ted Childs,
Fiona Connery,
Dr Derek Cooke,
Josh Dynevor,
Gordon Flemyng,
Lucy Gannon,
Stevie Groves,
Charles Hubbard,
John Hudson,
Jonathan Hudson,
Fiona Johnston,
Barry Ledingham,
Nick Lockett,
Julian Murphy,
Simon Shepherd,
Tony Virgo,
Deborah Waight,
Kevin Whately,
C.J. Wills.

PUBLISHER'S ACKNOWLEDGEMENTS

Boxtree would like to thank the following people for their co-operation in the production of this book:

Roy Barraclough
Adam Berman
Amelda Brown
Christopher Brown
Amanda Burton
Elizabeth Chadwick
Esther Coles
Dr Derek Cooke
Sara Cragg
Thomas Craig
David Credell
Peter Dalton
Maurice Denham
Tony Doyle
Hazel Ellerby
Beth Goddard
Jaye Griffiths
David Harrison
Sharon Hinds
Agatha Husle
Jonathan Hyde
George Irving
Donna King
David Kitchener
Caroline Langrishe
Jacqueline Leonard
Judy Loe
Donal McCann
James Masters
Dearbhla Molloy
Natalie Morse
Samantha Morton
Madelaine Newton
Bill Nighy
Richard Platt
Shaun Prendergast
Simon Shepherd
Sylvia Syms
Melanie Thaw
Chris Walker
Kevin Whately
Frank Windsor
Kendal Wood

PRE-INTERMEDIATE

coursebook

Lindsay Clandfield

with additional material by Amanda Jeffries

About Global

Lindsay Clandfield is a teacher, teacher educator and lead author of Global. He was born in England, grew up in Canada, taught at a university in Mexico, lives in Spain and has trained teachers from around the world. He is also the creator of the popular blog **Six Things** (www.sixthings.net), a collection of lists about ELT.

Six quotes that inspired global

True education means fostering the ability to be interested in something.

Sumio Iijima, Japanese physicist

It is books that are the key to the wide world; if you can't do anything else, read all that you can.

Jane Hamilton, American author

The English language is nobody's special property. It is the property of the imagination…

Derek Walcott, Caribbean poet

The important thing is not to stop questioning.

Albert Einstein, German-American physicist

The mind is not a vessel to be filled, but a fire to be kindled.

Plutarch, Greek historian

If you are going to write another coursebook for the English language, please try to do something a bit different.

An English teacher who wishes to remain anonymous

Global Pre-intermediate by numbers:

10 units 160 pages 10 extracts from famous novels 53 vocabulary sections 35 explanations of English grammar 10 functional English lessons 27 accents from around the world in Global Voices 200 audio clips 30 video clips 150 interactive activities 100s of curious and interesting facts

Content highlights

1 Individual & Society

Surprising origins and facts about everyday objects
Six Degrees of Separation by John Guare
CCTV is watching you!

2 Eating & Drinking

Tastes Comforting Secrets of the world's top kitchens **The people behind the drinks** Water and the human body

3 Art & Music

Discovered! Works of art found in unexpected places *The Picture of Dorian Gray* by Oscar Wilde The history of sound recording *High Fidelity* by Nick Hornby

4 Hopes & Fears

When I grow up… children's hopes for the future The aid worker: a profession of hope Famous dystopias in literature Reactions to… *An Inconvenient Truth*

5 Work & Leisure

Profile: An Indian call centre worker Bad bosses and work issues The serious leisure perspective Ten facts about amusement parks

6 Science & Technology

The science of happiness The worst jobs in science *Frankenstein* by Mary Shelley Going, going, gone … Online auctions

7 Time & Money

A brief history of time zones A Tale of Two Cities by Charles Dickens A lifetime of financial concerns A different kind of bank

8 Home & Away

Famous homes and their infamous occupants *Dracula* by Bram Stoker The cat came back *The Beach* by Alex Garland New kinds of tourism

9 Health & Fitness

The common cold Milestones of modern medicine Olympic tales

10 New & Old

Brave New Words by Kerry Maxwell New places in a new world Old but loved: the Trabant Two classic board games

Global English

by **David Crystal**

page 15 Same language but different
page 39 The power of music
page 63 All work and no play
page 87 The English language and the number four
page 111 Sports English

Contents

Unit		Grammar	Reading texts	Listening texts	Vocabulary	Speaking and Pronunciation
UNIT 1	**Individual** page 6	Word order in questions (p7) *What* and *How* questions (p9)	Surprising origins and facts: The identity (ID) card (p7)	Descriptions of people (p8)	Everyday objects (p6) Describing people (p8) EV *look* and *look like* (p8)	Describing people (p8) False identities (p9) (P) The alphabet (p7)
	Society page 10	Present simple, frequency adverbs (p11) Present continuous (p13)	It's a small world … the six degrees of separation theory (p10) Readers' response CCTV is watching you (p13)	Descriptions of personal relationships (p10) Explanation of the six degrees of separation theory (p10)	People you know (p10) EV *in touch* (p10) EV *place* (p12)	Family and friends (p11) Arguments for and against CCTV (p12) (P) Linking words (p13)
		Function globally: **Common social expressions** (p14) **Global English:** **Same language but different** (p15)		**Writing:** **A personal description** (p16) **Study skills:** **Being a good language learner** (p17)		
UNIT 2	**Eating** page 18	Countable / uncountable nouns, quantifiers (*some, any*) (p19) Quantifiers (*a lot of, a little, a few, not enough, much, many*) (p20)	Tastes comforting (p18) Ten secrets … from the world's top kitchens (p20)	Talk on Zao Shen (p21)	Food (p18) In the kitchen (p21) EV *taste* (p18)	Food questionnaire (p18) How do you make it? (p19) Food tips (p20) Describing a kitchen (p21) (P) /k/ and /tʃ/ (p21)
	Drinking Page 22	The infinitive (p23) The infinitive of purpose (p24)	The people behind the drinks (p22)	Talk on water and the human body (p24)	Containers and drinks (p22) The human body (p24)	What do you like to drink …? (p22) Drinks questionnaire (p25) (P) /tə/ and /tuː/ (p25)
		Function globally: **Eating out** (p26) **Global voices:** **Food that makes you think of home** (p27)		**Writing:** **A description of food and drink** (p28) **Study skills:** **Evaluating your language learning** (p29)		
UNIT 3	**Art** Page 30	Past simple and past continuous (p32)	Discovered! True stories of how valuable works of art were found in unexpected places (p30) *The Picture of Dorian Gray* by Oscar Wilde (p33)		Works of art (p30) Furniture and furnishings (p32) EV *discover* (p30)	Describing works of art (p30) Retelling stories (p32) (P) Past simple regular verbs (p33)
	Music page 34	*Used to* (p35)	*High Fidelity* by Nick Hornby (p37)	Lecture on the history of sound recording (p35) Talk on music in film and TV (p36)	Audio and video (p34) Feelings (p36) EV Saying and writing decades (p35) EV *just* (p37)	Describing pictures (p34) (P) *Used to* (p35) Music (p37)
		Function globally: **Agreeing and disagreeing** (p38) **Global English:** **The power of music** (p39)		**Writing:** **A scene from a short story** (p33) **A review** (p40) **Study skills:** **Conversation partners** (p41)		
UNIT 4	**Hopes** page 42	Future hopes and plans (p43) Future plans and intentions (*be going to*, present continuous) (p45)	When I grow up … (p42) Pandora's box (p45)	Interview with two aid workers (p44)	Adjectives and synonyms (p42) Global issues (p44)	My hopes and plans (p43) Foreign aid (p44) Hope (p45) (P) Word stress (p44)
	Fears page 46	Prediction and ability (*will, be able to*) (p47) Future time clauses (p49)	Things will get worse … famous dystopias in literature (p46)	Conversation about *An Inconvenient Truth* (p48)	Phrasal verbs with *get* (p47) Geographical features (p48) EV *-ed* / *-ing* adjectives (p48)	Climate change questionnaire (p49)
		Function globally: **Making offers and decisions** (p50) **Global voices:** **Reasons why people learn English** (p51)		**Writing:** **An email to a friend** (p52) **Study skills:** **Using your dictionary: finding the right entry** (p53)		
UNIT 5	**Work** page 54	*Have* (p55) Modal verbs (p56)	Profile of an Indian call centre worker (p54)	Conversations between bosses and employees (p56)	Work (p54) Work issues (p56) EV *job* and *work* (p54)	Jobs (p54) Job characteristics (p57) (P) Contractions (p57)
	Leisure page 58	*-ing* verbs (p59) Present perfect, *have been / have gone* (p60)	Ten facts about … amusement parks around the world (p60)	Presentation about 'The serious leisure perspective' (p58)	Leisure activities (p58) EV *play* (p58)	Ten questions about leisure (p61) (P) /ŋ/ (p59) (P) Past participles (p61)
		Function globally: **Turn-taking** (p62) **Global English:** **All work and no play** (p63)		**Writing:** **Leisure time** (p59) **A CV** (p64) **Study skills:** **Recording new words and phrases** (p65)		

EV - Extend your vocabulary **(P) - Pronunciation**

Unit		Grammar	Reading texts	Listening texts	Vocabulary	Speaking and Pronunciation
UNIT 6	**Science** page 66	Comparatives with *- er* and *more* (p67) Comparatives (*a bit / much / as … as*) (p68)	The science of happiness (p66) *Fitter Happier* (p67) *Frankenstein* by Mary Shelley (p69)	Conversation about the worst jobs in science (p68)	Noun formation (p69) EV Metaphors for *happy* (p66)	Happiness (p66) Guessing jobs (p68) Dangerous knowledge (p69) (P) The schwa (p67)
	Technology page 70	Superlatives (p70) Phrasal verbs and objects (p73)	Going, going, gone … (p70) The Luddites (p73)	Website addresses (p71) Conversations about computer problems (p72)	Compound nouns (p70) Phrasal verbs (p72) EV Other ways of saying *yes* (p72)	Website addresses (p71) Modern technology (p73) (P) Phrasal verbs, sentence stress (p72)
		Function globally: Finding things in common (p74) **Global voices:** The most important technological advance (p75)		**Writing:** Describing advantages and disadvantages (p76) **Study skills:** Personalising language learning (p77)		
UNIT 7	**Time** page 78	Present perfect with *for* and *since* (p79)	A brief history of time zones (p78) *A Tale of Two Cities* by Charles Dickens (p81)	Talk on the concept of time (p80)	Prepositions of time (*in, on, at*) (p78) Time expressions (p80)	The best time to … (p78) Time-saving inventions (p81) It is the best of times because … (p81) (P) /aɪ/ and /eɪ/, sentence stress (p80)
	Money page 82	Present perfect with *yet* and *already* (p82)	A lifetime of financial concerns (p82) A different kind of bank (p84)		Money, verb phrases (p82) EV *borrow* and *lend* (p85)	Describing pictures (p84) A bank loan (p85) (P) /ʌ/ (p83)
		Function globally: Shopping in a market (p86) **Global English:** The English language and the number four (p87)		**Writing:** Giving your opinion (p88) **Study skills:** Managing your study time (p89)		
UNIT 8	**Home** page 90	Passive voice (p91)	Bram Stoker's *Dracula* (p91) The cat came back (p92)	Famous homes (p90)	Animals (p92) Prepositions of movement (p93) EV *house* and *home* (p90)	A tour of your home (p90) Animals (p92) (P) /h/ (p90)
	Away page 94	First conditional (p95) Second conditional (p97)	Travel guidebooks (p94) *The Beach* by Alex Garland (p95) New kinds of tourism (p96)	Conversations with travel guides (p94)	Adjectives and prepositions (p96) EV Words that mean *trip* (p94)	Beach resorts (p95) Describing photos (p96) If you could go anywhere … (p97) (P) Sentence stress (p97)
		Function globally: Speaking on the telephone (p98) **Global voices:** Homes where you live (p99)		**Writing:** A dialogue (p91) A description of a town (p100) **Study skills:** Learning words with prepositions (p101)		
UNIT 9	**Health** page 102	Modal verbs of advice (p103) *Could / couldn't, had to / didn't have to* (p105)	Milestones of modern medicine (p104)	Talk on the common cold (p102) Advice on cures for the common cold (p103)	Feeling ill (p102) Medical treatment (p104)	The common cold (p102) (P) *ch* and *gh* (p102) (P) Word stress (p104) Sports questionnaire (p107)
	Fitness page 106	Past perfect (p107) Reported statements (p109)	Olympic losers (p106)	Conversation at the doctor's (p108)	Sport (p106) *Say, tell* and *ask* (p109) EV *win* and *beat* (p106)	A visit to the doctor (p108) Fitness questionnaire (p109)
		Function globally: Describing illness (p110) **Global English:** Sports English (p111)		**Writing:** A sick note (p103) An online post (p112) **Study skills:** Using your dictionary: exploring collocations (p113)		
UNIT 10	**New** page 114	Defining relative clauses (p115) Definite article (*the*) (p117)	*Brave New Words* by Kerry Maxwell (p114) New places in a new world (p116)	Interview with Kerry Maxwell on *Brave New Words* (p114)	New words in context (p114) Places (p116) EV Words that mean *new* (p116)	Famous quotes (p117)
	Old page 118	Verb form review (p119) *Both, neither* (p120)	Old but loved: the Trabant (p118)	Two classic board games (p120)	Transport (p118) Games (p121) EV Words that mean *make* (p120)	Transport (p118) Driving questionnaire (p119) A board game (p121) (P) Consonant clusters (p118) (P) Sentence stress and intonation (p121)
		Function globally: Ending a conversation (p122) **Global voices:** Your favourite words in English (p123)		**Writing:** Definitions game (p115) A report on studies (p124) **Study skills:** Evaluating your pronunciation (p125)		

Communication activities: Student A: (p126) Student B: (p128) **Additional material:** (p130) **Grammar focus:** (p132) **Audioscript:** (p152)

Individual & Society

Part 1

Vocabulary
Everyday objects

Reading
The Identity Card

Grammar
Word order in questions

Pronunciation
The alphabet

Vocabulary

1 Look at the pictures and read the information. Match each object to a word in the box. There are three words you do not need.

chewing gum credit card glasses
key ring lipstick mobile phone
pen umbrella

2 Do you have any of these things with you today? Which ones? Tell a partner.

Reading

1 1.01 Read and listen to the text on page 7 about another everyday object: the identity card. What kind of information about an individual can you find on an identity card?

2 Read the text again and find examples of …

1 a historical reason for ID cards.
2 countries with no ID cards.
3 a material used in ID cards.
4 information on an ID card.
5 biometric information on an ID card.

3 Does your country have identity cards? What information do they contain?

Surprising origins and facts: Everyday objects

a

Origin: Egypt, more than 5000 years ago
Cleopatra used one made from dead insects.

b

Origin: United States, 1973
The first model weighed 0.79 kg and measured 25cm.

c

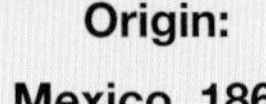

Origin: Mexico, 1860
It comes from the chicle plant. The original idea was to use it to make car tyres.

d

Origin: United States, 1950
The first one was the Diner's Club card. People used it to pay in New York restaurants.

e

Origin: Italy, 13th century
The early models helped people to see but they caused headaches because they were so heavy.

Surprising origins and facts: The identity (ID) card

Grammar

__Are__ ID cards obligatory?
__Do__ all countries __have__ ID cards?
__What is__ a biometric ID card?
__What did__ people __use__ ID cards for?

- in questions the verb goes before the subject
- in present simple or past simple questions, the auxiliary verb *do / did* goes before the subject and the infinitive goes after the subject
- question words (*What, Where, Who,* etc.) go at the start of a question

1 Complete the questions by putting the words in the correct place.

1	do you do?	what
2	you speak any foreign languages?	do
3	what your name?	is
4	what's phone number?	your
5	you have any children?	do
6	where you born?	were
7	where did you to school?	go
8	where do live?	you
9	you married?	are
10	what your date of birth?	is

2 Match the questions in exercise 1 to the topics in the box.

Name	Profession
Address	Marital status
Phone number	Children
Date of birth	Education
Place of birth	Languages

3 Choose five questions from exercise 1. Work in pairs and ask each other the questions.

G Grammar focus – explanation & more practice of word order on page 132

What were the first ID cards?

The first ID cards were, in fact, paper identity documents, which appeared in the 18th century.

What did people use the first ID cards for?

People used the first ID cards to travel to different countries. The ID card was the first passport.

Do all countries have ID cards?

No, they don't. There are more than a hundred countries in the world with ID cards. But several English-speaking countries don't have a national ID card system. These countries include the UK, the US, Canada, Australia, Ireland and New Zealand.

What do ID cards look like?

ID cards are usually made of plastic and can fit inside a person's wallet.

What information do governments put on ID cards?

Most ID cards contain the person's name, date of birth, signature and a photograph.

Some cards contain other information such as the person's address, phone number, nationality, profession and marital status.

What is a biometric ID card?

More modern ID cards now contain biometric information, for example, fingerprints or digital images of people's eyes.

Pronunciation

1 1.02 Listen to three people spelling personal information. Write the words they spell.

2 Work in pairs. A: spell the words to B.

- your last name
- the name of the street you live on
- two words from this lesson

3 Swap roles and repeat.

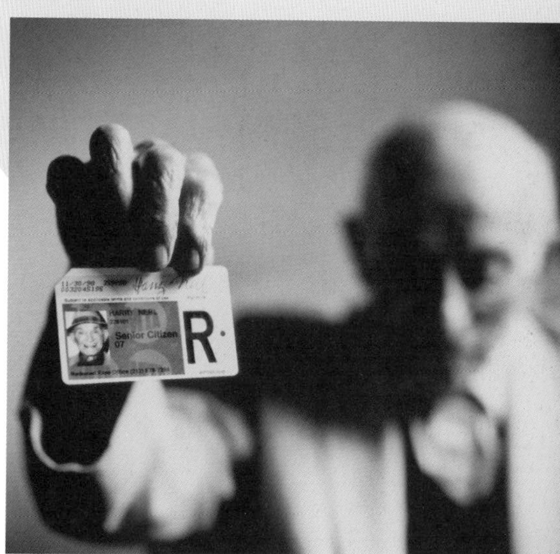

Individual & Society

Part 2

Speaking & Vocabulary
Describing people

Listening
Identity parade

Grammar
***What & How* questions**

Speaking
False identities

Speaking and Vocabulary

1 Think of someone you know very well and describe this person to a partner. Use the phrases below to help you.

- This is …
- He's / She's …
- He's / She's got … eyes and … hair.
- He's / She's … years old.

2 Write the words in the box under the correct headings below.

bald beard blond curly fair in her twenties medium-height middle-aged overweight scar short shoulder-length slim straight young

3 Think about the person you described in exercise 1. Can you add any more details to the description?

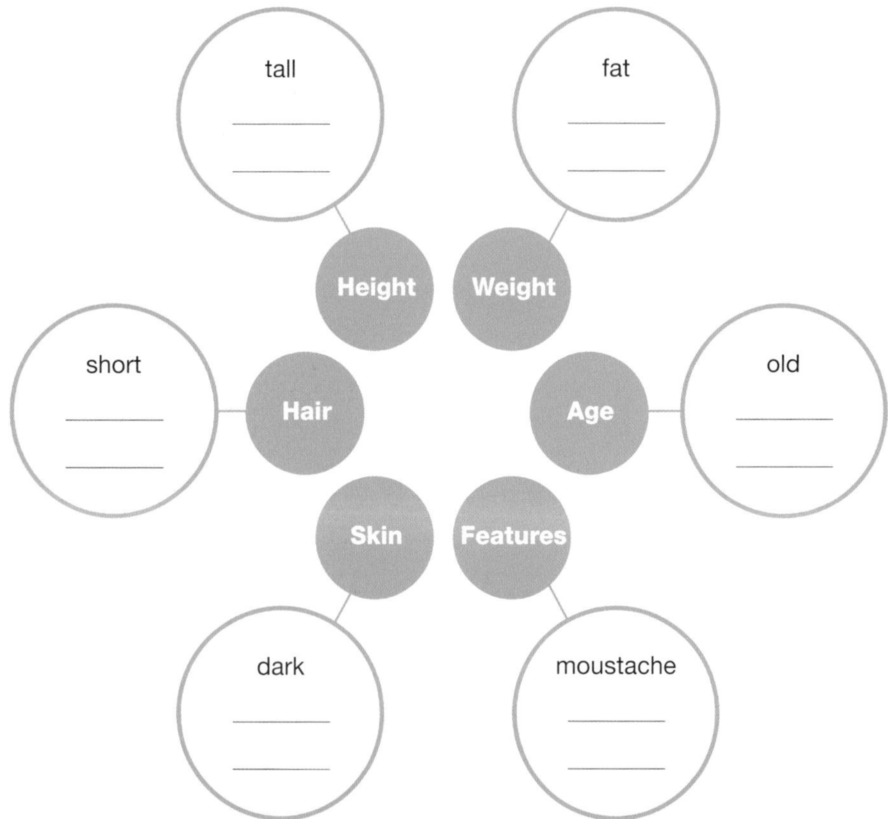

Listening

1 1.03–1.06 Listen to four conversations and choose the correct photo a–j on page 9 for each one.

2 Listen again and answer the questions. There is one question for each conversation.

1 Does the woman like the photo?
2 How old is the baby?
3 What is different about Bella?
4 What colour is the man's hair?

3 Work in pairs. A: choose one of the photos and describe it to your partner. B: try to guess the correct photo. Then swap roles and repeat.

Extend your vocabulary – *look* and *look like*

We use *look* + adjective to describe a person's appearance.

He looks thin.
She looks good.

We use *look* + *like* + noun phrase to compare someone's appearance to someone or something else.

She looks like her mother.
He looks like a film star.

Choose the correct option in each pair of sentences.

1	He looks like his father.	He looks his father.
2	Are you OK? You look like tired.	Are you OK? You look tired.
3	I look horrible in this photo.	I look like horrible in this photo.
4	That chair doesn't look like comfortable.	That chair doesn't look comfortable.

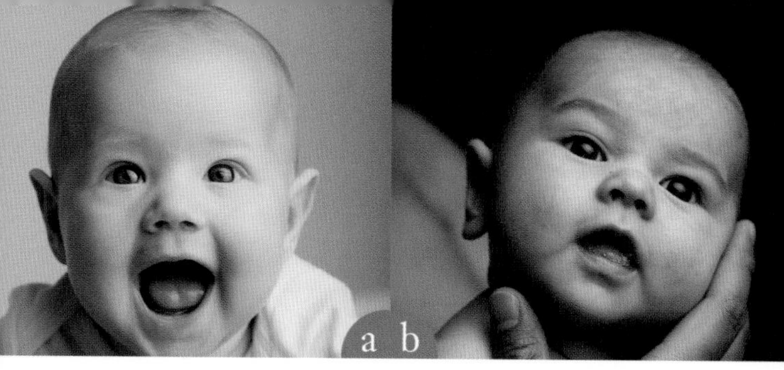

Grammar

How old is he?
What kind of car does he drive?
What colour are his eyes?

- use *how* + adjectives such as *old*, *tall*, *long* to ask for more detail
- use *what* + *kind of* / *sort of* + noun to ask for information about the noun
- also use *what* + *colour* / *time* / *size* to ask for specific detail

1 Complete the questions below with the correct question words.

how   how many   how much
what kinds   what sort

Q&A: IDENTITY THEFT

1 ________ **safe is your identity?**
The answer is: not safe, if you look at the statistics for identity theft.

2 ________ **of crime is identity theft?**
Identity (ID) theft occurs when someone steals your identity. It's one of the biggest new crimes in the world today.

3 ________ **people are victims of identity theft every year?**
Experts think that millions of people are victims around the world. In the US alone, it's around nine million people every year.

4 ________ **does identity theft cost?**
ID theft is big business and costs billions of dollars to national economies.

5 ________ **of identity theft are there?**
There are different types: using your credit card; getting a phone in your name or getting a government document, eg a driving licence, are some examples.

Q&A:

2 Put the words in the correct order to make questions.

1 colour are your eyes what?
2 hair colour what your is?
3 hair how long your is?
4 month what birthday is your?
5 old you how are?
6 street live you do on what?
7 tall you are how?

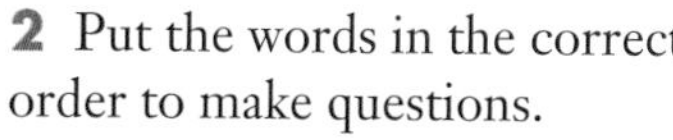
Grammar focus – explanation & more practice of *what* and *how* on page 132

Speaking

1 Write this information on a piece of paper and give it to the teacher.

- your full name
- your address
- your birthday

2 You are going to *steal* someone's identity. Take a piece of paper from the teacher and do not show it to anybody. This is your new identity.

3 Work in pairs and ask each other questions from exercise 2. Find out your partner's false identity.

Part 3

Vocabulary & Listening
People you know

Listening & Reading
Six degrees of separation

Grammar
Present simple, frequency adverbs

Speaking
Family & friends

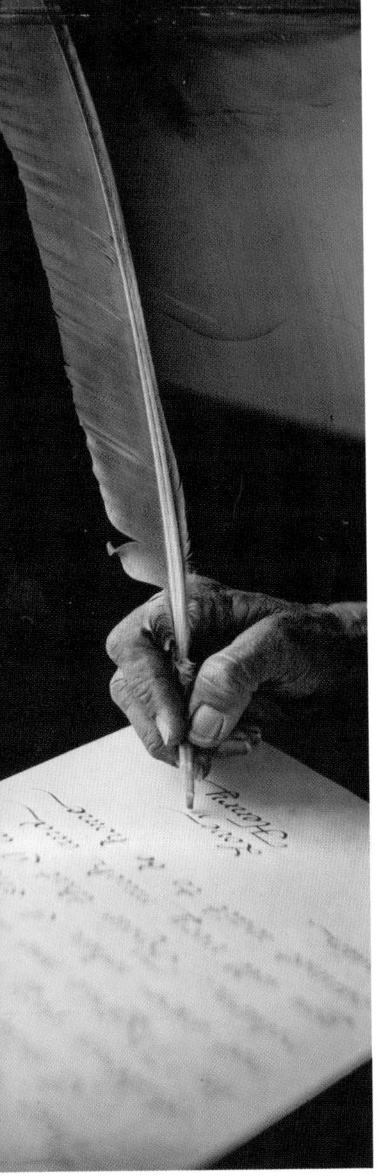

Vocabulary and Listening

1 Work in pairs and make a list of the people you know in the class. Tell each other what you know about them.

2 1.07 Listen to a woman talking about people she knows. Write the words in the box under the correct names.

acquaintance classmate colleague friend neighbour

Sofia ________ **Hans** ________

Ken ________ **Pilar** ________

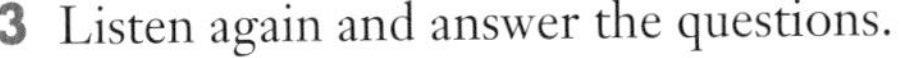

3 Listen again and answer the questions.

1 Where is Becky's neighbour?
2 Does Becky know Hans well?
3 Does she work with Ken?
4 How does she know Sofia?

4 Copy the diagram above and write the names of people you know. Write the relationship underneath each name. Then work in pairs and tell each other about the people.

This is Louise. She's my neighbour.

Jorge is a colleague from work.

Listening and Reading

1 1.08 Read and listen to the extract from the play *Six Degrees of Separation* on page 11. Do you know this theory?

2 1.09 Listen to an explanation of the theory. Draw lines between the names below to show which people are connected.

you
John
Jane
The Ambassador
Mary
Robert
The Secretary General of the United Nations
Mr Smith

3 Listen again. Explain the link between …

1 you and John.
2 Jane and Robert.
3 Mr Smith and the Ambassador.

4 Work in pairs and discuss these questions.

Do you think this theory is true? Are you connected to a famous person in any way? Tell your partner.

My wife's sister has met the President.

I work with a man. His son's teacher went to school with a famous singer.

Extend your vocabulary – *in touch*

If you are *in touch* with someone you see, speak to or write to them.

He is often in touch with important people.

You can *lose touch* with a person if you don't see, speak or write to them any more. You are then *out of touch* with that person.

I lost touch with a lot of my school friends many years ago. We are out of touch now.

Keep in touch or *stay in touch* are informal expressions you can use to tell someone you want to be in contact.

See you soon. Let's keep in touch.

Complete the sentences with an expression using *touch*.

1 She's still ______ with her grandmother. She writes to her every week.
2 I'm ______ with my school friends. I never see them.
3 A: See you later.
B: OK, ______.
4 He doesn't want to ______ with his family. He calls them every month.

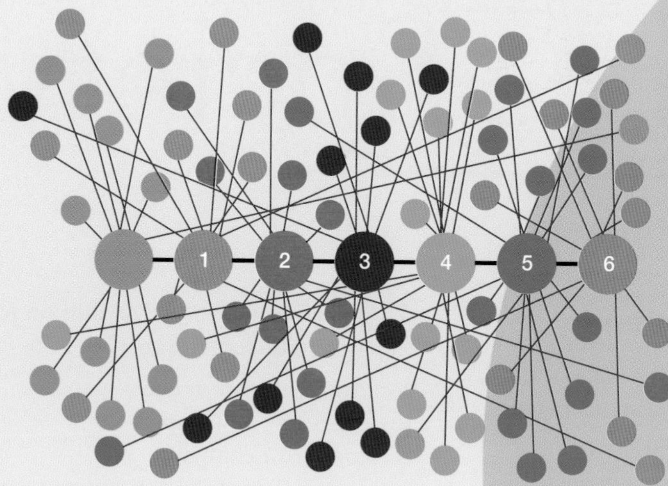

It's a small world ... the six degrees of separation theory

I read somewhere that everybody on this planet is separated by only six other people. Six degrees of separation between us and everyone else on this planet. The President of the United States, a gondolier in Venice, just fill in the names. ... I am bound – you are bound – to everyone on this planet by a trail of six people.

From *Six Degrees of Separation* by John Guare.

Grammar

*Robert **works** for a big hotel in the city centre.*
*Mr Smith **knows** many people.*
*He **sometimes has** lunch with the ambassador.*
*He **is often** in touch with important people.*

- use the present simple to talk about habits and routines and for things that are always true
- add *s* to regular verbs when talking about *he / she / it*
- use frequency adverbs to say how often something happens
- frequency adverbs go between the subject and the verb except with the verb *to be*

1 Complete the text about online social networks using the correct form of the words given.

Keeping in touch

One way people often ________ (*keep*) in touch with friends and family is using the internet. People ________ (*use*) social networking sites. These are special websites. Every member ________ (*have*) their own page.

Let's look at Jim, for example. Jim ________ (*be*) always in touch with his network of friends. He ________ (*not write*) emails, he ________ (*put*) information on a social networking site every day. Jim often ________ (*take*) photos of his family and ________ (*put*) them on his webpage. His friends ________ (*look*) at Jim's page and ________ (*see*) the information and photos. They then ________ (*send*) him messages.

2 Complete the sentences by putting the word or phrase in the correct place.

1 Becky talks to her parents on the phone. (*three times a week*)
2 She is very friendly with the neighbours. (*always*)
3 She goes out with her colleagues. (*often*)
4 She uses the internet to keep in touch with people. (*every day*)

G Grammar focus – explanation & more practice of the present simple on page 132

Speaking

Work in pairs.
A: turn to page 126.
B: turn to page 128.

Part 4

Speaking & Reading
CCTV is watching you

Grammar
Present continuous

Pronunciation
Linking words

Speaking and Reading

1 Read the information below about CCTV cameras and answer the questions in pairs.

1 Do any of the facts surprise you?
2 Do you have CCTV in your town? Where?
3 Do you think that CCTV cameras are a good idea?

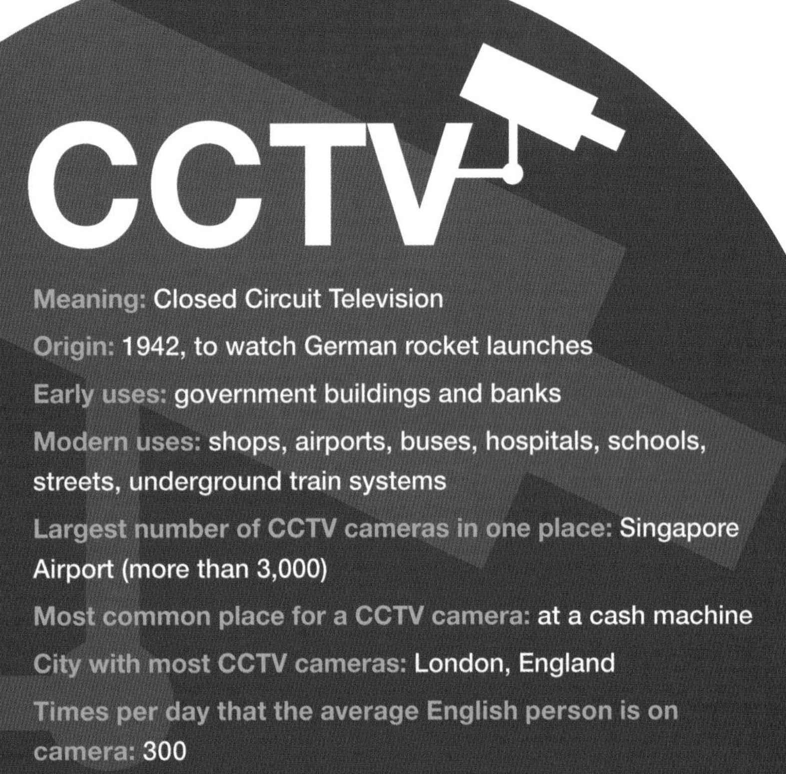

CCTV

Meaning: Closed Circuit Television

Origin: 1942, to watch German rocket launches

Early uses: government buildings and banks

Modern uses: shops, airports, buses, hospitals, schools, streets, underground train systems

Largest number of CCTV cameras in one place: Singapore Airport (more than 3,000)

Most common place for a CCTV camera: at a cash machine

City with most CCTV cameras: London, England

Times per day that the average English person is on camera: 300

2 Quickly read *Readers' response* on page 13. What kind of texts are they?

a advertisements in a newspaper
b letters to a newspaper
c emails to a company
d messages from the government

3 Read the texts again and answer the questions.

1 Who works at night in a shop?
2 Who thinks the article is not fair?
3 Who talks about the police?
4 Who mentions other ways of watching people?

4 Work in pairs. Find two arguments in favour of and two arguments against CCTV cameras in the texts. Which arguments do you agree with?

Extend your vocabulary – expressions with *place*

Place is a very common word in English expressions.

If something *takes place*, it happens.

The festival takes place in October.

If something is *out of place* it does not belong or is uncomfortable.

I felt out of place there, I didn't know anybody.

Look at the highlighted expressions in the texts on page 13. Match them to their meanings or uses 1–5 below.

1 to explain the first point in an argument
2 instead of
3 everywhere
4 a particular position or part of town
5 that something is not appropriate for you

Readers' response

CCTV is watching you

First identity cards, and now cameras all over the place. They are watching our every move. Soon they will listen to our phone calls and read our emails and letters. Do we have any private life left?

Rajit Gadh

Your article, CCTV is watching you, gives a very negative view of CCTV cameras. In the first place, the truth is that we are living in a dangerous society and people need to feel safe. You also don't mention how crime is going down in neighbourhoods with CCTV. You only give one side of the argument!

Philip Richards

So we have CCTV cameras in our neighbourhood. I really don't understand it. This is a very quiet place and there are no problems here. Personally I believe that this is just another example of government invasion of our privacy.

Martha Klein

The problem with the cameras isn't the technology, it's how people are using the technology. If the police are using the cameras to find information about criminals, what is the problem with that? It's not our place to say how they should do their job.

Kenneth Thomas

My co-workers and I agree with CCTV cameras. We work in a 24-hour shop and I usually work late. We have two cameras in the shop and we are putting in two more now. We don't have a lot of money. The cameras give us protection in place of security guards.

Tatyana Ivanov

Grammar

*CCTV cameras **are watching** you.*
*We **are putting** in two more cameras now.*
*We **agree** with CCTV cameras.*

- use the present continuous to talk about things that are happening now or around now
- use the present continuous to talk about temporary situations
- we do not usually use stative verbs such as *agree, believe, know, like, need* with the present continuous

1 Underline the correct form of the verbs in the letter.

I *am looking / look* out of my window at work right now and I can see two CCTV cameras. These cameras *are belonging / belong* to the company, and they watch our every move. I *am not understanding / don't understand* why we *are needing / need* them. I *am not liking / don't like* them.

Lola Sule

2 Think of three people you know. For each person, write two or more sentences about …

- what they do.
- what they are probably doing now.

My brother Graham works as a secondary school teacher.

He's probably teaching a history class right now.

3 Work in pairs and compare your sentences. Ask one question about each person on your partner's paper.

Where is your brother teaching?

G Grammar focus – explanation & more practice of the present continuous on page 132

Pronunciation

1 **1.10** Listen to five sentences. How many words do you hear in each? (contractions = two words)

2 Listen again and write the sentences. Then practise saying them. Pay attention to linking the words together.

3 Work in pairs and imagine a context for each sentence. Think about:

- Who is speaking?
- Where are they?
- What do they say next?

Function globally common social expressions

Warm up

Work in pairs and choose two or three situations from the list below. Roleplay a short conversation for each situation.

Situations

1 You are meeting for the first time.
2 You are friends. It's late and you would like to go home.
3 A is working and B is the customer. B: you want some help.
4 You work together. It's A's first day. B: introduce yourself.
5 You are classmates. It's the end of the week and you are saying goodbye.
6 A: it's your birthday. B gives you a present.
7 You don't know each other. A: you bump into B who drops something.

Useful phrases

- How are you?
- Nice to meet you.
- Have a good weekend.
- Excuse me.
- Thank you very much!
- See you tomorrow.
- I'm sorry.

Listening

1.11–1.14 Listen to four conversations. Match each one to a picture and a situation.

Language focus: social expressions

Read the phrases and cross out the response that is **not** correct.

1 How are you?
a Fine thanks. b Very well, thank you.
c I'm nice.
2 Hi, I'm George.
a Fine to meet you. b Nice to meet you.
c Pleased to meet you.
3 Have a good weekend.
a You too. b Thanks. c Yes, please.
4 Excuse me.
a Yes, can I help you? b You're welcome.
c Yes?
5 Thanks for everything.
a You're welcome. b No problem.
c Yes, please.
6 See you tomorrow.
a You too. b Bye. c See you.
7 I'm sorry.
a That's all right. b It's OK.
c You're welcome.

Speaking

Work with a new partner and choose **one** of the tasks below.

A Repeat the warm up activity using the new expressions you have learnt.

B Look at the audioscript on page 152 and choose one of the conversations. Practise it and try to memorise it. Then continue the conversation.

Global English

Same language but different

by David Crystal

We use language to express our thoughts, form relationships with others, and build communities. The focus is always on the individual. If you study language you study people, and people are as different as chalk from cheese. So their language will be different too.

Sometimes it's regional background that makes the difference. If you hear someone say *That's a bonny wee child*, the speaker is probably from Scotland, because words like *wee* (little) and *bonny* (pretty) are hardly ever used anywhere else. And someone who says *My car's hood and windshield were damaged* probably has an American background; someone from the UK would say *bonnet and windscreen*.

Often it's social background that makes the difference. In the 1950s in Britain there was a lot of publicity about how upper-class (U) people used different words from those used by other classes (non-U). U speakers had *luncheon* (or *lunch*) in the middle of the day and *dinner* in the evening. Non-U speakers had *dinner* in the middle of the day. *Luncheon* is rare today, but there is a still a social divide between *lunch* and *dinner*.

Above all, these days, it's the technology that makes the difference. The internet allows people to express their individuality in ways that were inconceivable a few years ago. Emails vary from highly formal (*Dear Professor Crystal*) to highly informal (*Yo, Dave!!*). Older people often keep the rules of punctuation and capitalisation they once learned; younger people often try out new ways (*i dont think so – LOL*).

But times are changing. As more older people start to use the internet, they are also using the latest abbreviations more and more. BRB (Be right back).

Glossary

background (*noun*) – the type of family, social position or culture that someone comes from

BRB (*verb*) – internet abbreviation for *Be right back*; you use this to say informally that you will return soon

LOL (*verb*) – internet abbreviation for *laughing out loud*; you use this to say informally that you think something is funny

Warm up

1 Are these sentences true (*T*) or false (*F*) for you?

- I speak more than one language.
- I speak differently at work to how I speak at home.
- My language has many different dialects.
- There is more than one language in my country.
- Rich people speak differently to poor people.

2 Work in pairs and compare your answers. Do you agree?

Reading

1 Read the text *Same language but different*. What three factors does the author mention?

a differences in geography
b differences in social class
c differences in diet
d differences in technology

2 Read the text again and decide if these sentences are true (*T*) or false (*F*).

1 People are very different, so language is different.
2 *Hood* and *windshield* are British English words.
3 U speakers had lunch in the evening.
4 Technology always makes language very formal.
5 Young people don't use capital letters in the same way as older people on the internet.
6 Young people are inventing new ways of using capital letters.

Language focus

Find words or expressions in the text with these meanings.

1 to be very different (lines 2–3)
2 uncommon (line 14)
3 most importantly (line 16)
4 impossible to think about or imagine (line 17)

Speaking

Do you think the differences in English that the author talks about are true for your language? Think of some examples. Use the questions below to help you.

- How do people start and finish emails in your language? Is it formal or informal?
- Are there different parts of your country that use different words to mean the same thing? Can you give an example and explain it in English?
- Are there abbreviations on the internet in your language like *LOL* or *BRB*?

UNIT 1 Writing a personal description

Reading

1 Read Constanza's description of herself.

Is it …

a an email to a friend?
b an introduction for a social networking site?
c a letter of application for a job?

2 Is there anything in the description that's true for you?

Hi! My name is Constanza Ximena Jara Castro, but people call me Coti for short. I'm twenty years and single. I born in Valdivia, in the south of Chile, but now I live in Santiago, the capital city. I study journalism in the university and I like very much this course.

We are five people in my family – my parents, my two elder sisters and me. We also have got a dog called Kalu. My father's job is a photographer and my mother is teacher.

In my free time I like swimming, listening music and seeing friends. In the future I hope to go to USA for do a Master's and my ambition is to work as a journalist for a national newspaper.

Writing skills: looking for errors in your work

1 Read a corrected copy of Constanza's description and find twelve differences.

2 Which of these errors do you sometimes make?

3 Do you usually check your writing for errors before giving it to a teacher?

Hi! My name is Constanza but people call me Coti for short. I'm twenty years old and single. I was born in Valdivia, in the south of Chile, but now I live in Santiago, the capital city. I am studying journalism at university and I like this course very much.

There are five people in my family – my parents, my two elder sisters and me. We also have a dog called Kalu. My father is a photographer and my mother is a teacher.

In my free time I like swimming, listening to music and seeing friends. In the future I hope to go to the USA to do a Master's and my ambition is to work as a journalist for a national newspaper.

Language focus: joining sentences

1 Join the sentences using *and*, *but* or *so*.

I have a dog called Lucky. I have a cat called Mimi.
I have a dog called Lucky and I have a cat called Mimi.

1 I'm short and slim. I have long curly black hair.
2 My sister trained as a teacher. She's unemployed at the moment.
3 I'm thirty years old. I'm married with two children.
4 Clodagh isn't a common name. People often don't know how to spell it.
5 I have three sisters. I don't have any brothers.
6 I was born in a small village. I find living in a big city very strange.

2 Read the joined sentences. Cross out any words that you don't need.

I have a dog called Lucky and ~~I have~~ a cat called Mimi.

Preparing to write

Make notes about yourself for a social networking site. Use the topics in the box to help you and include your own ideas.

Name Age Birthplace Town Occupation
Family Free time Ambitions

Writing about names

- My full name is Alejandro Gustavo Donoso Jimenez.
- People call me Alex for short.
- My nickname is Chacho.
- I was named after my grandfather.
- I have a sister called Andrea and a brother called Pablo.
- I have a dog whose name is Pepe.

Writing

Write your description and check it for errors. Then work in pairs and swap your descriptions. Try to correct each other's work.

Global review

Grammar

1 Complete the questions with the correct words.

1 ________ married? No, I'm single.
2 ________ speak English? Yes, a little.
3 ________ your phone number? It's 07051-459-216.
4 ________ you do? I'm a teacher.
5 ________ is your car? It's red.

2 Complete the sentences with the correct form of the verb in brackets.

1 A: Excuse me, can you help me?
B: I'm sorry, I ________ (*try*) to work right now.
2 I ________ (*not / know*) many people in this town.
3 My brother ________ (*not/ like*) his boss, so he ________ (*look*) for a new job.
4 My mother ________ (*not / speak*) any foreign languages.

Vocabulary

1 Find and correct six spelling mistakes.

acquaintance bald clasmate colleage freind heigth identity keyring middle-aged neigbour proffession umbrella

2 Look at the pictures. Correct three mistakes in each description.

1 This is Carlos. He's bald and overweight, and he's got a beard.
2 This is Veronica. She's middle-aged, with short dark curly hair.

1

2

Speaking

Work in groups of three. A: throw a dice to choose a person in the box. B and C: ask questions about the person. Ask about name, age, job, family and what they look like. Then swap roles and repeat.

1 A good friend
2 A neighbour
3 A family member
4 Your first friend
5 A new colleague or classmate
6 A good teacher

Study skills

Being a good language learner

1 Read the learning questionnaire. How often are these statements true for you? Give yourself a score for each question. Not usually = 0 points Sometimes = 1 point Usually = 2 points

* I try to practise using English as often as I can outside the classroom. ___
* I am willing to take risks and am not afraid of making mistakes. ___
* I am organised in the way I manage my learning. ___
* I think about how I learn best. ___
* If I don't understand something, I try to guess. ___
* I notice my mistakes and try to learn from them. ___
* I set goals and monitor my progress. ___
* If I am not sure about something, I ask for help. ___
* I regularly review what I have learnt. ___
* I try to use English to communicate my ideas. ___

2 Add up your total score and read what it means below.

16–20	Congratulations! You are already an excellent language learner. Keep up the good work!
11–15	You already have some very good language learning strategies. Now think how you can improve even more.
6–10	You are starting to use the right strategies but need to be more consistent.
0–5	Maybe you are finding it difficult to make progress. Try some of the strategies above and you could see a big difference.

3 Work in pairs and discuss the questions.

- Which of the strategies in the quiz do you use most?
- Which do you need to use more?
- Give your partner suggestions about things to do.

4 Write two new things you will try to become a better language learner.

Eating & Drinking

Part 1

Vocabulary & Speaking
Food

Reading
Tastes comforting

Grammar
Countable / uncountable nouns, quantifiers (*some, any*)

Speaking
How do you make it?

Vocabulary and Speaking

1 Write the words in the box under the correct heading below.

bitter breakfast cook dinner
eat fresh lunch salty serve
snack spicy sweet taste

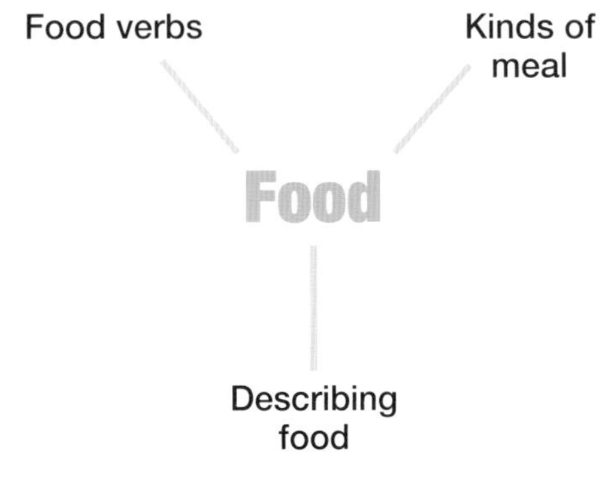

2 Work in pairs and choose five questions from the list below. Then ask each other the questions.

- What meals do you eat with your family?
- Who prepares the food in your family?
- What do you like to eat on special occasions, eg your birthday?
- What did you have to eat last night?
- How often do you buy food? Where do you do the shopping?
- Do you eat out a lot? What kind of food do you like to eat at a restaurant?
- What did you have to eat this morning?
- Do you have a favourite food when you are sad? What is it?

A: *I'm going to ask you some questions about food and eating.*
B: *OK.*
A: *What meals do you eat with your family?*
B: *I usually have breakfast and dinner with my family. I have lunch at work.*

Reading

1 1.15 Read and listen to *Tastes comforting* on page 19. Do you have a name for this kind of food in your language?

2 Read the text again and make notes about each kind of comfort food under the headings *name*, *country* and *ingredients*.

3 Work in pairs and tell each other about the four kinds of comfort food in the text.

4 Do you have a comfort food? Tell your partner about it.

5 You are going to read more information about comfort food in different countries.
Work in pairs. A: turn to page 126. B: turn to page 128.

Extend your vocabulary – *taste*

You can use the noun *taste* when you describe a flavour.
This chocolate has a very sweet taste.
It is also the name of one of the five senses (*sight, hearing, smell, touch and taste*).
You can use the verb *to taste* in the following ways:
taste + adjective
taste + *like* / *of* + noun
It tastes sweet / bitter / delicious / awful.
It tastes like chicken.
This water tastes of apples.
You can say *It tastes delicious* to give a compliment about food.

Complete the sentences with your own ideas.

- ... has a sweet taste.
- I like food that tastes ...
- I think ... tastes awful.

tagine

Tastes comforting

The expression comfort food is only around forty years old. It means a kind of familiar, simple food. People associate comfort food with good feelings, with childhood or with home.

Comfort food exists in all cultures. Some examples of popular comfort food from around the world include:

Roti *– a kind of bread served with vegetables or lentils (popular in India).*

Ramen *– a dish of noodles with vegetables and meat in a soup (popular in Japan).*

Tagine *– a slowly cooked dish of meat and vegetables (popular in North Africa).*

Poutine *– a dish of fried potatoes with cheese and meat sauce (popular in French Canada).*

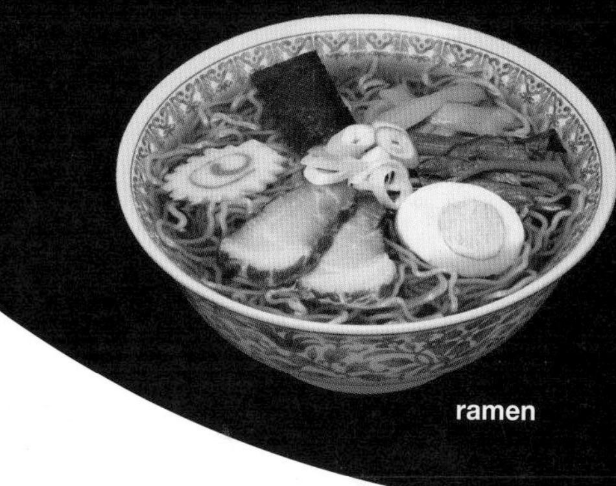

ramen

Grammar

*It's **a dish** of pasta and meat. We are making **two dishes** like this.*
*There is some **meat** in the dish.*
*I like **coffee**. Can I have **a coffee** please?*
*We have **some meat** but we don't have **any vegetables**.*

- countable nouns can be singular or plural
- uncountable nouns do not have a plural form
- some words can be countable or uncountable
- use *some* and *any* with plural nouns or uncountable nouns
- we usually use *some* in affirmative sentences and *any* in negative sentences and questions

1 Look at these words from the texts. Decide if each one is countable, uncountable or if it can be both.

bread casserole cheese chocolate cracker lentil meat noodle pasta pizza potato sandwich steak sweet toast vegetable

2 Choose the correct word to complete the texts.

My comfort food

When I'm feeling sad, I always eat *any / some* chicken soup. Very hot chicken soup with pasta. There isn't *any / a* better dish for me.

Last summer I studied English in Scotland and stayed with *a / some* host family. Scottish food was OK, but they didn't have *a / any* good bread. Two weeks later a friend from Germany visited and brought me *some / any* delicious *Roggenbrot* bread. It was my comfort food.

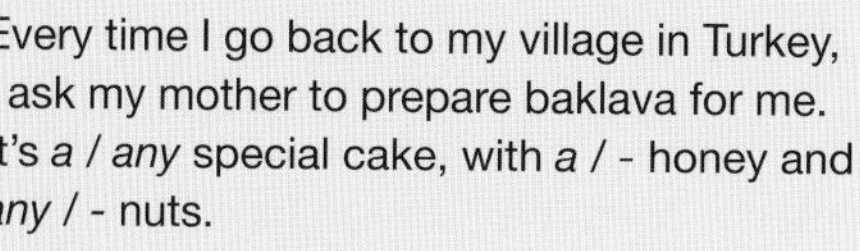

Every time I go back to my village in Turkey, I ask my mother to prepare baklava for me. It's *a / any* special cake, with *a / -* honey and *any / -* nuts.

Grammar focus – explanation & more practice of nouns on page 134

Speaking

1 Think of a dish that you like and make some notes about it. Use the headings below to help you.

Ingredients
Who usually prepares it
When you eat it
Why you like it

2 Work in pairs and tell each other about your dishes.

I'm going to tell you about arroz con costra. It's a Spanish dish and it's one of my favourites. It's a rice dish. My father usually makes it in the summer. You cook it with some meat …

Eating & Drinking

Part 2

Reading & Speaking

Ten secrets ... from the world's top kitchens

Grammar

Quantifiers (*a lot of, a little, a few, not enough, much, many*)

Vocabulary & Speaking

In the kitchen

Pronunciation

/k/ & /tʃ/

Listening

Zao Shen

Reading and Speaking

1 Work in pairs and ask each other these questions.

1 Can you cook?
2 Do you like cooking?
3 What dishes can you make?
4 Who is the best cook you know?

2 1.16 Read and listen to *Ten secrets … from the world's top kitchens*. Which secret or secrets are about …

a food preparation?
b food storage?
c eating?
d cleaning?
e the kitchen?

3 Did you know any of these tips? Tick (✔) the ones you knew.

4 Do you know any other good food tips? What are they?

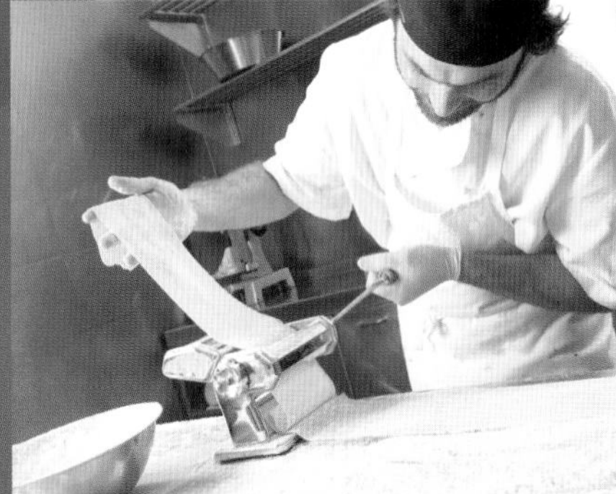

1 To give soup a beautiful golden colour, add some onion skin. Remember to take it out of the soup before you eat it.

2 Too much salt in a sauce? Add a little sugar or sparkling water.

3 Eggs will stay fresh if you store them with the pointed end down.

4 To clean a pan after cooking fish, put some cold tea in the pan for ten minutes first.

5 If you want a lot of juice from a lemon, cut it in half and put it in the oven for a few minutes first.

6 Lots of green bananas? Leave them in a bowl with a red tomato next to them.

7 When you cut an onion, put some bread under your nose. You may feel silly, but you won't cry.

8 Do you eat too much food at mealtimes? Turn off the lights. Dim lighting makes you want to eat less.

9 To see if pasta is cooked, throw a piece against the fridge. If it sticks on the fridge, it's cooked.

10 To make your kitchen smell good, put a little orange peel in the oven at 180°C for fifteen minutes.

Ten secrets … from the world's top kitchens

Grammar

*Do you eat **too much food** at mealtimes?*
*Put it in the oven for **a few minutes**.*
*If you want **a lot of juice** from a lemon …*
***Too much salt** in a soup?*

- use *a little* and *much* with uncountable nouns
- use *a few* and *many* with plural countable nouns
- use *a lot of* and *(not) enough* with plural nouns and uncountable nouns
- use *too much / many* to say there is more than you want

1 Read the sentences below about a busy head chef. Match the sentences 1–5 to the meanings a–e.

1 He is always a few minutes late for work.
2 He has a lot of friends at the restaurant.
3 He eats too many cakes and biscuits.
4 He doesn't get enough sleep.
5 He has enough work at the moment.

a He doesn't need any more.
b He should eat less.
c He isn't early.
d He's often tired.
e He has eight or nine.

2 Complete the questions with *much* or *many*.

In a typical day …

- how ______ meals do you eat?
- how ______ coffee do you drink?
- how ______ time do you spend in the kitchen?
- how ______ portions of fruit do you eat?
- how ______ water do you drink?
- how ______ junk food or fast food do you eat?

3 Work in pairs and choose **four** questions from the list above. Then ask each other the questions. Use the expressions in the box to help you.

a little	a lot	not many
not much	too many	too much

Grammar focus – explanation & more practice of quantifiers on page 134

Vocabulary and Speaking

1 Describe the differences between these three kitchens.

Useful language

- bowl
- glass
- oven
- spoon
- fire
- kettle
- saucepan
- toaster
- frying pan
- mug
- sink

Useful phrases

- This kitchen looks like it's in …
- There are … in this kitchen and … in that kitchen.
- I think this picture is more interesting. I prefer …

2 Which kitchen do you prefer? Why?

Pronunciation

1 1.17 Listen to the words below. Which have the /k/ sound, which have the /tʃ/ sound and which have both? Which word does not have a /k/ or a /tʃ/ sound?

chill	chocolate	cloth	cook	cup
fork	knife	picture	quick	watch

2 Listen again and repeat. What are the common spellings for /k/ and /tʃ/?

Listening

1 Look at the picture of Zao Shen. Which country do you think he is from? Who do you think he is?

2 1.18 Listen to a short talk about Zao Shen and answer the questions.

1. Who is Zao Shen?
2. Can you name one thing he does?
3. Where can you see pictures like this?

3 Are there any important beliefs about food or kitchens in your culture? What are they?

THE KITCHEN-GOD

Part 3

Speaking & Vocabulary
Containers and drinks

Reading
The people behind the drinks

Grammar
The infinitive

Speaking and Vocabulary

1 Work in pairs. How many correct phrases can you make with the words in the box?

a	glass cup mug bottle carton can	of	coffee cola juice milk tea beer water wine

Language note: some uncountable nouns can be countable if we believe there is a container, eg *two coffees* means *two cups of coffee*.

2 Work in pairs and ask each other these questions.

What do you like to drink …
- on a hot summer's day?
- in the morning, with breakfast?
- after dinner?
- in the winter, when it's cold outside?
- when you feel sad or miserable, as a comfort drink?

What other drinks do you like? When?

Reading

1 Look at the photos and names of different people on page 23. Do you know any of the names? What drinks are they associated with?

Useful phrases

- I don't know this name.
- I think this is …
- This is the name of a kind of coffee / water / beer.

2 1.19 Read and listen to the text *The people behind the drinks*. What do all the drinks have in common? Choose the best answer.

a They are all more than 100 years old.
b They are all cold drinks.
c They are not English drinks.

3 Read the text again and complete the sentences with the names of the drinks.

1 ________ sponsors a famous book.
2 ________ and ________ are from France.
3 ________ and ________ are hot drinks.
4 ________ was given as a present.
5 ________ and ________ were named after monks.

4 Do you know any of these drinks? Which ones?

Grammar

*He **wanted to make** a new drink.*
*It was **difficult to understand**.*

- use the infinitive after some verbs: *agree, forget, need, try, want*
- use the infinitive after adjectives

1 Read the extract from George Orwell's *A nice cup of tea*. Complete the rules by writing *to* or nothing (–) in each gap. Do you agree with his rules?

A nice cup of tea

It isn't easy to make a good cup of tea.
First of all, you should ______ use Indian or Ceylonese tea.
It's important ______ make tea in small quantities – in a teapot.
You need ______ make the teapot hot first.
Don't ______ put hot water in a cold pot.
Strong tea is the best kind of tea. One strong tea is better than twenty weak teas.
After you ______ put the tea in the pot, stir it. Or shake the pot.
Try ______ use a good breakfast cup for your tea. Tea is best in a good cup.
Don't forget ______ put the tea in the cup before you ______ put the milk in.
Tea is meant ______ be bitter. Don't put sugar in a nice cup of tea.

2 Write some rules for how to make a drink or some food that you know.

3 Work in pairs and tell each other your rules.

A nice …
It's important to …
You need to …
The best … to eat/drink is …
Try to use …
Don't forget to …

G Grammar focus – explanation & more practice of the infinitive on page 134

The people behind the drinks

Perrier
Dr Louis Perrier was a doctor and politician in the south of France. At the end of the 19th century he got a job with a company that made special mineral water in a bottle. The water was originally popular in the UK and the US, but is now available around the world.

Cappuccino
The espresso coffee with hot milk has always had the Italian name cappuccino. It is more than three hundred and fifty years old and is now famous around the world. The name comes from a group of monks in Italy, the Capuchin monks.

Guinness
In 1759 an Irishman called Arthur Guinness started making beer in a small brewery in Dublin. He eventually created a dark beer called Guinness, which became Ireland's national beer. The Guinness company now owns many different products, the most famous being the *Guinness Book of World Records*, first published in 1955.

Earl Grey Tea
The Earl, Charles Grey, was British Prime Minister from 1830–1834. During his time in office, he received some special tea as a gift from China. The tea became very popular in Britain, and eventually people gave it the name Earl Grey tea.

Dom Pérignon
Dom Pérignon (1638–1715) was a blind Benedictine monk from Épernay, France. His senses of taste and smell helped him to improve the wines made at his monastery. It was Dom Pérignon who put the bubbles in champagne.

Glossary
blind (*adjective*) – unable to see
brewery (*noun*) – a place where people make beer
monk (*noun*) – a man who lives in a religious community away from other people

Eating & Drinking

Part 4

Vocabulary
The human body

Listening
Water & the human body

Grammar
The infinitive of purpose

Pronunciation
/tə/ & /tuː/

Speaking
Drinks questionnaire

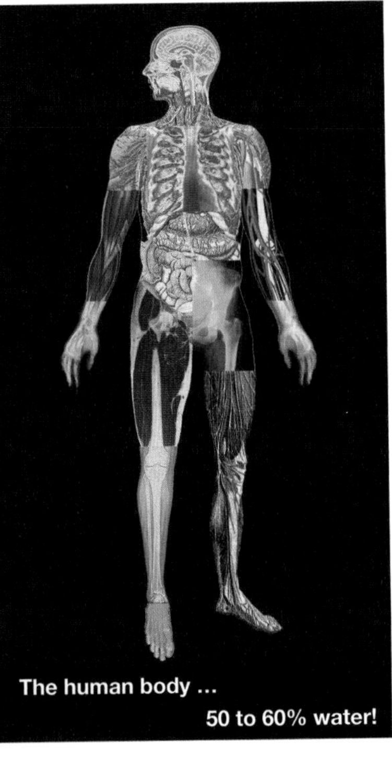
The human body ... 50 to 60% water!

Vocabulary

1 How many parts of the body can you name in English? Work in pairs and complete the words below.

_ rm	b _ ck	e _ r
elb _ w	f _ ng _ r	f _ _ t
ha _ r	h _ nd	he _ d
k _ ee	l _ g	n _ se

2 Look at the words in the box. Decide if each part is inside (*I*) or outside (*O*) the body. Write I or O.

blood ___ bone ___ brain ___
heart ___ muscle ___
nails ___ skin ___

3 Work in pairs. How many parts from exercise 2 can you see in the picture?

Listening

1 You are going to hear a talk about water and the human body. First check you understand the words in the box.

breathe convert factor
nutrients temperature waste

2 1.20 Listen to the talk and write the parts of the body that you hear.

3 Listen again. What do the numbers mean?

a few days 2 ⅔ 22%
75% 85–95% 92%

4 How much water do you drink? Do you think you drink enough water? Tell a partner.

Grammar

Human beings need to drink water ***to live****.*
What does water do ***to help*** *the body?*

- we use the infinitive to say why we do something

1 Look at the pictures of different objects below. Describe what each object is for using the phrases in the box.

breathe underwater drink with
make ice cubes purify water
serve drinking water water plants

You use this to water plants.

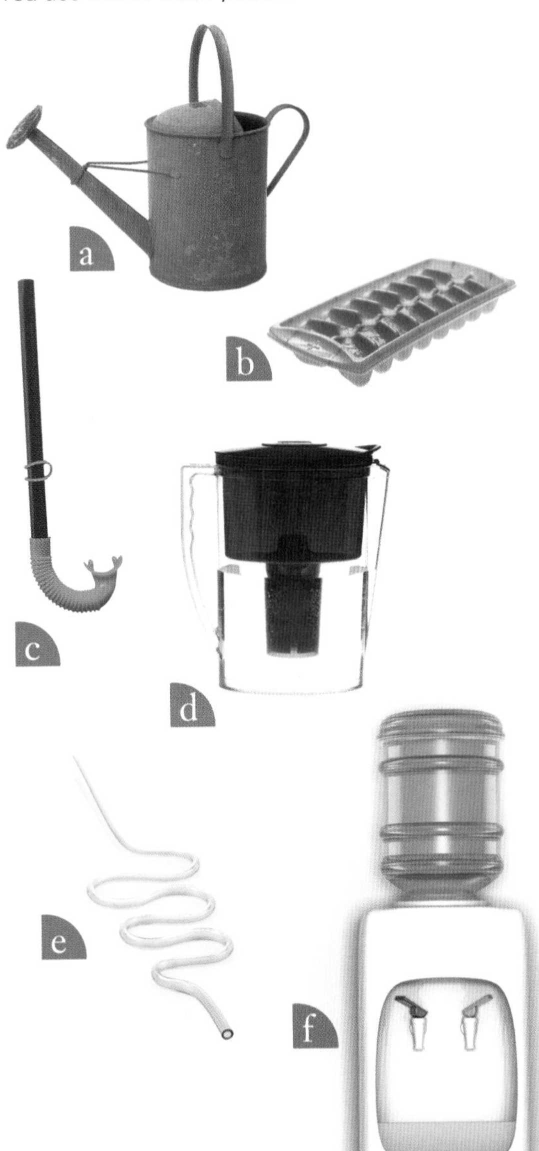

2 Complete *More water facts* with *to* + a verb from the box.

flush grow have produce provide

More water facts

Around 2.5% of the planet's water is fresh water. The rest is salt water.

It usually takes between 50 and 100 litres ______ a shower.

It takes 5 to 10 litres ______ the toilet.

You need 1,900 litres of water ______ one kilogram of rice.

You need 100,000 litres of water ______ one kilogram of beef.

On average, it costs €23 ______ safe and clean water for one person.

About 1.1 billion people do not have access to clean drinking water. That's about 1 in 6 people.

3 Work in pairs. Complete the sentences in as many different ways as you can.

I went to the shop to …

People use water to …

He's learning English to …

G **Grammar focus** – explanation & more practice of the infinitive of purpose on page 134

Pronunciation

1 1.21 Listen and circle how the underlined word is pronounced in each sentence.

It's too cold. /tə/ /tuː/

You need to drink more water. /tə/ /tuː/

2 1.22 Listen to the story below then practise saying the sentences. Pay attention to the pronunciation of /tə/ and /tuː/.

Last summer I went to Tunisia

It was too hot, and I needed something to drink.

I was hungry too.

I went to a shop to buy some water.

I didn't know how to ask for water.

I didn't have enough money to pay for it.

I spoke to the owner.

And he gave it to me for free.

He gave me some oranges too.

Speaking

1 Use the prompts to make questions.

- How much water / every day?
- Do / too little water?
- Do / water before you go to bed?
- Do / bottled water or tap water?
- How many bottles / week?

2 Work in pairs and choose one of the tasks below.

A Ask each other the questions from exercise 1.

B Make a similar questionnaire about a different drink, eg tea or coffee. Use the questions in exercise 1 to help you. Then interview another pair.

Function globally eating out

Warm up

1 Look at the pictures of four different places to eat. Work in pairs and describe the similarities and differences between them.

Useful language

- fast food
- self-service buffet
- flight attendant
- tray

Useful phrases

- I think this is in …
- It looks like a / an …
- In this picture they're … and in this picture they're …
- This one looks the most comfortable / expensive / interesting.

2 Have you been to any places like these? Which photo do you like the best?

Listening

1 1.23–1.25 Listen to three conversations. Match each one to a photo. There is one photo you don't need.

2 Listen again and answer the questions.

Conversation 1: Who is the reservation for?
Who is ready to order: the man or the woman?

Conversation 2: What is the problem with the food?
What size drink does the man have?

Conversation 3: Does the woman have anything else to drink?
Where does she have to pay?

Language focus: eating out

1 Put the words in the correct order to make useful phrases. Which phrases do customers say? Mark them with a ***C***.

1 would to order you what like?
2 here think I there's a mistake.
3 the I have could bill?
4 your meal you did enjoy?
5 medium small, or large?
6 reservation we've a got.
7 over have to pay you there.
8 thanks lovely, it was.
9 for two, table please a.

2 1.26 Listen and check your answers. Then listen and repeat the phrases.

Speaking

Work in groups of three. A and B: you are customers. C: you work in a restaurant.

Turn to page 130 and choose a restaurant menu. Then roleplay a conversation. Use the new expressions you have learnt.

Global voices

Warm up

1 Complete the sentences with the words in the box. Use a dictionary to help you.

beetroot boil candy fry kebab lamb sweets

1 ______ is a kind of meat.
2 A ______ is a sort of meat dish.
3 ______ is a kind of vegetable.
4 ______ and ______ are sweet food made with sugar.
5 ______ and ______ are two ways of cooking food.

2 What other words could you use to complete these sentences?

Listening

1 You are going to listen to six people talking about food that makes them think of home. Try to match the names of food to the countries.

borsch candy kebab pizza schnitzel tortilla

1 Iran ______
2 Italy ______
3 Russia ______
4 Germany ______
5 US ______
6 Spain ______

2 **1.27–1.32** Listen and check your answers.

3 Listen again and match the speakers 1–6 to the phrases a–f.

Speaker 1: Mo, Iran ___
Speaker 2: Gianfranco, Italy ___
Speaker 3: Elena, Russia ___
Speaker 4: Marlies, Germany ___
Speaker 5: Matt, US ___
Speaker 6: Sonia, Spain ___

a And it is very tasty really.
b I think it is a very simple dish.
c Of course not Pizza Hut but Napoli pizza.
d They remind me of growing up in the United States.
e Typical traditional food.
f You most often have it with French fries.

Language focus: listing ingredients

Choose the correct sentence.

1 a It consists of rice and lamb.
  b It consists with rice and lamb.
2 a It's made from eggs and potatoes.
  b It's made for eggs and potatoes.
3 a It's of vegetables, and meat and pasta.
  b It's made with vegetables, and meat and pasta.
4 a It is got rice and fish in it.
  b It has got rice and fish in it.

Speaking

1 Choose three of the topics below. Write one example of each on a piece of paper.

- a typical food or drink from your country
- a food or drink that you don't like
- a food or drink that you liked when you were a child
- a food or drink from another country that you like

2 Work in pairs and swap your lists. Can you guess the categories?

3 Tell each other more about the food or drinks on your lists.

Useful phrases

- It consists of …
- It's made from …
- It's delicious! / It tastes really good.

UNIT 2 Writing a description of food and drink

Reading

1 Read Gustavo's description of food in Brazil. Choose the best title for each paragraph.

a Drinks in Brazil
b Mealtimes
c Invitation to Brazil
d Food around Brazil

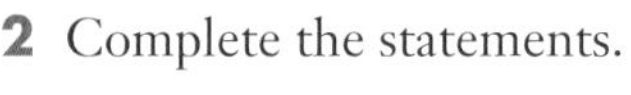

2 Complete the statements.

1 In Brazil, people tend to eat ______ meals a day.
2 The main meal of the day in Brazil is ______.
3 The national dish is ______.
4 The most typical drinks are ______.
5 Food and drink in Brazil are ______.

1 ______________

In my country, people normally have three meals a day: breakfast, lunch and dinner. We also tend to have a lot of snacks between meals. For breakfast, we usually have coffee with milk and eat bread. We also like to eat fruits such as bananas, papaya, melon or watermelon, and to drink juice or yoghurt. Lunch is the main meal of the day. We generally eat a portion of beans and rice with beef, chicken or fish and salad. Dinner is similar to lunch but we tend to eat quite late, between seven and ten in the evening.

2 ______________

The food in Brazil varies from region to region. Here in São Paulo, we like to eat feijoada with rice and meat on Wednesday or Saturdays. Feijoada is our national dish and it is cooked with beans and dried meat. In Minas Gerais, cheese bread is a speciality. In Bahia, the food is very spicy and hot. In the north of Brazil, people eat a lot of fish but in the south, it is common to have barbecues and to drink a kind of tea that is served very hot.

3 ______________

I think that coffee is the most typical beverage in Brazil. People drink coffee almost all the time; for breakfast, at work, in restaurants and so on. We also like to drink beer, and on special occasions or for celebrations, we drink caipirinha. Caipirinha is a drink made with pinga or vodka mixed with sugar or honey and crushed lemons.

4 ______________

If you come to Brazil, you will enjoy our delicious and varied food and drink. Welcome to Brazil!

Language focus: describing habits

1 Notice how we describe habits.

We *normally / generally / usually* have coffee with milk.
People *like to / tend to* eat quite late.
It is *common /customary* to have barbecues.

2 Complete the sentences.

1 We ______ to have our main meal in the evening.
2 It is ______ to use chopsticks when we eat.
3 On special occasions, people ______ to eat out.
4 People ______ have a sandwich for lunch.
5 It is ______ for families to eat together.
6 We ______ use fresh ingredients to prepare meals.

Writing skills: using commas

Use commas …

a to separate prepositional phrases.
In my country, people normally have three meals a day.
b to separate items in a list.
breakfast, lunch and dinner

1 Find more examples of a and b in the text.

2 Add commas to these sentences.

1 In China typical dishes are rice noodles and dumplings.
2 Noodles are made with flour eggs and water.
3 For breakfast people tend to have coffee bread and jam.

Preparing to write

1 Make notes about food and drink in your country. Use the paragraph titles to help you.

Mealtimes Typical dishes Drinks

2 Work in pairs and share your ideas.

Describing meals and dishes

- The main meal of the day is …
- Our national dish is …
- A speciality / typical dish is …
- Our main / staple food is …
- Our most typical drink is …
- On special occasions, we have …

Writing

Write a description of food and drink in your country for a class magazine. Use your notes and the useful phrases above to help you.

Global review

Grammar

Correct the mistakes in eight of these sentences and tick (✔) the two that are correct.

1 I need get more sleep.
2 English people drink a lot tea.
3 You drink too many coffee.
4 I use a coffee machine for make my coffee.
5 How much biscuits do you want?
6 Could I have a few sugar in my tea, please?
7 This chocolate tastes bitter.
8 I have too little eggs to make a cake.
9 Don't forget buy some noodles.
10 It's important to eat enough fruit and vegetables.

Vocabulary

Circle the correct option to describe each picture.

1 *bottle / carton / can* of juice
2 *mug / glass / cup* of coffee
3 *plate / frying pan / saucepan*
4 *spoon / fork / knife*
5 *oven / sink / microwave*
6 *finger / arm / elbow*
7 *knee / foot / back*
8 *nail / muscle / bone*
9 *casserole / vegetable / toast*
10 *cook / serve / taste*

Speaking and Writing

1 Work in groups of three and ask each other the questions.

- What did you eat and drink yesterday?
- Do you have a healthy diet?

Useful phrases

- I eat a lot of …
- I eat / drink too much / many …
- I don't eat enough …

2 Work in pairs. You are going to have a party for everyone in the class. Write a list of the food and drink you need to buy. Then compare your list with another pair.

Study skills

Evaluating your language learning

1 Work in pairs. Look back at the unit you have just studied. Tell each other which parts you found easy or difficult.

2 Think about what you have learnt in this unit. Mark the statements a, b, c or d.

a confidently and accurately
b quite confidently and accurately
c with help from my notes or my teacher
d with difficulty

I can ...

* describe my eating and drinking habits ___
* ask about eating and drinking habits ___
* talk about quantities ___
* describe things in a kitchen ___
* pronounce the sounds /k/ and /tʃ/ ___
* find information in a short reading text ___
* talk about containers and drinks ___
* understand a simple listening passage ___
* describe how to make a dish or drink ___
* describe purpose using *to* + infinitive ___

3 Work in pairs and compare your answers.

4 Look at how Stefan has evaluated his language ability. Underline the phrases which describe ability.

I think I'm quite good at understanding reading texts in the book. Sometimes I find it difficult to understand the listening passages. I'm not very good at grammar but my pronunciation is quite good. I need to expand my vocabulary, especially everyday English. I need more practice in speaking.

5 Work in pairs and describe your ability in the areas below. Make suggestions about how to improve.

Grammar	Reading
Vocabulary	Listening
Pronunciation	Speaking
Social situations	Writing

6 Write a letter to your teacher. Say what you have found easy and difficult in the classes so far. Describe your general language ability.

UNIT 3 Art & Music

Part 1

Vocabulary & Speaking
Works of art

Reading
Discovered!

Speaking
Art

Vocabulary and Speaking

1 Match the words to the pictures a–h.

cave art   old manuscript   painting
photograph   sculpture   self-portrait
sketch   statue

2 Work in pairs and describe the pictures. Use the words in exercise 1 and the useful phrases to help you.

Useful phrases

- This picture shows …
- I think this is a picture of …
- It looks as if + clause …
- This is from + time / place …
- I (really) like / don't like this picture …

a

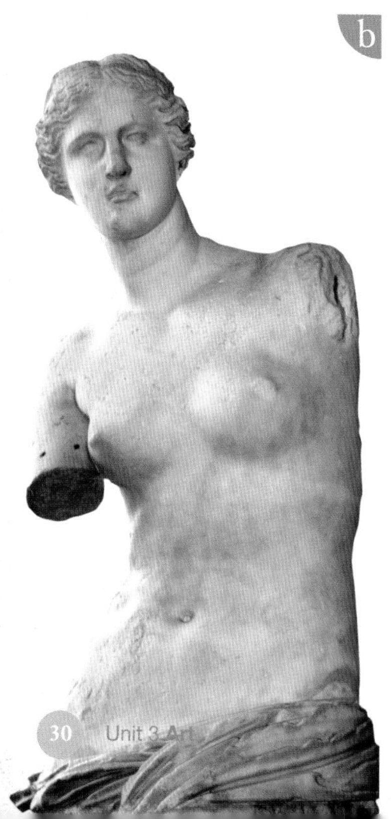

b

Reading

1 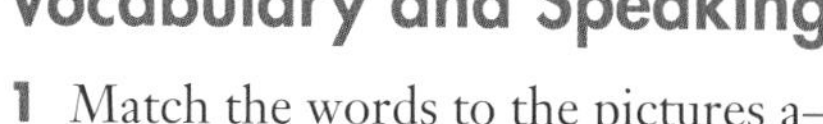 1.33 Read and listen to *Discovered!* on page 31 and match each text to a picture. There are four pictures that you do not need.

2 Read the texts again and complete the sentences with one or more words.

1 The *Venus de Milo* is a statue of ________.
2 The *Venus de Milo* is now in ________.
3 Some Mexican workers discovered a sculpture while they were installing ________.
4 The sculpture is now in ________.
5 The couple from Milwaukee thought their Van Gogh painting was ________.
6 *Vase with Flowers* sold for ________.
7 The man found the Declaration of Independence while he was shopping at ________.
8 The manuscript was inside a ________.

c

Extend your vocabulary – *discover*

Words in the same family:
discover – verb
discovery – noun
discovered – adjective
undiscovered – adjective

Complete the sentences with the correct form of *discover*.

1 The archaeologists made an important ______ near the town castle.
2 We only want to ______ the truth.
3 News flash: Picasso sketches ______ in church basement.
4 The painting was ______ until the dealer noticed it on the wall.

Speaking

Work in pairs and choose **one** of the tasks below.

A Tell your partner about an object that is important in your family. Use these questions to help you prepare.

- What is the object?
- How old is it?
- Where did it come from?
- Why is it important to you?

B Ask each other these questions.

- Do you like art? What kind of art do you like?
- Do you have any art in your house? What is it? Who is it by?
- Have you ever been to an art gallery? Which one?

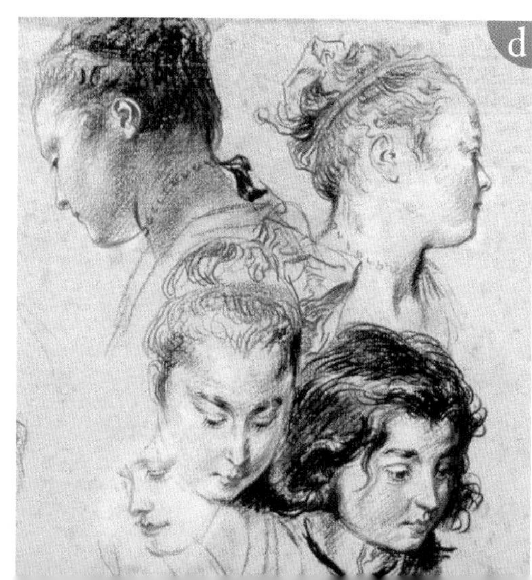

d

Discovered!

True stories of how valuable works of art were found in unexpected places

In a field

In 1820 a Greek peasant named Yorgos was working in his field on the island of Milos when he found several blocks of stone. Under the stones were four statues: three figures of the God Hermes and one of Aphrodite, the goddess of love. Three weeks later a group of French archaeologists arrived by ship. They bought the Aphrodite and took it to France. The king, Louis XVIII, called it *Venus de Milo* and gave it to the Louvre. It is now one of the most famous works of art in the world.

Under a street

On February 21, 1978, workers were putting down electrical cables on a busy street corner in Mexico City when they discovered a huge sculpture of the Aztec moon goddess Coyolxauhqui. It was more than four hundred years old and is now in the Museum of the Great Temple in Mexico.

On a wall

A man and his wife from Milwaukee, US, asked an art dealer to look at a painting they had in their home. While he was walking through the house, the dealer saw a different painting. The couple thought this was a reproduction of a Vincent Van Gogh, but it was in fact the original. On March 10, 1991, the painting *Vase with Flowers* sold for $1.4 million.

At a market

A man from Philadelphia was shopping at a flea market when he saw a wooden picture frame he liked. He paid $4 for it. When he got home he took the old picture out of the frame and found an old document behind it. It was a copy from 1776 of the American Declaration of Independence. The copy sold for $2.4 million in New York in 1991.

Glossary

archaeologist (*noun*) – a person who studies ancient societies

dealer (*noun*) – a person who sells a particular product

flea market (*noun*) – a market where old things are sold at low prices

peasant (*noun*) – a poor person who works on another person's farm

reproduction (*noun*) – a copy of something

Art & Music

Part 2

Speaking
Retelling stories

Grammar
Past simple & past continuous

Vocabulary
Furniture & furnishings

Reading
The Picture of Dorian Gray

Pronunciation
Past simple regular verbs

Writing
A scene from a short story

Speaking

1 Work in pairs. Tell each other what you remember about the works of art from page 31. Use the phrases below to help you.

A Greek peasant was working in his field when …

In 1978 a group of Mexican workers were putting down electrical cables when …

One day an art dealer went to visit a man and his wife in Milwaukee. While he was walking through the house …

A man from Philadelphia was shopping at a flea market when …

2 Check your answers in the texts.

Grammar

1 Write the past simple form of the verbs in the box. All the verbs are in the text on page 31.

arrive ask buy discover find
get pay see sell take

2 Put the verbs into two groups, regular and irregular verbs.

Three weeks later a group of French archaeologists ***arrived*** *by ship.*
Yorgos ***was working*** *in his field.*
While he ***was walking*** *through the house, the dealer* ***saw*** *a different painting.*

- use the past simple to talk about completed actions in the past
- use the past continuous to talk about an action in progress in the past
- the past continuous is common with a simple past action when one action interrupts the other

3 Complete the texts with the past simple or past continuous form of the verbs in brackets.

In a hole in the ground

In 1978 workers ________ (*dig*) behind an old casino in Dawson City, Yukon when they ________ (*discover*) more than 500 films from 1903 to 1929. The films ________ (*be*) in perfect condition because of the cold temperatures.

In an attic

In 1990 Barbara Testa, a librarian, ________ (*find*) 665 pages of an old book while she ________ (*look*) through a trunk in her attic. The book ________ (*be*) the original manuscript of the great American novel *Huckleberry Finn* by Mark Twain.

As a bicycle rack

Every day employees of the God's House Tower Museum in Southampton, UK ________ (*put*) their bicycles against a black rock in the basement. In 2000 two Egyptologists ________ (*visit*) the museum. They ________ (*examine*) other items when they ________ (*see*) the black rock. They ________ (*identify*) it as a 2,700-year-old statue of the Egyptian King Taharqa.

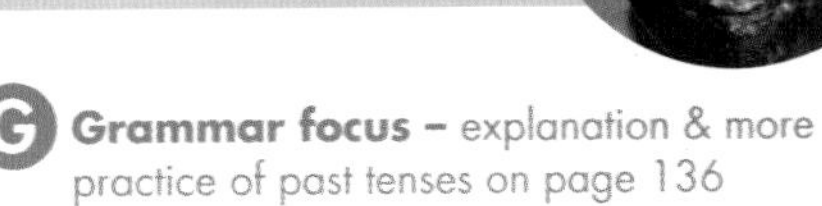

Grammar focus – explanation & more practice of past tenses on page 136

Vocabulary

1 Which of these things can you see in the picture on page 33?

armchair carpet coffee table
curtains lamp mirror shelf
sofa wall window

2 Which things do you have in your house? Where are they?

The Picture of Dorian Gray

Dorian decided to go to bed and went slowly towards his bedroom. He walked along the hall and through the library. Basil's portrait of Dorian was on a wall in the library. Suddenly Dorian stopped and looked at the portrait. He was surprised. The painting looked different. The face in the painting had changed. Yes, it had changed! Quickly, Dorian opened the curtains. Sunlight came into the room. Dorian looked closely at the picture and saw that the face was different. It looked unkind and cruel. A huge mirror hung on another wall. Dorian looked in the mirror at his own face. He saw a beautiful young man. He had not changed. What was happening to the picture?

Suddenly Dorian remembered the day that Basil finished the picture. Dorian remembered his wish. He remembered his own words.

'I wish that I could always be young. I wish that picture could grow old instead of me. I would give anything and everything for this to happen. I would give my soul!'

Why did the face in the picture look cruel and unkind? Was his wish coming true? Was the picture changing?

The Picture of Dorian Gray (1890) is one of Oscar Wilde's most famous novels. The main themes are the purpose of art and the obsession with youth and beauty.

Glossary

cruel (*adjective*) – causing pain to people
huge (*adjective*) – extremely large
soul (*noun*) – the spiritual part of a person
wit (*noun*) – the ability to use words in a clever way that makes people laugh

Reading

1 1.34 Read and listen to an extract from the book *The Picture of Dorian Gray*. What was happening?

2 Work in pairs. Choose two of these questions and then discuss them.

- Have you read this book? Would you like to?
- Dorian makes a wish by saying: 'I wish that I could always be young. I wish that picture could grow old instead of me.' Would you make the same wish as Dorian? Why?
- Do you think people are too concerned with being young in today's society?
- 'Your personality is written on your face.' What does this quote mean? Do you agree with it?

Pronunciation

1 1.35 Listen to some sentences from the text. Tick (✔) the verbs that have an extra syllable in the past tense.

1 decide – decided ___
2 walk – walked ___
3 stop – stopped ___
4 look – looked ___
5 open – opened ___
6 remember – remembered ___

2 Practise saying the verbs and the past tense forms.

3 How do you pronounce the past tense of these verbs?

asked discovered hated finished listened loved needed started wanted worked

Writing

1 Read the opening sentences from four short stories.

Mark was sitting in the most comfortable armchair when he heard the strange noise again.

I was happy when I received the sculpture, but I didn't know its secret.

As she was looking at the photograph, she was certain she saw the eyes move.

It was the most beautiful painting, and the most dangerous.

2 Choose one of the sentences and continue the story. Write two or three more sentences.

3 Work in pairs. Swap your stories and add another sentence to your partner's story. Then return the story to your partner.

Oscar Wilde **(1854–1900)**

Oscar Wilde was an Irish writer of plays, poetry and novels. He was famous for his wit and commentary on the society of Victorian London.

Art & Music

Part 3

Speaking
Describing pictures

Vocabulary
Audio & video

Listening & Writing
The history of sound recording

Grammar
Used to

Pronunciation
Used to

a

b

Speaking

1 Look at pictures a and b. Make some notes on the differences between them. Use the useful language and phrases to help you.

Useful language

- classical music
- conductor
- guitarist
- play
- concert hall
- drummer
- orchestra
- rock group

Useful phrases

- This looks like …
- The picture at the top / bottom shows …
- Maybe / perhaps it's in …

2 Work in pairs and describe the differences between the pictures.

3 Work in pairs and ask each other these questions.

- What kind of music do you like?
- Where do you usually listen to music? At home, at work, on the bus etc?
- Do you listen to music while you are working or studying? What kind of music?

Vocabulary

1 Rearrange the letters to make the correct words.

▶ yapl  wirend  staf wadfror

■ pots ❚❚ saupe ⏏ cejet

2 1.36 Listen and check your answers. Then repeat the words.

3 Match the words to the pictures on page 35.

audio cassette ___
CD ___
DVD player ___
headphones ___
MP3 player ___
record ___
record player ___
video cassette ___

Do you have any of these things at home?

4 1.37 Complete the instructions with the words in the box. Then listen and check your answers.

button down off on plug up watch

Right, to use this DVD player, first you _____ it in here. To turn it _____, just press this _____. Now press eject and put the disc in the tray. Close the tray and press play to _____ the film. To turn _____ the volume, use this button. If it's too loud, turn _____ the volume with this button. And, to turn it _____, press here.

5 Work in pairs. Make a similar set of instructions for a CD or MP3 player.

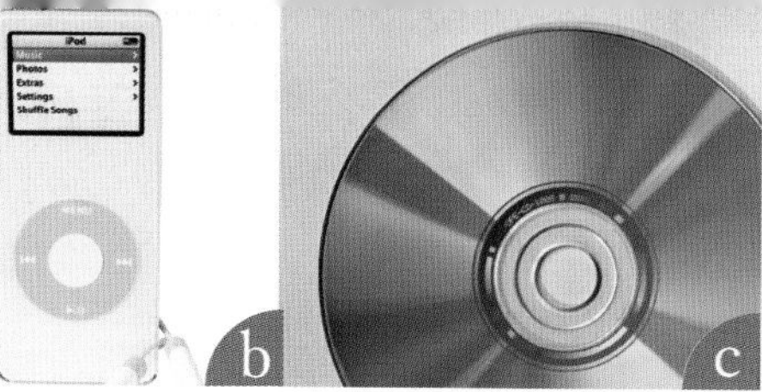

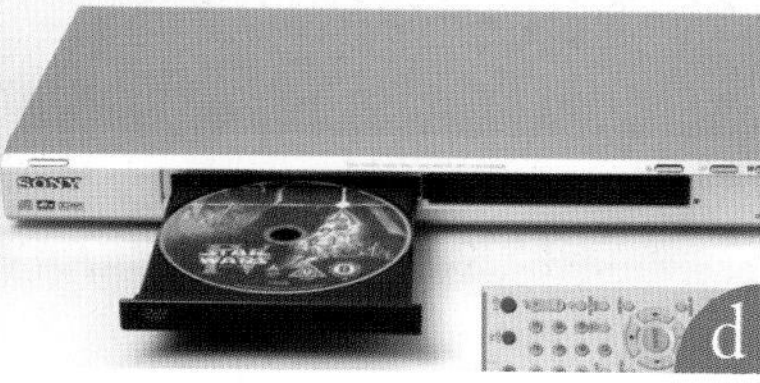

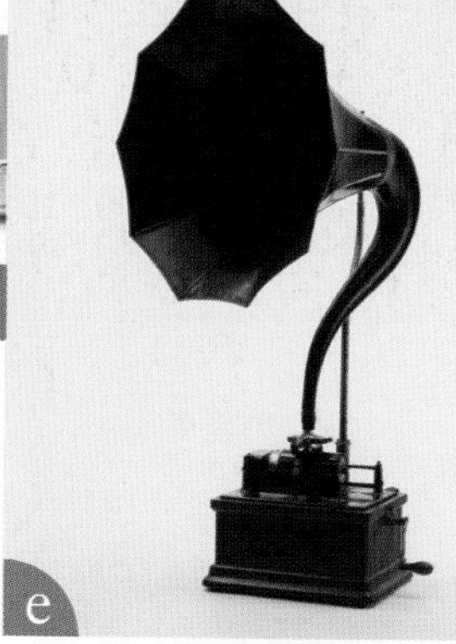

Listening and Writing

1 You are going to hear a lecture about the history of sound recording. Before you listen, list the words from vocabulary exercise 3 in order from oldest to newest.

2 **1.38** Listen to the lecture and check your answers.

3 Listen again and complete the notes.

History of
sound recording

The first: Thomas Edison in ______.

Edison predicts sound recordings for office dictation, speaking ______, education, talking ______ and music.

1900s: people play ______ on ______ players.

1920s: first films with sound – called ______.

______: Philips introduces audio cassette.

1963: first ______ opens in Los Angeles.

1970s–1980s: VHS video, cassette Walkman and ______ – ends era of the record.

Early 1990s: DVD

1996: first digital music player sold in ______.

2001: Apple iPod, a popular ______, appears.

Current music devices can store ______ songs, video and ______.

Extend your vocabulary – saying and writing decades

In English we can use the phrase *the nineties* to describe the years from 1990 to 1999.

I was at university in the nineties.

In informal writing we can write *the 90s*.

The years 2000 to 2010 are sometimes called *the noughties*.

Complete the sentences with the correct decades.

1 I don't like music from ______ (1980–1989).
2 I was born in ______ (1960–1969).
3 I was at school in ______ (1970–1989).

Grammar

*People **used to** listen to music on vinyl discs.*
*Vinyl records **used to** be popular.*
*They **didn't use to** have CDs.*

- use *used to* to talk about regular actions in the past which don't happen now
- use *used to* to talk about situations in the past which aren't true now
- the negative of *used to* is *didn't use to*

1 Look at the picture below and rewrite the sentences with *used to.*

In those days families were bigger.

In those days families used to be bigger.

1 Most women were housewives.
2 People didn't have lots of things.
3 Most families didn't have a television.
4 Some families had a radio in the living room.

2 Make questions with *did* and *use to*. Add two more questions.

1 What music ______ you ______ listen to?
2 Where ______ you ______ go to school?
3 ______ you ______ have long hair?

3 Work in pairs and ask each other the questions.

G **Grammar focus** – explanation & more practice of *used to* on page 136

Pronunciation

1 **1.39** Listen and repeat these sentences. Pay attention to the stressed words.

My <u>brother</u> <u>used</u> to <u>play</u> the <u>guitar</u>.
I <u>didn't</u> <u>use</u> to <u>listen</u> to <u>classical</u> <u>music</u>.

In connected speech, *used to* is pronounced /juːstə/.

2 Underline the stressed words in grammar exercise 1.

3 **1.40** Listen and check your answers. Then repeat the sentences.

Art & Music

Part 4

Vocabulary
Feelings

Listening
Music in film & TV

Speaking & Reading
High Fidelity

Vocabulary

1 Match the words in bold to the words in the box with similar meanings.

I was feeling **cheerful** today because …
… makes me feel very **calm**.
Last week I was **miserable** because …
I'm **frightened** of …
… makes me **sleepy**.
I'm always **anxious** when …

angry	bored	excited	happy	
relaxed	sad	scared	tense	tired

2 Complete the sentences in exercise 1 so they are true for you.

3 1.41 Listen to four short pieces of music. How do they make you feel?

4 Imagine one of the short pieces of music is part of a scene from a film. Listen again and answer the questions.

- Where is the scene?
- Who is in the scene?
- How do they feel?
- What is happening?

5 Work in pairs and tell each other about the scene you imagined.

Listening

1 1.42 Listen to the composer Andy Price talking about how he uses music in films and TV programmes. Tick (✔) the feelings he mentions.

angry	calm	excited	happy
sad	safe	scared	tense

2 Listen again and choose the correct answers.

Music *used to be / has always been* an important part of film and television.

If you want an audience to feel *scared / angry* then use violins, played very quickly and on a high note.

Gentle music on a guitar, piano or violin is good for *love scenes / death scenes*.

Choral music (people singing) can make an audience feel *tense / sad*.

When the character of Robin Hood appears in the programme you can hear *trumpets / guitars*.

The orchestra *used to play / usually plays* in front of a large screen showing the film.

3 Work in pairs and compare your answers.

Andy Price is a composer for theatre, film, television and advertisements. His work includes the music to the BBC programmes *Robin Hood*, *Score* and *The Six Wives of Henry VIII*. He has won many awards for his work.

Extend your vocabulary – using *just*

You can use *just* in spoken English in different ways.
For emphasis:
Just turn it off!
To mean *only*:
It just makes me bored.
To mean *exactly*:
He is just like his father.

Put *just* into the following sentences. What does *just* mean in each one?

1 Be quiet, please.
2 It was a mistake.
3 Thank you for the CD, it's what I wanted.

Speaking and Reading

1 Work in pairs. Write down the names of all the pop groups you can think of in one minute.

2 Work with another pair and compare your lists. Then answer these questions.

- Is pop music popular in your country?
- Who listens to pop music?
- Do you like pop music?

3 1.43 Read and listen to the extract from Nick Hornby's *High Fidelity*. How does pop music make the writer feel?

4 Work in pairs and discuss these questions.

- Do you think the author is being serious or funny?
- The writer thinks British people are very scared of violence in videos.
  Do people in your country worry about this? Do you think it is a problem?

High Fidelit

What came first, the music or the misery? Did I listen music because I was miserable? Or was I mise because I listened to music? Do all those record you into a melancholy person?

People worry about kids playing with guns, and teenagers watching violent videos; we are scared th some sort of culture of violence will take them over. Nobody worries about kids listening to thousands – li thousands – of songs about broken hearts and rejecti and pain and misery and loss. The unhappiest people know are the ones who like pop music the most …

Nick Hornby (1957–)
Nick Hornby is one of Britain's most popular contemporary authors. He frequently writes about sport and music. Many of the characters in his books have aimless or obsessive personalities.

High Fidelity (1995) is set in London and is about Rob, a man who works in a record shop. His girlfriend has left him. In the rest of the book, Rob examines his past relationships with women and with music. There was a film of the book in 2000 and a Broadway musical in 2007.

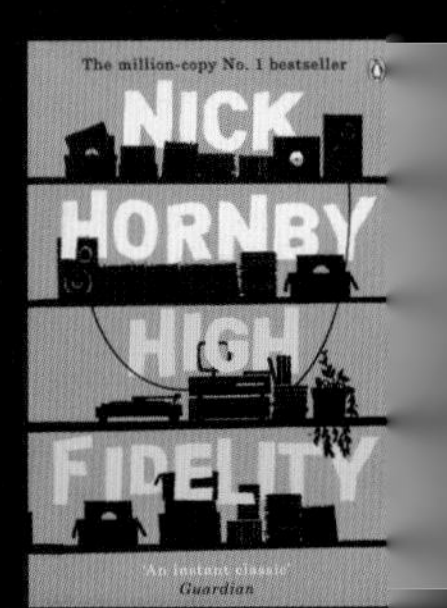

Glossary:
melancholy (*noun*) – a feeling of being very sad and having no hope
miserable (*adjective*) – extremely unhappy

UNIT 3 Function globally agreeing and disagreeing

Warm up

1 Work in pairs and look at the pictures from four different films. Match the pictures to the types of film in the box.

action comedy drama horror musical
romantic comedy science fiction thriller

2 Describe the similarities and differences between the pictures.

3 What kinds of films do you like?

Useful language

- costumes
- martial arts
- in black and white

Useful phrases

- I think this one is a / an …
- I've seen / I've never seen …
- This could be from India / Germany …

Listening

1 1.44–1.46 Listen to three conversations about films and match each one to a situation. There is one situation you don't need.

a An interview situation, perhaps on television or on radio.
b A couple deciding what to rent at a DVD shop.
c Two friends coming out of the cinema.
d A teacher giving his opinions about films to a class.

2 Listen again and answer the questions.

Conversation 1: Did they both like the film?
Conversation 2: What kinds of films do they talk about?
Conversation 3: What kind of film does the woman want to see?

Language focus: agreeing and disagreeing

1 Read the sentences and mark *A* for agreeing, *D* for disagreeing or *I* for in between.

I agree. ___
Absolutely. / Definitely. ___
I don't agree (at all). ___
Well, maybe but … ___
You're absolutely right. ___
That's what I think too. ___
Oh please! ___
That's right. ___
I sort of agree / disagree but … ___
Exactly. ___

2 1.47 Listen and check your answers. Then listen and repeat the phrases. Try to copy the intonation.

Speaking

Work in pairs and choose **one** of the tasks below.

A Complete these sentences with your own ideas.

- Two great films are ________ and ________.
- Two great actors are ________ and ________.
- The best musician from my country is ________.
- The worst kind of music today is ________.

Compare your ideas with your partner. Do you agree or disagree?

B Decide how much you agree or disagree with these statements.

- Music used to be much better.
- Hollywood always produces the same kinds of films.
- There is a lot of exciting new art around today.
- Art galleries and museums are important for society.

Compare your opinions with your partner. Do you agree or disagree?

Global English

The power of music

by David Crystal

Music has the power to engage all the emotions – from excitement to relaxation, from tears to laughter. But why does it have such power over us? The clue lies in babies.

The word *lullaby* has been in English since the Middle Ages. It's one of several, such as *rockaby* and *hushaby*, which show how generations of mothers have helped their children fall asleep through music.

Babies can hear in the womb about two months before they're born. Newborns prefer their mother's voice to that of a stranger. And they show preferences in music too. One research study played the same tune to a group of mothers every day throughout pregnancy; another group of mothers didn't hear the tune. When all the babies were born, their heart-rate was monitored while the tune was played to them. Only the 'musical' babies reacted to the tune.

There's something special about the music of the voice. From the moment a baby is born, the mother talks to it in an unusual way. Her voice ascends and descends from very high to very low – almost like singing in speech. And infants soon copy. You can hear them trying to sing from around nine months of age.

Glossary

clue (*noun*) – a piece of information that helps you to understand something

longer (ad*verb*) – more time

monitor (*verb*) – to regularly check something

stranger (*noun*) – someone who you do not know

Melody, of both speech and music, is especially significant. In another study, infants were shown two pictures of their mother. In one she was singing and in the other she was speaking. They looked for longer at the singing one.

Singing also simplifies our vocal behaviour: words are often shorter, sounds are clearer and repeat more often, and they often rhyme. Nursery rhymes work so well because they combine these effects – clear rhythm, repeated sounds and rhyme. In the music of speech lies the foundation of poetry.

Warm up

1 Complete the nursery rhyme with the words in the box. Do you know this rhyme?

all blows fall

Rock-a-bye baby on the tree top,
when the wind ___
the cradle will rock,
when the bough breaks
the cradle will ___,
down will come baby,
cradle and ___.

2 Can you remember any nursery rhymes in your language? What are they?

Reading

1 Read the text. Which sentence is the best summary?

a Music and poetry are linked.
b We are affected by music from a very young age.
c Babies are more sensitive to music than adults.
d Lullabies are an English invention.

2 Read the text again. What do these words refer to?

1 it (line 2)
2 It (line 3)
3 that (line 6)
4 it (line 11)
5 them (line 12)
6 one (line 18)
7 they (line 21)
8 they (line 22)

3 Which of the facts in the text do you think are the most interesting? Compare your ideas with a partner.

Language focus

Look at the words in the box and put them into two groups: *music* or *babies*. Then translate them into your language.

born infant melody musical nursery pregnancy rhyme singing tune womb

Speaking

Work in pairs and ask each other these questions.

When you were a child …

- did your mother or father sing to you? What songs?
- did you have a favourite record or group? What was it?
- did you play an instrument? Which one?
- did you have music class at school? Did you enjoy it?
- did you use to sing? What songs?

UNIT 3

Writing a review

Reading

1 Read Stefano's review of a concert he went to and answer the questions.

1 Who gave the concert?
2 What sort of singer is he?
3 Where was the concert held?
4 What happened during the concert?
5 Did Stefano enjoy the concert?

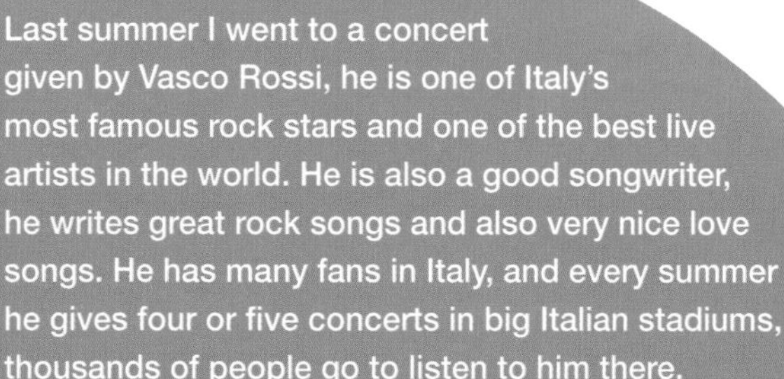

Last summer I went to a concert given by Vasco Rossi, he is one of Italy's most famous rock stars and one of the best live artists in the world. He is also a good songwriter, he writes great rock songs and also very nice love songs. He has many fans in Italy, and every summer he gives four or five concerts in big Italian stadiums, thousands of people go to listen to him there.

The concert took place in Rome's Olympic stadium, there were very many people there, all the tickets were sold out. I arrived at the stadium at three o'clock in the afternoon, I had to queue for six hours, I was very excited to see Vasco Rossi. The concert started at 9 o'clock in the evening, it went on for a very long time, maybe three or four hours. When Vasco Rossi started the concert everybody shouted, in the middle of the concert the crowd sang with him, it was very nice.

When the concert finished there were many security guards, everybody went home very quickly but without problems. I was very tired, I also went straight home, I was happy because of the excellent concert.

2 Would you enjoy the concert? Why?

Writing skills: sentences

1 You cannot join sentences with a comma. You need to start a new sentence using a full stop and capital letter. Stefano wrote:

Last summer I went to a concert given by Vasco Rossi, he is one of Italy's most famous rock stars.

He should write:

Last summer I went to a concert given by Vasco Rossi. He is one of Italy's most famous rock stars.

2 Find 12 more places where Stefano has joined sentences with a comma.

3 Join some of the sentences using *and*, *but* or *so*.

Language focus: adjectives

Make your writing more interesting by avoiding words like *nice*, *good* or *great*. Use your dictionary to find different words.

Improve Stefano's writing by using these words in the text.

moving   powerful   talented   tender and expressive

Preparing to write

1 Think of a concert you have been to or would like to go to. Make notes about it. Use the useful phrases below to help you.

Paragraph 1: Who was the concert given by? Give some information about the performer.
Paragraph 2: Where did the concert take place? Who was in the audience? What happened during the concert? How did you feel?
Paragraph 3: What happened at the end? How did you feel?

2 Work in pairs and share your ideas.

Describing a concert

- The concert was given by …
- It was a live / open air / sell-out concert.
- It took place in a stadium / a concert hall / a field.
- The hall was full /packed / half empty.
- The audience cheered / clapped / shouted.
- The music was brilliant / powerful /moving.
- I felt excited / moved / happy.

Writing

Write a review of a concert. Use your notes to help you.

Global review

Grammar

1 Complete the sentences with the past simple or past continuous form of the verbs in brackets.

1 How much ________ (*you / pay*) for that painting?
2 I ________ (*not / pay*) anything. It was a present.
3 When we ________ (*arrive*) at the cinema, our friends ________ (*wait*) for us.
4 My grandfather ________ (*find*) a valuable manuscript while he ________ (*work*) in his attic.
5 He ________ (*sell*) it to the museum for more than half a million dollars.

2 Complete the sentences with the correct form of *used to* and the words in brackets.

1 What kind of music ________ (*you / listen*) to when you were a child?
2 I ________ (*listen*) to pop music. I ________ (*not / like*) classical music then, but I do now.

Vocabulary

1 Read the definitions and complete the words.

1 a large group of musicians who use instruments to play classical music o ______
2 you can listen to live music here c ______ h ______
3 an image of a person or animal, made of stone, metal or wood s ______
4 you usually put books on these s ______
5 a comfortable object to sit on a ______

2 Complete the sentences with the correct word.

1 I used to be *angry / tense / frightened* of horses.
2 Sanna always has a happy face – she's a *sad / cheerful / scared* person.
3 I hate exams – they make me *anxious / relaxed / sleepy*.
4 As a child I used to feel very *miserable / bored / excited* about going on holiday – it was the best week of the year.

Speaking and Writing

1 Work in pairs. You are ill in bed and feeling miserable. Tell your partner how to find your favourite music and play it on your music player. Then swap roles and repeat.

2 Work in small groups. Write four sentences about your childhood using *used to* or *didn't use to*. One must be false. Take it in turns to read out your sentences and try to guess which one is false.

Study skills

Conversation partners

1 Work in pairs and discuss these questions.

- How often do you speak English outside class every week?
- In what situations do you speak English? For example, with friends or family, at work, in social situations etc.
- What do you talk about?
- How can speaking outside class help to improve your speaking ability?

One way to practise speaking is to meet with a conversation partner between classes. Your partner can be someone from your English class. You can use some of your time together to practise what you have learnt in class.

2 Work in pairs. Make arrangements to meet as conversation partners this week.

* Decide on a time and place to meet.
In school, before or after the class?
In one person's house at the weekend?
In a bar or café in the evening?
On the phone?

* Decide how long you will meet for.
For fifteen minutes?
For half an hour?
Some other length of time?

* Decide which of these topics you would like to talk about. Add your own ideas.
Finding out about each other.
Your taste in art, music or books.
Things you used to do in a previous school.
Feelings that you had this week.
Some things that you did this week.
Instructions for using something.
________________________.

3 Make some notes after the meeting.

- What was the most helpful or interesting part of the meeting?
- What was difficult?
- What will you do differently next time?

UNIT 4 Hopes & Fears

Part 1

Vocabulary
Adjectives & synonyms

Reading
When I grow up ...

Grammar
Future hopes & plans

Speaking
My hopes & plans

Vocabulary

1 Look at the phrases below. Put them in order from most important (1) to least important (4). Compare your answers with a partner.

being **good-looking** being **intelligent**
being **rich** having **good** health

2 Match the words in bold in exercise 1 to the words in the box with similar meanings. There are two words in the box that you don't need.

awful beautiful clever excellent handsome smart terrible wealthy well-off wonderful

3 Look at the two extra words. What are they synonyms of?

4 Look at your list from exercise 1. Do you think your order was different in the past? How about in the future? Complete the sentences and then compare with a partner.

When I was younger I probably thought … was more important.
… will be more important when I'm older.

Reading

1 Read the text *When I grow up*. What are the children talking about?

a Their hopes for their own lives and their families
b Their hopes for the world
c Both a and b

2 Read the text again. Which quotes are the most interesting for you? Choose two quotes and tell a partner.

3 Work in pairs. Choose two of these questions and then discuss them.

- Do you think these children are optimistic or pessimistic about the future?
- Do children in your country have similar hopes?
- Did you have similar hopes when you were a child?

WHEN I GROW UP ...

I want to live with my mum as long as I can.

I hope to have a rich husband.

I'd like to be super intelligent.

I hope that people in my area say sorry when they do something bad.

I hope we have more places where you can sit and talk without the sound of cars.

I'd like to have lots of money.

To put the world's money together and give Africa water.

I hope to have a lot of money.

I'm planning to travel and learn different languages.

I want to help my father pay for things.

I'd like thousands of people to watch me on TV.

My family is going to find a box of treasure.

I hope that my mum meets someone and has a baby.

Grammar

*I **hope** to have a lot of money.*
*I **would like** to be super intelligent.*
*I am **looking forward to** being older.*
***I'm going to** be a fun but good teacher.*

- use *hope, plan, want* and *would like* to talk about future hopes that aren't definite
- use the infinitive after *hope, plan, want* and *would like*
- use *look forward to* to talk about definite future plans
- use *be going to* to talk about things you have already decided to do

1 How many correct sentences can you make with the words in the table? Use the text to help you.

I	'm -	hope going looking forward planning want would like	to	get getting	a good job.

2 Complete the text using the correct form of the words given.

The hopes of children

In a survey of English schoolchildren, researcher Cathie Holden found that, for their personal future, the majority of boys and girls hope *to go / going to* university or college. They also all hope *getting / to get* a good job. More boys are planning *to pass / pass* their driving test than girls, and more girls are looking forward to *have / having* children.

For their local area, children in the report said they hope for less violence and fewer poor people. They also said that they would like *have / to have* more parks and places to play. The majority of boys and girls are looking forward to *living / live* in a world without wars and an important number of them said they would like things *to get / getting* better in the developing world.

G **Grammar focus** – explanation & more practice of future tenses on page 138

Speaking

1 Choose **three** of the ideas in the box that you would like to talk about.

- A place you hope to visit one day
- Something you hope you **don't** do in the future
- Something you're not looking forward to
- A person you'd like to meet one day
- A person you're going to see today

2 Work in pairs. A: tell B about your ideas. B: ask for more information.

3 Swap roles and repeat.

I'm planning to have one child and spend lots of time with him or her.

I want to be good-looking.

I'd like my dad to understand me one day.

No wars because my brother's dad will die, he's in the army.

I'm going to be a fun but good teacher.

I'd like to have less pollution in my city.

I want to have a nice house.

I'm looking forward to being older and not having to listen to my parents any more.

I'd like to make a difference.

I'm going to get a good wife.

I'd like people to grow up but never die.

I want to be wise.

For the world to be more human.

UNIT 4

Hopes & Fears

Part 2

Speaking & Listening

A profession of hope

Vocabulary & Pronunciation

Global issues, word stress

Grammar

Future plans & intentions (*be going to*, present continuous)

Reading & Speaking

Pandora's box

Josh Gross and Helle Hansen are based in Denmark. In terms of foreign aid, Denmark is one of the most generous countries in the world. There are many NGOs (Non-Governmental Organisations) in Denmark that work on projects in Latin America and Africa.

Speaking and Listening

1 Study the graph about foreign aid below. Then work in pairs and discuss the questions.

- Does anything about the graph surprise you?
- Do you know any aid organisations? What are they?
- Have you ever given money to an aid organisation?
- Do you think rich countries should give more money in foreign aid?
- Do you know anyone who works for an aid organisation?

2 **1.48** Listen to two aid workers talking about their next job. Put the interviewer's questions and comments in the correct order.

How did you become aid workers? ___
What is the most important thing in your job? ___
So, tell us about yourselves. 1
Thanks for your time. ___
What are you going to do there? ___

3 Listen again. What do these words mean in the listening?

Danish	Guatemala
two years ago	village

4 Would you like to work for an aid organisation? Why?

Vocabulary and Pronunciation

1 Match the words in the box to the definitions below.

disease	homelessness	hunger	
natural disasters	pollution	poverty	war

1 people do not have enough money
2 people do not have a place to live
3 people do not have enough food
4 people are sick
5 countries are fighting each other
6 weather or environmental problems such as floods (too much water) or earthquakes (when the earth moves)
7 the air, water or land is dirty

2 Complete the pronunciation chart with the words from exercise 1.

O	Oo	oO	Ooo	oOo
war	natural	___	___	___
	___		___	___

3 **1.49** Listen and check your answers. Then repeat the words.

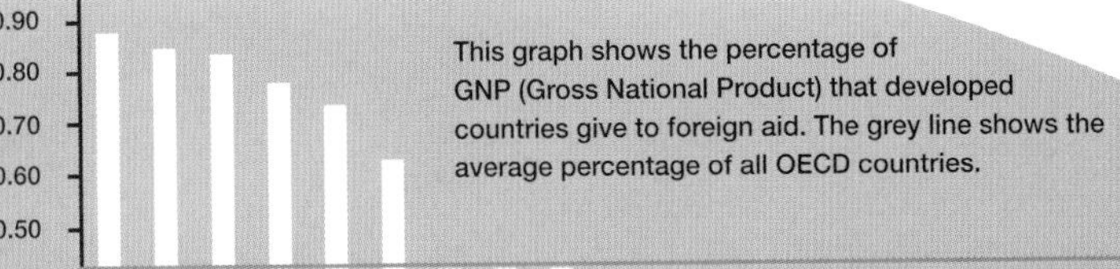

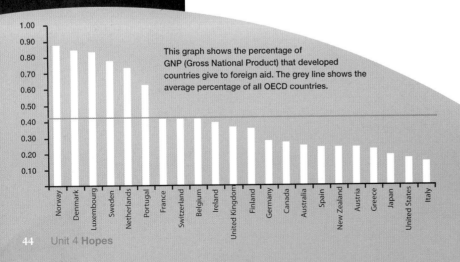

This graph shows the percentage of GNP (Gross National Product) that developed countries give to foreign aid. The grey line shows the average percentage of all OECD countries.

Grammar

*We **are going to work** with the children there. The organisation **is starting** a new project in Guatemala next year.*

- use *be going to* to talk about things you have already decided to do
- use the present continuous to talk about future plans, often when they are already arranged

1 Read the text and decide if the underlined parts are correct or incorrect. Then correct the mistakes.

A new project

Susana works for a Spanish NGO in Madrid. The organisation is start a project next month in Ethiopia. Susana is going for work with a local women's organisation in the country. Together they are going to develop an educational project for pregnant women. Susana is going to travel to Ethiopia with a group of doctors. 'I'm a bit nervous, but I've been to Africa before and I know Ethiopia,' she says. 'It's going to being a great project.'

2 Complete the questions with the present continuous or *be going to*.

1 A: What ________ (*do*) after class?
   B: Meeting a friend.
2 A: ________ you ________ (*go*) away next summer?
   B: No, I'm staying here.
3 A: ________ you ________ (*read*) an English book this year?
   B: Yes, I am. I have a detective novel I want to read.
4 A: ________ you ________ (*work*) tomorrow?
   B: Yes, I am. I start at 8am!
5 A: ________ you ________ (*study*) English next year?
   B: Yes, I think so.

3 Work in pairs and ask each other the questions from exercise 2.

G Grammar focus – explanation & more practice of future tenses on page 138

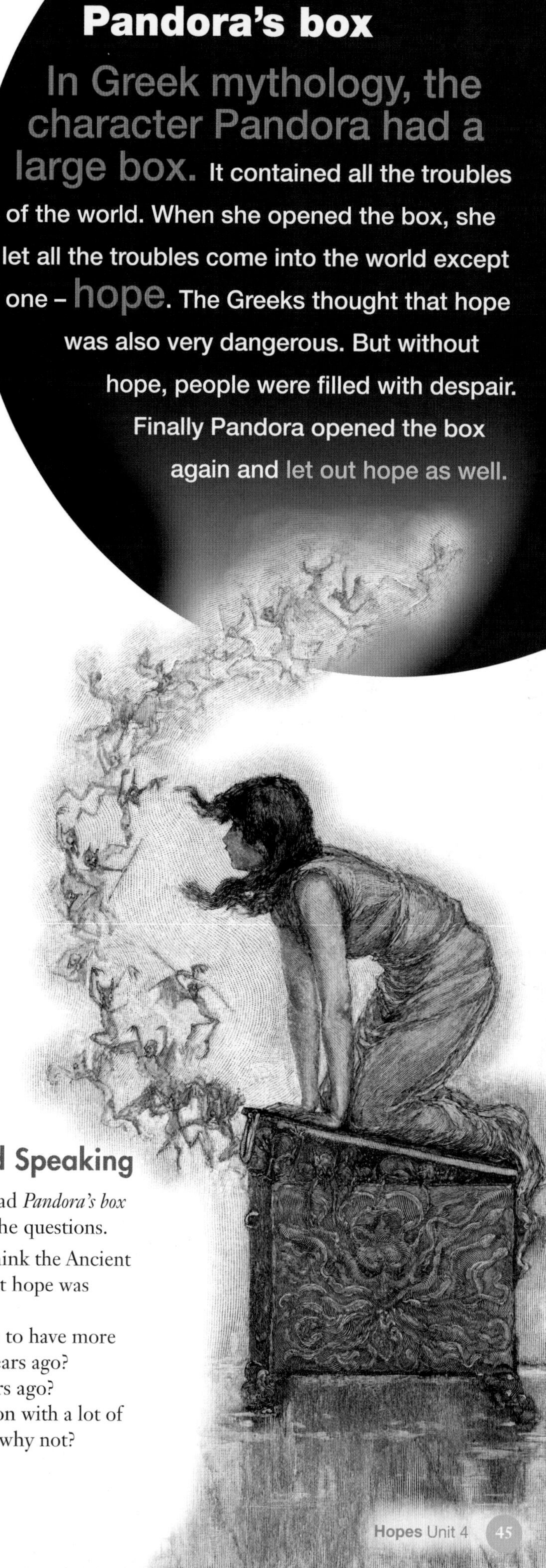

Pandora's box

In Greek mythology, the character Pandora had a large box. It contained all the troubles of the world. When she opened the box, she let all the troubles come into the world except one – hope. The Greeks thought that hope was also very dangerous. But without hope, people were filled with despair. Finally Pandora opened the box again and let out hope as well.

Reading and Speaking

Work in pairs. Read *Pandora's box* and then discuss the questions.

- Why do you think the Ancient Greeks thought hope was dangerous?
- Did people use to have more hope twenty years ago? A hundred years ago?
- Are you a person with a lot of hope? Why or why not?

Part 3

Reading
Things will get worse

Grammar
Prediction & ability (*will, be able to*)

Vocabulary
Phrasal verbs with *get*

Reading

1 Which novels do students in your country usually have to read at school? Did you read them?

2 Look at the titles below of three famous books that students in many English-speaking countries often study. Do you know any of these books?

3 1.50 Read and listen to the summaries and tick (✔) the features they have in common.

a The story happens in the future.
b The government controls everything.
c The story happens in England.
d People are happy.

4 Read the summaries again and decide if the sentences refer to *1984*, *Brave New World* (*BNW*) or *A Handmaid's Tale* (*HT*).

1 Women won't be able to have children. ___
2 There'll be only three countries in the world. ___
3 There will be a nuclear disaster. ___
4 We won't have wars. ___
5 Babies will be born in factories. ___
6 The government will control people's thoughts. ___
7 Love will be a crime. ___
8 People won't get sick from disease. ___

5 Look at the sentences in exercise 4. Do you think these things will happen in the future? Tell a partner.

Useful phrases

- It's possible.
- I don't think …
- Maybe …
- I'm sure … won't …
- I'm sure … will …
- I hope not.

Things will get worse …
Famous dystopias in literature

Nineteen Eighty-Four

The author: George Orwell (1903–1950), English

The novel is set in the future, but it is the year 1984. Winston Smith lives in London, part of the country Oceania. There are three countries in the world: Oceania, Eurasia and Eastasia. Big Brother is the leader of Oceania. The government controls everything, even people's thoughts. Winston works for the government, but he is getting tired of his boring life. He meets Julia, another worker, and they fall in love – a crime in Oceania. The government discovers their secret, and Winston and Julia must go to the Ministry of Love, a centre for enemies of Big Brother.

Brave New World

The author: Aldous Huxley (1894–1963), English

London, 600 years in the future. The Controllers are the rulers of the world. People don't know war, poverty, disease or pain. They enjoy leisure time, sports and pleasure, but they are not free. The Controllers create babies in factories. Adults are divided into five social classes, from the intelligent *alphas* to the worker *epsilons*.
When a man from a wild area of the world gets to London, he criticises the society. In the end, he has to choose between joining them or dying.

Glossary

dystopia (*noun*) - imaginary place or situation where everything is very bad
infertile (*adjective*) – not physically able to have children
pollution (*noun*) – chemicals and other substances that have a harmful effect on air, water or land
revolution (*noun*) – a situation in which people completely change their government or political system
totalitarian (*adjective*) – controlling a country and its people in a very strict way
underground resistance (*noun*) – a secret organisation that fights against the group that controls their country

A Handmaid's Tale

The author: Margaret Atwood (1939–), Canadian

In the future a revolution replaces the government of the United States with the totalitarian Republic of Gilead. Because of pollution and nuclear accidents, many women are infertile. New laws create the job of handmaid, a woman who can have babies for rich families.
This is the story of Offred, a handmaid. Offred works for Fred, a commander, and his family. She wonders if she can get away, and learns about an underground resistance from another handmaid. But there isn't much time. If Offred doesn't get pregnant soon, she knows they will send her to the dangerous colonies.

Grammar

There ***will*** *be only three countries in the world.*
Women ***won't be able to*** *have children.*

- use *will* and *won't* to talk about future predictions
- use *will / won't be able to* to talk about ability or possibility in the future

1 Read the text about *Fahrenheit 451*. Complete the summary below by rewriting the underlined sentences with *will / won't* or *will / won't be able to.*

Fahrenheit 451

The author: Ray Bradbury (1920–), American

It is 24th century America. The government controls society through the media. It is criminal to be an intellectual. People can't read or own books, as books are against the law. The population gets all their information from the television. They don't know their history. Guy Montag is a fireman. Firemen don't stop fires, they start them. They burn books at a temperature of 451 degrees. One day Montag meets the young Clarisse, who makes him question the society he lives in. Soon Montag gets interested in the books he is supposed to destroy.

In Ray Bradbury's vision of the future …
the government will control society through the media.

2 Read the definition of *utopia*. Write five predictions for a future utopia.

utopia (*noun*) – an imaginary place or situation in which everything is perfect

G Grammar focus – explanation & more practice of prediction & ability on page 138

Vocabulary

1 Look at these phrases with *get* from the summaries. Write them next to the correct meanings of *get* in the table below.

1 Winston works for the government, but he is *getting tired* of his boring life.
2 When a man from a wild area of the world *gets to London* …
3 If Offred doesn't *get pregnant* soon …
4 The population *gets all their information* from the television.
5 Soon Montag *gets interested* in the books …

Meaning of *get*	Examples		
become	*getting tired*		
receive			
arrive			

2 Match the phrasal verbs with *get* to the correct definitions.

1 get around — a return (from a journey)
2 get away — b travel
3 get back — c get out of bed
4 get together — d leave / escape
5 get up — e spend time with someone

3 Work in pairs and ask each other the questions.

Imagine it's a perfect, utopian world …

- What time do you get up every day?
- What time do you get back home from work?
- Where do you get away when you need a holiday?
- How often do you get together with friends and family?
- How do you get around? What kind of transport do you use?

Part 4

Vocabulary
Geographical features

Listening
An inconvenient truth

Grammar
Future time clauses

Speaking
Climate change questionnaire

Vocabulary

1 Look at the pictures and complete the words with the correct vowels.

2 1.51 Listen and check your answers. Then repeat the words.

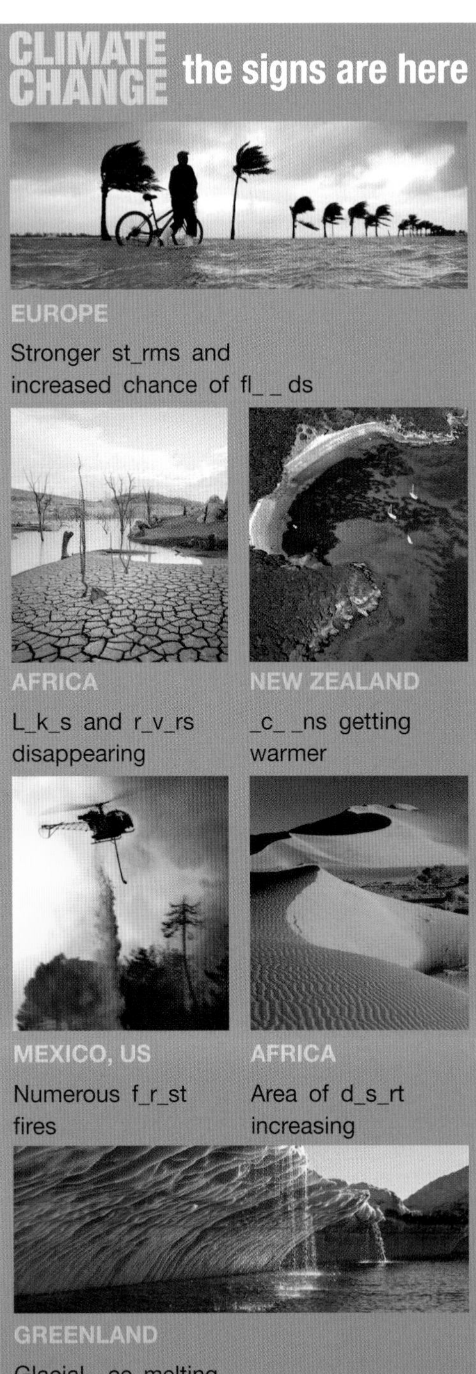

CLIMATE CHANGE the signs are here
EUROPE
Stronger st_rms and increased chance of fl_ _ds
AFRICA
L_k_s and r_v_rs disappearing
NEW ZEALAND
_c_ _ns getting warmer
MEXICO, US
Numerous f_r_st fires
AFRICA
Area of d_s_rt increasing
GREENLAND
Glacial _ce melting

Listening

1 Look at the film poster on page 49. How does the poster describe the film? What do you think it is about?

2 1.52 Listen to people talking about the film and check your answer.

3 Listen again. Are the statements true (*T*) or false (*F*)?

Speaker 1: He saw the film a few years ago.
Speaker 2: She didn't know about global warming and climate change before she saw the film.
Speaker 3: He liked the film.
Speaker 4: He thinks it's a typical Hollywood film.
Speaker 5: She doesn't believe that climate change is happening.
Speaker 6: He thinks it's important for young people to see it.

4 Have you seen this film? Would you like to?

Extend your vocabulary – *–ed* / *–ing* adjectives

Terrified describes how we feel.
I was terrified by the film.
Terrifying describes things or situations that make us feel terrified.
It was a terrifying experience.
We can use this rule for many adjectives: *bored / boring, frightened / frightening, interested / interesting, surprised / surprising.*

Choose the correct words to complete the dialogues.

1 A: Did you see the film?
B: Yes, I did. It was long, and really *bored / boring*.

2 A: So, was he angry?
B: No. He was very *relaxed / relaxing* about the whole thing. I was *surprised / surprising*.

3 A: I'm a bit nervous about the heat this summer.
B: I know what you mean. It's a *worrying / worried* situation.

By far
the most terrifying film
you will ever see.
an inconvenient truth
A GLOBAL WARNING
PG
PARAMOUNT CLASSICS

Grammar

After you see this film, you will think differently.
If we reduce carbon emissions, we will reduce global warming.

- after future time clauses such as *after*, *before*, *when* and *if* we use a present tense

1 Complete the sentences with the present simple or future simple of the verbs in brackets.

1 If we ________ (*not do*) something now, we ________ (*have*) serious problems in the future.
2 If you ________ (*look*) at the ten hottest years, you ________ (*see*) they happened in the last fourteen years.
3 When this climate change ________ (*happen*) I ________ (*be*) dead.
4 You ________ (*think*) differently after you ________ (*see*) it.

2 Work in pairs and complete the sentences with your own ideas.

After class finishes …
I … before the end of this year.
If the weather is good tomorrow …
When I have enough money …

G Grammar focus – explanation & more practice of future time clauses on page 138

Speaking

1 Read the questions below and think about your answers.

How to reduce your carbon footprint

1 Do you use energy-saving light bulbs? How many?
2 Do you recycle anything? What?
3 Do you ever walk / take the bus instead of driving? How often?
4 Do you use a lot of hot water at home? What for?
5 Do you buy things with lots of packaging? What?
6 Have you ever planted a tree? When?

2 Work in pairs and ask each other the questions. If your partner answers *yes*, ask the follow-up question.

3 Look at the information in the table and tell your partner how much carbon they will save if they make these changes.

Action	Carbon saving
Change to energy-efficient light bulbs	68 kg per year
Recycle half of your household waste	1,095 kg
Walk instead of driving	0.5 kg per km
Wash your clothes in cold water	225 kg per year
Reduce your household waste by 10%	544 kg
Plant a tree	907 kg

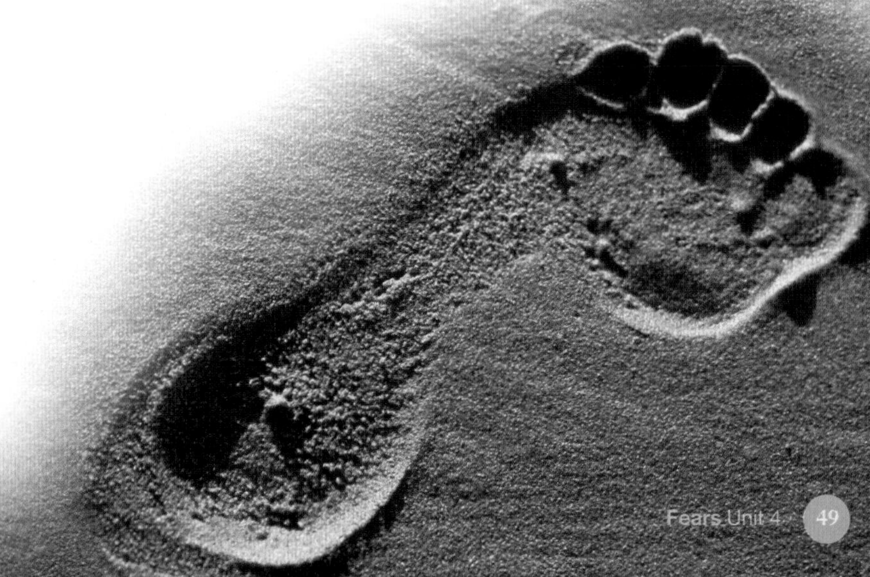

UNIT 4

Function globally making offers and decisions

Warm up

Work in pairs and choose three situations from the list below. Roleplay a short conversation for each situation.

Situations

1 A: you are talking to a friend (B). Your train to the airport leaves in 5 minutes. You're late!
B: your car is parked outside.

2 A: you arrive at your destination and get off the train.
B: you are carrying a very heavy bag.

3 A: you are in the train station café with a friend (B).
B: you don't have enough money to pay for the coffees.

4 A: you are at the train station but have missed your train. You want to buy a ticket for the next train.
B: you work in the ticket office.

Listening

1 1.53–1.55 Listen to three conversations. Match each one to a situation in the Warm up. There is one situation you don't need.

2 Listen again and answer the questions.

Conversation 1: How much is the bill?
Conversation 2: How is the man going to get to the airport?
Conversation 3: What train is the woman going to take?

Language focus: offers and decisions

1 Read the information in the table. What verb do we often use to make offers and decisions?

Offers	I'll carry those books for you.
	Shall I pay for this?
	Let me take that for you.
Decisions	I'll take the next train.
	I won't take the train. I'll take a taxi.

Language note: *shall* is usually used only in questions and with *I* or *we*.

2 Complete the offers or decisions with *will* or *shall* and a verb from the box. There is one verb you don't need.

carry have help pay take

1 A: Are you ready to order?
B: Yes. I ______ a salad.

2 A: I don't understand this.
B: That's all right. I ______ you.

3 A: The next train is in twenty minutes.
B: ______ we ______ it or wait?

4 A: Here, let me take those bags.
B: Thanks, but it's OK. I ______ them.

3 1.56 Listen and check your answers. Then listen and repeat the phrases.

Speaking

Work with a new partner and choose **one** of the tasks below.

A Repeat the warm up activity using the new expressions you have learnt.

B Look at the audioscript on page 154 and choose one of the conversations. Practise the conversation and try to memorise it.

Global voices

Warm up

1 Read ten reasons why people learn English. Choose the top 3 and the bottom 3 for you.

I'm learning English because …

1 I'd like to get a job with a multinational company.
2 I want to understand songs, TV programmes or films in English.
3 I hope to get a job with a company in the USA.
4 I'd like to be an English teacher.
5 It will be helpful for my career.
6 I'm planning to get a job in the tourism industry.
7 I want to meet other English-speaking people and make friends.
8 It's important for my studies.
9 It's a world language and it's important to know.
10 I like English and American culture.

2 Work in pairs and compare your answers. Can you think of any other reasons why people learn English?

Listening

1.57–1.62 Listen to six people talking about why they are learning English. Which reasons from exercise 1 do they give? Write the numbers.

1 Abdul, Libya ___
2 Olga, Russia ___
3 Mert, Turkey ___
4 Naif, Saudi Arabia ___
5 Arthur, France ___
6 Dain, South Korea ___

Abdul, Libya

Olga, Russia

Mert, Turkey

Naif, Saudi Arabia

Arthur, France

Dain, South Korea

Language focus: synonyms

Read the sentences from the listening. Which word in the box has a **different** meaning to the word in bold?

1 Well I believe English is very important **nowadays**. Naif, Saudi Arabia

actually currently now these days

2 I'm learning English because it will be helpful for my **career**. Abdul, Libya

job profession university studies work

3 We need to study English. It is **essential**. Dain, South Korea

important necessary obvious vital

Speaking

1 Read the questions about learning English. They are typical questions from international English speaking exams. Choose three questions you can answer.

- How long have you been learning English?
- Why are you learning English?
- How important is English in your country?
- How will English be useful to you in the future?

2 Think about your answers and practise what you want to say.

3 Work in pairs and ask each other the questions.

UNIT 4 Writing an email to a friend

Reading

1 Read two emails between friends. What do they arrange to do?

Hi Pamela,

I am writing to invite you to go to the cinema with me this weekend. I would like to see *La Vie en Rose*.

It is a drama starring Marion Cotillard and it has had very good reviews. It is the true story of the famous French singer, Edith Piaf. I have heard that the music is beautiful and the acting is brilliant.

We could meet in front of Cinemark at Higienópolis Mall at four o'clock on Saturday. Would that be convenient for you?

Yours sincerely

Laura

Hello Laura,

I would love to go to the cinema with you. That would be wonderful. I would really like to see this film. My sister has seen it and she says it is great. I will see you at four o'clock.

Pamela

2 Would you like to see this film? Why?

Writing skills: informal style

1 Are these statements true (*T*) or false (*F*)?

In emails to friends …

a do not use contractions such as *I'm*, *it'll*.
b use informal salutations such as *hi*, and endings such as *cheers*.
c we can miss out salutations and endings.
d we must write in paragraphs.

2 Laura and Pamela have not used contractions in their emails. Make 13 changes to the emails.

3 Mark these expressions formal (*F*), quite informal (*Q*) or informal (*I*).

Hello Laura	Dear Laura	Hi Laura
Best wishes	Cheers	Yours sincerely
Bye for now	Regards	Yours

Language focus: making invitations and arrangements

1 Mark these expressions formal (*F*) or informal (*I*).

1 I am writing to invite you to go to the cinema.
2 How do you fancy going to the cinema with me?
3 I'm afraid I'm busy tomorrow.
4 Unfortunately I am busy tomorrow.
5 Would it be convenient to meet on Friday evening?
6 What about meeting outside Pizza World?
7 I'd love to see the film.
8 I would very much like to see the film.
9 That would be wonderful.
10 That sounds great.
11 I look forward to seeing you on Friday.
12 See you on Friday.

2 Read the emails again and change any expressions that are too formal.

Preparing to write

Work in pairs and tell each other about a film you have seen recently. Use the useful phrases below to help you.

Describing a film

- It's a western / comedy / drama / thriller / musical.
- It's an action film / a horror film / a documentary.
- It's about …
- It's had brilliant / good / quite good / poor reviews.
- It stars Marion Cotillard and it's directed by Olivier Dahan.
- The acting / photography is wonderful / poor.

Writing

Work with a new partner. Write an email to your partner inviting them to see a film. Describe the film and suggest a time and a place to meet. Then swap your emails and write replies.

Global review

Grammar

Complete the sentences with the correct words.

1 What *do you do / are you doing* next weekend?
2 I hope *getting / to get* together with some friends.
3 I would like *to learn / learning* another language.
4 I *'ll buy / 'm going to buy* a new car at the weekend.
5 When I *buy / will buy* my new car, I *will able / will be able* to get around more.
6 Are you looking forward to *go / going* to university?
7 Next month I *will start / am starting* a new job.
8 If the world's temperature *gets / will get* warmer in the next few years, glacial ice *melts / will melt*.

Vocabulary

Put the words into the correct boxes. There are two words you do not need.

clever desert flood forest fire homeless lake
ocean poor storm war wealthy well-off

Natural disasters	People with a lot of money
People helped by aid organisations	**Geographical features**

Speaking and Writing

1 Work in groups of three. Ask each other about your plans for the times below.

- after class
- this evening
- the weekend
- next summer

Try to find one plan that is the same for everybody.

2 Work in pairs. Write a list of five things people could do to reduce their carbon footprint. Then compare your list with another pair.

Study skills

Using your dictionary: finding the right entry

1 Work in pairs and look at the phrases below. Which word would you look up in the dictionary to find the meaning of each phrase?

1 global warming
2 get away
3 fall in love
4 against the law

2 Look up the words to see if you were right.

* The most important word in an expression is called the *keyword*. Keywords are often nouns, but can also be verbs, adjectives or adverbs.
* Some words in a dictionary have more than one entry. This might be because the same word can belong to two classes:
  an ***orange*** dress (*adjective*) — eat an ***orange*** (*noun*)

3 Find two different word classes for each of these words.

1 heat ______
2 pretty ______
3 fair ______

Sometimes words have the same spelling but different meanings or different pronunciations.

4 Find two meanings and pronunciations for these words.

1 tear ______
______
2 close ______
______

Some words have many meanings.
These are listed at the beginning of an entry.

green (*adjective*)
1 like grass in colour
2 with lots of plants
3 caring for nature
4 not ready to be eaten
5 not experienced
6 of the Green Party

5 Choose the best meaning of *green* in the sentences below.

1 She is campaigning for ***green*** issues such as reducing packaging and the use of cars.
2 We need more ***green*** areas in our town.
3 He is too ***green*** to manage the company.

Work & Leisure

Part 1

Speaking
Jobs

Vocabulary
Work

Reading & Speaking
Profile of an Indian call centre worker

Grammar
Have

Speaking

1 Read the quote about work in the United States.

"When you go to work, if your name is on the building, you're rich. If your name is on your desk, you're middle class. If your name is on your shirt, you're poor."
Rich Hall, American comedian and writer

2 Work in pairs and discuss these questions.

- What does this quote say about jobs in America?
- Is this true in your country?
- Look at the jobs in the box. Which ones would / wouldn't you like? Decide on the top three and the bottom three.

builder	doctor	disc jockey (DJ)
journalist	lawyer	
manager in a fast food restaurant		
musician	nurse	police officer
politician	security guard	shop assistant
teacher	waiter	

Vocabulary

1 Read the texts below and replace the underlined words and phrases with words in the box. Use your dictionary to help you.

bonus	employ	hiring	an interview
salary	training	wages	

Job possibilities at a multinational company
We give work to 6,000 people and need more
We offer a good starting money, plus end-of-year extra money
English and computer skills needed

Local supermarket is now giving jobs
No experience necessary, we will provide teaching of the skills
Excellent money per hour and good working environment
Contact Andrew Grau for a talk about the job

2 Work in pairs and discuss these questions.

- Have you ever been to a job interview? How was it?
- Is there a minimum wage in your country? What is it?
- Do you know anyone who works night shifts? What do they do?
- What is a good starting salary in your opinion?

Reading and Speaking

1 Read the introduction to *Profile of an Indian call centre worker* on page 55 and answer the questions.

1 Do you know what a call centre worker does?
2 Have you ever spoken to one?

2 Read the rest of the text. What does she say about …

1 her feelings about the job?
2 the hours she works?
3 the people she talks to?

Extend your vocabulary – *job* and *work*

You can use both *job* and *work* to talk about what someone does to get paid.
Do you like your job / work?
What kind of job / work do you do?
Work is uncountable with this meaning, so you cannot say ~~a work~~ or ~~works~~.
Complete the sentences with *job*, *jobs* or *work*. Sometimes more than one answer is possible.

1 Rajeshwari has a good ______.
2 She likes her ______.
3 I have two ______.
4 Many young people don't have any ______.
5 Do you have a ______?

3 Work in pairs and choose **one** of the tasks below.

A Tick (✔) two pieces of information in the text you think are interesting or unusual. Then compare with your partner.

B How would you describe Rajeshwari? Write three words. Then compare with your partner.

Profile of an Indian call centre worker

The English newspaper, *The Observer*, interviewed Rajeshwari Singh, a 20-year-old call centre worker. Rajeshwari lives and works in New Delhi, India. This is what she said about her work.

Companies like using call centres because they are cheaper and can give 24-hour service.

I was so happy when I got this job. It was my first ever interview but they hired me. That night my dad bought chocolates and sweets and we had a small party. He was very proud.

With bonuses, my starting salary is 16,000 rupees (£190) a month.

There are 350,000 call centre workers in India.

I sell landlines to Americans. People can get angry. They say 'You people are taking the jobs from our hands.' I say that it's not my fault if Americans are expensive to employ.

My alias is Katie Jones. That's a little lie, I suppose, but a good lie. If I had to use my own name, I'd lose five minutes at the beginning of every call spelling it out, and I don't have a lot of time.

When you have voice training, you have to speak in an American accent all the time or you lose it. When I call home, my parents say 'I don't believe it, it's not you any more!'

Call centre workers answer the phone or make telephone calls for large companies.

Night shifts destroy your life. I don't get home from work until five in the morning, and I don't sleep until six.

You have to dress well even though people can't see you. It's a question of self-confidence. People can pick that up from your voice. And there are 4,000 people in the office to look at you.

There are a lot of Indians living in America and Britain. Sometimes you talk to people who say 'No English. Hindi? Hindi?' and you realise you're talking to an Indian, and often you get so confused you forget how to speak Hindi.

I miss my parents. I can't tell them when I feel upset because they'd come right away to Delhi and take me home.

Many banks, ticket companies and telephone companies are using call centres in other countries.

Glossary

alias (*noun*) – a different name that somebody uses instead of their real name

landline (*noun*) – a telephone line that is not a mobile phone

pick up (*phrasal verb*) – to notice something that is not very obvious

upset (*adjective*) – sad, worried or angry about something

Grammar

1 Look at sentences 1–8 and match them to the uses of *have* a–e below.

1 I have got a job as a call centre operator. b
2 I have worked at the company for ten years. ___
3 We had a small party. ___
4 I have voice training. ___
5 I have to use my own name. ___
6 I don't have a lot of time. ___
7 I have to speak with a US accent. ___
8 I have to dress well. ___

We can use *have*:

a to talk about possessing or owning something.
b as an auxiliary with *got* to talk about possessing or owning things.
c as an auxiliary with *to* to say what is necessary or obligatory.
d as an auxiliary in the present perfect.
e to talk about actions or experiences.

Language note: we can only use the contracted forms of *have* when it is the auxiliary verb, not when it is a main or modal verb.

2 Read the sentences with *have* and insert contractions where they are possible.

1 I have a brother and a sister.
2 I have never been to a job interview.
3 We have English class on Thursday morning.
4 I have got a good English dictionary.
5 I have had more than one job in my life.
6 I have breakfast with my family every morning.

Grammar focus – explanation & more practice of *have* on page 140

Work & Leisure

Part 2

Listening & Vocabulary
Work issues

Grammar
Modal verbs

Pronunciation
Contractions

Speaking
Job characteristics

Listening and Vocabulary

1 Look at the cartoon about a bad boss. What is the joke? Do you think it is funny?

2 **1.63–1.66** Listen to four bosses talking to their employees. Number the topics in the order you hear them.

a meal	___	the computer	___
dress code	___	the weekend	___

3 Listen again and choose the correct alternative to complete each sentence.

Conversation 1: Someone has called (*in / out / for*) sick.
Conversation 1: You can take next Saturday (*away / off / on*).
Conversation 3: You are (*on / for / at*) company time, and you must respect that time.
Conversation 4: Of course you can go (*on / in / at*) your lunch break now.

4 Which do you think are bad bosses? Why?

Grammar

1 Look at sentences 1–6 and complete the rules a–d below.

1 You ***have to*** work this Saturday.
2 You ***can*** take next Saturday off.
3 You ***mustn't*** wear jeans to work.
4 You ***don't have to*** wear a jacket and tie.
5 You ***can't*** send personal messages with this computer.
6 You ***must*** arrive on time.

a We use _*have to*_ and _*must*_ to talk about rules and things that are necessary.
b We use ________ and ________ to say when something is not allowed.
c We use ________ to say that something is not necessary.
d We use ________ to say that something is possible or allowed.

Language note: modal verbs are followed by an infinitive without *to*.

2 Complete the texts with the words in the boxes. Use each word only once.

can don't have to must

Dress-down Friday

In many financial companies in Britain, employees ________ wear a suit or other formal clothes. Some workplaces have a *dress-down* day, usually on a Friday. On this day, people ________ dress so formally. They ________ wear whatever they like.

can can't mustn't

Work computers

According to a 2006 survey by the American Management Institute, 78% of American companies have rules about email, instant messenger and blog use. Workers ________ use their computers for work, but they ________ send personal email messages or instant messages. Also, they ________ download programs onto work computers.

can don't have to have to

Flexitime

A study of the 68 biggest Australian companies found that 93% offered flexitime hours to their employees. Under flexitime, workers ________ work a fixed number of hours in a week, but they ________ start and finish at the same time every day. If they come to work earlier, they ________ leave earlier.

3 Complete the sentences about your job. If you do not work, use one of the jobs on page 54.

Every day I have to … at work.

I don't have to … at work.

At work, I can usually …

I can't … at work.

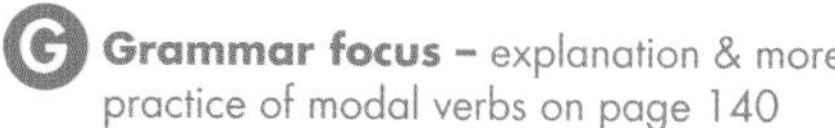
Grammar focus – explanation & more practice of modal verbs on page 140

Pronunciation

1 1.67 Listen to the pairs of sentences. Can you hear the differences?

1 You can't wear that.
  You can wear that.
2 She can't come to class today.
  She can come to class today.
3 You must use your books.
  You mustn't use your books.

> **Language note:** in British English, *can't* is pronounced /kɑːnt/.

2 1.68 Listen and circle the word you hear. Then practise saying the sentences.

1 Workers *mustn't / must* use the computers on the first floor.
2 You *can't / can* take your lunch break at two o'clock.
3 I really *must / mustn't* answer emails more quickly.

Speaking

1 Read the job characteristics in the box and tick (✔) the ones which are important to you.

> **What's important for you in a job?**
>
> You earn a lot of money.
> You don't have to wear a uniform.
> Your work is interesting.
> You can work flexible hours (you can start and finish when you like).
> You can take regular breaks.
> You have to work with the public.
> You can be your own boss.
> You can work close to home.
> You don't have to work on Saturdays or Sundays.
> You have job security (you don't have to worry you will lose your job).

2 Work in pairs and share your ideas. Decide on the five most important characteristics of a job.

A: *For me, the most important things in a job are …*
B: *OK. For me, the most important things are …*
A: *What do you think the top five are?*
B: *I think …*

3 Work with another pair and compare your lists. Do you agree? Make a new list of the five most important characteristics.

Useful language

What do you think is the most important?
I think that … is more important than …
What about you?
I disagree. I think … is more important.
I agree. Let's put it on the list.

Part 3

Vocabulary
Leisure activities

Listening
The serious leisure perspective

Grammar
***-ing* verbs**

Pronunciation
/ŋ/

Writing
Leisure time

Vocabulary

1 Match the verbs in the box to the nouns.

chat collect cook do
go for play read watch

______ books the newspaper
______ exercise the gardening
______ a walk a drink with friends
______ stamps coins things
______ television a film the news
______ video games chess sport
______ with friends on the phone
______ a meal dinner vegetables

2 Work in pairs and tell each other which of the activities you do.

I watch television every night.
I hardly ever read the newspaper.

3 Look at the chart showing how Americans spend their leisure time. Then work in pairs and discuss the questions.

- Is there anything that surprises you?
- Is it similar to how you spend your leisure time?

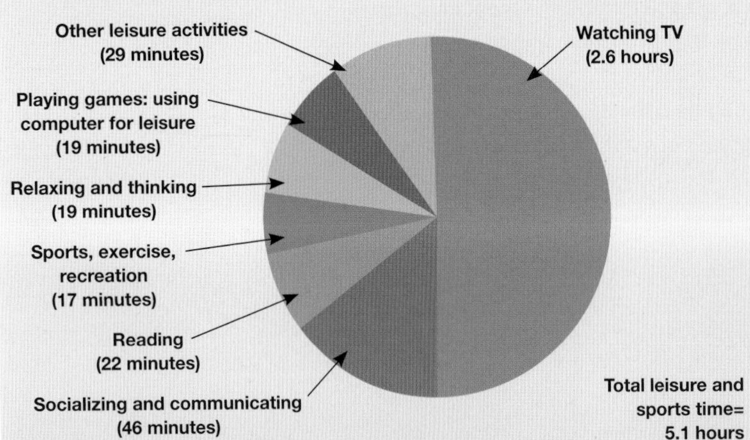

Listening

1 1.69 You are going to hear a presentation about *The serious leisure perspective*. Listen and put the slides on page 59 in the correct order.

2 Listen again and answer the questions.

1 What are some examples of casual leisure?
2 Why do people enjoy casual leisure?
3 Why does leisure have a bad reputation?
4 What are some examples of serious leisure?
5 Why does the speaker think serious leisure is important?

3 Work in pairs and ask each other these questions.

- Which do you prefer, casual or serious leisure activities?
- Do you know anyone who has a serious leisure pursuit? What is it?

Extend your vocabulary – *play*

Words in the same family:
play – verb
player – noun
playful – adjective

Complete the sentences with the correct form of *play*.

1 He is an excellent football ______.
2 I ______ computer games until very late last night.
3 She is a very ______ child.

Grammar

1 Look at sentences 1–3 and answer the questions a–c below.

1 Watch***ing*** television is casual leisure.
2 He's good at swimm***ing***.
3 People enjoy do***ing*** leisure activities.

a What is the subject in sentence 1? Replace the subject with another activity from the listening.
b What kind of word comes before the *-ing* form in sentence 2?
c What other verbs can go before the *-ing* form in sentence 3?

2 Write the *-ing* form of the verbs in the box. Then put them into three groups according to their spelling.

cut cycle do make play
run smoke stop swim
take watch work

3 Complete these sentences with your own ideas using the *-ing* form. Then work in pairs and share your ideas.

… is very relaxing.
I'm not very interested in …
I'm good at …
I don't enjoy … alone.
Some people find … a lot of fun, but I think it's boring.

G Grammar focus – explanation & more practice of *-ing* forms on page 140

Pronunciation

1 1.70 Listen and repeat the sentences. Pay attention to the underlined sounds. What is the most common spelling of /ŋ/?

1 Relaxing and watching TV are my favourite things.
2 I think English is a difficult language.
3 No thanks, I'm stopping smoking.

2 Work in pairs. Read your sentences from grammar exercise 3 to each other. Pay attention to the /ŋ/ sound.

Writing

1 Choose one of the activities in the box below and write a short paragraph about it.

- an activity you enjoy doing
- an activity you used to do but stopped doing
- a sport you like watching
- something you aren't very good at doing
- an activity you hate doing

2 Work in pairs. Swap papers and write two questions about your partner's activity. Then return the papers.

3 Read your partner's questions and rewrite the paragraph. Include the original information and the answers to your partner's questions.

Part 4

Reading

Ten facts about ... amusement parks

Grammar

Present perfect, *have been* & *have gone*

Pronunciation

Past participles

Speaking

Ten questions about ... leisure

Reading

1 Look at the two pictures. Do you like either of these things?

2 Quickly read *Ten facts about amusement parks around the world* and find the answers to the questions.

1 Where did the roller coaster come from?
2 Where was one of the first amusement parks?
3 What do modern amusement parks have?
4 How much money do amusement parks make?
5 What is the most popular amusement park outside the United States?
6 What is an *imagineer*?

3 Have you ever been to an amusement park? Is there one in your country?

Grammar

*They **have built** eleven parks around the world.*
*I **have been** to an amusement park.*
***Have** you **ever been** to an amusement park?*

- use the present perfect to talk about an unspecific time in the past
- use the present perfect to talk about experiences
- use *ever* in questions about experiences
- *ever* means the same as *in your life*

Language note: *She has **been** to Tivoli Gardens.* This means she has come back. *She has **gone** to Tivoli Gardens.* This means she is still there.

1 Complete the two texts with the past simple or present perfect form of the verbs in brackets.

Dale Johansson is a photographer of amusement parks. He ________ (*visit*) more than 50 different parks in 20 countries and ________ (*take*) photos of each one. He first ________ (*become*) interested in amusement parks when his father ________ (*take*) him to one when he was a child.

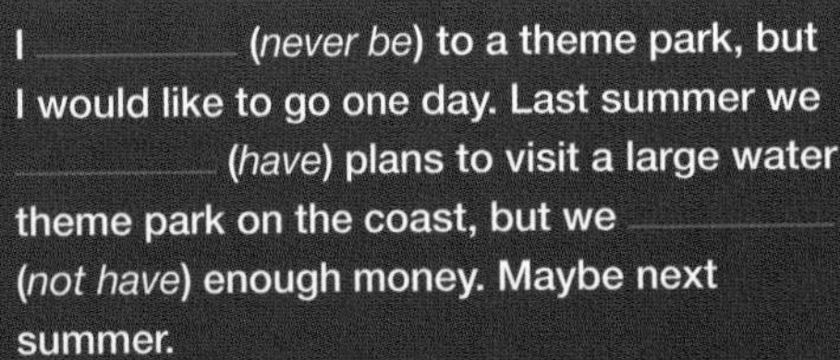

I ________ (*never be*) to a theme park, but I would like to go one day. Last summer we ________ (*have*) plans to visit a large water theme park on the coast, but we ________ (*not have*) enough money. Maybe next summer.

roller coaster

2 Complete the dialogues with *been* or *gone*.

1 A: Where has he ______?
B: I don't know. He was here just a minute ago.
A: Oh no.

2 A: We've ______ on this ride three times.
B: I know, but it's great. Isn't it great?
A: Hmmm.

3 A: Where's Marco?
B: He's ______ on his break. He'll be back in fifteen minutes.
A: He can't do that!

4 A: Have you ______ here before?
B: Sorry, I don't understand. What?
A: Is this your first time here?

3 Work in pairs. Imagine you hear one of the dialogues at an amusement park. Who is speaking? How do they feel? Add two more lines and then act out the dialogue.

G **Grammar focus** – explanation & more practice of the present perfect on page 140

merry-go-round

Pronunciation

1 Put the past participles in the box into four groups depending on their sound.

been	bought	brought	come	
done	driven	eaten	forgotten	
ridden	seen	swum	taught	won

/ən/ /ʌm/ or /ʌn/ / ɔːt/ /iːn/

2 1.71 Listen and check your answers. Then repeat the words.

Speaking

1 1.72 Listen to the stress and intonation in this question.

Have you ever <u>been</u> to an <u>amusement park</u>?

2 Work in pairs. Look at the leisure questionnaire and say the ten questions. Use *Have you ever* + past participle. Pay attention to the stress and intonation.

3 Work in pairs and ask each other the questions. If your partner answers *yes*, ask two follow-up questions. Use the ideas in the box below to help you.

A: *Have you ever been to an amusement park?*
B: *Yes, I have.*
A: *Did you like it?*
B: *Yes, I loved it.*
A: *Who did you go with?*
B: *I went with my family.*

Did you like it?	What?	When?	
Where?	Who with?	Why?	Why not?

Ten facts about … amusement parks around the world

Amusement parks are leisure places for adults, teenagers and children.

People often think amusement parks are an American invention, but they originally come from Europe. Tivoli Gardens in Copenhagen, Denmark, is one of the oldest European amusement parks.

The first roller coaster was invented in Russia in the 1600s. People went down snowy hills on blocks of ice.

The world's fastest roller coaster is the *Formula 1 Racecoaster* at Germany's Nürburgring. It travels at 217 km per hour.

Modern amusement parks usually have rides, roller coasters and eating areas. There is often a common theme to make visitors feel as if they are in a different world.

Amusement parks are big business. In the United States alone, amusement parks make an annual profit of $11 billion. More than 30% of Americans have been to an amusement park.

Walt Disney created the first Disney theme park, an amusement park with several sections, in 1955 in California, US. The Disney Corporation has built eleven Disney theme parks around the world.

The most popular amusement park in the world is Walt Disney World in Florida.

The most popular park outside the US is Disneyland in Tokyo. Four of the top ten amusement parks are in Asia.

The people who invent Disney amusement park rides have a special name. They are called *imagineers*.

Ten questions about … leisure

1 … be to an amusement park?
2 … ride on a roller coaster?
3 … buy tickets for a sports event?
4 … be to a rock concert?
5 … stay at a health spa?
6 … see a circus?
7 … do a dangerous sport?
8 … drive a very fast car?
9 … be to a water park?
10 … visit a zoo?

Function globally turn-taking

Business meeting | Job interview | Parent-teacher meeting | Residents' association meeting

Warm up

Look at the pictures of four different meetings. Work in pairs and ask each other the questions.

- Who is speaking in each photo? What are they talking about?
- Have you ever been in one of these situations? When?
- Choose one of the pictures and think of two rules for that situation.

  At a business meeting people have to arrive on time.

  Somebody has to take notes.

Listening

1 1.73–1.75 Listen to three conversations and match each one to a picture. There is one picture you don't need.

2 Listen again and choose the correct answers.

Conversation 1: The woman wants to know about ...

a the books.
b the children.
c his son.

Conversation 2: The man needs to arrive at ...

a seven in the evening.
b seven in the morning.
c the European offices.

Conversation 3: The man doesn't like ...

a the wages.
b the dress code.
c the woman.

Language focus: turn-taking

1 Read the audioscript on page 155. Find examples of a speaker turn-taking. This could be ...

a asking a new question in the conversation.
b asking permission to speak.
c adding something to the conversation.

2 Make three turn-taking questions or sentences using the words in the box. You can use each word more than once.

add ask a question can could
here I just may say something

Speaking

Choose **one** of the tasks below.

A Work in pairs and choose one of the conversations from the listening. Write the next three or four lines. Then read the conversation together. Use the new expressions you have learnt.

B Work in groups of three. A: choose a question and answer it. B: ask a question or give more information. C: continue. Use the new expressions you have learnt.

- What is most important in a job?
- What would be the ideal relaxing weekend?
- Is it necessary to speak English for work?
- Is it easy for young people to get jobs?
- Should there be more leisure facilities for young people?

Useful language

- Excuse me.
- Pardon me.
- Sorry, but ...

Global English

All **work** and no **play**

by David Crystal

There's an old saying in English: *All work and no play makes Jack a dull boy*. Or Jill. Psychologists tell us we need a balance between work and play to have a healthy lifestyle. And it is the same for language.

One of the most noticeable features of work language is the technical vocabulary, or jargon, that people use. Outsiders won't understand it. A doctor might look at the face of someone who's had a fall and say to a colleague 'That's a nasty perorbital haematoma'. If you were the patient, and heard this remark, you might be worried. But basically all it means is you've got a black eye.

Every profession has its jargon - law, banking, sport, physics, language teaching ... Thousands of specialised terms might be used. They add precision. And they also make people feel they belong together. You know you're a member of a group when you can comfortably *talk shop*.

Jargon also saves time. That's why doctors say such things as *BP* and *SOB* (blood pressure, shortness of breath). It's quick and convenient.

But they shouldn't use such terms to the patient. Work language and leisure language are two very different things. That's the argument of the Plain English Campaign, which wants specialists to speak clearly when talking to the public.

It's easy for people to use jargon carelessly and annoy people. It's worse when it's used deliberately, to mislead the public. That's why we get so angry when we hear people using it to hide the truth. A politician once admitted that something he had said was 'an instance of plausible deniability'. In other words, he'd told a lie!

Glossary

carelessly (*adverb*) – without thinking about what you are doing, so that you cause problems or damage

dull (*adjective*) – boring

mislead (*verb*) – to make someone believe something that is incorrect or not true

outsider (*noun*) – someone who does not belong to a group or organisation

talk shop (*verb*) – to talk about your work, especially in a way that is boring for other people

Warm up

1 Think of two or three examples of jargon in your language and write them on a piece of paper.

2 Work in pairs and share your ideas. Explain what your jargon means in English.

Reading

1 Read *All work and no play*. What is the main topic of the text?

a plain English
b technical vocabulary
c doctors and language
d radio and television

2 Read the text again and decide if the statements are true (*T*) or false (*F*).

1 Psychologists say that work is more important than play.
2 Jargon is language that everybody understands.
3 Jargon can be useful.
4 Jargon is precise language and it can make communication quicker.
5 The Plain English Campaign wants people to use more jargon.
6 We get angry when people use jargon to tell lies.

Language focus

Find words or expressions in the text with these meanings.

1 the correct relationship between two things (line 2)
2 to make something more clear or specific (2 words) (line 10)
3 easy (line 14)
4 people in general (2 words) (line 19)
5 used for saying something in another way (3 words) (line 25)

Speaking

Do you think there is too much jargon in your language? Can you think of some examples? Do you think campaigns like Plain English are a good idea?

Writing a CV

Reading

Read the CV and put the headings in the correct places.

Date of birth   Email address
Education and qualifications   Interests
Referees   Skills   Work experience

CURRICULUM VITAE: Ahmed al-Qadi

(1) ____________ : al-qadi22@hotmail.com
(2) ____________ : 18–08–1987

(3) ______________________
2003–2005
Al Hussein College, Amman, Jordan
General Secondary Education Certificate
Average score: 88.5%

2005–2009
Applied Science University, Amman, Jordan
B.Sc. in Management Information Systems
GPA Score: 90.5% (Evaluation: Very Good)

(4) ______________________
2009–Present
Jordan Telecom: database assistant

(5) ______________________
English: intermediate
Jordanian driving licence
Modern programming and database management

(6) ______________________
Travelling, understanding other cultures, football

(7) ______________________
Mr Firas Al-Jabali, Head of Information Services, Jordan Telecom
Dr Omar Yassin, Head of Management Information Systems, Applied Science University, Amman, Jordan

Writing skills: setting out a CV

Correct the spelling and punctuation mistakes in this CV.

CURICULUM VITAE: Nathalie Baekelandt

Email adress   n.baekelandt @wanadoo.fr
Date of Birth   17 / 12 / 88

Education and Califications
University of Lille BA Hons Economics

Work Expereince
Personal Assistant to Project Manager, EDF Energy.
Duties – booking appointments, taking minutes, record-keeping

Skils   English: fluent
    Computer literate

Interests   Aerobics, dance, swimming, photography, theatre

Referrees On request

Language focus: writing dates

Different countries write dates in different ways.
In Britain, the order is day, month, year.

16–01–2008 or *16/01/08*
16 Jan 2008 or *16th January 2008*

In the US, the order is month, day, year.

01–16–2008 or *01/16/08*
Jan 16 2008 or *January 16th 2008*

Complete the table.

UK	US
22nd November 1995	
	Feb 14th 2000
	05–28–1982
02–10–95	

Preparing to write

Work in pairs and make notes on what you would write under each of the CV headings.

Describing skills

- IT literate (Word, Excel, Powerpoint)
- French: fluent / intermediate / elementary
- Current driving licence
- Basic first aid

Writing

Write your CV. Use your notes and the useful phrases to help you.

Global review

Grammar

1 Complete the sentences with the correct form of the verb in brackets.

1 ________ (*you /ever / be*) to the US?
2 Yes, I ________ (*go*) there last year.
3 I hate ________ (*write*) letters, but ________ (*chat*) to friends on the phone is great fun.
4 I ________ (*never / ride*) a camel, but I ________ (*see*) one in a zoo.

2 Complete the job description for a shop assistant using *can*, *have to*, *don't have to* or *mustn't*.

1 You ________ be polite to customers.
2 You ________ have a driving licence.
3 You ________ arrive late.
4 You ________ earn a bonus if you sell a lot of goods.

Vocabulary

Match the words on the left to the ones on the right.

play	a walk
do	television
go for	a meal
chat	exercise
collect	on the computer
read	a magazine
watch	stamps
cook	on the phone

Speaking

1 Work in small groups. Think of three leisure activities you enjoy and mime them. The others try to guess the activities.

A: *I think you like playing tennis.*

B: *Yes, that's right. / No, that's not right.*

2 Work in small groups. Talk about a job you do or would like to do.

- Talk about the things you have to do.
- Talk about the good and bad parts of the job.

Study skills

Recording new words and phrases

1 Work in pairs and discuss these questions.

- Where do you write down new English words and expressions that you learn?
- When do you write down new words and expressions?
  - a In class?
  - b When you are reading?
  - c When you are doing homework?
  - d At some other time?
- What information do you write down about the words? Show your partner.
- How do you use your vocabulary notes when you have written them?

2 Look at how three Polish students have recorded new words from this unit. What are the differences between them?

upset = przygnębiony   take off = wziąć (sobie) wolne
chess = szachy   amusement park = park rozrywki

upset /ʌp'set/ adj. sad, worried or angry about something. I miss my parents. I can't tell them when I feel upset.
take time off work = wziąć (sobie) wolne z pracy
You can take next Saturday off.

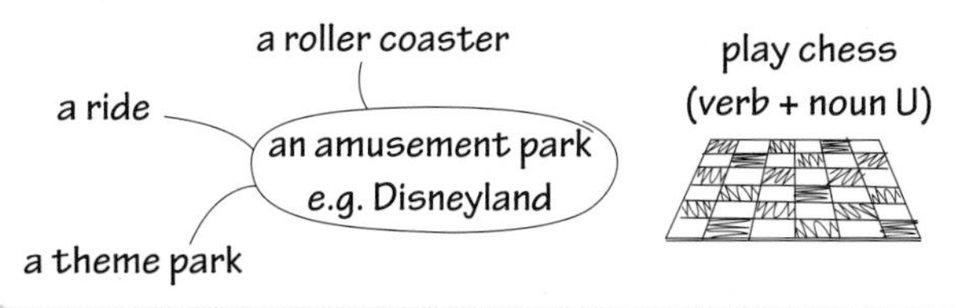

3 Work in pairs and discuss the questions.

- Which method do you prefer?
- How can the different ways help?
- If you record words in a different way, why is that?

4 This week try recording vocabulary in a different way. How will you do it?

Science & Technology

Part 1

Writing & Speaking
Happiness

Reading
The science of happiness

Grammar
Comparatives

Pronunciation & Reading
The schwa /ə/

Writing and Speaking

1 Write down five things that make you happy.

2 Work in pairs. Compare your lists and discuss these questions.

- Which items do you have in common?
- Is there anything you would like to change in your list?
- What do you think makes people happy?
- On a scale of 1 to 10 how happy are you?

Reading

1 Read the article *The science of happiness* and put the headings in the correct place.

Climate and happiness
Measuring happiness
Money and happiness
What makes people happy?

The science of happiness

Everyone wants to be happy. Some argue that the main reason people do the things they do is to become happier. Others argue that happiness is a basic human right. But what is happiness? What really makes people happy?

1 ______

Social scientists usually calculate happiness simply by asking how happy people are. They ask people the question 'How happy are you from 1 to 10?' Ed Diener, an expert on happiness from the University of Illinois, says that this is a valid way of getting information about people's happiness.

2 ______

In one study, researchers asked people in different parts of a country 'How satisfied are you with your life?' People in parts of the country with nicer weather said they were more satisfied with their lives. They said they lived better than people from a city with bad weather.

3 ______

Researchers have examined the relationship between money and happiness for many years. They conclude that very poor people are less happy than rich people. But lots of money doesn't make you happier. If you have a home, food and clothes, extra money doesn't automatically make you more content.

4 ______

According to researchers, there are three things which make people happy:

1 Having close relationships with people – family and friends. The closer and deeper the relationships are, the better for your happiness.
2 Believing in something. This could be religion, a spiritual outlook or a special philosophy in life.
3 Having objectives that you find enjoyable and interesting. This means that your life has a purpose.

2 Read the text again. Look at the answers and complete the questions.

1 Q: How ______ ______ ______ happiness?
A: By asking people how happy they are.
2 Q: Which ______ ______ ______ satisfied with their lives?
A: Those who live in warmer parts of the country.
3 Q: Does money ______ ______ ______?
A: If you have a home, food and clothes then no, it doesn't.
4 Q: What three things ______ ______ ______?
A: Family and friends, belief in something and enjoyable objectives.

3 Match the highlighted words in the text to the definitions.

1 officially acceptable
2 something that makes you happy
3 meaning
4 your general view of things
5 to discover a number or result using mathematics

4 Do you agree with what the text says about happiness? Do you think it is possible to measure happiness?

Extend your vocabulary – metaphors for *happy*

We often use words that mean *high up* or *moving upwards* when we want to describe feeling happy or hopeful.

We often use words that mean *low down* or *falling* when we want to describe feeling sad.

Look at these expressions. Is each person feeling happy or sad?

1 That news really lifted my spirits.
2 My heart sank when I saw him.
3 I feel pretty low today.
4 I'm on top of the world.
5 I'm walking on air.
6 She's a bit down today.

Grammar

Lots of money doesn't make you ***happier****.*
People with close family relationships were ***more satisfied than*** *people with no family.*
People said they ***lived better*** *in warm countries.*

- use comparative adjectives to compare two people or objects
- use adjective + *er* for short adjectives and *more* + adjective for longer adjectives
- use comparative adverbs to compare two actions

Complete the texts with the comparative form of the adjectives in brackets.

Health and happiness

Scientists say that happy people are ________ (*healthy*) than unhappy people. They also live ________ (*long*) and ________ (*good*) lives and are ________ (*fit*). One study found that ________ (*happy*) people live up to nine years longer.

Research in the United States suggests that married couples with children are ________ (*satisfied*) when their children are ________ (*young*). When researchers asked married couples about happiness with teenage children they said their lives were a lot ________ (*stressful*).

A survey of British men and women between 1993 and 2003 found that many people said their lives were ________ (*enjoyable*) as they became older. It showed that men were ________ (*content*) than women in their teenage years, but women were ________ (*happy*) than men ________ (*late*) in life.

G **Grammar focus** – explanation & more practice of comparatives on page 142

Pronunciation and Reading

1 2.01 Listen to the words and phrases. How are the underlined sounds pronounced?

fitter happier more productive
comfortable regular exercise
patient better driver

2 Listen again and repeat the words.

3 The words in exercise 1 come from a song by the English rock group *Radiohead*. Work in pairs. A: read the first line of the song. B: read the second line. Pay attention to the underlined schwa sounds.

4 The songwriter said that this song is about people in Britain in the 90s. Do you think he liked the 90s? Would you say the same about your country in the 90s?

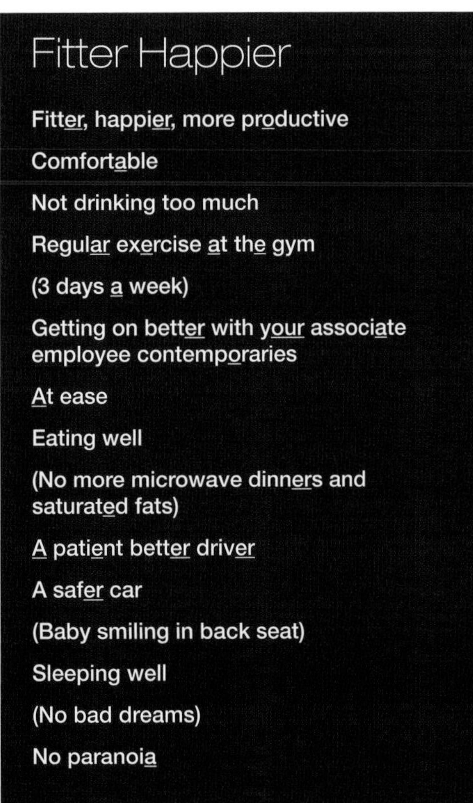

Fitter Happier

Fitter, happier, more productive
Comfortable
Not drinking too much
Regular exercise at the gym
(3 days a week)
Getting on better with your associate employee contemporaries
At ease
Eating well
(No more microwave dinners and saturated fats)
A patient better driver
A safer car
(Baby smiling in back seat)
Sleeping well
(No bad dreams)
No paranoia

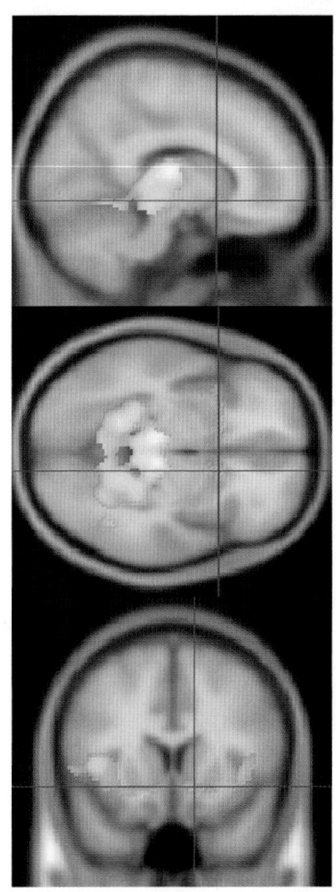

Part 2

Speaking & Listening
Someone has to do it

Grammar
Comparatives (*a bit, much, as … as*)

Vocabulary
Noun formation

Reading & Speaking
Frankenstein

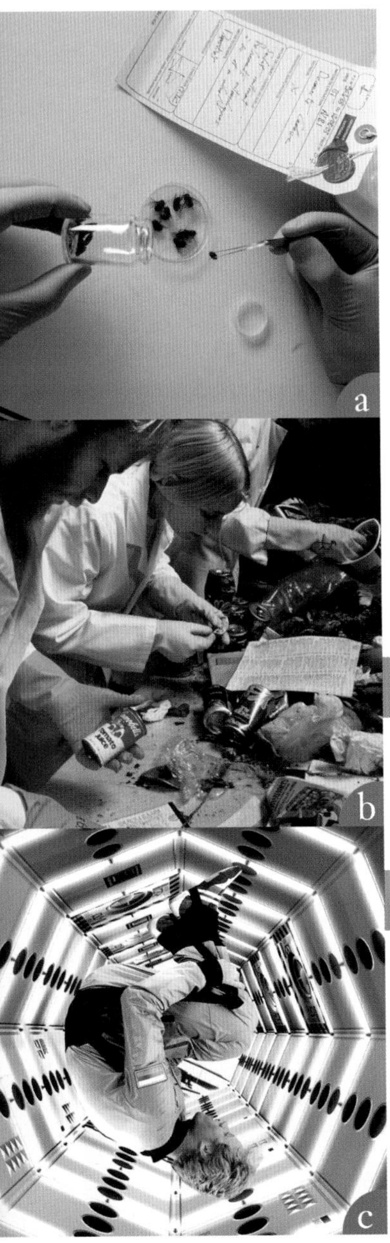
a
b
c

Speaking and Listening

1 Work in pairs. Look at pictures a–c and discuss what you think the jobs are.

2 Read the text below and match the jobs to the pictures. Then discuss what you think these people do in their jobs.

Someone has to do it … in the name of science

The American magazine *Popular Science* looked at all the possible jobs you could have in science, and they picked out the worst ones. Here are three of them:

Garbologist – studies rubbish

Forensic entomologist – studies insects in the bodies of dead people

Gravity research subject – participates in experiments to study the effects of zero gravity on the human body

Language note: *garbage* is American English and *rubbish* is British English.

Useful language

- dirty
- flies
- rubbish
- experiments for space travel
- gloves
- turns around and around

Useful phrases

- Maybe he / she …
- It looks like he / she works in …
- He / she probably …
- This looks …

3 2.02–2.03 Listen to two people talking about their jobs. Which two jobs do they talk about?

4 Listen again and choose the correct answers.

1 Speaker 1 stayed in bed for …
 a the summer. b 50 days. c 15 days.
2 They paid speaker 1 …
 a $6,000. b $600. c $60,000.
3 Speaker 2 thinks her work …
 a is disgusting. b is interesting. c is boring.
4 Speaker 2 is finishing a project on …
 a office rubbish. b restaurant rubbish. c office and restaurant rubbish.

5 Do you think these jobs are bad? Which is the worst, in your opinion?

Grammar

Office rubbish is ***less disgusting*** *than restaurant rubbish.*
It's ***not as bad as*** *you think.*
It's ***a bit more difficult*** *than that.*
She works ***much faster*** *than him.*

- use *less* + adjective to mean not as much
- use (*not*) *as* + adjective + *as* to make comparisons
- use *as* + adjective + *as* to say that two things are the same
- use *a bit* or *much* to modify comparative adjectives and adverbs

1 Read the sentences from the listening and choose the alternative that is closest in meaning.

1 Office garbage is much less disgusting than restaurant garbage.
 a Restaurant garbage is much more disgusting than office garbage.
 b Office garbage is much more disgusting than restaurant garbage.
2 My job isn't as bad as people think.
 a My job is worse than people think.
 b My job is better than people think.

2 Complete the sentences with your own ideas.

I speak English a bit better now than …
The weather today is a bit less … than …
English is a bit easier than …
I think … is much more … than …
I don't believe … is as … as people say.

3 Work in two groups. Group A: turn to page 127. Group B: turn to page 129.

G Grammar focus – explanation & more practice of comparatives on page 142

Vocabulary

1 Match each word to a suffix to make a new noun.

Word	Suffix	New noun
happy	-ist	happiness
science	-er	
relation	-ence	
exist	-ness	
research	-ship	

2 Make new nouns from the words in the box. Which noun endings are used for jobs?

economy friend paint nervous
silent teach tour weak

3 Complete the text with the correct form of the words.

The **NASA** researcher

My wife Karen is a ________ (*research*). She won a ________ (*scholar*) from NASA to research a special project. She is studying the possible ________ (*exist*) of life on other planets. She loves the work, except for the ________ (*lonely*). She works alone in a little office. She listens in complete ________ (*silent*) for unusual radio signals from space.

Reading and Speaking

1 2.04 Read and listen to the extract from the book *Frankenstein*. What was the problem with the science experiment?

2 Work in pairs and discuss this question.

- One of the themes of *Frankenstein*, and of many science fiction stories, is *dangerous knowledge*. Do you think scientific knowledge can be dangerous? Think of some examples.

Mary Shelley (1797–1851) was an English romantic novelist. She is best known for the novel *Frankenstein*, which she wrote when she was 19 years old. Some critics have called her the first English science fiction author.

***Frankenstein* tells the story of the scientist Dr Frankenstein and how he wishes to create life from a dead body, but how he creates a monster instead.**

The body moved and I went nearer. I held out my arms and smiled. The man sat up and turned his head. His eyes were open.

I thought to myself 'Oh, God. What have I done? What has gone wrong?'

The man's skin was wrinkled and yellow. His eyes were yellow and dry. His thin, black lips opened in a terrible smile. I had made a Monster!

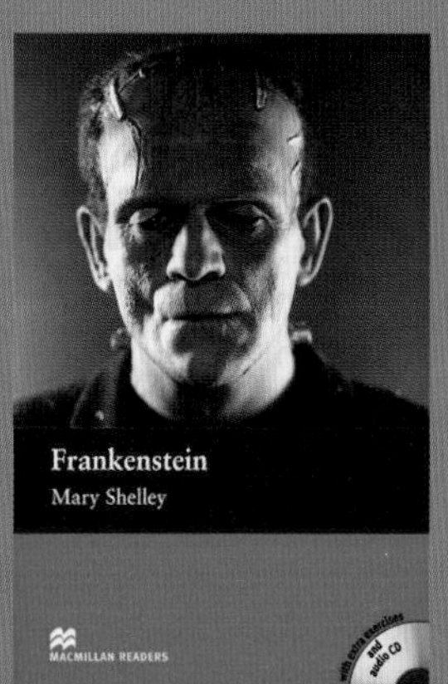

Frankenstein

Science & Technology

Part 3

Vocabulary
Compound nouns

Reading
Going, going, gone

Grammar
Superlatives

Listening & Speaking
Website addresses

Vocabulary

1 Look at the photo. How many of the things can you name in English?

2 Match the words in A to the words in B to make compound nouns. Which things can you see in the picture?

A	B
computer	phones
head	top
key	site
lap	screen
memory	board
mobile	message
mouse	stick
text	phone
web	pad

3 2.05 Listen and repeat the words. Underline the stress in each compound noun. Which one is different?

Reading

1 Work in pairs and ask each other the questions.

- Do you use the internet often? What for?
- Which websites do you often visit?

2 You are going to read about online auctions. Tick (✔) the words you think you will see.

businessman buy dangerous
expensive global internet
jet kidney river sell

3 2.06 Read and listen to *Going, going, gone* on page 71 and check your answers.

4 Read the text again and answer the questions.

1 What do people do in online auctions?
2 How many people use eBay?
3 Name five unusual things that people have sold or tried to sell on eBay.

5 Have you ever bought or sold anything on the internet? Would you buy anything in an online auction?

Grammar

Online auctions are among ***the biggest*** *businesses on the internet.*
Of all the online auction sites, eBay is probably ***the most famous****.*
It is one of ***the most popular*** *websites I've heard of.*

- use superlative adjectives to compare two or more people or objects
- use adjective + *est* for short adjectives and *the most* + adjective for longer adjectives
- we often use superlatives with the present perfect tense

1 Complete the sentences with the correct word.

1 Online auctions are popular because you can find *the strangest / stranger* things there.
2 Many things online are *the cheapest / cheaper* than the same things in a shop.
3 I prefer buying from shops because I think it's *the safest / safer* than buying on the internet.
4 I think online shopping is *the best / better* way to get things.
5 The founder of eBay is one of *the richest / richer* men in America.

2 Complete the sentences with the superlative form of the adjectives.

1 What's ________ (*long*) time you've ever spent on the internet?
2 Who's ________ (*funny*) person you've ever spent time with?
3 What's ________ (*cold*) place you've ever been to?
4 What's ________ (*strange*) thing you've ever eaten?
5 What's ________ (*good*) film you've ever seen?

3 Work in pairs. Choose **three** of the questions from exercise 2 and ask each other.

G Grammar focus – explanation & more practice of superlatives on page 142

Online auctions and the eBay phenomenon

Online auctions are among the biggest businesses on the internet. These are sites that use the technology of the internet to allow people to buy things from each other. People can buy and sell almost anything online now. Of all these online auction sites, eBay is probably the most famous. Let's look at the numbers.

241,000,000 +

Ten years after eBay started in 1995 there were more than 241 million registered users, making it one of the most popular websites on the planet.

4th

With more than 200 million registered users, eBay's population is almost as big as that of Indonesia, which has the world's fourth biggest population.

£1.81

Many people have tried to sell fake items or silly things online. One man tried to sell the internet for a million dollars. Nobody wanted it. Another person tried to sell the meaning of life. It sold for £1.81.

$4.9 million

One of the most expensive items sold on eBay was a Gulfstream II private business jet for $4.9 million. One of the largest items ever sold was a World War II submarine. It was sold by a small town in New England that decided it did not need it any more.

50,000

In 2004 a 50,000-year-old mammoth appeared on eBay. The Dutch owner of the animal sold it for £61,000. It was one of the most unusual things sold on eBay.

1999

People have tried to sell all sorts of human body parts on the internet. In 1999 a human kidney went on sale on eBay. The website cancelled the auction and stops any auctions that aren't ethical.

Glossary

ethical (*adjective*) – considered to be right

fake (*adjective*) – made to look like something else

mammoth (*noun*) – an animal similar to an elephant with long hair that lived a very long time ago

submarine (*noun*) – a ship that can travel under the water

Listening and Speaking

1 2.07 Listen and write the email and website addresses you hear. Which of these websites do you know?

Useful phrases

.	dot
/	slash
@	at
learn_English	learn underscore English
learn-English	learn dash English

2 Write five website or email addresses that you know – they can be real or invented.

3 Work in pairs and read the addresses to each other. Write the addresses as you listen.

Part 4

Speaking & Listening
Computer problems

Vocabulary & Pronunciation
Phrasal verbs, sentence stress

Grammar
Phrasal verbs & objects

Reading & Speaking
The Luddites

Speaking and Listening

1 Read the quotes about computers below. Work in pairs and tell each other if you agree with them and why.

Computers are useless. They can only give you answers.
Pablo Picasso, Spanish artist

I do not fear computers. I fear the lack of them.
Isaac Asimov, American science fiction writer

Think? Why think? We have computers to do that for us.
Jean Rostand, French scientist and philosopher

Computers are like dogs. They smell fear.
Simon Alexander, American comedian

2 2.08–2.12 Listen to five conversations about computer problems and number the problems in the order you hear them. There is one extra problem.

computer screen	email
internet connection	password
printer and printing	saving work

3 Listen again and choose the correct answers.

1 What did the man change in conversation 1?
  a a cable b the mouse
  c the computer screen
2 How does the man feel at the end of conversation 2?
  a happy b worried c frustrated
3 What's wrong with the man's email in conversation 3?
  a there's a virus
  b there's too much email
  c he needs a password
4 Who saves their work in conversation 4?
  a the woman b the man
  c the woman and the man
5 What happened to the woman's password in conversation 5?
  a she forgot it b she changed it
  c she doesn't have one

Extend your vocabulary – other ways of saying yes

Here are some common ways of saying *yes*.
Yep and *yeah* are informal ways of saying *yes*.
Definitely is a stronger way of saying *yes*.
That's right is used instead of *yes* to respond to a question or statement.
I'm afraid so is used when you think the person hopes you will say *no*.

1 Look at the audioscript on page 155. Find an example of each way of saying *yes*.
2 Write five questions to ask your partner. You want them to answer *yes*.
3 Work in pairs and ask each other the questions. Answer *yes* in different ways.

Vocabulary and Pronunciation

1 Complete the sentences from the listening with the words in the box.

down (x2) in on out (x2) up

1 Now **log** ______ to the system.
2 **Shut** ______ the computer and leave it.
3 The laptop's **gone** ______ again.
4 **Type** ______ your username and password.
5 When I try to **print** ______ a document the computer **prints** ______ a different document.
6 You should really **back** ______ all your work.

2 2.13 Listen and check your answers.

3 Listen and repeat the sentences. Try to copy the stress.

Grammar

*Turn **on** the computer.*
*Now **log on**.*
*Shut down **the computer**.*
*Shut **the computer** down.*
*Turn **it** on.*

- some phrasal verbs such as *turn on* can take an object
- other phrasal verbs such as *log on* do not take an object
- when the phrasal verb takes an object, it can usually go before or after the particle
- if the object is a pronoun, it can only go between the verb and particle

1 Tick (✔) the sentences that are correct.

1 a Pick up the phone.
b Pick it up.
c Pick up it.

2 a Can you print out them please?
b Can you print them out please?
c Can you print out the documents please?

3 a Turn them off.
b Turn off them.
c Turn off all the computers.

2 Circle the object of the phrasal verb in the sentences below. Sometimes there is no object.

Please sit down and open your books. (no object)
Did you plug in the computer?

1 Turn the volume up please.
2 Philip isn't here today. He called in sick.
3 I forgot to log on to the school system.
4 Look up the words in the dictionary.
5 Write the words down in your notebook.
6 My flight takes off at seven o'clock tonight.

3 Look at the sentences again. If there is an object, replace it with a pronoun.

Did you plug it in?

G Grammar focus – explanation & more practice of phrasal verbs on page 142

The **Luddites**

One of the most famous anti-technology movements was the Luddite movement in 19th century England. The Luddites were organised groups of workers who were losing work to the new textile machines. They went out at night and destroyed the machines with hammers. Today the term *luddite* is used in English to talk negatively about people who are anti-technology.

Glossary

movement (*noun*) – a group of people who work together for a particular reason

textile (*noun*) – any type of woven cloth

Reading and Speaking

1 2.14 Read and listen to the text about the Luddites.
What kind of people were they?

2 Read the statements and mark your opinion next to each one. 1 = strongly disagree, 4 = strongly agree

Modern technology …	
• makes us work harder, not less hard.	1 2 3 4
• is giving away our privacy.	1 2 3 4
• has taken away more jobs than it has created.	1 2 3 4
• has made us safer.	1 2 3 4
• is giving us too much information, so it's difficult to know what is true.	1 2 3 4
• has to be free for everyone.	1 2 3 4

3 Work in pairs. Discuss your opinions and try to give reasons for them. Are you a modern *Luddite*?

I agree that modern technology makes us work harder. In my job, I have to answer lots of emails and messages, and I have to do it more quickly than before.

Function globally finding things in common

a b c d

Warm up

1 Look at the pictures of four situations. Work in pairs and describe the similarities and differences between them.

Useful language

- chatting
- laptop
- on a train
- diary
- in an airport
- suit

Useful phrases

- I think they are on a train.
- They look like friends / colleagues / strangers.

2 What do you think the people in each picture are talking about? Choose one of the pictures and write a short conversation. Then present your conversation to another pair.

Listening

1 2.15 Listen to a conversation between two people in a taxi. Where are they going? What happens at the end?

2 Listen again and tick (✔) the things they have in common.

1 They are both going to the Technology Conference. ___
2 They have both been to San Francisco before. ___
3 They are both from Germany. ___
4 They both went to school in England. ___
5 They both work for ABT Technology. ___
6 They have both been to conferences before. ___
7 They are both staying at the conference hotel. ___

Language focus: finding things in common

Look at the highlighted expressions in the audioscript on page 155. Then complete the rules with *so*, *too* or *neither*.

We use ***so*** / ***neither*** when we have something in common.

Use ______ + auxiliary + *I* for affirmative statements.

Use ______ + auxiliary + *I* for negative statements.

We also use *me* + ***too*** / ***neither***.

Use *me* + ______ for affirmative statements.

Use *me* + ______ for negative statements.

Language note: when we don't have something in common, we can respond with the short form.

A: *I am from Scotland.* B: *I'm not.*
A: *I live in the city centre.* B: *I don't.*
A: *I've never been to an art gallery.* B: *I have.*

Speaking

1 Look at the topics in the box. Write five true sentences about yourself. Use the phrases to help you.

Topic	Phrases
You & your family	I live with … I'm married / single …
Food & drink	I like / don't like … I don't eat / drink …
Art & music	I have / haven't read / seen ... I listen to … I don't like …
Hopes & fears	I'm planning to … I'm afraid of …
Work & leisure	I work in … In my free time I …

2 Work in pairs. A: tell your partner about yourself. B: respond. Find three things you have in common. Use the new expressions you have learnt.

3 Swap roles and repeat the activity.

Global voices

Warm up

1 Put the letters in the correct order to make words for technological advances.

treniten velsietoni limboe nohep
pmretuco lenap

2 Why are these advances important or useful? Complete the sentence for each of the advances above.

I think the … is important / useful because …

Listening

1 2.16–2.22 Listen to seven people talking about technological advances. Which advance from exercise 1 is each person talking about?

1 Honor, England ______
2 Arthur, France ______
3 Sara, Italy ______
4 Antonis, Greece ______
5 Maxim, Russia ______
6 Starla, England ______
7 William, Ghana ______

2 Listen again. Which speakers give reasons for their choice? What reasons do they give?

Honor, England

Arthur, France Sara, Italy Antonis, Greece

Maxim, Russia Starla, England William, Ghana

Language focus: *and, so, because*

1 Read what Guy says about another technological advance. Complete the sentences with *and*, *so* or *because*. Use the explanations in brackets to help you.

I think the most important technological advance – well for me personally recently has been a hard disk recorder for recording TV programmes [says his opinion]

1 ______ it means I can record everything very easily [gives a reason]
2 ______ I can see exactly what I have recorded by looking at everything on screen [adds another reason]
3 ______ I don't have to find lots of video tapes and different things like that [adds more information]
4 ______ it is much easier now to record TV programmes than it was in the past [explains a consequence]
5 ______ because of digital television we have lots more programmes to choose from [adds another reason]
6 ______ there's much more variety and choice [explains a consequence]
7 ______ that means you need to record even more programmes than in the past. [explains a consequence]

2 2.23 Listen and check your answers.

Language note: in spoken English, it is very common to add lots of clauses together with words like *and*, *or*, *so*, or *because*.

Speaking

1 What is the most important or useful technological advance? Why do you think so? Make a few notes.

2 Work in pairs and present your ideas. Try to speak for at least one minute.

Useful phrases

- For me personally, the most important technological advance is the …
- I think the most useful advance is the … because …
- … and …
- … so that means …

UNIT 6 Writing describing advantages and disadvantages

Reading

1 Read Mohammed's essay on *The advantages and disadvantages of the internet*. Does he think there are more advantages or disadvantages?

2 Do you agree with his ideas? Can you think of other advantages or disadvantages?

The internet has revolutionised people's lives all over the world. People use the internet every day for their studies, to contact friends and family, and for pleasure. It has turned the world into a global village.

Using the internet has many advantages.

* You can send instant messages and contact people all over the world by email and in chat rooms.
* You can access huge amounts of useful information for your studies or for research.
* You can download games, music, videos, films and other software, often for free.

However, there are also certain disadvantages in using the internet.

* It can be dangerous to put personal information, such as credit card details, online.
* The internet is a good environment for hackers, who spread viruses and spy ware.
* There are some websites that are unsuitable for children.

In conclusion, despite the disadvantages, the internet brings huge benefits to our lives. It is hard nowadays to imagine a world without the internet.

Language focus: listing points

1 Look at a corrected version of the second paragraph of Mohammed's essay. What is different?

Using the internet has many advantages. First of all, you can send instant messages and contact people all over the world by email and in chat rooms. In addition, you can access huge amounts of useful information for your studies or for research. Another important advantage is that you can download games, music, videos, films and other software, often for free.

2 Change the third paragraph in the same way. Use some of the useful phrases below to help you. Remember to use commas.

Listing points

- Firstly ... / First of all ...
- Secondly ...
- In addition ...
- As well as that ...
- Another advantage is that ...
- Finally ... / Lastly ...

Writing skills: getting ideas

Work in small groups and discuss this question.

When you want to get ideas for an essay do you ...

- read a book or article on the subject?
- do a keyword search on the internet?
- speak to other people?
- brainstorm all you know and think about the topic?
- write freely to express your ideas?
- use mind maps?
- do something else?

All of these methods can help. Try using a different one next time you write an essay.

Preparing to write

1 Work in pairs and choose one of the topics below.

clocks mobile phones satnavs television

2 Make a list of all the advantages and disadvantages.

3 Think about what to put in the introductory paragraph. For example, how and where the invention is used, its history, its effects on modern life etc.

4 Think about what you will write in the last paragraph. What is your conclusion? Are there more advantages or disadvantages? Why?

Writing

Write the essay. Use your notes and the useful phrases below to help you. Write four paragraphs:

a introduction, **b** advantages, **c** disadvantages, **d** conclusion.

Introducing advantages and disadvantages

- There are several advantages / disadvantages of ...
- However, there are also some / certain disadvantages.
- One of the main advantages / disadvantages is ...

Global review

Grammar

Circle the corrct options. Sometimes both are correct.

1 Where do I *plug in the computer / plug the computer in*?
2 If you don't want to lose your documents, it's a good idea to *back them up / back up them*.
3 Your computer is much *better / more better* than mine.
4 Tom works *harder /less hard* than his sister.
5 Shopping online is *more convenient / convenienter* than going to the supermarket.
6 The Nile is *the most long / the longest* river in the world.
7 Your job isn't *as well-paid as / as well-paid than* mine.
8 Time passes *faster / more fast* than you think.
9 Germany is a bit *less colder / less cold* than Norway.

Vocabulary

Read the definitions and put the letters in the correct order to make the correct words.

1 you use this to type documents on a computer
yebadrok ______
2 you store and carry computer information on this
rymome kicts ______
3 a small computer that you can carry around
potpal ______
4 you use these to listen to music without making a noise
nohapsheed ______
5 your computer sometimes does this if there is a problem
thus wond ______
6 a relationship with a friend
sprifidhen ______
7 the state of being happy
shipspane ______
8 a person who does a study to find new information
screeherra ______

Speaking

1 Work in pairs and find three differences between the items below. Which do you prefer and why?

- emails and text messages
- laptop computers and desktop computers
- mobile phones and landlines

2 Work in pairs. A: your partner has never seen one of the items below. Describe it and explain how it works. Then swap roles and repeat.

- a computer
- a printer

Study skills

Personalising language learning

1 Look at how Atsuko has recorded new words and grammar from the unit.

nervous (adj.) feeling excited and worried, or slightly afraid. Get nervous about / of something.
** I get nervous when I have to speak in class.*
** My sister used to be nervous of ducks.*
outlook (n. sing.) Your general attitude to things. Share the same outlook on something.
** Fumie and I share the same outlook on friendship.*
back up (verb T) to make a copy of information on your computer.
** I must remember to back up my work on a memory stick.*

**My hair is much longer than Fumie's hair.*
**I prefer summer to winter because I love sunbathing.*

If you can relate new language to yourself, your experiences or your ideas, it often makes it easier to remember.

2 Think of three words or phrases you have learnt this week. Write a true sentence about yourself or your life using each word or phrase.

1 ______
2 ______
3 ______

3 Write one true sentence about yourself or your life using a comparative structure and one using a superlative structure.

1 ______
2 ______

4 Work in pairs and read out your sentences. Ask questions to find out more information from your partner.

Remember to write sentences personalising new language when you record it in your vocabulary notebook or grammar notes.

UNIT 7 Time & Money

Part 1

Vocabulary & Speaking
Prepositions of time (*in, on, at*)

Reading
A brief history of time zones

Grammar
Present perfect with *for & since*

Vocabulary and Speaking

1 What do the letters mean? Solve the time puzzle.

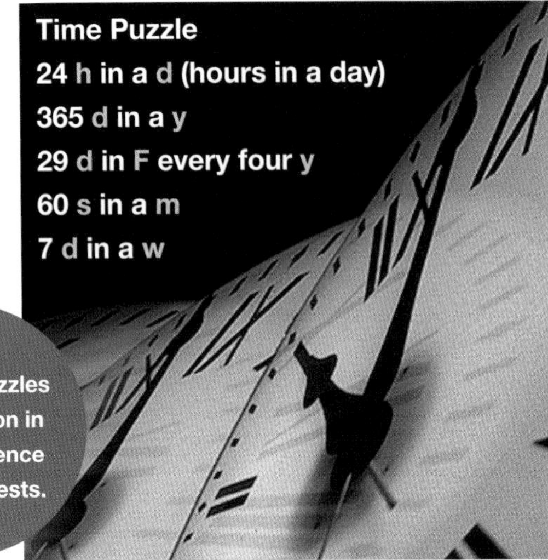

Time Puzzle
24 h in a d (hours in a day)
365 d in a y
29 d in F every four y
60 s in a m
7 d in a w

These kinds of puzzles are common in IQ (Intelligence Quotient) tests.

2 Here are three other *time numbers*. Can you make more puzzle items with them?

60 12 52

3 Complete the rules with the expressions in the box.

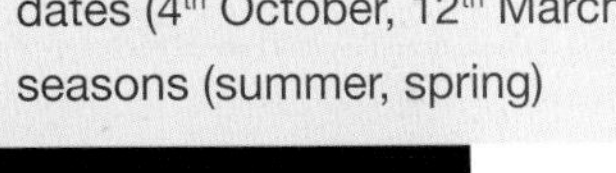

dates (4th October, 12th March)	specific times (6 o'clock, eight-thirty)
seasons (summer, spring)	years (1999, 2005)

Use ***in*** with months (*February, December*), times of the day (*the afternoon, the evening*), ________ and ________.
Use ***on*** with days (*Monday, Friday*) and ________.

Use ***at*** with ________ and certain time expressions (*the weekend, night*).

4 Choose five questions and write your answers on a piece of paper. Use a preposition + a time expression.

What's the best time to …
- go on holiday?
- wake up on a day when you aren't working?
- do homework or study?
- visit your home town?
- watch television for films or series?
- get married in your country?
- do exercise?

5 Compare your answers with a partner. Ask why.

A: *The best time to get married is in June.*
B: *Why?*
A: *Because the weather is always good in June.*

Reading

1 Work in pairs and discuss the questions.
- How many time zones are there in your country?
- Can you name a country where it is the middle of the night right now?
- Can you name a country that is one day behind you right now?

2 2.24 Read and listen to *A brief history of time zones* on page 79. Are these statements true (*T*) or false (*F*)?

1 Time zones have existed for 500 years.
2 Greenwich Mean Time and Coordinated Universal Time are the same thing.
3 China has always had the same number of time zones.
4 Jet lag makes you tired.
5 There is only one internet time.

3 Work in pairs and choose **one** of the tasks below.

A Choose three pieces of information from the text that you think are the most interesting. Compare with your partner.

B Discuss the questions.
- Have you visited a place with a different time zone? Where? When?
- Have you ever had jet lag?
- Do you know any good ways to avoid jet lag?

A brief history of **time zones**

Origin The idea of time zones has not existed for very long. People used to measure time using the shadow of the sun. For years, each country used its own time, and local times used to be very different from one place to another. After the 19th century people began to travel more. There was a lot of confusion about times. Countries needed a single, standard time. In 1884 members from 27 countries met in Washington, US to create a system of time zones. The world has had a time zone system for less than 200 years.

GMT, CUT, DST The time zone system starts with the Prime Meridian, an invisible line through Greenwich, England. This time is called GMT (Greenwich Mean Time) or CUT (Coordinated Universal Time). Many countries also observe daylight saving time, or summer time. This is the time of year when people change their clocks.

Different zones Some large countries have more than one time zone. The United States has ten time zones and Russia has eleven. China used to have five time zones but changed to one single zone in 1949. This means that when you cross the border from China to Afghanistan, you have to change your watch by four hours! Some countries have differences of less than one hour. For example, when you go across the border from India to Nepal you change your watch by only 15 minutes.

Jet lag If you travel across many time zones by plane, you may get jet lag. Jet lag is the feeling of being very tired because you have travelled across parts of the world where the time is different.

Internet time The spread of the internet has also increased communication between people from different countries. The Swiss company Swatch introduced internet time so that people on the internet would all use the same time. Greenwich has had its own internet time, called GET (Greenwich Electronic Time), since the year 2000.

Grammar

*We **have had** standard time **for** less than 200 years.*
*Greenwich internet time **has existed since** 2000.*

- use *for* and *since* with present perfect to talk about unfinished time
- use *for* with a period of time
- use *since* with a point in time
- do not use *in* + a time expression with the present perfect tense

1 Complete the text with *for*, *since* or *in*.

A brief history of … watches

The idea of a portable object that tells the time has been around ______ five hundred years.

______ the past, people held watches in their hands. They were later called pocket watches, because you could put them in your pocket.

The wristwatch has existed ______ 1880, and electronic watches first appeared ______ the 1950s. Digital watches have existed ______ 1970.

Watches have been sold as jewellery ______ more than a hundred and fifty years. A watch is often considered a traditional gift idea for a man.

2 Complete the sentences with the present perfect and *for* or *since*.

1 I ________ (*live*) in this town ________ ten years.
2 I ________ (*study*) English ________ I was twelve years old.
3 I ________ (*be*) in class ________ eight o'clock.
4 I ________ (*know*) the teacher ________ two years.
5 I ________ (*have*) my watch ________ my twentieth birthday.
6 I ________ (*know*) my oldest friend ________ we were at primary school together.

3 Complete the sentences with your own ideas and compare with a partner.

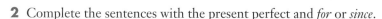

G Grammar focus – explanation & more practice of *for* & *since* on page 144

UNIT 7

Time & Money

Part 2

Vocabulary
Time expressions

Listening
The concept of time

Pronunciation
/aɪ/ & /eɪ/

Speaking
Time saving inventions

Reading & Speaking
A Tale of Two Cities

Vocabulary

1 Match the phrases in bold to the pictures. Which ones do you think are funny?

1 I think he **spends** too much **time** in front of the television.
2 It looks like Tom's worked **overtime** again.
3 Well, it **saves time** in the mornings!
4 Have you ever thought this job is a **waste of time**?
5 Advantage #1: lots of **free time**.

2 Look at the words and phrases in bold. What are they in your language?

a

b c

d

e

Listening

1 2.25 Listen to a talk about the concept of time in English. Finish the sentence to summarise the main point of the talk.

Time is ...

2 2.26 Match 1–4 to a–d to make sentences. Then listen and check your answers.

1 The concept of time in the English language ...
2 You can spend time and money ...
3 You can give someone your time, ...
4 We can convert time into money ...

a and money into time.
b is connected to money.
c just like you can give them money.
d or save it.

3 Are there similar expressions for time in your language?

Pronunciation

1 2.27 Listen and repeat the sounds and words.

/aɪ/, time /eɪ/, save

2 2.28 Listen and tick (✔) the word that has a different sound. Listen again and repeat the words.

1	fly	gym	why	eye
2	time	smile	life	machine
3	mobile	might	friend	height
4	save	waste	mail	money
5	great	break	meat	paper

3 Look at the words in exercise 2. What are some common spellings for /aɪ/ and /eɪ/?

4 2.29 Listen and repeat the proverbs. Do you have any similar proverbs in your language?

1 Time flies when you're having fun.
2 Time waits for no man.
3 So many things, so little time.
4 Life is short and time is swift.

A Tale of Two Cities

It was the best of times, it was the worst of times, it was the age of wisdom, it was the age of foolishness, [...] it was the spring of hope, it was the winter of despair, we had everything before us, we had nothing before us ...

A Tale of Two Cities is a romantic adventure set in London and Paris. It happens in the years just before the French Revolution, a time of great changes in Europe.

Actor Sir John Martin-Harvey playing Sidney Carton, the main character in the story (1926).

A Tale of Two Cities **is a historical novel. The story is invented, but the background is based on real events.**

Glossary

foolishness (*noun*) – stupid behaviour

wisdom (*noun*) – knowledge and experience

Speaking

1 Work in pairs and choose the five most important inventions from the list. Then rank them from 1 (most important) to 5 (least important).

Top Time-saving Inventions

The hairdryer	The personal computer
The internet and email	The photocopier
The microwave oven	The plane
The mobile phone	The washing machine

Useful phrases

- I think …
- Why do you think so?
- Because … used to take a very long time.
- I agree / disagree.

2 Compare your list with another pair. Do you agree?

3 Can you think of other things that save time?

Reading and Speaking

1 2.30 Read and listen to the first lines of *A Tale of Two Cities*.

2 Work in pairs. Some people say that the first line of the extract could be about the times we live in now. Do you agree? Are we living in the best of times and the worst of times?

3 Complete the sentences with your own ideas.

It is the best of times because …

It is the worst of times because …

4 Compare your ideas with another pair.

Charles Dickens (1812–1870)

Considered one of the greatest English novelists in history, Dickens came from a very poor family. His books often talk about the situation of poor people in Victorian England.

Part 3

Vocabulary
Money, verb phrases

Reading
A lifetime of financial concerns

Grammar
Present perfect with *yet & already*

Pronunciation
/ʌ/

Vocabulary

1 Match the words in the box to the pictures.

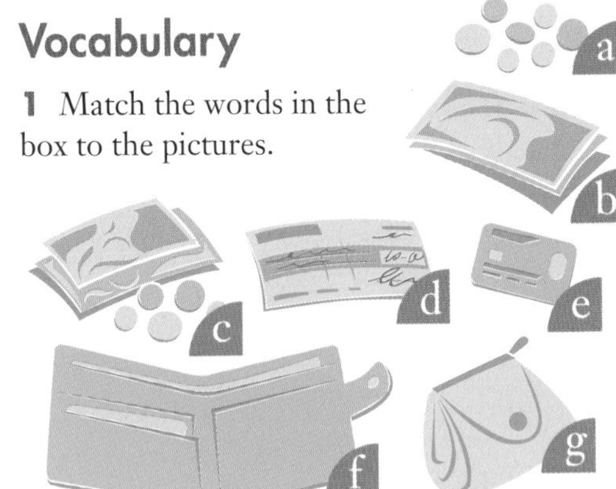

cash cheque coins
credit card notes purse wallet

2 Cross out the option that is not possible.

1 You earn a a salary b money c the lottery.
2 You can spend money a on clothes b on food c in the bank.
3 You can take out a loan a from a bank b from your wallet c for a car.
4 You owe money a to a friend b to the bank c for your wallet.
5 People pay a electricity bills b water bills c money bills.

3 Look at the questions about money. Which questions would you **not** normally ask someone you don't know very well?

1 How much do you earn?
2 Where's the nearest cash machine?
3 Can you lend me some money?
4 How much did your jacket cost?
5 How much do you spend every week on food?
6 Do you have change for a five (dollar/euro/pound) note?
7 How much cash do you have with you now?
8 Do you owe a lot of money?

4 Compare your answers with a partner.

Reading

1 Look at the title of the text on page 83. What do you think it is about?

2 Read the text and check your answer.

3 Read the text again and answer the questions.

1 How much does the child's toy cost?
2 Does the university graduate have a job?
3 When does the family man pay the bills?
4 Where do the young couple work?
5 What has the heir done with her money?
6 Do the retired couple have money problems?

4 What are common money concerns for people your age?

Grammar

*I've **already** saved €3.*
*I haven't started work **yet**.*

- use *already* to emphasise something has happened before now
- use *yet* to talk about something that has not happened, but will probably happen soon

1 Find examples of *yet* and *already* in the text and complete the rules.

We use *yet* and *already* with the ______ tense.
We use ______ in affirmative statements.
We use ______ in negatives and questions.

2 Work in pairs. Look at the *to do* list and make sentences with *yet* or *already*.

She has already done the shopping.
She hasn't paid the bills yet.

do the shopping ✓
pay the bills
call work about a day off
do English homework ✓
go to the bank ✓
phone parents

3 Make your own *to do* list. Write down six things. Include …

- three things you haven't done yet, but would like to do this week.
- three things you have already done this week.

4 Compare your list with a partner. Ask questions.

A: *Have you done your homework yet?*

B: *Yes, I have.*

A: *Have you visited your parents yet?*

B: *No, I haven't.*

A: *When are you going to visit them?*

G Grammar focus – explanation & more practice of *yet* & *already* on page 144

Pronunciation

1 2.31 Listen and repeat the sound and words.

/ʌ/, sun, mother

2 2.32 Tick (✔) the words that have the /ʌ/ sound. Then listen and check your answers.

brother bus buy
cost home money some

3 2.33 Read and listen to the poem below.

4 Work in pairs. Read the poem, one line each at a time.

Routine

More work.
Less fun.
More money.
More buying.
More fun.
Less money.
More work.
Less fun.
More money.
More buying.
More fun.
Less money.
More work.

Stuart Doggett

A lifetime of financial concerns

As we get older our money concerns change, but they don't go away…

The retired couple

'My wife and I stopped work last month. We haven't received any money from the government yet but we have our savings, and we've already paid for our house. When the money comes, we'll travel. We've always wanted to go to France. Maybe now we can.'

The university graduate

'I haven't started work yet and I owe $10,000. How am I going to pay this money back?'

The family man

'Our situation has become more difficult since we had our second child. Everything is getting more and more expensive. We really don't look forward to the end of the month when we have to pay everything.'

The heir

'With the money my uncle left me, I've already paid for my house and a new car. I'm going to put the rest in a special bank account for my children.'

The eight year old

'I've already saved €3. Two more and I can buy the toy I want!'

The young couple

'Our friends often ask us: "Have you bought a place yet?" Well, we've already visited three banks and none of them want to help us. It's crazy, houses are so expensive here. We're thinking of living outside the city centre, but that means we have to commute and we don't really want that.'

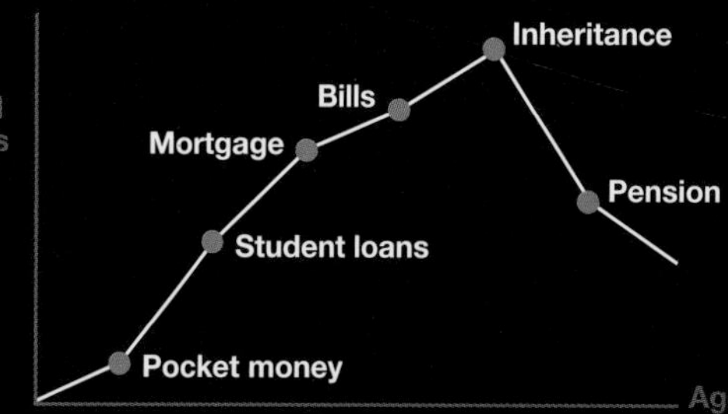

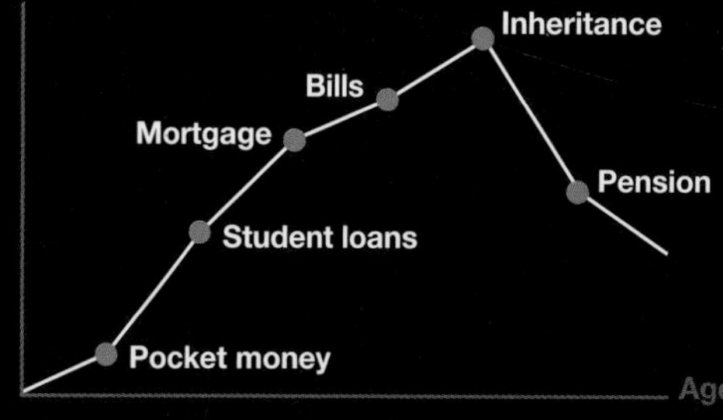

Part 4

Speaking
Describing pictures

Reading
A different kind of bank

Speaking
A bank loan

Speaking

Look at the pictures of people meeting at a bank. Work in pairs and describe the similarities and differences between them.

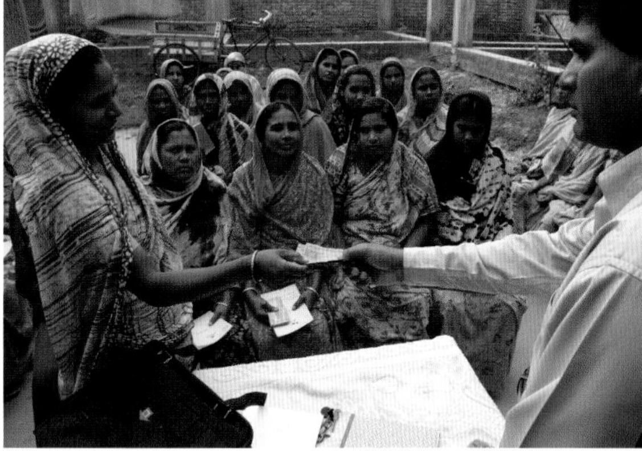

Useful language

- formal clothes
- married couple
- outside
- group of women
- modern office
- traditional clothes

Useful phrases

- In this picture … but in this picture …
- In this picture they are wearing … but in this one they are wearing …
- This picture was probably taken in … while this one was taken …

I made a list of people who needed just a little bit of money. And when the list was complete, there were 42 names. The total amount of money they needed was $27. I was shocked.
Muhammad Yunus

Reading

1 2.34 Read and listen to *A different kind of bank*. Find two differences between a Grameen Bank and a normal bank.

A different kind of bank

This is not charity. This is business: business with a social objective, which is to help people get out of poverty.
Muhammad Yunus

The Grameen Bank in Bangladesh is very different from a normal bank. In the words of its founder, Muhammad Yunus, **normal banks work on the principle 'the more you have, the more you can get.** In other words, if you have little or nothing, you get nothing.' The Grameen Bank system works on the principle that the person who has nothing is the first person who should get a loan from the bank.

The bank was started as a project in 1976 by Yunus. It gives people very small loans, called microcredit. In 1983 the Grameen Bank Project became an independent institution and the bank is now owned by its borrowers. There are more than seven million people who borrow from the Grameen Bank and 97% of them are women. It has more than 2,000 branches covering 79,000 villages. In normal banks, people go to the bank for a loan. In Grameen banks, the bank workers go and visit people in the villages. The bank often lends money to groups of women to start their own small businesses.

The Grameen bank system works very well in Bangladesh. Borrowers pay back more than 98% of the loans, and the bank has made a profit almost every year. It uses its profits to help with natural disasters.

In 2006 the Nobel committee gave Mohammad Yunus the Nobel Peace Prize for his work with the bank.

Glossary

branch (*noun*) – an office representing a large company
charity (*noun*) – an organisation that gives money and help to people who need it
founder (*noun*) – someone who starts an organisation
poverty (*noun*) – a situation where people do not have enough money to pay for basic needs

2 Read the text again and choose the correct answer.

1 The Grameen Bank thinks that … should get loans first.
   a rich people b people with nothing
   c women
2 It lends … to people.
   a small amounts of money
   b large amounts of money
   c no money
3 Most of the people who borrow from the bank are …
   a women. b poor.
   c both women and poor.
4 Grameen Bank workers meet the borrowers …
   a in their offices. b in the capital city.
   c in their villages.
5 The bank gets back … of the money it lends.
   a a bit b almost all c all

3 What do you think of the Grameen bank? Is it a good idea?

Extend your vocabulary – *borrow* and *lend*

If we *borrow* something from someone, they give it to us and we agree to give it back.

I need to borrow some money from the bank.

If we *lend* something to someone, we give it to them and they agree to give it back to us.

The bank is going to lend me some money.

Complete the sentences with the correct form of *borrow* or *lend*.

1 My pen isn't working. Can I ______ yours?
2 She ______ him two thousand euros for the car. He hasn't paid it back yet.
3 I don't have enough money for the bus. Could you ______ me some?
4 We didn't have enough chairs, so we ______ some from the neighbour.

Speaking

1 Read the situation below.

Situation

The bank has lent your learning institution €12,000 to modernise the facilities. The director has asked you for suggestions on how to spend the money. What does your institution need?

2 Work in small groups and discuss what you are going to buy. Remember that your budget is €12,000. Write down your final list of items.

3 Present your plan to another group. Give reasons for your decisions.

Useful phrases

- We need …
- We don't need …
- … is more important than … because …
- I don't think … is as important as … because …
- I don't think … is very important because …
- We have decided to spend … on … because …

CD players
€150 each

Computers
€1,000 each

Electronic whiteboards
€1,000 each

Food and drink machine for students
€2,500

Modern desks and chairs
€ 1,500 per classroom

Nice chairs for the teachers
€150 each

Painting and decoration
€400 per classroom

Televisions with DVD players
€400 each

Function globally shopping in a market

Warm up

1 Look at the pictures of four different markets. Work in pairs and describe the similarities and differences between them.

Useful phrases

- This stall sells …
- I think this market is in …
- The stallholder is …

2 Which market could you see in your country?

Listening

1 2.35–2.37 Listen to three conversations. Match each one to a photo.

2 Listen again and answer the questions.

Conversation 1: What does the man want?
How much is the final price?
Conversation 2: What does the woman buy?
Conversation 3: What does the woman want?
Why is she sad at the end?

Language focus: shopping

1 Correct the mistakes in these sentences.

1 How much it is?
2 I can help you?
3 I just looking thanks.
4 Have you a red shirt?
5 You can to have it for a hundred and twenty-five.
6 I take it.
7 No, thanks. I leave it.
8 That very expensive.

2 2.38 Listen and check your answers. Then listen and repeat the phrases.

Speaking

Work in pairs and choose **one** of the tasks below.

A Choose one of the markets and roleplay a conversation. Use the new expressions you have learnt.

B Choose three things (eg your book, your pencil, your phone). You are going to try and *sell* them to your partner. Decide a price for each thing.

Try and sell your things to your partner. Use the new expressions you have learnt.

Global English

The **English language** and the number **four** by David Crystal

If there's a number you should remember when thinking about the way the English language has changed over time, it is the number four.

The first boats carrying Angles, Saxons and Jutes from the north of Europe arrived in several parts of the British Isles in 449 AD. The different dialects they spoke gave us the earliest form of English – Old English, or Anglo-Saxon. Exactly 400 years later, King Alfred 'the Great' was born. He is especially famous in the history of English, because it was thanks to his planning that Old English literature survived.

In 1400, Chaucer died, leaving us the literary highlight of Middle English, *The Canterbury Tales*. Soon after, a major sound change began which affected many English vowel sounds. This 'Great Vowel Shift' is the main reason that Chaucer's language sounds so different from the English we use today.

In 1600, when Shakespeare was writing, roughly 4 million people spoke English in Britain. Today, around 400 years later, 400 million people speak English as a mother tongue, and four times as many speak it as a second or foreign language.

Glossary

Angle, Saxon, Jute (*noun*) – the names of Germanic peoples who lived in England

dialect (*noun*) – a way of speaking a language that is used only in a particular area or by a particular group

shift (*noun*) – a change in something

Timeline of the English Language

449 AD ______________

787 AD **Viking raids** began in England – Scandinavian influence on English names for people and places

849 AD ______________

1066 **Norman invasion** of England. The French language influences English in many ways.

1400 ______________

1400s–1500s ______________

1476 **First printing press** set up in England. Standard writing system starts to develop.

1600 ______________

1600s English comes into contact with other languages through **colonisation**.

1800s Time of the **Industrial Revolution** and **British Empire**. Huge changes in English.

1884 New English Dictionary project begins – will become the **Oxford English Dictionary**.

late 1900s Rise of the internet and **globalisation**. English becomes world language.

2000 ______________

Warm up

Look at the timeline for the English language. Tick (✔) the bold phrases that you have heard of before.

Reading

1 Read the text *The English language and the number four*. Find three reasons why the number four is important.

2 Read the text again and complete the timeline with information from the text.

Language focus

Choose the option with the same meaning as the underlined phrases.

1 <u>exactly 400</u> years later
  a 400 b 390–410
2 <u>roughly 4 million</u> people
  a 4 million b 3.8–4.2 million
3 <u>around 400</u> years later
  a 400 b 395–405
4 400 million speak English as a mother-tongue, and <u>four times as many</u> speak it as a second or foreign language
  a 100 million b 1,600 million

Speaking

Work in pairs and discuss the questions.

- Can you think of any examples of how your language has changed? For example, a word or phrase that doesn't exist anymore.
- What other languages have an influence on your language? Can you give examples?
- Does your language have an influence on any other languages? Which ones?

Writing giving your opinion

Reading

1 Read Tayse's essay on *Life today is too fast and people don't have enough time for what is important*. Does she agree with the statement?

(1) ________________.
People have too many things to do and spend all their time rushing from place to place. We travel by car and plane, communicate by email and mobile phone, and get information immediately on the internet. Even our food nowadays is often fast food.

(2) ________________.
We worry about work and our obligations, and consequently become stressed and ill. We spend our time earning more money and buying more and more things, and so we lack time for what is important. We rarely spend time with friends and family or stop to relax or have fun.

(3) ________________.
We should spend more time seeing our friends and family. We also need to think about relaxing and enjoying ourselves, even for a few hours a day. We need to find time to listen to music, read books for enjoyment, and enjoy our hobbies. We can't let life pass us by.

2 Read the essay again and put the sentences in the correct places. How do the sentences help us to understand each paragraph?

a I believe it is important to realise that there are other things in life as well as work and money.
b As a result of this, we save time but end up filling it with other things.
c It is certainly true that for many people, especially in big cities, life today is too fast.

3 Do you agree with Tayse's opinions?

Writing skills: organising your ideas

Look at Tayse's essay plan below. Put the points in each paragraph in the correct order.

1 Life today too fast
- *a too many things to do – always rushing*
- *b life in big cities too fast*
- *c transport, communication, internet, food*

2 Don't have enough time for what is important
- *a no time for friends and family*
- *b earn money – buy things*
- *c worry about obligations – become stressed*
- *d save time but fill it with other things*

3 Conclusion – what to do
- *a spend more time with friends & family*
- *b can't ~~let~~ life pass us by*
- *c relax, have fun – music, reading, hobbies*
- *d need to realise other things are important*

Language focus: giving your opinion

Complete these sentences from the text.

1 ________ realise that there are other things in life as well as work and money.
2 ________ spend more time seeing our friends and family.
3 ________ find time to listen to music.
4 ________ let life pass us by.

Preparing to write

1 Work in pairs and choose one of the statements below to write about. Do you agree with the statement?

- Schools and universities do not teach students enough about how to manage their time.
- The love of money is the root of all evil.

2 Write three paragraph headings and then write notes under each heading.

Saying what you think

- It is (certainly) true that …
- I (personally) believe that …
- It is my opinion / view that …

Writing

Write your essay. Use your notes and the useful phrases to help you.

Global review

Grammar

1 Complete the sentences with the correct word.

1 My birthday is ______ November 12th.
2 What are you doing ______ the weekend?
3 The best time to get married is ______ the spring.
4 I've lived in my house ______ six years.
5 I've studied French ______ last year.
6 I've had this purse ______ I was ten years old.

2 Put the words in the correct order.

1 yet / bill / paid / electricity / you / the / have?
2 gave / me / a / bank / loan / the.
3 saved / three / have / I / already / euros.
4 fun / flies / you're / time / having /when.

Vocabulary

1 Match the words on the left to the ones on the right.

jet	money
student	jam
pocket	watch
over	lag
traffic	loan
cash	time
wrist	machine

2 Put *owe*, *borrow* or *lend* in each gap.

1 Could you ______ me ten dollars, please?
2 I need to ______ some money from the bank.
3 How much do I ______ you for the tickets?

Speaking

1 Work in groups of three. Talk about yourselves using *for* and *since* and try to find three things that are the same for all of you.

*I've known Maria **for** three years.*

*I've had my watch **since** January.*

*We've all studied English **for** two years.*

2 Work in groups of three and discuss your English classes. Find three things you've already studied, and three things you haven't studied yet.

*We've **already** studied the present perfect.*

*We haven't practised writing letters **yet**.*

3 Work in pairs and ask each other these questions.

- What do you usually spend your money on?
- Do you save money? How? What for?
- How do you like to spend your free time?

Study skills

Managing your study time

1 Answer the questions about study time. Then discuss your answers with a partner.

1 When do you study best?
  a In the morning.
  b In the afternoon or evening.
  c Late at night.
2 What do you do with homework?
  a Do it straight away.
  b Do it when you are ready.
  c Do it at the last minute.
3 How do you study outside class?
  a Just do your homework.
  b Re-read the work done in class.
  c Do other work as well.
4 When do you re-read your notes?
  a Before meals.
  b Travelling to school or work.
  c Before going to sleep.

Top tips for study time

- ★ Find the time when you work best, and study then.
- ★ Re-read the work you have studied in class. Little and often is best, e.g. ten minutes a day.
- ★ Use spare moments to re-read your class work, eg before meals, between classes, on the bus or waiting for an appointment.
- ★ Decide what is most important.
- ★ Make a work plan and follow it.
- ★ Don't waste time thinking about work – do it straight away!

2 Make a study plan for next week. Use your answers to exercise 1 and the Top tips to help you.

- What will you do?
- When will you do it?

UNIT 8 Home & Away

Part 1

Speaking
A tour of your home

Pronunciation
/h/

Listening
Famous homes

Grammar
Passive voice

Reading & Writing
Bram Stoker's Dracula

Speaking

Draw an outline of the rooms in your house or flat. Then work in pairs and take your partner on a *tour* of your home.

Useful language

- balcony
- bedroom
- front door
- kitchen
- study
- bathroom
- dining room
- hall
- living room
- toilet

Useful phrases

- This is the …
- Over here there's a …

Pronunciation

1 2.39 Listen and repeat the sound and the word.

/h/, home

2 2.40 Listen to the sentences. Underline the words with the /h/ sound.

Home is where … the heart is.
happy memories are.
you hang your hat.
the hard drive is.
your hopes are.

3 Listen again and repeat the sentences. Which one do you like the best?

a

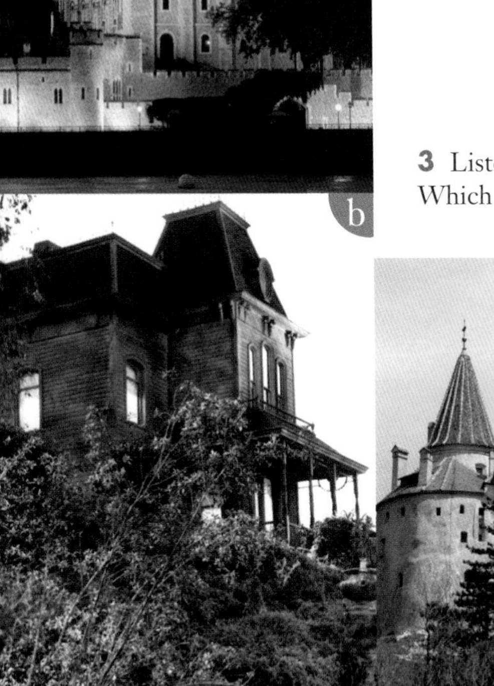
b

c

Listening

1 Look at the pictures of three famous homes. Where are they? Who do you think lived there? Use the words in the box to help you guess.

castle Dracula film set ghost haunted prince prisoner tower

2 2.41–2.43 Listen to people talking about these homes and check your answers.

3 Listen again. Are the statements true (*T*) or false (*F*)?

Conversation 1:

a The tower was built more than 900 years ago.
b The young princes were put in the tower by their uncle Richard III.

Conversation 2:

a The house was used in a film.
b The house is never open.

Conversation 3:

a The castle is still occupied by the government.
b Dracula never saw the castle.

4 Are there any famous homes in your town? Where are they? Who lived there?

Extend your vocabulary – *house* and *home*

A *house* is a building that people live in.
She lives in that big house.
Someone's *home* is the place where they live.
That flat is the home of a large family.

Complete the sentences with *house* or *home*.

1 I'm going ______ after class.
2 Please do exercise 3 for ______ work.
3 See that big red ______ over there? My father lives there.
4 I'll do the shopping and cleaning, but you do the other ______ work.
5 Hi, I'm not at ______ at the moment. Please leave a message.

Grammar

People say the tower ***is haunted.***
The castle ***was returned*** *to its owners.*

- we use the passive voice when we want to focus on the action, not the person who does the action
- we also use the passive voice when we do not know who does the action or it is not important

1 Read the sentences from the listening and decide if they are active (*A*) or passive (*P*).

1 The Tower of London was built in 1078.
2 Their uncle put them in the tower.
3 It was used in the film *Psycho*.
4 People believe that Vlad Tepes – the original Dracula – lived here.
5 It is visited every year by thousands of people.

2 Complete the texts with the correct form of *to be*.

Official residences
around the world

The Palacio de la Moncloa is the official residence of the Spanish prime minister in Madrid. It *was / is* destroyed during the Spanish Civil War, but it *was / is* rebuilt afterwards.

Abdeen Palace, in central Cairo, *is / was* built in 1874 for the Egyptian royal family. Today it *is / was* used as an official residence for the president and a museum.

The Lodge, located in Canberra, Australia, *is / was* built in 1926. It *was / is* meant to be a temporary home for the Australian prime minister. Now it is the official one.

The official residence of the president of Ukraine is Mariyinsky Palace in Kiev. It *is / was* constructed in the 18th century and *is / was* used as military headquarters between 1917 and 1920.

The Zhongnanhai is a group of buildings in Beijing, China. It *is / was* used as an official residence of the head of state in the past. Today, when foreign politicians come to visit, they *were / are* welcomed there.

Grammar focus – explanation & more practice of the passive on page 146

Bram Stoker's Dracula

As Jonathan Harker approaches the castle doors, they open. An old man, carrying a lamp, enters the room.

Dracula: Welcome to my home.

Harker: Count Dracula?

Dracula: I am Dracula, and I bid you welcome, Mr Harker, to my house. Come in.

Dracula: You will, I trust, excuse me that I do not join you. But I have already dined and I never drink ... wine.

The novel *Dracula* was written in 1897 by the Irish novelist Bram Stoker. There have been many adaptations of the novel for film. The 1992 film *Bram Stoker's Dracula* was directed by Francis Ford Coppola.

Reading and Writing

1 Read the scene from the film *Bram Stoker's Dracula*.

2 Work in pairs and write the next three lines of the dialogue. Then present your scene to another pair.

Language note: *I bid you welcome* is a formal, literary way of saying welcome.

UNIT 8 Home & Away

Part 2

Vocabulary & Speaking
Animals

Reading
The cat came back

Vocabulary
Prepositions of movement

Vocabulary and Speaking

1 Look at the pictures of different animals. Would you keep any of these animals in your home? Which ones?

budgie cat dog goldfish hamster
horse mouse rabbit snake spider

2 Which of these animals have …

a tail? eight legs? fur?
big ears? fins? wings?

3 Work in pairs and ask each other these questions.

- Did you have a pet as a child? What was it?
- Are you afraid of any of these animals?

Reading

1 Do you prefer cats or dogs? Why? Tell a partner.

I prefer … because they are friendlier / more intelligent / more interesting.

I don't like cats or dogs.

2 Read the introduction to *The cat came back* on page 93 and discuss the questions in pairs.

- Do cats have any special meaning in your country?
- Do many people keep them as pets? What is the most common pet?
- In English, people sometimes say that cats have nine lives. Does this expression exist in your language?

3 Quickly read the rest of the text and choose the best subtitle.

a True stories of cats who lived in different countries.
b True stories of cats who travelled a long distance to come home.
c True stories of cats who loved their owners.
d True stories of cats who travelled a long distance to leave home.

4 2.44 Read and listen to the text and complete the sentences with the names of the cats.

1 _____ lived in the USA.
2 _____ came home after about two months.
3 _____ and _____ came back home after a week.
4 _____ went to his owners' second home.
5 _____ was happy but very dirty.

5 Find words in the text with these meanings.

1 so important that you should not criticise it (introduction)
2 the official line that separates two countries (paragraph 1)
3 very dirty (paragraph 2)
4 the sound a cat makes when it's happy (paragraph 2)

6 Which story do you think is the most surprising? Do you know any unusual pet stories?

The cat came back

Archaeologists estimate that humans and cats have lived together for more than 9,000 years. In Ancient Egypt, cats were considered sacred animals and protectors of the home. Today there are an estimated 500 million domestic cats in the world, making cats one of the most common animals in the home. It's common to say that cats have nine lives because of their strange ability to survive, as the following true stories show.

Minosch – travelled 2,400 km through Germany. In 1981 Mehmet Tune, a Turkish man living in Germany, went to Turkey with his cat and family for a holiday. At the Turkish border Minosch disappeared. Sixty-one days later, back in northern Germany, the family heard a noise at the door. It was Minosch.

Howie – walked 1,900 km across Australia. In 1978 this three-year-old cat walked home from the Gold Coast in Queensland, Australia, to Adelaide. The trip took a year. Kirsten Hicks, the cat's owner, said that although he was filthy and bleeding, Howie was actually purring.

Ernie – travelled 965 km to Texas. In September 1994, Chris and Jennifer Trevino's cat Ernie jumped out of a pick-up truck while it was travelling down the motorway. The cat was 965 km away from home. A week later, Ernie walked back into the Trevino family home in Victoria, Texas.

Gringo – travelled 780 km down to the French Riviera. The Servos family lost their pet cat Gringo from their home in northern France in December 1982. The following July they learnt that the cat was in the south of France. Gringo had travelled through France and arrived at the Servos's summer home a week later. The neighbours took care of him until the Servos family arrived.

Vocabulary

1 Look at the pictures and complete the sentences with the correct prepositions from the box.

across	across	
along	down	in
into	out of	past
through	up	

2 2.45 Listen and check your answers. Then cover the sentences and try to retell the story.

1 Ernie jumped ______ the truck and walked ______ the highway.

2 He went ______ a bridge, and ______ some fields.

3 He walked ______ the river, but fell ______ by accident.

4 He ran ______ some sleeping dogs.

5 He climbed ______ a tree to sleep and climbed ______ again the next morning.

6 He walked ______ the family home one week later.

UNIT 8 Home & Away

Part 3

Reading
Travel guidebooks

Listening
Conversations with travel guides

Grammar
First conditional

Reading & Speaking
The Beach

Reading

Read *A quick guide to the world's most famous guidebooks* and complete the sentences with the names of the guidebooks.

1 ________ became famous for its restaurant reviews.
2 ________ was written by a soldier.
3 ________ was the first modern guidebook.
4 ________ and ________ were written for people without a lot of money.

Which of these guidebooks did you know about already?

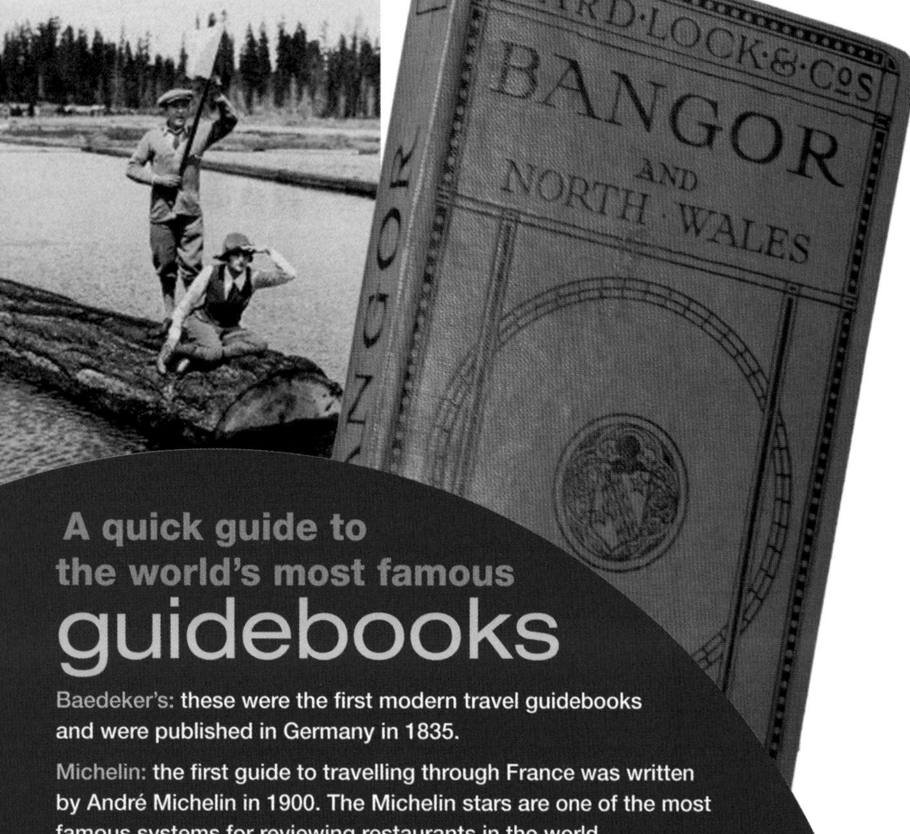

A quick guide to the world's most famous guidebooks

Baedeker's: these were the first modern travel guidebooks and were published in Germany in 1835.

Michelin: the first guide to travelling through France was written by André Michelin in 1900. The Michelin stars are one of the most famous systems for reviewing restaurants in the world.

Frommer's: the book *Europe on $5 a day* was written in 1957 by Arthur Frommer, an American soldier, and was one of the first budget travel guides.

Lonely Planet: the *Lonely Planet* guidebooks were started by Tony and Maureen Wheeler in 1973. They were originally written for budget travel in Asia, but now cover almost every country in the world.

Listening

1 2.46–2.48 Listen to three conversations between tourists and travel guides / agents. Choose the correct situation for each one. There is one place you don't need.

beach   city centre   market   travel office

2 Listen again and choose the correct answers.

Conversation 1: The man wants to travel …
a to the USA. b this month.
c next month.

Conversation 2: The tower is …
a the newest building in the city.
b the tallest building in the city.
c the oldest building in the city.

Conversation 3: The guide persuades the man to …
a buy a carpet. b have lunch.
c visit the city.

Extend your vocabulary – words that mean *trip*

A *trip* is when we go somewhere and come back again.

A *drive* is a trip in a car. A *flight* is a trip in a plane.

A *journey* is a long trip from one place to another.

A *tour* is a trip to a place where there are interesting things to see.

A *ride* is a short trip in a car or bus or on a bicycle or motorcycle.

Replace the underlined words with other words that mean *trip*.

1 I went for a <u>trip</u> in my brother's new car.
2 They were very tired and had jet lag after the third <u>plane trip</u>.
3 He took me for a <u>trip</u> in his new Volkswagen.
4 She's saving money for her next <u>trip</u> across Europe.

Grammar

*If you **go** up the tower, you **won't** regret it.*
*If you **buy** one of these carpets now, I **can** get a good price for you.*
***I'll** ask **if** you **like**.*

- use the first conditional to talk about a possible future situation
- use the present simple in the *if* clause
- use *will*, *can* or *might* plus verb in the main clause
- the *if* clause can be the first or second clause in the sentence

1 Complete the sentences from the listening with the correct phrase.

1 If you *travel / will travel* this month, *you'll / you* get an extra 20% discount.
2 If you *will go / go* up the tower, you *won't / don't* regret it.
3 *We'll / We* go there later if you *will want / want*.
4 If you *buy / will buy* two, she *will give / gives* you a big discount.

2 What is the difference between these sentences?

a If I go to London, I'll buy an English guidebook.
b If I go to London, I might buy an English guidebook.
c If I go to London, I can buy an English guidebook.

3 Work in pairs. Read the situations and complete the sentences with your own ideas.

1 You want to go somewhere this weekend. (sunny or raining?)
If it's sunny, we'll …
2 You have won a big prize (a trip for two or money?)
If we win the trip for two, we …
3 Your friend is going to have a baby and you want to buy a present. (boy or girl?)
If it's a boy …

G Grammar focus – explanation & more practice of the first conditional on page 146

The Beach

In *The Beach*, the main character Richard finds a secret community of travellers in Thailand. They live on a perfect beach, a place that is not in any guidebooks. Here Sal, a woman who lives there, explains the idea behind the secret community to Richard.

'Of course this is more than a beach resort. But at the same time, it is just a beach resort. We come here to relax by a beautiful beach, but it isn't a beach resort, because we're trying to get away from beach resorts. Or we're trying to make a place that won't turn into a beach resort. See?'

'No.'

Sal shrugged. 'You will see, Richard. It really isn't that complicated.'

Reading and Speaking

1 Check you understand the phrase *beach resort*. Are there any beach resorts in your country? Do you like them?

2 2.49 Read and listen to the text. Then work in pairs and discuss the questions.

- What do Sal and the others want to avoid? Why?
- Do you often visit places that are popular with tourists?
- Are there any places in your country that have too much tourism? Where?

Alex Garland (1970–) is an English writer of novels and films. He wrote his first novel *The Beach* in 1996 when he was 26 years old and it became a classic. It was made into a film in 2000.

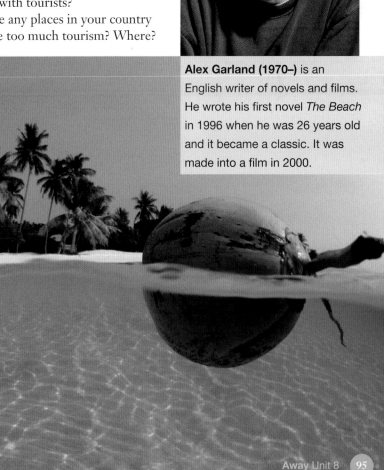

Home & Away

Part 4

Speaking
Describing photos

Vocabulary
Adjectives & prepositions

Reading
New kinds of tourism

Grammar
Second conditional

Pronunciation & Speaking
Sentence stress

Speaking

Work in pairs. Look at the pictures below and describe them. How do you think they are connected?

Useful language

- ancient
- disaster area
- operating theatre
- castle
- kitchen
- storm

Useful phrases

- It looks a bit like …
- This picture shows … while this one shows …
- This picture looks nicer / more interesting / more boring than …

Vocabulary

1 Complete the sentences with the correct prepositions.

about at in of of with

1. I'm interested ______ historical and cultural places.
2. I'm bored ______ beach holidays; we go to the beach every year.
3. I'm worried ______ the situation and I want to help.
4. I'm fond ______ sand, sea and sun.
5. I'm not good ______ cooking, but I want to learn.
6. I'm a bit afraid ______ old castles and places like that.

2 Match the sentences in exercise 1 to the pictures from the speaking activity. More than one answer may be possible.

3 Complete the sentences in exercise 1 with your own ideas.

Reading

1 Read the text *New kinds of tourism* on page 97. Which kind of tourism does each picture show?

2 Read the text again and put the sentences in the correct places in the text.

a. This kind of tourism involves going to a different country for health care and at the same time enjoying more typical tourist attractions.
b. New Zealand has benefited from this kind of tourism since the film *The Lord of the Rings* was made there.
c. The increase in the number of tourists also means an increase in the kinds of tourism now available.
d. Cooking holidays are growing in popularity, especially in countries like Italy and France.
e. This kind of tourism is not very popular with local residents for obvious reasons.

3 What is your opinion of these different kinds of tourism? Write a number for each one. 1 = very acceptable, 5 = completely unacceptable

Then compare your ideas with a partner.

I think … is very acceptable.

I have some problems with …

I think … is unacceptable.

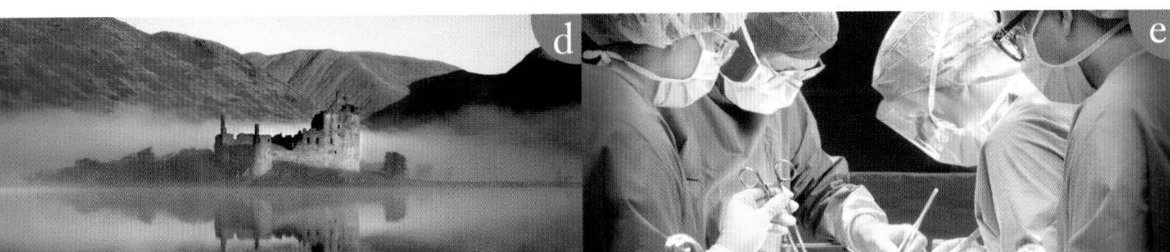

New kinds of
tourism

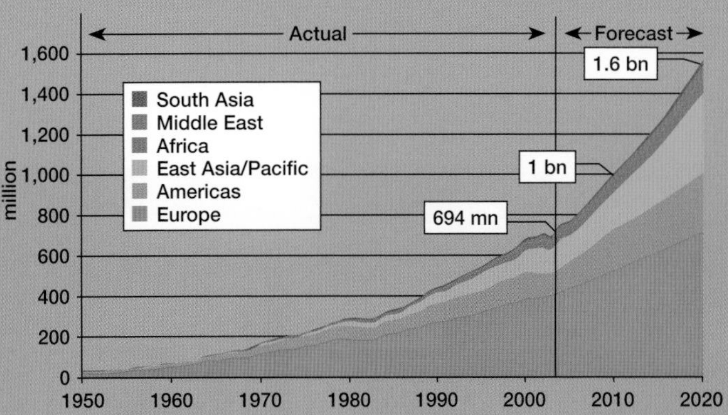

Would you do it if you had the chance?

People are travelling more than ever before. The World Tourism Organisation (UNWTO) predicts that by 2020 the number of international travellers will be more than 1.6 billion people per year (see chart). ______ Here are four different kinds of tourism that have appeared recently.

Medical tourism

Medical tourism can be for a variety of things, from operations to visits to the dentist or even cosmetic surgery. __a__ A few of the popular countries offering medical tourism are India, Cuba, Thailand, Argentina and Jordan. In Kenya they even offer medical safaris.

Culinary tourism

Nearly all tourists eat in restaurants, and dining is one of the top three tourist activities. But if you were in a country famous for its food, would you learn how to cook it? Welcome to the more extreme form of culinary tourism, where people go to another country to learn how to prepare its food. ______

Disaster tourism

Disaster tourism involves visiting the site of a disaster. Examples include tours to New Orleans after Hurricane Katrina, to parts of Thailand after the tsunami or tourist visits to ground zero in New York.

______

Literary tourism

Another growing area of tourism is literary tourism. This is a kind of cultural tourism and there are several types. It can be connected to the life of an author, for example visiting the author's home or favourite places, or connected to the lives of characters in a story. It can also be a visit to a place where a film was made.

______

Glossary

cosmetic surgery (*noun*) – medical operations that improve someone's appearance

ground zero (*noun*) – a place where a lot of people have been killed

health care (*noun*) – the services that look after people's health

safari (*noun*) – a journey, especially in Africa, to see wild animals in their natural environment

tsunami (*noun*) – a very large wave that is caused by an earthquake under the sea

Grammar

1 Look at sentences 1–3 and answer questions a–c below.

1. *If* you *were* in a country famous for its food, ***would*** you ***learn*** how to cook it?
2. *If* I *went* to Morocco, I ***would visit*** the market in Medina.
3. We ***wouldn't visit*** the disaster area *if* we *were* in New Orleans.

a What tense are the verbs in the underlined parts of the sentences?
b What form of the verb follows *would* in the other part of the sentences?
c Are these real or unreal situations?

2 Which sentence in each pair is about an unreal situation?

1 a We'll go if we have the money.
  b We'd go if we had the money.
2 a Would you visit there if you could?
  b Will you visit there if you can?
3 a I'd never visit a disaster zone.
  b I'll never visit a disaster zone.

G Grammar focus – explanation & more practice of the second conditional on page 146

Pronunciation and Speaking

1 2.50 Look at this question. Only the stressed words are written. Listen and write the missing words.

______ you ______ go anywhere ______
______ world, where ______ ______ go?

2 Listen again and repeat the question. Then work in pairs and ask each other.

3 Work in pairs and ask each other the questions in the box. Pay attention to the stressed words.

Language note: *would you* is often pronounced /wʊdjuː/ or /wʊdjə/ in fast connected speech.

- If you could work or study in another country, would you do it? What country would you prefer?
- If some foreign friends visited you for one day and wanted to see some sights, where would you take them?
- What would you do if your son or daughter told you they wanted to travel on their own?
- If you went to England, would you buy souvenirs? What would you buy? Who for?

Function globally speaking on the telephone

Warm up

Work in pairs. Roleplay a short phone conversation for each situation.

Situations

1 A: phone B. You can't go to work today. Say why.
2 B: phone A. You have a problem in your kitchen. You want A to come and fix it.
3 A: phone B. You would like to reserve a room in B's hotel for two nights.
4 B: phone A. Tell A about a fantastic holiday you have just returned from.

Listening

2.51–2.54 Listen to four short phone conversations. What is the man trying to do? What happens at the end?

Language focus: telephone English

1 Put the words in the correct order to make useful phrases.

1 about calling the English learning holiday I'm.
2 Mrs Knight can speak to I?
3 please a moment, just.
4 call back I'll.
5 a message I can take?
6 Greenway hello, Holidays.
7 Pablo Alonso is hello, this.
8 you put I'll through.

2 2.55 Listen and check your answers. Then listen and repeat the phrases.

3 Look at sentences 1–8 in exercise 1 and match them to the functions a–h below.

Which phrase do you use …

a when you answer the phone?
b to say who you are?
c to say the purpose of your call?
d to politely ask the other person to wait?
e to connect one caller to another?
f to ask to speak to someone?
g to ask if the other person wants to leave a message?
h to say you will call again later?

Speaking

Work in pairs and choose **one** of the tasks below.

A Repeat the warm up activity using the new expressions you have learnt.

B Prepare a phone conversation. Use the diagram below to help you. Then practise your conversation.

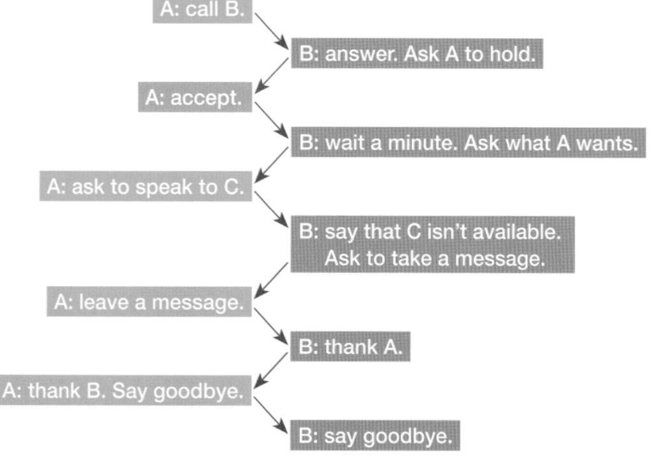

A: call B.
B: answer. Ask A to hold.
A: accept.
B: wait a minute. Ask what A wants.
A: ask to speak to C.
B: say that C isn't available. Ask to take a message.
A: leave a message.
B: thank A.
A: thank B. Say goodbye.
B: say goodbye.

Global voices

cottage terraced houses

block of flats

Warm up

1 Look at the pictures of different homes. Work in pairs and describe the similarities and differences between them.

2 Are any of the pictures similar to homes in your country?

Listening

2.56–260 Listen and cross out the topic the speaker **doesn't** mention.

1 David, Georgia
 a blocks of flats b houses in the villages c house prices
2 Elena, Russia
 a big houses b house prices c rooms in a house
3 Valeria, Bolivia
 a blocks of flats b coloured houses c homes in Oxford
4 Katie, Northern Ireland
 a terraced houses b blocks of flats c varied homes
5 Bea, England
 a house prices b living rooms c house mates

David, Georgia Elena, Russia
Valeria, Bolivia Katie, Northern Ireland Bea, England

Language focus: adverbs of degree

1 Put the adverbs of degree into three groups.

+	++	+++
________	________	________
________	________	________

a bit extremely fairly quite slightly very

2 Match the speakers 1–5 to the summaries a–e. Then listen again and check your answers.

1 David, Georgia ___
2 Elena, Russia ___
3 Valeria, Bolivia ___
4 Katie, Northern Ireland ___
5 Bea, England ___

a The homes in my country are quite varied. They have different pretty colours.
b Homes in my country are very big; in the cities there are blocks of flats, and in the country there are more houses.
c In my country many young people share a big house together; homes are quite large.
d Flats in my country are extremely expensive, much more expensive than flats in Great Britain.
e Terraced houses in my city are fairly typical. They have two rooms upstairs and two rooms downstairs.

3 Which sentences in exercise 2 are true for your country?

Speaking

1 Choose **one** of the topics below. Make some notes using the questions to help you.

- Homes in your country and homes in Great Britain / USA. Different? How?
- An extremely big house you have visited. Whose? Where? What's it like?
- A part of your city where the buildings are quite ugly. Where? What do they look like?
- A part of your country where homes are fairly cheap. Where? How much? Why?

2 Work in pairs and tell each other about your topic.

I'm going to tell you about an extremely big house I've visited. It's a friend's house, and it is outside the town. It has many bedrooms, and a very large living room …

Writing a description of a town

Reading

Read Aneta's description of her town and answer the questions.

1 What are the town's main attractions?
2 What does Aneta like and dislike about the town?
3 Would you like to visit the town? Why?

Hi Mariko

How are you? I hope you are well. I'm so glad you are coming to stay with me next month. Will be great to see you again.

Let me tell you a bit about my town. Is called Rajec and is in the north of Slovakia, near the Mala Fatra mountains. Is not a large town (are about 7,000 inhabitants) but is very old and beautiful. The main attraction of the town is the 16th-century Town Hall. Is also a medieval square in the centre of the town, as well as lots of historical buildings. Outside the town are also thermal baths, and a golf course and tennis courts.

The worst thing about Rajec is that is a bit quiet and isn't much to do at night. Is no cinema, and are not many bars and restaurants. But what I like best is the countryside around the town. Is wonderful to go walking there in the summer. Are mountains nearby, as well as a small lake.

Anyway, that's all for now. I'm looking forward to seeing you soon.

Love,

Aneta

Language focus: *it* and *there*

1 Aneta has forgotten to use *it* seven times and *there* seven times. Write the words in the correct places in her description.

***It** will be great to see you again.*

2 Complete the rules using *it* or *there*.

a Use ______ to talk about something for the first time.
______ is an old Town Hall. ______ aren't many bars.

b Use ______ to talk about something you have already mentioned.
______ is very old. ______ is near the mountains.

Writing skills: giving more information

Make your writing more interesting by giving more information about places.

Put the clauses with *where* in the best place in the email.

1 …, where people go skiing in the winter
2 …, where you can go for a day trip
3 …, where you can go fishing
4 …, where you can enjoy the natural hot water all year round

Preparing to write

Work in pairs and ask each other the questions. Use the useful phrases below to help you.

1 What's your town called?
2 What sort of town is it?
3 Where is it exactly?
4 What is it like?
5 What are the main attractions?
6 What can you do there?
7 What is the worst thing about the town?
8 What do you like best about the town?

Describing a town

- It's a small / medium-sized / large town / city / village.
- It's historical / modern / touristy / a bit quiet / quite lively.
- It's in the north / in the south-east / in the centre of …
- It's on the coast / near the capital city.
- There are lots of shops / no historical buildings.
- There's a medieval castle / no shopping centre.
- There's a lot / not much / nothing to do (at night).

Writing

Write an email like Aneta's to describe your town to a friend. Use your answers from above to help you.

Global review

Grammar

Complete the sentences with the correct words.

1 The Tower of London *was built / was build / built* in 1078.
2 Every year, Dracula's Castle *visited / visit / is visited* by thousands of tourists.
3 People *do not permit / is not permitted / are not permitted* to take photographs too close to 10 Downing Street.
4 I'm bored *at / with / on* my job so I'm going to leave.
5 If you *don't / won't / wouldn't* hurry, you'll miss the bus.
6 I would visit Brazil if I *have / had / would have* enough money.
7 You'll never pass the exam if you *don't / won't / didn't* study.
8 You *will / can / could* see lions if you went on safari.

Vocabulary

1 Read the definitions and complete the words.

1 an animal with a very long neck g ______
2 the biggest animal in the world w ______
3 an insect that makes honey b ______
4 a book that tells you about places to visit g ______
5 something you pack before you travel s ______

2 Complete the directions using the correct prepositions.

Go (1) ______ the road,
(2) ______ the bridge and
(3) ______ the church.

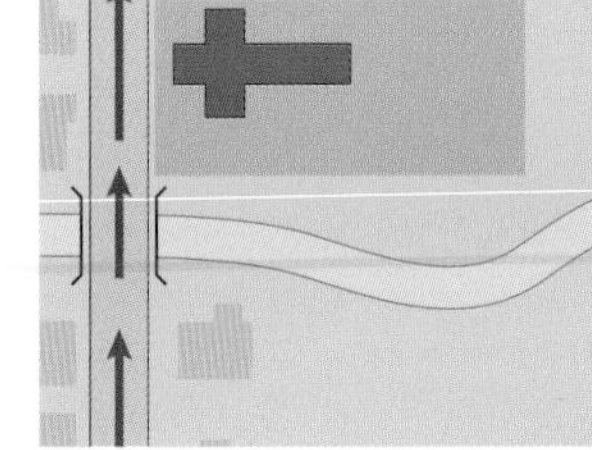

Speaking

1 Work in pairs and ask each other the questions.

- If you could live anywhere in the world, where would you live, and why? What would your house be like?
- Where would you go if you could travel anywhere in the world? What would you do there? What could you see?

2 Work in pairs. You are going on holiday together. Discuss and decide where you are going.

A: you want to go to a tropical beach. Think of some reasons why.
B: you want to go to a city. Think of some reasons why.

Useful phrases

- A: If we go to Hawaii, we can …
- B: Yes, but … is boring. If we go to …, we can …

Study skills

Learning words with prepositions

1 Work in pairs. Can you remember which prepositions were used in these sentences?

1 Hi, I'm not ______ home ______ the moment.
2 The castle is known ______ Dracula's Castle.
3 If you were in a country famous ______ its food, would you learn how to cook it?
4 You are going ______ a three-day trip.

When you learn new words, it is a good idea to learn them with the preposition they are used with.

interested ***in*** ***at*** *home* *go* ***on*** *a trip*

2 Look up these adjectives in your dictionary. Write the preposition they are used with and an example sentence from the dictionary.

Similar *to*

Their situation is very similar to ours.

1 different ______
______
2 married ______
______
3 related ______
______
4 keen ______
______

3 Use a dictionary to find out whether these words are used with *to*, *for* or *on*.

1 go ______ holiday
2 go ______ a drive
3 go ______ the cinema
4 go ______ a drink
5 go ______ safari
6 go ______ a picnic
7 go ______ a cruise
8 go ______ a concert
9 go ______ lunch
10 go ______ a tour

UNIT 9 Health & Fitness

Part 1

Speaking & Listening
The common cold

Vocabulary
Feeling ill

Pronunciation
Ch & gh

Listening
Cures for the common cold

Grammar
Modal verbs of advice

Writing
A sick note

Speaking and Listening

1 Work in pairs and ask each other the questions.

- How often do you get a cold?
- Have you had a cold yet this year?
- Do you ever take time off work or school with a cold?

2 Try to complete the information about the common cold with the numbers in the box. There are two numbers you don't need.

24–48 hours	2 months	2–5	50
200+	2–3 years	$3.5 billion	6–10

In numbers …
the common cold

- the number of viruses that cause the common cold
- the average number of colds an adult gets every year
- the average number of colds a child or baby gets every year
- the average time you have a cold before you feel the symptoms
- the average time in your life you will have a cold
- the cost of the common cold in the US every year (from lost time at work and school)

3 2.61 Listen and check your answers.

Vocabulary

1 Complete the sentences with the correct word.

1 *What's / How's* <u>the matter</u>?
2 I *feel / have* <u>tired</u>.
3 I've *got / feel* a <u>headache</u>.
4 I've got a *hurt / sore* <u>throat</u>.
5 My <u>back</u> *hurts / is hurts*.
6 I have a *blocked / blocking* nose.
7 *I'm / I've* always <u>sneezing</u>.

Language note: when you talk about feeling ill you can use *I have* or *I've got*.

2 Replace the underlined words in exercise 1 with the words in the box. There may be more than one possible answer.

cough	coughing	fever
head	leg	sick
stomach ache	toothache	wrong

3 Work in pairs. A: turn to page 127.
B: turn to page 129.

Pronunciation

1 2.62 Listen to the groups of words. Which word has a different *ch* or *gh* sound?

1	cheap	chicken	choose	machine
2	character	catch	technique	headache
3	tough	enough	ought	cough

2 Write the words from exercise 1 in the correct columns.

/f/	/k/	/tʃ/	/ʃ/	silent

3 2.63 Listen and repeat the sentences. Pay attention to the *ch* and *gh* sounds.

1 I've had enough of this cough.
2 I think I caught it from Charles.
3 He's had a headache for ages.

4 2.64 Read and listen to the poem below. How many different pronunciations of *ough* are there?

I take it you already know
Of tough and bough and cough and dough.
Others may stumble but not you,
On hiccough, thorough, slough and through.
…
A dreadful language? Man alive,
I'd mastered it when I was five.

5 Try to read the poem aloud.

Listening

1 Read the quote about the common cold. What advice would you give to someone with a cold?

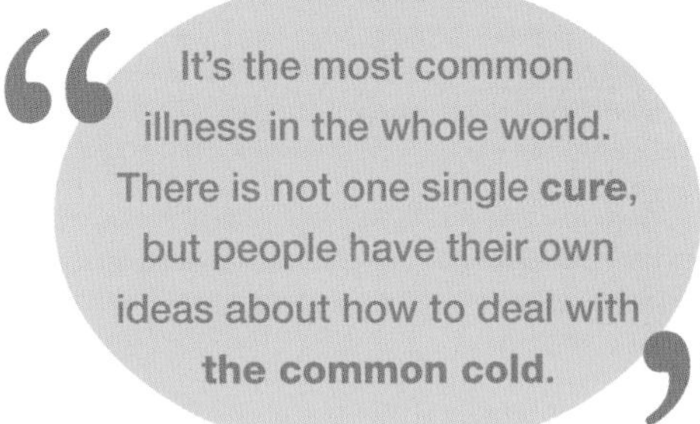

It's the most common illness in the whole world. There is not one single **cure**, but people have their own ideas about how to deal with **the common cold.**

2 2.65 Listen to the different people answering the same question. List the pictures above in the order that you hear them: eg b, …

3 Choose one of the verbs in the box. Listen again and make notes on the advice you hear with that verb.

breathe	drink	eat	
go	stay	take	wash

4 Compare your notes with a partner. Then check the audioscript on page 157.

Grammar

You ***should*** *eat garlic.*
You ***shouldn't*** *do any exercise.*
You really ***ought to*** *wash your hands regularly.*
You ***must*** *stay in bed.*

- use *should* to give advice and make suggestions
- we can also use *ought to*, but *should* is more common
- *must* is similar to *should* but is stronger

1 Use the pictures and your own ideas to give advice to someone with a cold.

I think you should …

I don't think you should …

2 Make new sentences with the words in brackets.

Can't sleep at night? Advice for insomniacs …

Drinking coffee before bed is a very bad idea. (*mustn't*)

You mustn't drink coffee before bed.

1 Try taking a warm bath before bed. (*should*)
2 Sleep on a good bed. (*should*)
3 It's a good idea to see a doctor if the problem continues. (*ought to*)
4 Smoking before you go to bed isn't a good idea. (*shouldn't*)
5 Try to get some exercise during the day. (*should*)

G Grammar focus – explanation & more practice of modal verbs on page 148

Writing

1 Read the three situations and choose **one**.

Situations

1 You have been invited to a party tonight, but you don't feel well. Write a note to your friend. Explain the situation and apologise.
2 You have a special exam tonight but you don't feel well. Write a note to your professor. Explain the situation and ask if you can do the exam another time.
3 You don't feel well today and you can't go to work. Write a note to your co-worker. Explain the situation and ask them to change shifts with you.

2 Work in pairs and swap your sick notes. Write a short reply and give the person some advice.

Useful language

- I'm sorry but I can't …
- I'm sorry but I won't be able to …
- I'm not feeling very well.
- I've got …
- I think I've got …
- Sorry to hear that you're not feeling well.
- Don't worry, we / you can …
- Get better soon.

UNIT 9 Health & Fitness

Part 2

Vocabulary
Medical treatment

Pronunciation
Word stress

Reading
Milestones of modern medicine

Grammar
Could / couldn't, had to / didn't have to

Vocabulary

1 Complete the questions with the correct form of the verbs.

Have you ever …
______ an operation?
______ in a hospital overnight?
______ a bone?
break have stay

Do you …
______ a check-up with your doctor?
______ the dentist? How often?
______ any pills?
go for take visit

Are you afraid of …
______ injections?
______ to hospital?
______ ill?
become go have

2 Choose one question from each box. Work in pairs and ask each other the questions.

Pronunciation

1 Put these words into groups with the same number of syllables. Then mark the stressed syllable.

alcohol	Arabic	hospital
medical	operation	originally
pharmacy	preservation	translation

2 2.66 Listen and follow *Arab influences on medicine* to check your answers. What do you notice about the last syllable of the words?

3 2.67 Listen and repeat the words from exercise 1.

Avicenna, Prince of Physicians (980–1037)

Arab influences on MEDICINE

The world of **medicine** was influenced greatly by the Arab world.

The first **pharmacies** and **medical** schools were developed in Damascus, Cairo and Cordoba.

The Arabs were also the first to use **alcohol** to treat illnesses. The word **alcohol** is **originally** an **Arabic** word.

In 977 one of the biggest **hospitals** in the world was founded in Baghdad. More than 20 doctors performed **operations** there.

The world of **Arab medicine** is also responsible for the **translation** and **preservation** of important **medical** works by Ancient Greeks, such as Hippocrates.

4 Work in pairs and practise reading the text. Each person reads one line each. Pay attention to the word stress.

Reading

1 The words in the box are from a text called *Milestones of modern medicine*. Check you understand what they mean.

anaesthesia antibiotics disease DNA vaccines

2 What do you think the text is about? Choose one answer.

a important discoveries in medicine
b the most serious diseases in medicine
c a competition between doctors

3 2.68 Read and listen to the text on page 105 and check your prediction.

4 Read the text again and complete the sentences with the names of the milestones.

1 ______ helped identify many diseases.
2 ______ reduced deaths from dirty water.
3 ______ reduced deaths by infection.
4 ______ helped doctors with operations.
5 ______ was invented to treat rabies.
6 ______ were discovered by accident.

5 The *British Medical Journal* asked doctors to vote for the most important milestone. Which do you think won?

Milestones of MODERN MEDICINE

In 2007 the *British Medical Journal* asked doctors and nurses from around the world what the most important discoveries in modern medicine were. Here are some of the finalists.

Anaesthesia Before anaesthesia patients had to be awake during operations. At the end of the 1800s, drugs were developed that stopped the feeling of pain. Operations became much easier for doctors and much less painful for patients.

Antibiotics In 1928 Alexander Fleming accidentally discovered that penicillin kills bacteria. This had an enormous impact on medicine. Doctors could treat infections properly. Antibiotics were first produced on a massive scale during World War 2.

DNA The structure of DNA was discovered in the 1950s by two scientists, James Watson and Francis Crick. Crick was a British physicist and Watson, who was American, studied ornithology (birds). The discovery of DNA has helped to identify many diseases and has changed modern medicine.

Germ theory Before 1847 doctors didn't have to wash their hands before an operation. Ignaz Semmelweis, a doctor from Vienna, realised that women in labour could be dying from infections passed on by the hands of their doctors. This became the germ theory of disease. At the end of the 19th century, infection caused 30% of deaths. By the end of the 20th century it caused less than 4%.

Sanitation As cities grew in the 1800s, so did pollution. Dirty water caused many diseases. This turned attention to water systems and sanitation was born. Clean water helped death rates fall by the beginning of the last century.

Vaccines Louis Pasteur created the first vaccine for rabies in 1885. Vaccines have saved millions of lives over the last century and will continue to do so for years to come.

Glossary

bacteria (*noun*) – very small living things. Some types of bacteria cause diseases

identify (*verb*) – to recognise something and to understand what it is

infection (*noun*) – a disease that is caused by bacteria or by a virus

labour (*noun*) – the process by which a baby is pushed from its mother's body when it is being born

rabies (*noun*) – a serious disease passed from animals to humans

sanitation (*noun*) – conditions and processes relating to the water supply and human waste

Grammar

Doctors ***could*** *treat infections properly.*
Doctors ***didn't have to*** *wash their hands.*
Patients ***had to*** *be awake during operations.*

- use *could* and *couldn't* to talk about things that were or were not possible in the past
- use *had to* and *didn't have to* to talk about obligation or no obligation in the past
- the past form of *must* is *had to*

1 Complete the texts with *had to*, *didn't have to* or *could*.

The X-ray

Before 1900 if doctors wanted to know what was inside a person's body they ________ open it. In 1895 a German professor called Wilhelm Röntgen was experimenting with vacuum tubes. He discovered that he ________ see the bones inside his hand. He won the Nobel Prize for Physics in 1901.

Risks of smoking

In the past tobacco companies ________ put a warning on cigarettes. Doctors did not know that smoking ________ cause cancer. People began to realise that smoking kills after two important medical studies in the 1950s.

2 Work in pairs. Look at the words in the box and say what people *could*, *couldn't* or *had to* do before these inventions.

ambulance	anaesthesia
eye glasses	microscope
thermometer	wheelchair

G Grammar focus – explanation & more practice of *could* & *had to* on page 148

Part 3

Vocabulary
Sport

Reading
Olympic ...

Grammar
Past perfect

Speaking
Sports questionnaire

Vocabulary

1 Look at pictures a–i. What sports do they go with?

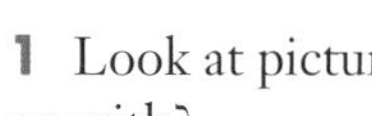

2 Look at the examples and complete the table with the names of sports from exercise 1.

play	go	do
squash	jogging	aerobics
		yoga

3 Read the clues. What sport is it?

This is a team sport. You play this sport outside. There are eleven players in the team. You have to pass the ball to other players with your foot. You have to kick the ball into the goal to get a point. You mustn't touch the ball with your hands.

4 Work in pairs. Choose a sport from this page and write some clues for it. Use the words in the box to help you.

dive goal hit hole individual
kick ride run throw wear

Reading

1 Do you watch the Olympic Games? Do you know when the next Olympic Games are? Do you know where they are? Tell a partner.

2 Quickly read the texts about the Olympics on page 107. What is the best way to complete the title?

a winners
b dreams
c losers
d records

3 Read the texts again. What do you think happened next? Write a sentence in each gap. Then compare your ideas with a partner.

4 Turn to page 130 to check your answers.

5 Do you know any interesting sport stories?

Extend your vocabulary – *win* and *beat*

We *win* a game, competition, election or prize.

She won the gold medal.

We *beat* someone in a game, competition or election.

He beat the other runners in the event.

Complete the sentences with the correct word.

1 She always *beats / wins* me at tennis.
2 He *beat / won* his first race when he was twelve years old.
3 Russia *beat / won* the USA for the gold medal.
4 I don't think I can *beat / win* him. He's too good.
5 We were *beaten / won*. The other team was better.

a judogi with black belt

b 1966 Brazil World Cup kit

c Olympic swimsuit

i pair of skis

d ball

e gloves

f clubs

g helmet

h net

Olympic ____

They are the world's fittest people. But even Olympic athletes have had their share of difficult, heart-breaking or just plain embarrassing moments ...

Short cut – 1904 Olympics, St Louis, USA

American Fred Lorz crossed the finish line of the Olympic marathon with a time of 3 hours and 13 minutes. He had beaten the second runner by 15 minutes. Lorz looked happy and fresh, and smiled for the photographers. Just before they gave him the gold medal, the race officials arrived to make a complaint. They took away the medal, and Lorz was banned from races for a year. ____

A helping hand – 1908 Olympics, London, England

The Italian Dorando Pietri was one of the unluckiest marathon runners. When he arrived in the stadium, he was very tired. The people were cheering, but Pietri couldn't continue. He fell down and got up again four times. Finally, around seven metres from the finish line, he fell down again and didn't move. Worried officials ran over and picked him up. He crossed the finish line and won the gold medal. But a few hours later the Olympic committee had to take it away from him again. They said he couldn't be the winner because ____

The extra distance – 1952 Olympics, Helsinki, Finland

Pakistani swimmer Mohammed Ramzan made history in the 1,500-metre swimming event. When all the other swimmers had finished, Ramzan continued going. He swam an extra 100 metres. ____

A new Olympic record – 2000 Olympics, Sydney, Australia

Eric Moussambani of Equatorial Guinea became one of the most loved athletes of the 2000 games. His race was the 100-metre freestyle swim. He jumped into the pool and started swimming. After the first 50 metres he was very tired. He went more and more slowly and almost stopped in the middle of the pool. The officials worried that he was drowning. But Moussambani continued and finally finished the race with a time of 1 minute and 52 seconds, the slowest in the history of the Olympics. Still, Moussambani was happy. ____

Grammar

*Ramzan **continued** but the other swimmers **had stopped**.*
*He **didn't win** the race because the officials **had helped** him.*

- use the past perfect to talk about an event in the past that happened before another event or before a specific time in the past

1 Complete the texts with the correct words.

couldn't go had lost told

1992 Olympics, Barcelona, Spain
A few minutes before his fight, Iranian boxer Ali Kazemi suddenly ____ the judges that he ____ in the ring. He ____ his gloves!

had fallen had thrown lost

1956 Olympics, Melbourne, Australia
Soviet rower Vyacheslav Ivanov only had his gold medal for a few minutes before he ____ it. He was so happy he ____ the medal into the air and it ____ into the lake.

2 Write reasons why these things might have happened. Then share your ideas with a partner.

The athlete stopped running and started crying.

Maybe she had lost the race. Maybe she had hurt her leg. Maybe she had won.

1 The football match was cancelled at the last minute.
2 The number one tennis player lost the first match of the tournament.
3 An important basketball player could not play in a game.

G Grammar focus – explanation & more practice of the past perfect on page 148

Speaking

1 Look at the sports questionnaire and write one more question.

2 Ask other students the questions. If someone answers *yes*, write their name and ask the follow-up question.

A: *Do you play a sport?*
B: *Yes, I do.*
A: *Which sport?*
B: *Volleyball.*

Glossary

ban (*verb*) – to say officially that someone is not allowed to do something
drown (*verb*) – to sink under water and die
embarrassing (*adjective*) – making you feel nervous, ashamed or stupid
official (*noun*) – someone with an important position in an organisation

Find someone who ...

plays a sport.	Which sport?
watches a sport on television.	Which sport?
is a fan of a team.	What team?
has been to a football match.	When?
hates sports.	Why?
used to play a team sport.	When? What sport?
doesn't do any sport.	Why not?
____	____

Part 4

Speaking
A visit to the doctor

Reading & Listening
At the doctor's

Grammar
Reported statements

Vocabulary
Say, tell* and *ask

Speaking
Fitness questionnaire

Speaking

1 Look at the pictures. What do you think is happening?

2 Work in pairs. Choose one of the pictures and prepare a short dialogue to go with it.

3 Present your dialogue to another pair.

Reading and Listening

1 2.69 Read and listen to the dialogue between a doctor and his patient. What is the good news and the bad news?

2 Cover the dialogue and try to remember. What did the doctor say …

1 about red meat?
2 about salt?
3 about coffee?
4 about exercise?
5 about work?

3 2.70 Listen to Mr Cartwright talking to his wife about his doctor's appointment. What information is the same and what is different?

D = Doctor **P** = Patient

D: Ah yes. Mr Cartwright. Please sit down. How are you feeling?
P: I'm fine, thanks.
D: I have the results of your tests.
P: Oh good!
D: Hm.
P: What's the matter?
D: Well, there's good news and bad news. Good news and bad news.
P: Give me the bad news first.
D: The bad news is, well, you aren't very fit. And you need to change your eating habits.
P: Do you mean a diet?
D: I'm afraid so, Mr Cartwright. I'm afraid so.
P: I see.
D: You can't eat any more red meat. It's really not good for your heart.
P: Oh.
D: You also have to stop putting salt on your food.
P: Er. No meat, no salt.
D: That's right. The other thing is coffee. Do you drink coffee?
P: Um, yes. Four or five cups a day actually.
D: Yes, well, only one cup of coffee a day from now on. One cup of coffee. And no sugar in the coffee, either.
P: Is that all?
D: No. You also need to do exercise. I have a daily exercise plan for you here.
P: Every day?
D: That's right, Mr. Cartwright. Daily means every day.
P: What's the good news, doctor?
D: The good news is that you are healthy enough to go back to work. You can start again tomorrow!
P: Oh.

Grammar

'You are healthy.' She **said** I **was** *healthy.*
'You can eat some red meat.' She **said** *I* **could** *eat some red meat.*

- use reported speech to say what another person said
- in reported speech, the verb often goes one tense *back*
  present simple → past simple
  present continuous → past continuous
  present perfect → past perfect
  past simple → past perfect
- other words such as pronouns can also change in reported speech

1 Change the sentences to direct speech. Then check your answers in the conversation on page 108.

The doctor told me she had the test results.
'I have the test results.'

1 I said I was fine.
2 She said that I wasn't very fit.
3 She told me that I couldn't eat any more red meat.
4 She told me that I also needed to do some exercise.

2 Change these sentences to reported speech. Then decide who said each one: the doctor or the patient.

'I've felt very ill for the last five days.'
The patient said he'd felt very ill for the last five days.

1 'You don't have a fever.'
2 'I've ordered some more tests.'
3 'I'm not feeling very well at the moment.'
4 'Going to work isn't a good idea.'
5 'I can give you a sick note.'
6 'I have a bad headache.'

G Grammar focus – explanation & more practice of reported statements on page 148

Vocabulary

1 Complete the story with *say*, *tell* or *ask*.

I went to the doctor last week.
He ______ me 'How do you feel?'
I ______ him I didn't feel very well.
He gave me some pills.
First, he ______ me I should take one green pill with a glass of water when I got up.
Then he ______ 'Take one red pill with a glass of water after lunch.'
Finally, he ______ that I should take a blue pill with a glass of water before bed.
I ______ the doctor 'What's the matter with me?'
He ______ me that I wasn't drinking enough water.

2 2.71 Listen and check your answers.

3 Complete the rules with *say*, *tell* or *ask*.

a ______ always takes an object such as *me*, *him*, *her*, *the people*.
b ______ never takes an object.
c ______ can take an object, but doesn't have to.

Speaking

1 Choose **four** of these questions. Then work in pairs and discuss the questions.

- Do you do any exercise?
- Do you prefer to exercise alone or with friends?
- Did you do a sport when you were younger? Which one?
- What are the best ways to keep fit?
- Do you have a family doctor? What's their name? How long have you been a patient?
- What food do you think is the healthiest?
- Do children in your country get enough exercise?

2 Work with a new partner. Report two things you learnt from your first partner. Use *said* or *told* plus reported speech.

Function globally describing illness

Warm up

Read the label. Find words or phrases with these meanings.

1 takes away pain for a short period of time (4 words)
2 a woman who is going to have a baby (1 word)
3 ask (1 word)
4 don't let children touch this (6 words)
5 might make you feel tired or sleepy (3 words)

How to read a drug label

Active ingredient
Acetaminophen 500g

Active ingredient tells you what chemicals are in the medicine.

Uses
Temporarily relieves minor pains due to
- headache
- backache
- the common cold
- toothache

Uses or *Indications* tell you what to use the medicine for.

Warnings
Do not use with alcohol. If you are pregnant, consult a doctor before use. Keep out of reach of children. May cause drowsiness.

This section tells you things you shouldn't do or take with this medicine.

Directions
Adults and children 12 years and older. Take two tablets every four to six hours as needed. Do not take more than 8 tablets in 24 hours.

This section tells you the recommended dosage – how much you should take and how often.

Listening

2.72 Listen to a conversation in a pharmacy. What is the man's problem? What does he buy?

cough syrup

tablets

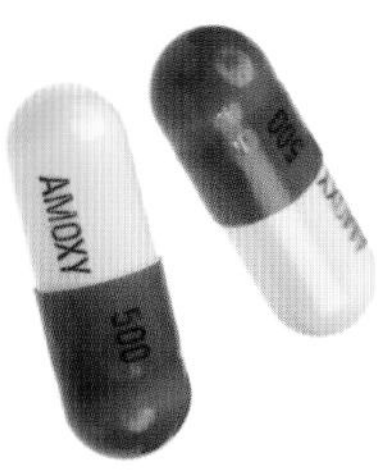

antibiotics

Language focus: talking about illness

Listen to the conversation again and complete the phrases with one or more words.

1 I ________ for a sore throat.
2 We ________ this syrup or these tablets.
3 ________ better?
4 How many ________?
5 How often ________?
6 ________ before mealtimes.
7 ________ allergic to any ________?
8 I'm afraid ________ a prescription for that.
9 You ________ a doctor if ________.

Speaking

Work in pairs and choose **one** of the tasks below.

A Look at the audioscript on page 157 and practise the conversation. Then create a similar conversation with different information.

B Roleplay a visit to the pharmacy. Use the new expressions you have learnt.

A: you are visiting another country. You don't feel well. Think of your symptoms.
B: you work in a pharmacy. Listen to A and suggest something for the problem.

Global English

Sports English

by David Crystal

Sports commentary is very familiar these days but it only arrived with the start of radio and television broadcasting. The term *sports announcer* was first used in 1923, soon followed by *sporting commentator* in the UK and *sportscaster* in the US. The modern British term, *sports commentator*, dates from the 1930s.

Sports commentating sounds easy, but it's difficult to do well, especially on radio, where a long silence can mean disaster. Detailed knowledge of the sport, keen observational skills, the ability to **think on your feet**, and above-average linguistic skills are essential. To make the job easier, commentators can use 'tricks of the trade' such as formulaic expressions. In horse racing there are certain things commentators always say at particular moments such as *They're off!*, *in the lead*, and *into the straight they come.* This means there is less for them to remember and it helps with fluency.

Each sport has its own style, reflecting the atmosphere and momentum, from the wild excitement of football (*It's a GO-O-O-AL*) to the quiet tones of snooker. There's distinctive grammar and vocabulary too. Commentaries are the perfect place to find the English present tense, both simple and continuous (*he's looking for a chance ... he scores ...*), and incomplete sentences (*Beckham to Kaka ... back to Beckham ...*).

But if you're looking for new vocabulary, you'll find more in the keep-fit disciplines, such as yoga (with its hundreds of words taken from Sanskrit), Pilates (with its unusual pronunciation taken from the name of its founder, Joseph Pilates, 'puh-lah-teez'), and the combination of yoga and Pilates *yogalates*. And that's just **the tip of the iceberg** of new linguistic blends. If you're into *exertainment* (exercise + entertainment) you'll know about the many kinds of *exergaming* (exercise + gaming). The neologisms keep your tongue linguistically fit too.

Glossary

above-average (*adjective*) – good, better than normal

discipline (*noun*) – a subject or sport

formulaic expression (*noun*) – an expression that has been used lots of times before

keen (*adjective*) – very strong

linguistic blend (*noun*) – a mixture of two or more words

neologism (*noun*) – a new word or expression, or an existing word with a new meaning

sports commentator (*noun*) – a person whose job is to give a description of a sporting event on television or radio as it happens.

Warm up

Read the definition of *sports commentator*. Are there any well-known sports commentators in your country? What are they famous for?

Reading

1 Read the text *Sports English*. Tick (✔) the topics that are mentioned. There are two topics you do not need.

a different words for sport
b sports commentary
c style of speaking
d winners and losers
e English grammar
f new vocabulary

2 Read the text again and find examples of …

a something you need to be a good sports commentator.
b a 'formulaic expression' that helps commentators sound more fluent.
c an example of an incomplete sentence used in sports.
d a 'keep-fit' sport.
e a neologism.

Language focus

1 Look at the expressions in **bold** in the text. Answer the questions below.

1 If you *think on your feet*, you …
   a are a very quick runner.
   b have good ideas and make decisions quickly.
   c get nervous in a difficult situation.
2 If we say something is *the tip of the iceberg*, it means …
   a there is a lot more of it that you can't see.
   b there is only a little bit of it.
   c it is a very dangerous thing.

2 Put each of the expressions into an example of your own. Tell a partner.

Speaking

Work in pairs and ask each other the questions.

- Do you enjoy listening to commentators?
- What sports do you like to watch?
- Do you do any *exergaming*?

UNIT 9

Writing an online post

Reading

1 Read the question from an online forum. Then read Darina's response and tick (✔) the suggestions she makes.

take exercise at home go for a walk
go on a diet have an exercise plan
join a gym spend a long time exercising
take up a new hobby/sport walk or cycle to work

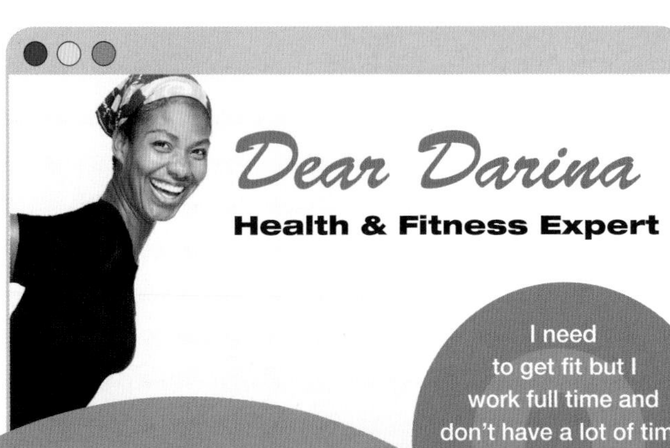

I need to get fit but I work full time and don't have a lot of time to take exercise. Can anyone out there help please?
Carla

Good question Carla. I had the same problem but I found some solutions. If you don't have much time, just try to be more active in your daily life. You could walk or cycle to work instead of taking the bus or driving. If you take a bus, why not get off one stop early and walk a bit longer? And try to go for a walk in your lunch break instead of sitting inside in front of a computer. It will make you feel a lot better!

If you have free time in the evening, consider joining an evening class. You could take up yoga, martial arts or dancing. That way you will meet people and have fun too! Alternatively, you could buy exercise equipment, a rowing machine or an exercise bike, and use it while you watch TV.

Most importantly, you should have a clear plan and stick to it. And you should exercise for a short time, but regularly. Hope this helps. Good luck and don't give up!

2 Do you do any of the things that Darina suggests? Which do you think is the best suggestion?

Writing skills: giving examples

We use *for example*, *for instance* or *like* to give examples.

1 Find three places in Darina's answer where she could use one of these phrases. Where would you put a comma?

2 Complete the sentences with the correct phrase.

1 Try not to use your car so much. You could walk or cycle to the supermarket, ________.
2 Why not take up a sport ________ tennis or swimming?
3 Consider getting up an hour early to take exercise. ________, you could go jogging, or go for a swim.

Language focus: giving advice

1 Look at Darina's response again and underline the phrases she uses to give advice.

2 Correct the sentences below.

1 Why you don't see a doctor?
2 Consider to go for a long walk.
3 You could starting a sport.
4 Just try be positive.
5 You should to watch less TV.

Preparing to write

1 Work in pairs and choose one of the problems below. Think of some solutions.

2 Work with another pair who chose the same problem. Did they think of the same solutions as you?

- I feel tired all the time.
- I'm having problems getting to sleep at night.
- My seven-year-old son loves fast food and unhealthy snacks. How can I get him to have a more healthy diet?

Writing

Write an online response like Darina's to give advice. Use your notes and the useful phrases below to help you.

Suggesting alternatives

- Instead of …, you could …
- Don't …; … instead!
- Alternatively, you could …
- Most importantly, you should …

Global review

Grammar

1 Put *had to, didn't have to, could* or *couldn't* in the gaps.

1 I broke my leg so I ________ stay in hospital for six weeks, and I ________ walk for two months.
2 I ________ have an X-ray because I hadn't broken any bones.

2 Complete the sentences with the past simple or past perfect form of the verbs in brackets.

1 Before the world ________ (develop) modern medicine, the Arabs ________ (found) many hospitals.
2 I ________ (feel) sick because I ________ (eat) too much chocolate.

3 Complete the sentences to report the conversation.

1 A: You're working too hard and you don't take enough exercise.
The doctor told me I ________________________________.
2 B: I'll give up my job and take up jogging.
I said I ________________________________.

Vocabulary

Complete the sentences with the correct word.

beat	feel	have	have	hurts
matter	see	sore	take	won

1 You look ill – what's the ______?
2 I ______ sick.
3 I've got a ______ throat.
4 You should ______ a doctor.
5 I have to ______ an operation.
6 I ______ a fever.
7 My back ______.
8 You should ______ two aspirin.
9 He ______ me at table tennis.
10 Manchester United ______ the football match.

Speaking and Writing

1 Work in pairs. Tell each other about a race, match or sporting event you have seen. Then work in a new pair and report what your partner told you.

2 Work in groups of four. Write down a real or invented problem. Then swap your papers and write advice using *should, shouldn't, must* or *mustn't*. Who gave you the best advice?

Study skills

Using your dictionary: exploring collocations

Collocations are words which are often used together.

catch a cold
(not ~~take~~ a cold)

a sore throat
(not a ~~hurt~~ throat)

1 Look at these entries in the *Macmillan Essential Dictionary*. Notice how the dictionary gives information about collocations.

health (*noun*)
1 the condition of your body, especially whether or not you are ill: *His health improved once he stopped working. She's had serious **health problems**. Lola is 85 and still **in very good health**. My father has been **in poor health** for some time.*

Adverbs often used with ill
critically, dangerously, desperately, gravely, seriously, severely + ill: used for saying that someone is very ill

2 Work in pairs. Try to guess which verb is **not** used with each noun below. Then check in a dictionary.

1	a get	b do	c make	d take	… exercise
2	a keep	b build	c get	d be	… fit
3	a call	b see	c order	d send for	… a doctor
4	a cause	b feel	c make	d relieve	… pain

3 Complete the sentences with the correct option. Then check your answers in a dictionary.

1 I have a *strong / heavy* cold today.
2 He was *strongly / violently* sick last night.
3 I had a *heavy / splitting* headache yesterday.
4 She is a *heavy / strong* smoker.

4 Use your dictionary to answer the questions.

1 You can *catch a cold*. What else can you *catch*?
____
2 You can have a *healthy diet*. What other adjectives go with *diet*? ________________
3 You can have a *sore throat*. What else can be *sore*?
____
4 You can *recover from an illness*. What else can you *recover from*? ________________

Remember to record collocations, not just words, in your vocabulary notebook.

UNIT 10 New & Old

Part 1

Reading & Listening
Brave New Words

Vocabulary
New words in context

Grammar
Defining relative clauses

Writing
Definitions game

Reading and Listening

1 Look at the book cover and read the introduction to *Brave New Words* on page 115. What do you think the book is about?

2 2.73 Listen to an interview with the author of the book. Number the topics in the order you hear them.

abbreviations ___
borrowing words ___
combining parts of words ___
combining words ___
giving new meanings to words ___

3 Listen again and match the example words to the categories in exercise 2.

brunch DVD mouse
text messages tsunami
virus windows

4 Can you think of any new words in your language? What are they? What do they mean?

Vocabulary

1 Work in pairs. Look at the pictures below and read the captions. Try to guess the meanings of the words in bold.

Useful language

- Maybe it means … • It could be a kind of …

2 Match the words in exercise 1 to the definitions below. There are two definitions you don't need.

a kind of car that produces carbon ___
the amount of greenhouse gases that an activity produces ___
a Japanese love story which is written for women ___
to search for something on the internet using the search engine Google ___
a number game from Japan which is now popular in English newspapers ___

3 Work in pairs and ask each other the questions.

- Do you ever google information on the web?
- Have you ever googled your own name?
- Have you ever done a sudoku puzzle?
- What are some ways of reducing your carbon footprint?

John tried to **google** information about Kenya for his next holiday.

His **carbon footprint** is bigger than yours.

Susan missed her stop because she was trying to finish her **sudoku.**

Brave New Words

Grammar

Kerry Maxwell is someone ***who*** *has written books about new words in English.*
Tsunami is a Japanese word ***which*** *has become used very frequently in English.*
Brunch is a meal ***that*** *people can have at 11 o'clock in the morning.*

- use relative clauses to give information about something or somebody
- if we are talking about a person, we use *who* or *that*
- if we are talking about an object, we use *which* or *that*

1 Complete the definitions with *who* or *which*.

1 An *emoticon* is …
 a a symbol ______ is used in email messages to show emotion.
 b a strong emotion ______ people have about computers.
 c a person ______ doesn't show their emotions.

2 An *internaut* is …
 a a person ______ works for a short time in an office.
 b a game ______ people play on the internet.
 c a person ______ spends a lot of time on the internet.

3 *Hinglish* is …
 a a person ______ comes from the country Hingland.
 b a language ______ is a mixture of English and Hindi.
 c clothing from India ______ you wear on your head.

2 Work in pairs. What is the correct definition of each word?

G **Grammar focus** – explanation & more practice of defining clauses on page 150

The English language is a dynamic phenomenon. Like your mobile phone or the grass in the garden, it is continually changing, constantly acquiring new characteristics. Many of these changes occur because of the way we live. As the world changes we need to find different ways of describing it, to fill the gaps in our vocabulary for new ideas.

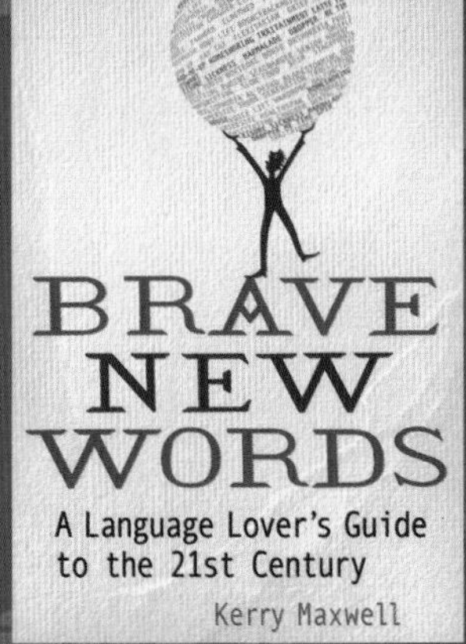

BRAVE NEW WORDS
A Language Lover's Guide to the 21st Century
Kerry Maxwell

Some of these words will stay in our vocabulary, others won't. Only time will tell. But the ways we make new words will continue, and will create many more new expressions in years to come.

Kerry Maxwell

Kerry Maxwell is a lexicographer – a person who writes dictionaries. She has worked on many dictionary projects, including the *Macmillan English Dictionary*. She lives in England.

Writing

Work in pairs and choose one of the boxes. You are going to write definitions for some new words.

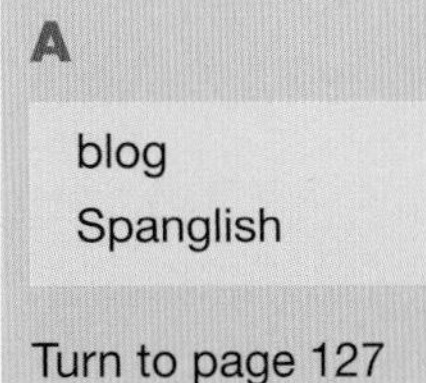

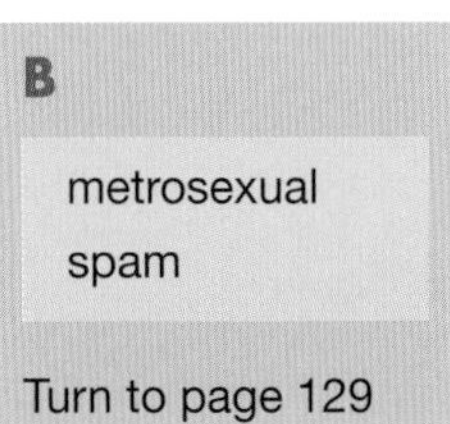

UNIT 10 New & Old

Part 2

Vocabulary
Places

Reading
New places in a new world

Grammar
Definite article (*the*)

Speaking
Famous quotes

Vocabulary

1 Put the words in order from small to large. Use your dictionary to help you.

capital city continent country ~~planet~~ state / province town village

2 Circle the word that does not belong in each group of words.

1	Africa	Asia	Armenia
2	Dallas	Italy	Frankfurt
3	Mars	Jupiter	Singapore
4	California	Canada	Washington
5	Tokyo	Liverpool	Paris

3 Choose a word from exercise 1 and write down some examples. Then include a word that does not belong. Work in pairs and tell each other your words. Say the odd one out.

Reading

1 Work in pairs. How many places in North America can you write down in one minute? Compare your list with another pair.

2 Read *New places in a new world* on page 117 and write the names in the correct places.

New Jersey New Mexico New Orleans Newfoundland New World New York

3 Read the text again and complete the sentences with the same place names.

1 ________ is not part of the US.
2 ________ is very big and dry.
3 ________ was nearly destroyed.
4 ________ has many people who travel somewhere else for work or school.
5 ________ was a Dutch colony.
6 ________ was visited by Vikings.

4 Find words in the text with these meanings.

1 a place where something is born
2 to start a city or organisation
3 very special or unusual
4 to travel regularly to and from work

5 Do you know any other place names that begin with the word *New*? What are they?

Extend your vocabulary – words that mean *new*

New is a very general word. We sometimes use words with more specific meanings that sound more natural in a particular context.

equipment, computers	*advanced, cutting-edge, modern*
ideas	*innovative, fresh*
films, books	*latest, recent*
something just bought and never used	*brand new*

Replace the word *new* in the dialogues with a more suitable word or phrase.

1 A: Is that your car?
B: Yes, it's *new*. I bought it yesterday.

2 A: Did you speak to Jeffrey about the project?
B: Yes, I did. It was very helpful. He has a lot of *new* ideas.

3 A: What did you see?
B: The *new* Tarantino film. It was OK.

New places in a new world

In the 15th century Pietro Martyr d'Anghiera, an Italian historian, was the first person to give the continent of America the name De Orbo Novo, which means the ____________. The prefix *New* for cities and regions of North America has since become very popular. Here we collect a few *new* places to live.

Nicknamed the Big Apple, ____________ is located in the American state of the same name. It's probably the most famous city in North America. Founded on Manhattan Island in the 17th century by the Dutch, it was originally called New Amsterdam.

____________ is a province in Canada. The province is in the east of the country, and the newest one to join Canada – it joined in 1949. Because of its position it was one of the first parts of North America that European voyagers discovered. The Vikings arrived here in AD 1000.

One of the largest states in the United States of America, ____________ is in the south-west of the country. It is a very dry state, and is covered in mountains and desert. The state was one of the original Wild West states, and the population is unique for its Spanish, American and Native American mix.

Capital of the state of Louisiana in the south, ____________ is famous for its multicultural history and nightlife. It is the birthplace of jazz. The city went through a dark period in its history in 2005 when it was almost destroyed by Hurricane Katrina.

Located in the north-east, ____________ is one of the original 13 states of the USA. Because it's so close to New York, people sometimes call it the bedroom state as hundreds of thousands of its people commute to and from the city for work or school every day.

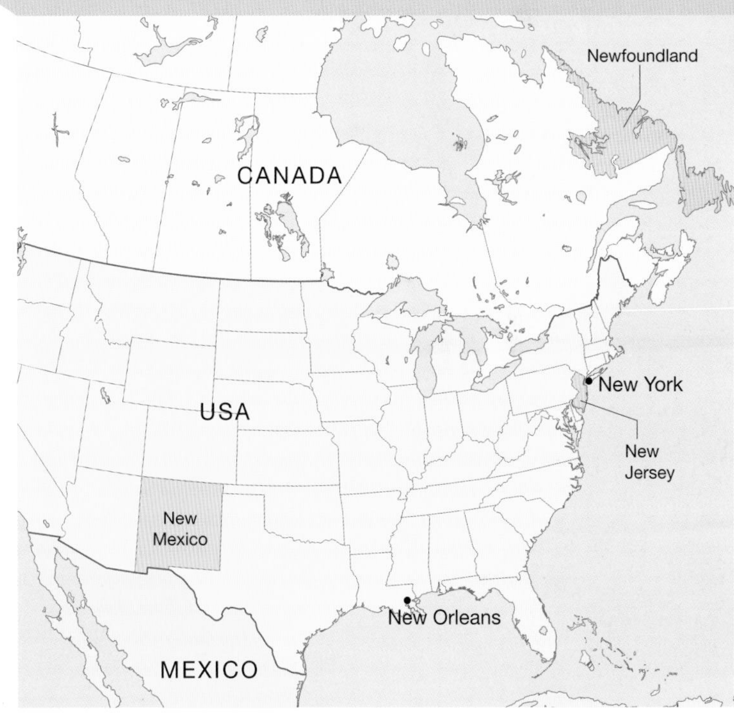

Grammar

1 Look at the highlighted examples of *the* in the text and match them to the rules a–d below.

We use *the* when …

a there is only one of this person or thing.
b this person or thing has been referred to before, in the text.
c it is part of a name.
d it is in a superlative phrase.

2 Choose the correct words to complete the texts.

New England is *a / the* region of *the / -* United States. It consists of *the / -* six states: Maine, New Hampshire, Vermont, Massachusetts, Rhode Island and Connecticut. New England was one of *a / the* first places *an / -* English people lived in America in 1620.

New Zealand is *a / the* country in the Pacific Ocean. It consists of two islands, *a / the* North Island and *a / the* South Island.

New Guinea is *an / the* island in the Pacific Ocean. It is *the / -* second largest island in *the / -* world. *An / The* island is divided into two parts – *the / an* Indonesian provinces of Papua and West Papua and *the / -* country of Papua New Guinea.

G **Grammar focus** – explanation & more practice of *the* on page 150

Speaking

1 Work in pairs. Read the incomplete quotes about America and try to finish them with your own ideas. Then work with another pair and share your ideas.

2 Which are the best quotes? Are they positive, negative or neutral about America?

3 Read the original quotes and find out who said them on page 130.

I think the most un-American thing you can say is …

America is a …

There is not a black America and a white America and Latino America and Asian America – there's …

All great change in America begins at the …

England and America are two countries separated by a …

UNIT 10 New & Old

Part 3

Vocabulary & Speaking
Transport

Pronunciation
Consonant clusters

Reading
Old but loved: the Trabant

Grammar
Verb form review

Speaking
Driving questionnaire

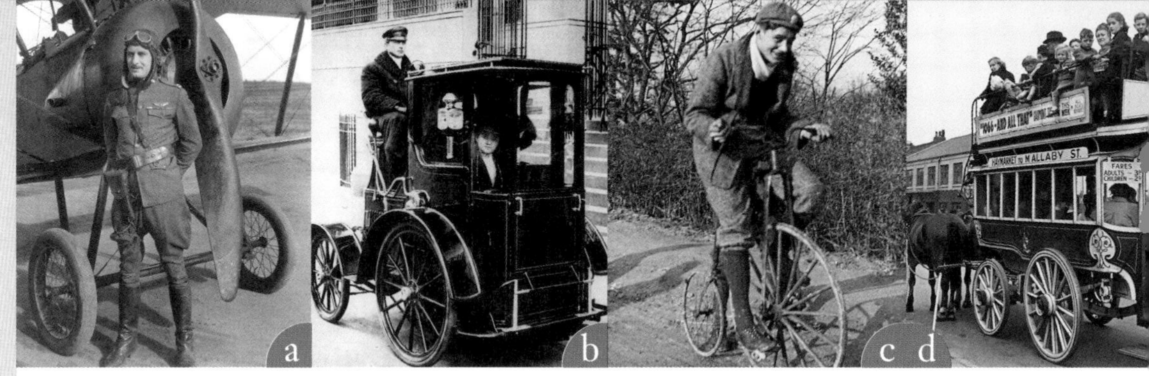

a b c d

e

f

g h

Vocabulary and Speaking

1 What different forms of transport can you see in the pictures?

2 Which of these forms of transport …

1 have **wheels**?
2 go on **tracks**?
3 have **wings**?
4 have an **engine**?

3 Tick (✔) the correct collocations to complete the chart.

	drive	ride	get on get off	get in get out of
a car				
a bus				
a motorbike				
a bicycle				
the underground				
a plane				

4 Work in pairs and ask each other the questions.

- Which of the forms of transport have you used?
- Which do you prefer?
- Are there any forms of transport that you never use?

Pronunciation

1 2.74 Listen and repeat the consonant clusters and words.

/pl/, plane
/tr/, tracks
/st/, stop
/str/, street

2 2.75 Listen and repeat the sentences.

1 The driver tried to drive the train off the tracks.
2 There are still school students at the bus stop.
3 The station is straight down this street.
4 Please don't play with the plastic planes.

Reading

1 You are going to read an article about an old car called the *Trabant*. Which of these words do you expect to see?

cheap communist fans fly
Germany jokes nostalgic
pollution smoke speed

2 2.76 Read and listen to *Old but loved: the Trabant* on page 119 and check your answers.

3 Read the text again and find …

1 three reasons why the Trabant isn't a very good car.
2 three reasons that show the Trabant is still popular.

4 Work in pairs and discuss the questions.

- Have you ever seen a Trabant?
- Are there any objects that make you nostalgic for the past? Which ones?

Old but loved: the Trabant

They're old, they're slow and they're noisy and smelly. So why are Trabants still popular?

They are still driving on Germany's roads, and have been in many popular films and music videos. The Trabant was East Germany's answer to the Volkswagen during communist times, and more than three million models were made before the fall of the Berlin Wall in 1989.

The name *Trabant* means *fellow traveller*. The first cars appeared in 1957. They were made from duroplast, a material made from recycled cotton from Russia. The Trabant needed 20 seconds to go from 0 to 100km per hour, and had a maximum speed of 112km per hour. The engine of the Trabant was special in two ways – it made a lot of noise and smoke and it produced a lot of pollution. Experts estimate that the Trabant produced five times more carbon monoxide than modern European cars.

Trabants – also called *Trabis* – have now become collectors' items, and have many fan clubs across Eastern and Western Europe. People say that the Trabi makes them nostalgic for old times. Even the smell of Trabi exhaust smoke is popular, and has been sold on the internet. Fan clubs celebrated the 50th anniversary of the Trabant in 2007, and many say there are going to be celebrations for the 75th anniversary in 2032. There are many jokes about the Trabant, but if this kind of popularity continues the Trabi will have the last laugh.

Q: How do you double the value of a Trabant?
A: Put petrol in it.

Q: Why is a Trabant the longest car?
A: There's 3 metres of car, followed by 15 metres of smoke.

Q: Why is the Trabant's rear window heated?
A: To keep your hands warm while you push it.

Glossary

exhaust (*noun*) – gases or steam that are produced by an engine as it works

model (*noun*) – a type of vehicle that a company makes

nostalgic (*adjective*) – remembering happy times in the past

Grammar

1 Look through the text and try to find examples of the verb forms below.

- regular and irregular past tense verbs
- a continuous tense
- the present perfect
- *going to* future
- a first conditional
- past simple passive

2 Complete the text below with the correct form of the verbs.

The Model T

The American Ford automobile company __________ (*exist*) since 1903, and is one of the biggest car manufacturers in the world.

One of its first cars __________ (*be*) the Model T. It __________ (*build*) by the Ford Motor Company from 1908 to 1927. The president of the company, Henry Ford, __________ (*want*) a car that was practical and not expensive for the American worker. The Model T __________ (*cost*) around $300 and __________ (*go*) up to 70km an hour. It was one of the first cars to be produced on an assembly line. By 1930 Ford __________ (*produce*) more than 10 million Model T cars, making it the most popular car in the world.

As newer cars came out in the 20s and 30s, people __________ (*start*) making jokes about the Model T. But today there __________ (*be*) still fan clubs of the Model T, and people still __________ (*drive*) them at old car shows.

3 Complete the questions with the correct form of the verbs.

1. When __________ (*do*) you get your driving licence?
2. __________ (*do*) you have a car? What kind?
3. What __________ (*be*) your first car?
4. What is the fastest you __________ (*ever travel*) in a car?
5. What is the furthest you __________ (*ever travel*) in a car?
6. __________ (*have*) you ever __________ (*have*) an accident?
7. If you __________ (*can have*) any kind of car, what __________ (*you choose*)?
8. __________ (*be*) the traffic bad where you live?
9. __________ (*be*) it difficult to find parking where you live?
10. Who __________ (*be*) the best driver in your family?

Grammar focus – explanation & more practice of verb forms on page 150

Speaking

Choose **six** of the questions from exercise 3 above. Work in pairs and ask each other the questions.

Part 4

Listening
Two classic board games

Grammar
Both, neither

Vocabulary
Games

Pronunciation
Sentence stress & intonation

Speaking
A board game

Listening

1 Look at the pictures of two classic board games. Do you know these games? Have you ever played them? Tell a partner.

2 2.77 Listen to a talk about the invention of these games. How many things do they have in common?

3 Listen again. What do these words and numbers mean?

Great Depression architect
by hand two or more 750 million+
200 million 80+ 25+

Extend your vocabulary – words that mean *make*

Make is a very general word. We sometimes use words with more specific meanings that sound more natural in a particular context.

things made in factories	*build, manufacture, produce*
buildings	*build*
problems, changes, effects	*cause, produce, generate*
new things	*design, develop, invent, create*

Replace the word *make* in the sentences with a more suitable word. More than one answer may be possible.

1 The traffic in the afternoon *makes* lots of problems.
2 They are *making* a new bank in the centre of town.
3 These cars are *made* in a Korean factory.
4 Alfred Butts *made* the game of Scrabble.
5 We've *made* a new computer program.

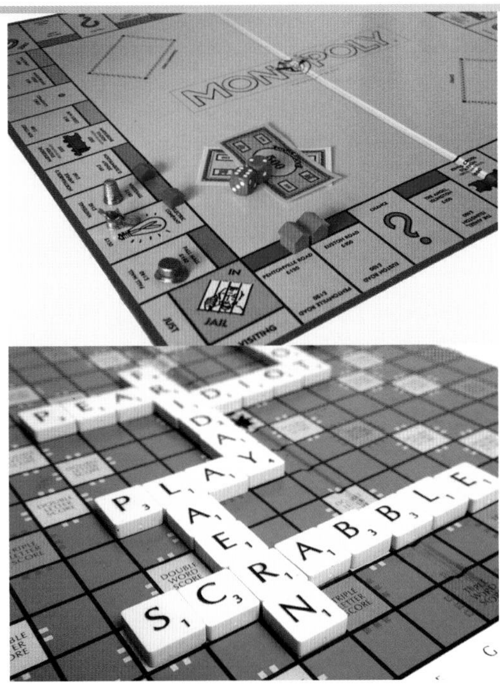

Grammar

***Both games are** successful today.*
***Neither game was** successful at first.*
***Both of them** are successful worldwide.*

- use *both* to talk about two things. *Both* is used with a plural noun and a plural verb
- use *neither* to say something negative about two things. *Neither* is used with a singular noun and verb
- use *both of / neither of* with a plural noun or pronoun

1 Work in pairs. Make sentences about Scrabble and Monopoly using these prompts plus *both* or *neither*.

1 games are American
2 inventors didn't have a job
3 games are played on a board
4 games were not accepted by toy companies at first
5 games are published in over 25 languages

2 Work in pairs. How many sentences can you make with these ideas in three minutes?

Both of us …
Neither of us …

G Grammar focus – explanation & more practice of *both* & *neither* on page 150

Vocabulary

1 Complete the texts with the words in the box.

board	dice	miss a turn	
money	points	square	turn

Scrabble

Scrabble is played with letters. Different letters are worth different ________.

Each player has seven letters per ________. You put the letters on the ________ and make words.

The object is to get as many points as possible. If you can't make a word with your letters, you ________.

Monopoly

In Monopoly, players roll a ________ and move their counter around the board.

Each ________ on the board represents a property. If you land on someone else's property, you have to pay them. The object is to collect property and make ________.

2 Look at the pictures of other classic board games. Match each sentence to one of the games.

1 The object is to **reach the end** of the board first.
2 You **move around the board** and answer questions.
3 There are sixty-four black and white **squares** on the board.
4 The objective is to **win** different coloured **pieces** when you answer correctly.
5 There are snakes and ladders on the board. You **go down** snakes and **up** ladders.
6 The object is to **capture** your opponent's king.

3 Work in pairs and discuss these questions.

- Have you ever played any of these games? Do you like them?
- What other board games do you know?

Pronunciation

1 Put the words in the correct order to make useful game phrases.

1 the roll dice
2 turn it's your
3 a card pick
4 turn miss a
5 again go
6 highest goes rolls first whoever
7 your is which piece
8 cheating no

2 2.78 Listen and check your answers. Then listen and repeat the phrases. Try to copy the intonation.

Speaking

Work in groups of three or four. You are going to play a board game. Turn to page 131 and read the rules. Then play the game.

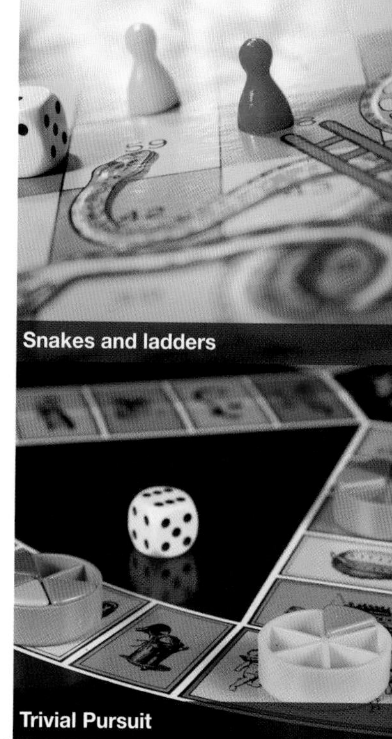

Snakes and ladders

Trivial Pursuit

Chess

Function globally ending a conversation

Warm up

Work in pairs and choose two of the situations below. Have a one-minute conversation for each situation.

Situations

1 You are strangers. It's very hot outside. A: start talking to B about the weather.
2 You are friends. A: you are learning to drive. Tell B about it.
3 You work together. A: you are going somewhere special on holiday. Tell B about it.
4 A: you are the boss. The company is closing. Tell B the bad news.

Listening

1 2.79–2.80 Listen to two conversations. Match each one to a situation above.

2 Listen again and answer the questions.

Conversation 1: How does each man feel?
Why do you think they feel this way?

Conversation 2: Does the woman have good memories of the past? Why?

Language focus: ending a conversation

1 Put the words in the correct order to make useful phrases.

1 going be I'd better
2 now really I go to have
3 off to rush sorry
4 I be going should

2 2.81 Listen and check your answers. Then listen and repeat the phrases.

3 2.82 Listen to the end of five conversations. Which words do you hear? Complete the words with the correct letters.

1 a _ _ _ _ y
2 r _ _ _ t
3 O _
4 w _ _ l
5 a _ _ r _ _ _ t

Speaking

Work in pairs and choose **one** of the tasks below.

A Repeat the warm up activity using the new expressions you have learnt.

B Create a conversation using **only** the words and phrases in the box. You can use each phrase more than once. Then practise the conversation.

Anyway. Bye. Goodbye. OK. OK, then. Right.
See you. Well. Well, I'd better … Yes, of course.

Global voices

Warm up

1 Write down three words you have learnt recently.

2 Work in pairs and give definitions for your words. Try to guess what your partner's words are.

Listening

1 2.83–2.89 Listen to seven people talking about their favourite words and expressions in English. Number them in the order you hear them.

awesome and legendary ___
gorgeous ___
harmony ___
love ___
Oh my god! ___
perhaps ___
you know ___

2 Listen again and choose the correct answers.

1 Arthur, from France, likes the expression because he hears it in *songs / movies*.
2 Diego, from Italy, thinks there *are / aren't* a lot of very interesting words in English.
3 Kristina, from Russia, heard people use her favourite word when they talked about *clothes / the weather*.
4 Elodie, from Switzerland, likes her favourite word because of the *spelling / pronunciation*.
5 Semih, from Turkey, says his favourite words make him feel *happy / funny*.
6 Bea, from England, thinks her favourite words are useful because *they give her time to think / they mean lots of different things*.
7 Guy, from England, likes his word because of the sound, the structure and because *it doesn't exist in any other language / it exists in lots of other languages*.

Arthur, France Diego, Italy

Language focus: *you know*

1 Bea talks about the expression *you know*. Read about how we use this expression in the box. Which uses did Bea talk about?

Language note: We can use *you know* …

a for emphasis.
*It's a difficult test, **you know**.*
b while we think about what to say next.
*This is a brand new phone. It's a, **you know**, phone with video and music and everything.*
c when we are giving extra information about something.
*Have you seen my English book? **You know**, the black one.*
d before we start to talk about a person or thing.
***You know** the Japanese restaurant near the school, well, it's closing.*

2 Add *you know* to the sentences below.

1 This is an old card game. (add emphasis)
2 I don't feel well. (add *a headache, sore throat*)
3 He won an Olympic medal. (add emphasis)
4 I had never heard that before. (begin with *You know*)
5 It was a big change in her life. (add *she was never the same again*)

Speaking

1 Write down two or three of your favourite words or expressions in English.

2 Work in small groups. Tell each other about your favourite English words or expressions and why you like them.

Useful phrases

- My favourite expression is ...
- I like it because ...
- I don't know why.
- I agree. It's a good word.
- I don't know. I don't like it very much.

Kristina, Russia Elodie, Switzerland Semih, Turkey Bea, England Guy, England

10 Writing a report on studies

Reading

1 Magdalena's new English teacher has asked her to write a report on her previous language course. Read her report. Did she enjoy the course? Why?

Last summer I studied English for one month in language school in Oxford. We had classes every morning for three hours and in the afternoons we had free time or went on excursions. My class was elementary level and there were twelve students in the class, from all over the world. I stayed with host family.

We studied book called *Move* and sometimes we played games and listened to songs. We did a lot of speaking and listening activities and we did some grammar exercises as well. There was study centre in the school. Sometimes I worked there in the afternoons.

I enjoyed the course very much. I really liked speaking with my classmates and our teacher was very patient and kind. I wasn't so keen on studying grammar. I think I made progress in my speaking, but I should try to speak more. I also need to improve my grammar and writing.

2 Fill in Magdalena's end-of-course report.

Magdalena has completed a ______ - month course at ______ level. She has worked hard, both in class and after class in the ______. She has made good progress, especially in her ______. However, she could still improve this, and also needs to work on her ______ and ______.

Language focus: *a* / *an* for new information

We use *a* or *an* when we write about a singular noun for the first time. Magdalena wrote:

Last summer I studied English for one month <u>in language school</u> in Oxford.

She should write:

Last summer I studied English for one month <u>in a language school</u> in Oxford.

Find three more places where Magdalena forgot to use *a* or *an*, and correct them.

Writing skills: giving reasons

Make your writing more interesting by giving reasons using *because* or *as*.

I enrolled on a language course as / because I wanted to improve my English.

1 Put these reasons in the correct places in Magdalena's report.

1 … because I wanted to practise speaking outside the class.
2 … as this was a good way to practise on my own.
3 … because the classes were always varied and never boring.
4 … as I am quite shy.
5 … as I still make a lot of mistakes.

2 Complete the sentences with a reason.

1 I want to improve my English as ______.
2 Sometimes studying English is difficult because ______.

Preparing to write

Work in pairs and make notes about your present English course. Use the useful phrases below to help you. Follow this format:

Paragraph 1: information about the course (level, length, number of students)
Paragraph 2: what you did during the course
Paragraph 3: feelings about the course, progress and areas to improve

Describing language activities and skills

- We did a lot of / some listening / speaking activities.
- We did a lot of / some grammar exercises / games / communicative activities.
- I really enjoyed speaking but I wasn't so keen on grammar.
- I need to improve my reading / writing / study skills.
- I need to extend my vocabulary / work on my pronunciation.
- I made progress in my listening / writing / grammar.
- I should try to speak more / be more accurate.

Writing

Write a report like Magdalena's for your next English teacher. Use your notes to help you. Check your report for *a* / *an* and correct past tense forms.

Global review

Grammar

The writer of this text has forgotten to use *the* eleven times. Put it in the correct places.

China is largest country in East Asia. Population of China is over 1.3 billion, and capital city is Beijing. One of most famous buildings in Beijing is *Forbidden City*. This is where last Emperor of China lived, and today it is visited by millions of tourists every year.

Sport is very popular in China, and 2008 Olympic Games were held in Beijing. Every morning many people practise *qigong* and *tai chi chuan* in city's parks. *Go* is another famous game that was invented in China. It is played with counters on a board, and objective is to control largest part of board.

Vocabulary

Complete the puzzle by reading the clues.

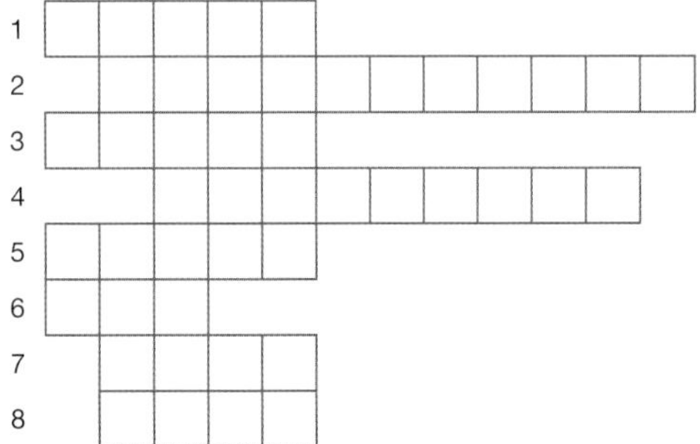

1 I've just bought a ______ new washing machine.
2 A fast form of public transport in a city.
3 Too much traffic can ______ pollution.
4 We should try to reduce our carbon ______.
5 You put your counters on this to play Scrabble.
6 You have to ______ on a bus before you travel.
7 When everyone else has played, it is your ______.
8 How do you get to work? I ______ a motorbike.

Speaking and Writing

1 Work in small groups. Describe a long journey you have made and list what you had to do. Who used the most forms of transport?

2 Work in pairs and find three new words you have learnt in this book. Then complete the definitions.

1 ________ This is a person who ________.
2 ________ This is a place where ________.
3 ________ This is a thing which ________.

3 Work with another pair and read your definitions. Try to guess the words.

Study skills

Evaluating your pronunciation

1 Work in pairs and discuss the questions.

1 How would you describe your pronunciation of English?
  a I speak like a native speaker.
  b My pronunciation is generally clear and comprehensible
  c I have a noticeable accent but my pronunciation is mostly comprehensible.
  d I have a strong accent and am sometimes hard to understand.
2 How would you like your pronunciation to be?
3 Which of these areas of pronunciation have you studied in this class?
  a vowel sounds
  b consonant sounds
  c consonant clusters
  d word stress
  e the relationship between sounds and spellings
  f sentence stress
  g rhythm
  h intonation
4 Which area is the strongest for you?
5 Which area do you need to work on most?

2 Work in pairs. Answer the questions.

1 Which is your favourite English sound?
2 Which is your least favourite?
3 Which sound do you find most difficult to pronounce?

3 Which of these strategies for improving pronunciation have you tried?

* Practise reading a short text aloud. Record it and listen to it, or ask a friend to listen and comment.
* Repeat the lines from a DVD or a song.
* Use a pronunciation book and CD.
* Practise repeating the pronunciation of new words with an electronic dictionary such as the Macmillan English Dictionary.
* Choose an area of pronunciation or a sound you want to improve. Focus on it for a few minutes every day when you are speaking.
* Other ideas.

4 Compare your ideas with a partner and decide how you can improve your pronunciation. What will you try?

Unit 1, Speaking (page 11)

1 Complete the questions with the correct word – *do* or *are*.

2 Ask your partner the questions.

3 Answer your partner's questions.

Family questions

- ______ you have a big family?
- How many brothers and sisters ______ you have?
- ______ you have family in other countries?
- ______ you in touch with them?
- How often ______ you in touch with your grandparents or grandchildren?
- ______ you have family reunions? How often?

Unit 2, Reading (page 18)

1 Read the text about vegemite. Are there any interesting or surprising facts in the text? Write them down.

2 Read the text again. Write down a few key words to help you tell your partner about the text.

3 Tell your partner about vegemite.

Vegemite

Vegemite is a dark brown food paste from Australia. You can put it on sandwiches, toast or crackers. It tastes salty and bitter and is not very popular in the world except in Australia and New Zealand. Vegemite has strong cultural associations in those countries, and many say it is a comfort food. Vegemite has very high levels of vitamin B, and during the 1940s the Australian army bought large amounts of it for the soldiers. According to the Prime Minister of Australia's website, Vegemite is 'the taste of Australia' and some Australians even take a jar with them when they travel to other countries.

jar of vegemite

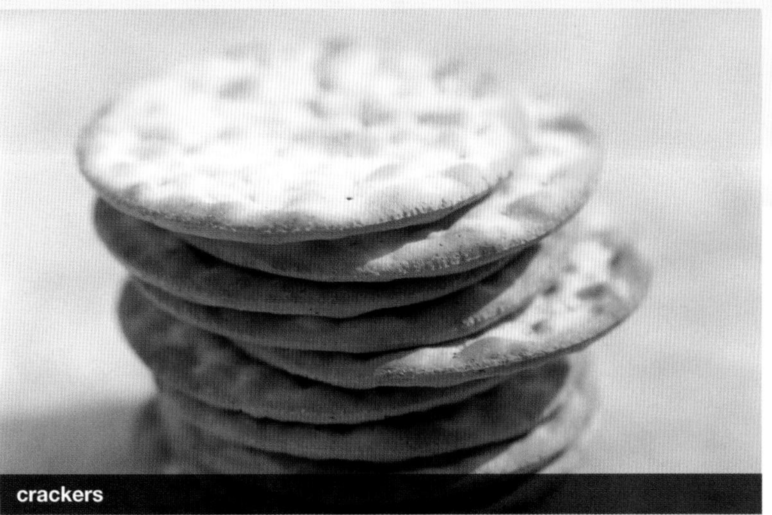
crackers

Glossary

bitter (*adjective*) – has a strong sharp taste that is not sweet

jar (*noun*) – a glass container for food, with a lid and a wide opening

paste (*noun*) – a food that is made by crushing meat, fish or vegetables

Unit 6, Grammar (page 69)

1 Write the questions for numbers 1–5 of the quiz. Use the comparative form of the adjective.

Which is faster, the speed of light or the speed of sound?

2 Work with a student from group B. Ask your questions.

3 Listen to questions 6–10 and try to answer them. Write the correct answers in the table.

	Column A		Column B	Answer
1	microscope	modern?	X-ray	microscope
2	speed of light	fast?	speed of sound	speed of light
3	theory that the Earth is round	old?	theory of gravity	theory that Earth is round
4	oil	expensive?	coal	oil, but coal is more polluting
5	hydrogen	heavy?	nitrogen	nitrogen is more than 10 times heavier than hydrogen
6	Jupiter		Saturn	
7	100°F		100°C	
8	one metre		one yard	
9	one megabyte		one gigabyte	
10	-40°F		-40°C	

Unit 9, Vocabulary (page 102)

1 Watch your partner and guess what's wrong.

2 Mime the symptoms below. Your partner must guess what's wrong.

1 You have a headache.
2 Your wrist hurts. / You have a sore wrist.
3 You're sneezing.
4 Your back hurts. / You've got a sore back.

Unit 10, Writing (page 115)

1 Read the definitions of the new words. Copy them down and then write two incorrect definitions for each word.

2 Work with a pair who chose different words. Read out your words and definitions.

3 Listen to the other pair's words and definitions and try to guess which is correct.

A blog is a diary or journal which is on the internet.
Spanglish is a language which is a mixture of Spanish and English.

Communication activities: Student B

Unit 1, Speaking (page 11)

1 Complete the questions with the correct word – *do* or *are*.

2 Answer your partner's questions.

3 Ask your partner the questions.

Friends questions

- How often ______ you talk to your neighbours?
- ______ you in touch with anybody you went to primary school with?
- ______ you go out with your colleagues from work or school?
- ______ you keep in touch with friends by email, phone, or face to face? How often?
- ______ you have any online friends or acquaintances?

Unit 2, Reading (page 18)

1 Read the text about popular comfort food for men and women. Are there any interesting or surprising facts in the text? Write them down.

2 Read the text again. Write down a few key words to help you tell your partner about the text.

3 Tell your partner about comfort food in North America.

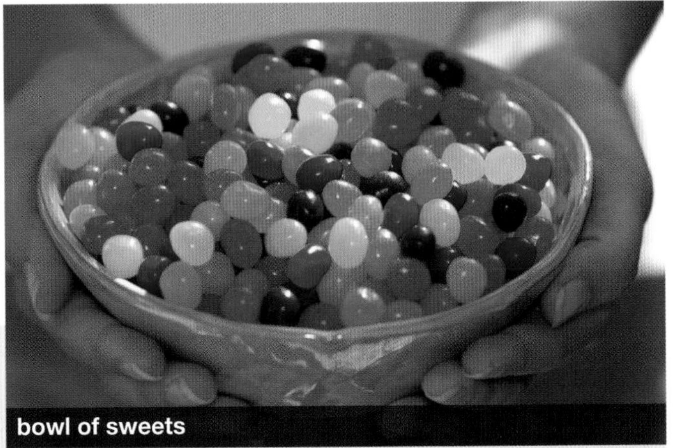
bowl of sweets

Comfort food for men and women

An article published in the American journal, *Physiology and Behavior*, shows differences between men and women and their choice of comfort food.

A survey of over 1,000 North Americans found that women often prefer snack-related comfort food while men prefer more meal-related comfort food. In particular, more women said they liked food like sweets and chocolate while men liked things such as pizza, pasta, steak or casseroles. Women often felt guilty and less healthy than men about their comfort food choices.

The researchers think that the differences between men and women may be because men like hot, prepared meals (that someone else made) while women look for easy comfort food that needs less preparation.

casserole

Glossary

casserole (*noun*) – a deep dish with a lid, used for cooking in the oven, or the mixture of food that is cooked

guilty (*adjective*) – ashamed and sorry because you have done something wrong

prefer (*verb*) – to like or want something more than something else

Unit 6, Grammar (page 69)

1 Write the questions for numbers 6–10 of the quiz. Use the comparative form of the adjective.

Which is further from the sun, Jupiter or Saturn?

2 Work with a student from group A. Listen to questions 1–5 and try to answer them. Write the correct answers in the table.

3 Ask your questions.

	Column A		Column B	Answer
1	microscope		X-ray	
2	speed of light		speed of sound	
3	theory that the Earth is round		theory of gravity	
4	oil		coal	
5	hydrogen		nitrogen	
6	Jupiter	far from the sun?	Saturn	Saturn
7	100°F	hot?	100°C	100°C; 100°F is only 37°C
8	one metre	long?	one yard	a metre is 1.09 yards
9	one megabyte	big?	one gigabyte	a gigabyte
10	-40°F	cold?	-40°C	they are the same temperature

Unit 9, Vocabulary (page 102)

1 Mime the symptoms below. Your partner must guess what's wrong.

1 You have a toothache.
2 You have a sore leg. / Your leg hurts.
3 You're coughing.
4 You've got a fever.

2 Watch your partner and guess what's wrong.

Unit 10, Writing (page 115)

1 Read the definitions of the new words. Copy them down and then write two incorrect definitions for each word.

2 Work with a pair who chose different words. Listen to their words and definitions and try to guess which is correct.

3 Read out your words and definitions.

A metrosexual is a young man who enjoys good clothes, an attractive home and a good personal appearance.
Spam are emails that are sent to many people and are not wanted.

Additional material

Unit 2, Function globally (page 26)

PIZZA PALACE

Pizza (choose your own toppings) ....
Mushrooms ....
Salami ....
Ham ....
Cheese ....
Tomato ....
Onion ....
Green or Red Pepper ....

Drinks ....
Cola ....
Water ....
Fruit Juice ....

The Liner Diner

Please wait to be seated.

- *Choose from our large self-service buffet.*
- *Great selection of fish and seafood. Ask your waiter for recommendations.*
- *Order your drinks and coffee from the waiter.*

BARNABY'S CAFÉ

Today's special
Cream of chicken soup
or
Green salad

Vegetarian lasagne
or
Traditional steak and potato pie

Dessert
Ice cream
Fresh fruit

Unit 9, Reading (page 106)

Short cut

He had travelled by car for 11 miles of the marathon!

A helping hand

Olympic officials had helped him cross the line.

The extra distance

Ramzan thought that he hadn't finished the race.

A new Olympic record

He had never swum in a pool of that size before.

Unit 10, Speaking (page 117)

1 Read the full quotes below. Do you think they are positive, negative or neutral about America?

2 Do you know any famous quotes about your country? Tell your partner.

“All great change in America begins at the dinner table.”

Ronald Reagan, former US President

“I think the most un-American thing you can say is 'You can't say that'.”

Garrison Keillor, American writer

“England and America are two countries separated by a common language.”

George Bernard Shaw, Irish writer

“America is a mistake, a giant mistake.”

Sigmund Freud, Austrian psychologist.

“There is not a black America and a white America and Latino America and Asian America – there's the United States of America.”

Barack Obama, US President

Unit 10, Speaking (page 121)

Rules

1 Play this game in groups of three or four. You need one coin and one board to play.
2 Each person needs a counter. Put the counters on the square marked Start.
3 Decide who is going first.
4 The first player tosses a coin. If the coin lands heads up, move your counter forward two squares. If the coin lands tails up, move your counter forward one square.
5 If you land on a grey square, follow the instructions. If you land on a red square, speak in English for one minute about the topic on the square.
6 The winner is the person who gets to the end of the board first.

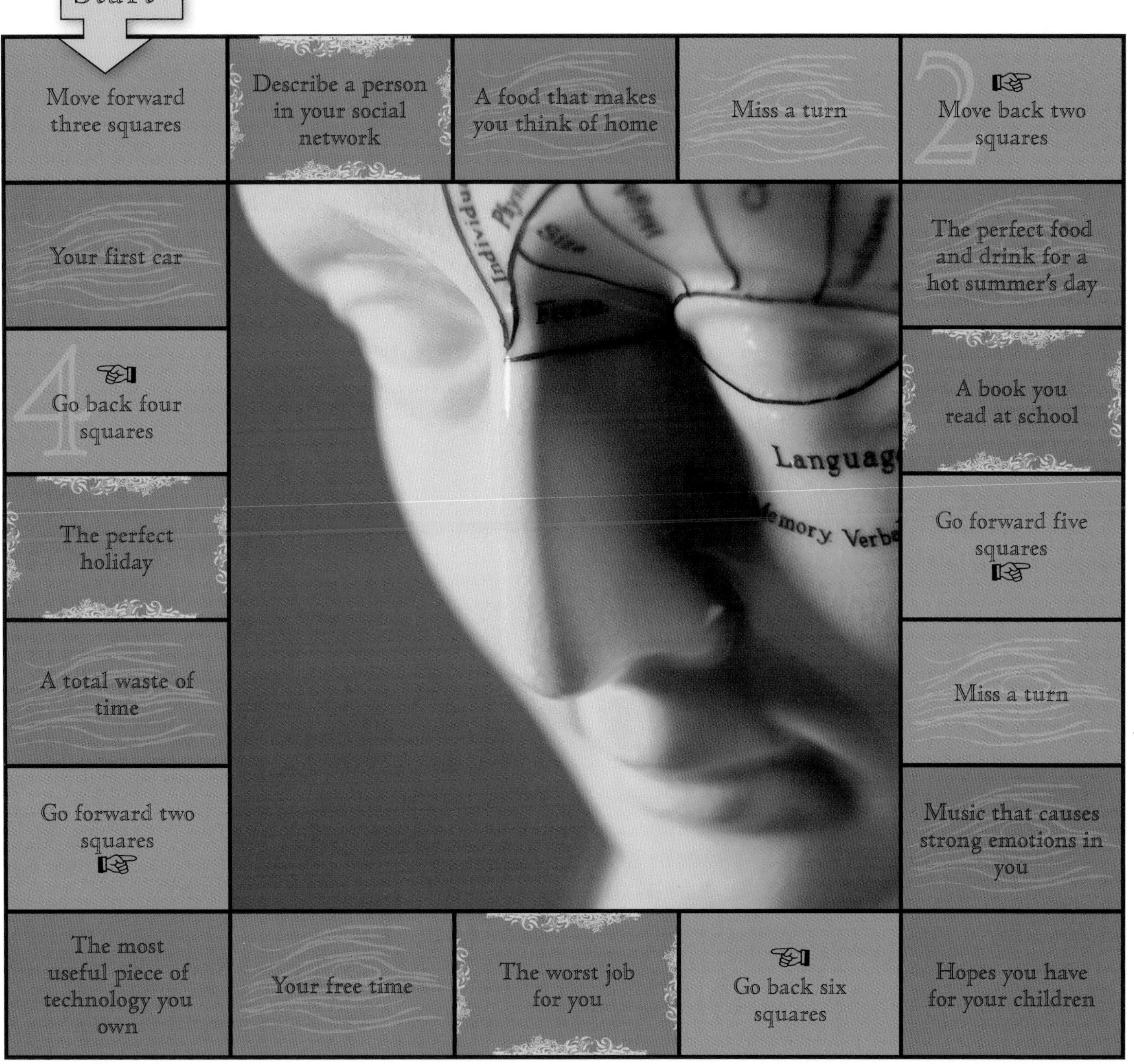
Start
Move forward three squares
Describe a person in your social network
A food that makes you think of home
Miss a turn
Move back two squares
The perfect food and drink for a hot summer's day
A book you read at school
Go forward five squares
Miss a turn
Music that causes strong emotions in you
Hopes you have for your children
Go back six squares
The worst job for you
Your free time
The most useful piece of technology you own
Go forward two squares
A total waste of time
The perfect holiday
Go back four squares
Your first car
Language
Memory Verbal

Grammar focus

Unit 1

Word order in question forms

Yes / No questions

In *yes / no* questions the verb goes before the subject:
*They **are** from Spain.* → ***Are** they from Spain?*

In present simple or past simple questions, the auxiliary verb *do / did* goes before the subject.
She speaks English. → ***Does** she speak English?*
She learnt French. → ***Did** she learn French?*

Wh- questions

Question words (*What? Where? Who? When? Why? How?*) go at the start of a question.
***Where** do you live? **When** were you born?*
***What** is your favourite sport?*

What and *How* questions

Use *how* and *what* with nouns and adjectives or adverbs to start questions.
***What** pets do you have?* ***What** kind of dog is it?*
***How** expensive was it?* ***How** often do you feed it?*

Use *like* in questions to ask about appearance or personality and characteristics.
*What does she look **like**? – She's tall and wears glasses.*
*What's that new restaurant **like**? – Noisy but the food is good.*

Present simple, frequency

Affirmative	Negative	Question	Short answers *Yes*	Short answers *No*
I / You / We / They **work**.	I / You / We / They **don't work**.	**Do** I / you / we / they **work**?	**Yes**, I / you / we / they **do**.	**No**, I / you / we / they **don't**.
He / She / It **works**.	He / She / It **doesn't work**.	**Does** he / she / it **work**?	**Yes**, he / she / it **does**.	**No**, he / she / it **doesn't**.

Use the present simple to talk about:
- habits and routines.
  *He **gets up** at seven o'clock.*
  *They **don't go** to bed late.*
- things that are always true.
  *The sun **rises** in the east.*
  *Water **boils** at 100°C.*

We use frequency adverbs and expressions of frequency with the present simple. Frequency adverbs (*always, usually, often, sometimes, hardly ever, never*) go between the subject and the verb, except with the verb *to be*.
*We **always** have lunch at 1 pm.*
*He is **always** late for class.*

Expressions of frequency (*every day, twice a week, on Mondays*, etc.) usually go at the end of the sentence. They go at the beginning of the sentence when we want to emphasise when or how often.
*We go shopping **on Saturdays**.*
***On Saturdays**, we go shopping.*

Present continuous

Affirmative	Negative	Question
I **am ('m) working**.	I **am ('m) not working**.	**Am** I **working**?
You / We / They **are ('re) working**.	You / We / They **are not (aren't) working**.	**Are** you / we / they **working**?
He / She / It **is ('s) working**.	He / She / It **is not (isn't) working**.	**Is** he / she / it **working**?

Use the present continuous to talk about:
- things happening now or about now.
  *We **are watching** TV.* *I'**m learning** English.*
- temporary situations.
  *He **is living** in London at the moment.*

The present continuous is often used with time expressions such as *now, these days, at the moment* and *this week / month / year*.

Some verbs (stative verbs) aren't used in the present continuous: *agree, appear, believe, forget, hate, hear, know, like, love, mean, need, own, prefer, realise, remember, see, seem, want*

Unit 1 Exercises

Word order in question forms

1 Decide if these questions are in the correct (✔) or incorrect (✘) order. Then correct the mistakes.

1 They are from Japan?
2 Where do your parents live?
3 Did learn you a language at school?
4 Who is your favourite actor?
5 Do like you chocolate?
6 How many students there are in the class?

2 Use the words to write the questions.

where born? Where were you born?
1 family from? ______
2 speak any languages? ______
3 job? ______
4 live? ______
5 married? ______
6 children? ______
7 play any sports? ______
8 favourite writers? ______
9 like music? ______

What and *How* questions

3 Write the questions.

How tall is he? He's nearly two metres tall.
1 What ______? My car's red.
2 How ______? I'm thirty.
3 What ______? My teacher's tall with short, dark hair.
4 How ______? The school is ten kilometres from here.
5 What ______? I have a Visa and an American Express.
6 How ______? It doesn't rain here very often.
7 What ______? She's nice, really friendly.

Present simple, frequency

4 Put the words in the correct order to make sentences.

his parents / on Sundays / my boyfriend / visits
My boyfriend visits his parents on Sundays.
1 check / every day / their email / they
2 TV / in the daytime / watch / hardly ever / we
3 goes / once a week / she / to the cinema
4 meet / at weekends / sometimes / I / colleagues from work
5 all evening / spends / he / on the internet / often
6 usually / my wife / before me / gets up
7 for a meal / go out / we / every Saturday night

Present continuous

5 Complete the dialogue with the correct form of the present simple or present continuous.

A: Where (1) ______ (*you / work*) at the moment?
B: In a hotel in Italy. My boyfriend (2) ______ (*live*) in Italy at the moment too.
A: (3) ______ (*you / like*) it there?
B: It's great. I (4) ______ (*prefer*) the lifestyle in Italy. In London everybody (5) ______ (*work*) long hours. People (6) ______ (*not enjoy*) life as much.
A: (7) ______ (*you / speak*) Italian?
B: Not very well, but I (8) ______ (*take*) classes now and I (9) ______ (*learn*) the language quite quickly. We (10) ______ (*not plan*) to go back to England for a while.

Unit 2

Countable / uncountable nouns, *some, any*

Countable and uncountable nouns

Countable nouns can be singular or plural. Most plural forms end in *s*.
Put it on your ***plate****. Where are the* ***plates****?*

Some plural countable nouns are irregular:
child – children
woman – women
man – men
Uncountable nouns don't have a plural form.
Do you take ***milk*** *and* ***sugar*** *in tea?*

Language note: Some words can be countable or uncountable.
I like coffee. (= the drink)
Can I have a coffee? (= a cup of coffee)

These are some common uncountable nouns: *accommodation, advice, bread, furniture, information, news, traffic, weather*

some and *any*

Use *some* and *any* with plural nouns or with uncountable nouns. We usually use *some* in affirmative sentences and *any* in negative sentences and questions.
Do you have ***any*** *plates?*
We need to buy ***some*** *milk.*

Use *a / an* with singular nouns.
I don't have ***a*** *plate. You need* ***an*** *egg for that recipe.*

a lot of, a little, a few, (not) enough, much, many

Use quantifiers before a noun to show the quantity or amount of something.

- *a little* and *much* are used with uncountable nouns: ***a little*** *coffee, too* ***much*** *sugar*
- *a few* and *many* are used with plural countable nouns: ***a few*** *apples, too* ***many*** *bananas*
- *a lot of* and (*not*) *enough* are used with uncountable nouns and plural nouns: ***a lot of*** *pasta,* ***not enough*** *vegetables*

Language note: *much / many* are usually used in negative sentences and questions or with *too*.
A lot of / lots of is usually used instead of *much / many* in affirmative sentences. *There's* ***a lot of*** *salt in this dish.*
We use *a lot* to answer the question *How much / many …?*

The infinitive with *to*

Use the infinitive with *to* after some verbs: *agree, arrange, decide, forget, hope, learn, manage, mean, need, offer, prefer, promise, refuse, remember, try, want, would like*
You need to eat slowly. Remember to add sugar.

Language note: we don't use *to* after modal verbs such as *can / can't* and *must*. (See Grammar focus 5 page 140 for more on modals.)
I ***can drink*** *one glass of wine, but no more.*

Use the infinitive with *to* after adjectives.
It's ***healthy to eat*** *salad. It's* ***good to try*** *different foods.*

Infinitive of purpose

We use the infinitive with *to* when we talk about the purpose of something or why we do something.
I eat lots of vegetables to get important vitamins. (= because I want to get)
You use a corkscrew to open wine. (= so that you can open)

Language note: We can use *in order to* instead of *to* in these sentences. *For* isn't used in these sentences.
I eat lots of vegetables ***in order to get*** *important vitamins.*
Not: ~~*I eat lots of vegetables for to get important vitamins.*~~

Unit 2 Exercises

Countable / uncountable nouns, *some, any*

1 Complete the sentences with *a / an*, *some* or *any*.

1 I'm going shopping. Do we need ____________ eggs?
2 Can I have ____________ large cola and two coffees please?
3 I'd like ____________ information about restaurants in the area.
4 There's ____________ bread left, but there isn't ____________ butter.
5 I'm making ____________ big cake for my son's birthday.
6 I need ____________ advice about vegetarian food.
7 Let's buy ____________ new furniture for the dining room.
8 I need ____________ onion for this dish.

a lot of, a little, a few, (not) enough, much, many

2 Underline the correct quantifier in each sentence.

1 A: I'm afraid there's too *much / many* milk in this.
B: Sorry, I forgot you only like a *few / little* in coffee.
2 A: How *much / many* biscuits would you like?
B: *A lot / A lot of*!
3 A: We have *lots of / much* space. Why don't you come and visit?
B: Thanks but I *don't have enough / have too little* days off.
4 A: My wallet was here *a little / a few* minutes ago!
B: I'm afraid there are *lots of / many* pickpockets here, sir.

3 Choose one of the dialogues in Exercise 1. Think about what is happening and who is speaking. Write the next two lines.

The infinitive with *to*

4 Read the text about a Japanese drink. Complete the text with *to* or nothing (–).

Sake is rice wine. The Chinese first learnt ___to___ make sake, but now it is the traditional drink of Japan. To make sake you need (1) ______ cook rice in water. It is important (2) ______ use a special kind of rice. You can (3) ______ serve sake warm or cold. In Japan people prefer (4) ______ drink warm sake in winter and cold sake in summer. You are meant (5) ______ drink sake with friends. Tradition says you mustn't (6) ______ pour sake for yourself. So if you drink sake in Japan, remember (7) ______ pour it only for other people.

Infinitive of purpose

5 Make six sentences.

1 I went to the baker's	to	a	meet our friends.
2 He looked round the café		b	celebrate her birthday.
3 She smiled at me		c	show she wasn't angry.
4 He went into the garden		d	buy some bread.
5 We cycled into town		e	find a good table.
6 They organised a party		f	pick some tomatoes.

Unit 3

Past simple and past continuous

Past simple

Affirmative	Negative	Question
I/You/He/She /It/We/They **worked**.	I/You/He/She /It/We/They **did not (didn't) work**.	**Did** I/you/he /she/it/we/they **work**?

-ed spelling

- for most verbs add *ed*: *look – look**ed***
- for verbs ending in *e*, add *d*: *smile – smile**d***
- for verbs ending in *y*, change the *y* to *ied*: *study – stud**ied***.
  (But verbs ending in vowel + *y* are regular: *play – play**ed***).
- for verbs ending in consonant-vowel-consonant, double the consonant and add *ed*, eg *stop – sto**pped***

Use the same form for all persons (*I, you, he, she, it, we, they*) except for the verb *to be*.
Some verbs have an irregular affirmative form:
have – had, go – went, see – saw, think – thought.
Use the past simple to talk about completed actions in the past.
*I **watched** a good film at the weekend.*
*I **bought** a book about history of art last week.*

Past continuous

Affirmative	Negative	Question
I **was working**.	I **was not (wasn't) working**.	**Was** I **working**?
You/We/They **were working**.	You/We/They **were not (weren't) working**.	**Were** you/we /they **working**?
He/She/It **was working**.	He/She/It **was not (wasn't) working**.	**Was** he/she/it **working**?

Use the past continuous to describe an activity or situation in progress in the past.
*He **was watching** a film on TV.*
We often use the past continuous for activities that are interrupted by a completed action. It is used in contrast with the past simple.
*He **was watching** a film on TV when the phone **rang**.*

X

watching a film *phone rang*

While is often used with the past continuous. *When* is often used with the past continuous and the past simple.
I fell asleep ***while*** I was reading a book.
I was reading a book ***when*** I fell asleep.

Used to

Affirmative	Negative	Question
I/You/He/She /It/We/They **used to work**.	I/You/He/She /It/We/They **didn't use to work**.	**Did** I/you/he /she/it/we/they **use to work**?

We use *used to* to talk about regular actions in the past which don't happen now.
*I used **to play** the guitar.* (= but I don't play it now)

We also use *used to* to talk about situations in the past which aren't true now.
*There **used to** be an art gallery in our town.* (= but there isn't one there now)

Language note: There is no present form of *used to*. We only use *used to* to talk about regular actions in the past.
Not: ~~I ***use to*** download music.~~

Unit 3 Exercises

Past simple and past continuous

1 Use the prompts below to write what was happening yesterday lunchtime in the park.

1. What / people / do / in the park / at midday yesterday?
2. two workers / dig / a hole
3. a man / read / a newspaper / on a bench
4. a woman / eat / a sandwich – but she / not enjoy / it
5. two children / play / hide and seek
6. an old woman / walk / her dog
7. two tourists / take / photos

2 Underline the correct form of the verb in each sentence.

1. We *were cleaning / cleaned* the windows when it *was starting / started* to rain.
2. While she *was looking / looked* in the mirror, she *was noticing / noticed* her first grey hairs.
3. It *was getting / got* dark when I *was switching on / switched on* the lights.
4. They *were dropping / dropped* the sculpture while they *were carrying / carried* it inside.
5. While she *was closing / closed* the curtains, she *was seeing / saw* somebody outside.
6. I *was painting / painted* the bedroom wall when I *was falling off / fell off* the ladder.

Used to

3 Complete the sentences with *used to* or *didn't use to* and an appropriate verb.

1. He ______________ to cassettes, he didn't use to listen to CDs.
2. He ______________ the violin, but now he plays the guitar.
3. He ______________ an MP3 player but he has one now.
4. He ______________ to classical concerts, he used to go to music festivals.
5. He ______________ miserable, now he feels relaxed and happy.
6. He ______________ opera but he likes it now.

Unit 4

Future hopes and plans

Use verbs such as *hope*, *plan*, *want*, *would like* (+ infinitive with *to*) to talk about future hopes that aren't definite.
*I **want** to work in a developing country.*
*I'**d like** to be an aid worker.*

Use *look forward to* (+ verb with *-ing*) to talk about definite future plans.
*I'm **looking forward to** working in Africa next year.*

Future plans and intentions (*going to*, present continuous)

Going to

Affirmative	Negative	Question
I am ('m) going to work.	I am not ('m) not going to work.	Am I going to work?
You / We / They are ('re) going to work.	You / We / They are not (aren't) going to work.	Are you / we / they going to work?
He / She / It is ('s) going to work.	He / She / It is not (isn't) going to work.	Is he / she / it going to work?

We use *going to* to talk about what we have already decided or intend to do in the future.
*He's **going to** train to be a doctor.* (= It is already decided)
*They're **going to** work for an NGO.*

Language note: *going to go* is often replaced by *going*.
*I'm **going to go** to France next year = I'm **going** to France next year.*

Present continuous

See Grammar focus 1 on page 132 for an explanation on how to form the present continuous.

Use the present continuous to talk about future plans, in particular for arrangements with a date and time, eg plans with friends or travel arrangements.
*I'm **meeting** friends this evening.* (= I've made an arrangement with them)
*We're **going to** Egypt on holiday this year.* (= We've already arranged the holiday)

Prediction and ability (*will, be able to*)

Will

Affirmative	Negative	Question
I / You / He / She / It / We / They will ('ll) work.	I / You / He / She / It / We / They will not (won't) work.	Will I / you / he / she / it / we / they work?

Use *will* to talk about predictions or beliefs about the future. It is often used with the verbs *think*, *hope* and *to be sure*.
*I think there'**ll be** a nuclear accident.*
*I'm sure there **will be** more homeless people in the future.*

Be able to

Use *will be able to* to talk about ability or possibility in the future. We don't use *will can*.
*We **won't be able to** stop pollution.*

Language note: compare *will* and *going to*.
*We're **going to** reduce carbon emissions.*
(= definite plan / intention)
*I think we'**ll** reduce carbon emissions.*
(= prediction, may or may not happen)

Future time clauses

Future time clause		Main clause
If When Before After As soon as	+ present tense (usually present simple)	future form (usually *will*)

Use future time clauses with a present tense to talk about future predictions.
***If** we **reduce** carbon emissions, we'**ll** reduce global warming.*
It is possible to change the order of the future time clause and main clause.
***When** you **see** the film, you'**ll** be really frightened.*
***Will** we have dinner **before** we **go** to the cinema?*

Language note: we use *if* for things that might happen but aren't certain. We use *when* for things that are certain.

Unit 4 Exercises

Future hopes and plans

1 Match the sentences.

1 She's a doctor. She wants
2 He's five years old. He hopes
3 I'm a teacher. I'm looking forward
4 I'm a student. I'm planning
5 They worry about pollution. They'd like
6 We're aid workers. We're looking forward

a to working on a new project in Latin America.
b to work for an environmental organisation.
c to fight disease in developing countries.
d to starting the new school year.
e to get a good job when I leave college.
f to get a bike for his birthday.

Future plans and intentions (*going to*, present continuous)

2 Complete the sentences. Use the correct form of *going to*.

1 We ____________ (*give*) our children a future!
2 This government ____________ (*not help*) our country!
3 When ____________ (*you / stop*) this war?
4 How ____________ (*we / feed*) our children?
5 We ____________ (*not give up*)!
6 Who ____________ (*help*) the poor?
7 I ____________ (*fight*) for what I believe!
8 Cars ____________ (*destroy*) our environment.

3 Complete the dialogues with the correct form of the present continuous.

1 A: They're holding a big climate change conference at the end of the year.
B: Where ____________?
2 A: When are you meeting Lisa again?
B: ____________ after work tomorrow actually.
3 A: I'm going on holiday in June.
B: Where ____________?
4 A: What time is David coming round?
B: ____________ today, I'm afraid.
5 A: Are you working on Saturday?
B: No, ____________ at all this weekend.

Prediction and ability (*will*, *be able to*)

4 Complete the text with *will* or *won't*.

What do we know about global warming? Well, global temperatures (1) ______ increase. Sea levels (2) ______ rise and in some areas there (3) ______ be floods. But in other areas there (4) ______ be enough rain. That means farmers in some areas (5) ______ be able to grow food any more. And some animals and plants (6) ______ be able to exist in changing environments, so there (7) ______ be fewer types of animals.

5 Underline the correct verb.

1 We *are having / will have* lunch with friends tomorrow.
2 I hope you *are going to enjoy / will enjoy* your visit.
3 What *are you going to do / will you do* this evening?
4 I'm sure we *will find / are finding* a solution.
5 She*'s going to be / will be* an engineer when she leaves school.
6 What time *will you meet / are you meeting* them?
7 What do you think *is happening / will happen* tomorrow?
8 I*'m going to check / 'm checking* my email in a minute.

Future time clauses

6 Complete the sentences with the correct form of the verb in brackets.

1 I think the baby ____________ (*start*) to cry as soon as we ____________ (*get*) on the bus.
2 If you ____________ (*do*) the shopping, I ____________ (*cook*) dinner.
3 You ____________ (*be*) shocked when you ____________ (*read*) that book.
4 After he ____________ (*finish*) work, he ____________ (*go*) to the airport.
5 She ____________ (*be*) upset if he ____________ (*forget*) her birthday.
6 I ____________ (*send*) you a text when we ____________ (*arrive*).

Unit 5

Have

Affirmative	Negative	Question
I/You/We/They **have** a car.	I/You/We/They **don't have** a car.	**Do** I/you/we /they have a car?
He/She/It **has** a car.	He/She/It **doesn't have** a car.	**Does** he/she/it **have** a car?

Use *have* as a main verb to talk about possessions, relationships or characteristics.
*I **have** two brothers.*
*She **has** dark hair.*

Language note: We can't use short forms when we use *have* as a main verb. Not: ~~*I've a cat.*~~

Instead of *have* we can also use *have got* for possession. *Have got* is often used in spoken and informal English.
*I've **got** two brothers.*
*She **hasn't got** dark hair.*
***Have** you **got** any money?*

Use *have* as a main verb with certain nouns to talk about actions or experiences. For example:
- have breakfast / lunch / dinner / a drink / a coffee
- have a party / a holiday / a swim / an accident / a good time
- have a chat / a conversation / a meeting
- have an illness / a headache / a problem

Modal verbs

Use *must* and *have to* to talk about things that are necessary. We often use *must* and *have to* for rules. *Have to* is often used for something which is necessary because of a law or because someone else says it.
*I **must** finish this report.*
*He **has to** give a presentation tomorrow.* (= His boss said so)

Use *must not (mustn't)* to express prohibition.
*You **mustn't** wear jeans and trainers in the office.*

Use *don't have to* to say that something isn't necessary, but it is possible or allowed.
*Men **don't have to** wear a tie at work.* (= but they can if they want to)
Use *can* to say that something is possible or allowed.
*You **can** buy food in the staff canteen. Or you **can** eat your own sandwiches there.*
Use *can't* to say that something is not possible or allowed.
*You **can't** eat lunch at your desk.*

-*ing* forms

The -*ing* form of the verb can be:
- the subject of a sentence

***Working** long hours is very stressful.*
***Playing** chess is very relaxing.*
- the object of some verbs, for example: *love, like, dislike, enjoy, mind, can't stand*

*I like **playing** basketball.*
*I can't stand **jogging**.*
- used after prepositions: *good / bad at, interested in, tired of, excited about, bored with, instead of, in spite of*

*He's very good at **skiing**.*
*I'm excited about **going** on holiday.*

Present perfect

Affirmative	Negative	Question
I/You/We/They **have ('ve) worked.**	I/You/We/They **have not (haven't) worked.**	**Have** I/You/We /They **worked**?
He/She/It **has ('s) worked.**	He/She/It **has not (hasn't) worked.**	**Has** he/she/it **worked**?

The present perfect is formed with the verb *have* + past participle. The past participle of regular verbs is the same as the past simple. (see Grammar focus 3 page 136). Irregular verbs often have different forms, eg go – went – gone.

Use the present perfect to talk about an unspecific time in the past. Compare the present perfect and the past simple.
*I **have been** to Disneyland.* (= no specific time, present perfect)
*I **went** to Disneyland last summer.* (= specific time, past simple)

We often use the present perfect with *ever* and *never* to talk about experiences up to the present.
***Have you ever been** to an amusement park?* (= at any time in your life)
***I've never been** on a roller coaster.* (= up to now)

Language note: *have been to* = have visited a place.

Compare: *She's **been** to Germany.* (= and now she has come back home).
*She's **gone** to Germany.* (= and she's still there).

Unit 5 Exercises

Have

1 Complete the sentences with the correct form of *have*.

1 She ____________ a baby yesterday – a little girl.
2 They ____________ got a car, they cycle everywhere.
3 We ____________ a party on Sunday evening. Would you like to come?
4 Do you know him? He ____________ glasses and he ____________ much hair.
5 I ____________ breakfast most days because I'm never hungry in the morning.
6 I'm afraid he ____________ got time right now.
7 We ____________ a printer at home so I bought one yesterday.
8 ____________ a minute, please Madam?

Modal verbs

2 Read the rules and choose the correct meaning.

1 Employees mustn't make private phone calls.
  a Private phone calls aren't allowed.
  b You can make private phone calls if you want.
2 Employees don't have to work fixed hours.
  a You need to work at the same time every day.
  b You choose when you work.
3 Employees have to follow the dress code.
  a You can wear what you want.
  b There are some clothes that you can't wear.
4 Employees can take breaks when they need them.
  a You take a break when you want to.
  b You need to tell the manager when you take a break.
5 Employees must clock in and out when they start and finish.
  a It's necessary to clock in and out.
  b It isn't necessary to clock in and out.
6 Employees can't call in sick without a doctor's note.
  a It's possible to call in sick without a doctor's note.
  b You need a doctor's note to call in sick.

-*ing* forms

3 Put the words in the correct order to make sentences.

1 type / he / without / looking / can
2 training / two / had / weeks / we / of
3 new / starting / she's / job / about / her / excited
4 part / looking / is / an / good / job / the / important / of
5 at / tea / work / hate / coffee / making / I / and
6 magazines / she's / working / instead of / always / reading

Present perfect

4 Write the dialogues with the correct form of the present perfect.

1 A: you / ever / try / skiing?
  B: Yes / we / go / skiing / in France / twice / so far.
2 A: what / you / done / with the remote control?
  B: I / not see / it / but / your mum / just / watch / a programme.
3 A: my son / stop / collecting / stamps.
  B: he / ever / think / about collecting / coins?
4 A: you / be / on holiday / this year?
  B: I / have / a busy year at work / so / I / not have / any time to relax.
5 A: She still / not finish / talking / on the phone.
  B: I hope / she / not call / that friend in Brazil.

2 Choose one of the dialogues. Think about what is happening and who is speaking. Write the next two lines.

5 Choose the correct ending.

1 They've built two amusement parks outside the city …
  a and they are going to build another.
  b two years ago.
2 They went on a roller coaster last summer and …
  a they love it.
  b they loved it.
3 She's been to the water park …
  a yesterday.
  b lots of times.
4 I've never been in a haunted house because …
  a I'm scared of the dark.
  b I was scared of the dark.
5 He bought a burger in the food area but …
  a it didn't taste very good.
  b it hasn't tasted very good.
6 We've visited a great theme park in South Korea …
  a when we were on holiday.
  b and one in Hong Kong too.

Unit 6

Comparative and superlative adjectives and adverbs

	Adjective	Comparative	Superlative
One syllable adjectives and adverbs: add *-er / -est*	fast slow big	fast**er** slow**er** big**ger**	the fast**est** the slow**est** the big**gest**
Adjectives ending in *e*: add *-r / -st*	nice	nice**r**	the nice**st**
Adjectives ending in *y*: change the *y* to *ie* and add *–r / -st*	dry	dr**ier**	the dr**iest**
Two or more syllable adjectives and adverbs that end in *-ly*: *more / most* + adjective or adverb	important quickly	**more** important **more** quickly	the **most** important the **most** quickly
Irregular adjectives and adverbs	good bad	**better** **well** **worse** **badly**	the **best** the **worst**

Language note: For one-syllable adjectives ending with one consonant, double the final consonant and add *-er / -est*.
Some two syllable adjectives, especially adjectives ending in *y* can be used in either form (*more* + adjective or with *-er / -est*)
angry – angrier / *more angry*

Use comparative adjectives to compare two things or people. Comparative adverbs compare two actions. *Than* is used after comparatives.
People in warm countries are ***happier*** *than people in cold countries.*
I can run ***faster*** *than you.*

Comparative adjectives and adverbs (*a bit, much, as … as*)

We can modify comparative adjectives and adverbs with *a bit* or *much*.
That DVD player is ***a bit*** *cheaper. This one is* ***much*** *cheaper.*

Use *(not) as … as* to make comparisons.
My job is ***as*** *exciting* ***as*** *yours.* (= both our jobs are equally exciting)
My job ***isn't as*** *exciting as yours.* (= your job is more exciting than mine)

Use *less* with longer adjectives to mean *not as much*.
She's ***less*** *intelligent than her sister.* (= her sister is more intelligent)

Superlatives

Use superlatives to compare someone or something in a group with all the other things in that group.
This computer is ***the cheapest*** *in the shop.*
Shopping online is ***the most convenient*** *method.*

Use superlatives with the present perfect.
My girlfriend is ***the most interesting*** *person* ***I've ever met.***

Use superlatives with *in the …*
The internet is ***the best*** *invention* ***in the*** *world.*
I'm ***the tallest*** *person* ***in the*** *class.*

Phrasal verbs and objects

A phrasal verb is a two-word verb consisting of a verb + a particle. Some phrasal verbs take an object and some phrasal verbs don't.
- verb + particle

Can you ***log on****?*
- verb + particle + object

Turn on *the computer.*

When phrasal verbs take an object, the object can usually go in two places:
- after the verb and particle

Turn on *the computer.*
- between the verb and particle

Turn *the computer* ***on.***

If the object is a pronoun, it can only go between the verb and particle:
Turn *it* ***on.***
Not: ~~*Turn on it.*~~

Unit 6 Exercises

Comparative and superlative adjectives

1 Write the comparative and superlative forms of the adjectives in the table.

Adjective	Comparative	Superlative
tall hot content safe good expensive enjoyable cheap beautiful heavy		

Comparative adjectives (*a bit, much, as ... as*)

2 Write comparisons using the prompts below.

1 he / be / patient / with the children / her
2 she / be / happy / now / last year
3 most people / get / a bit / fat / when / they / get / old
4 I / sleep / good / in my own bed / in a hotel
5 money / not be / as / important / health
6 this chair / be / much / comfortable / that one
7 some new robots / be / as / intelligent / humans
8 my home computer / starts / slowly / my work computer

Superlatives

3 Complete the sentences with the superlative form of the words in the box.

expensive fast good high popular strange

1 The blog of a Chinese film actress has the ____________ number of readers on the internet.
2 The ____________ name for @ is *elephant's trunk* in Danish.
3 The ____________ domain name cost $7.5 million.
4 Social networking is the ____________ growing sector of the internet.
5 'How to kiss' and 'Who is God' were the ____________ search questions in 2007.
6 Books are the things that sell the ____________ on the internet.

Phrasal verbs and objects

4 Complete the sentences with the correct phrasal verb.

1 The music is too loud.
Well, turn ____________!
2 The TV isn't working.
You need to plug ____________.
3 These web pages are really interesting.
Can you print ____________?
4 How do I put the word into the search engine?
Just type ____________.
5 The phone's ringing.
Well pick ____________!
6 The computer is frozen.
You have to shut ____________.
7 We need to find out train times.
Can you look ____________?
8 I've found his email address.
I'll write ____________.

Unit 7

Present perfect with *for* and *since*

for …	*since …*
years ages six months a long time	1999 the 1960s this morning 2pm he was a child

Language note: don't use the present perfect with time expressions like *in the 90s*, *in 2005*. Use the past simple with these expressions.

Use the time expressions *for* and *since* with the present perfect to talk about unfinished time. *For* states the length of time and *since* is used with the beginning of the time.
How long have you worked here?
I've worked here ***for*** *ten years.*
I've worked here ***for*** *ages.*
I've worked here ***since*** *2000.*
I've worked here ***since*** *I was 25.*

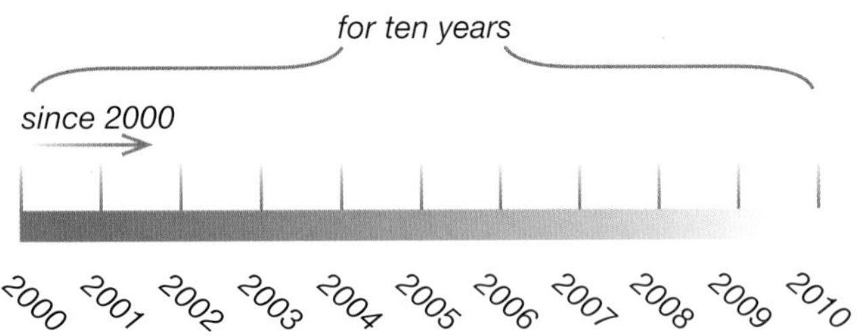

Present perfect with *yet* and *already*

Affirmative	Negative	Question
I/You/We/They have **already** eaten.	I/You/We/They haven't eaten **yet.**	Have I/you/we /they eaten **yet**?
He/She/It has **already** eaten.	He/She/It hasn't eaten **yet**.	Has he/she/it eaten **yet**?

Use *already* with the present perfect to emphasise that something has happened before now.

The structure is auxiliary + *already* + past participle. It is usually used in affirmative sentences.
I've ***already*** *been to the bank.*
I've ***already*** *checked our account.*

Use *yet* with the present perfect to talk about something that has not happened, but will probably happen soon.

Use *yet* in negatives and questions. *Yet* goes at the end of the sentence.
The money hasn't gone into my account ***yet****.*
Have you paid the bills ***yet****?*

Unit 7 Exercises

Present perfect with *for* and *since*

1 Complete the sentences with *for* or *since*.

1 I've had this job ____________ 2002.
2 She's known him ____________ 20 years.
3 We've wanted children ____________ ages.
4 I've liked travelling ____________ I went on my first school trip.
5 I've been working here ____________ a long time.
6 They haven't had anything to eat ____________ 6am.
7 We've had the same TV ____________ the 1990s.
8 I haven't seen her ____________ days.

2 Complete the text with the present perfect or the past simple form of the verb in brackets.

Microwaves (1) ____________ (*be*) a popular time saver for years. An American company (2) ____________ (*produce*) the first microwave in 1947 – it was almost 1.8 metres tall! Families (3) ____________ (*use*) smaller modern microwaves since the 1970s. But many people don't think it is safe. So, is microwaved food safe? The answer is 'yes' if you (4) ____________ (*cook*) the food for the right length of time. Microwaves (5) ____________ (*be*) particularly popular since companies (6) ____________ (*start*) producing freezer to microwave 'ready-meals' in the late 1980s. The UK (7) ____________ (*be*) the largest European consumer of microwave ready meals for years. But a report in 2008 (8) ____________ (*say*) British people are now starting to eat more healthily.

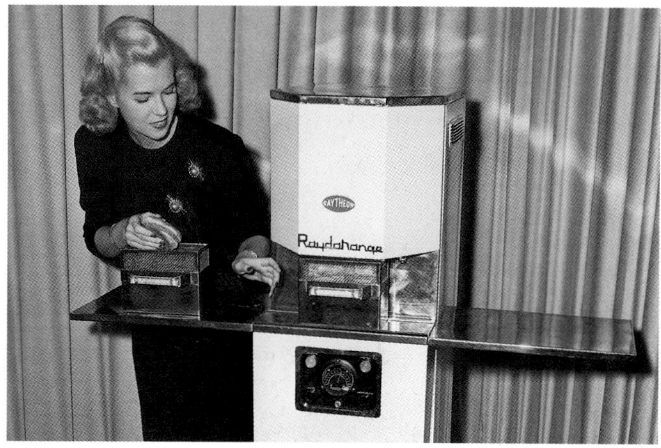

Present perfect with *yet* and *already*

3 Write the dialogues. Use *already* and *yet*.

1 A: you / pay / the electricity bill?
B: no but I / pay / the water bill.
2 A: we / not hear / about that loan.
B: I / call / the bank / twice about it.
3 A: we / spend / all our money for this month.
B: oh dear, / you / check / the lottery ticket?
4 A: our / railway shares / make / a profit.
B: good / but the water shares / not improve.
5 A: you / have / the letter about your inheritance?
B: no, the solicitor / not send / anything.

4 Correct the mistakes in these sentences.

1 Tom has lived in Germany for he was a child.
2 Has Emma got already married?
3 He hasn't done his homework already.
4 They have finished the book yesterday.
5 She's worked here since three months.
6 We haven't done this already.

Unit 8

The passive voice

Present passive		Past passive	
I **am** You/We/They **are** He/She/It **is**	**shocked.**	I **was** You/We/They **were** He/She/It **was**	**shocked.**

Form the passive with the verb *to be* + past participle.

Use the active voice to focus on the agent. (the person or thing who does the action)

agent *active verb* *object*
Zaha Hadid designed the building.

Use the passive voice to focus on the action.
*The building **was designed** in 2005.*

If we want to say who did the action we can use *by* + agent.
*The building **was designed** in 2005 by a famous architect.*

We use the passive when we do not know who did the action (the agent), or it is not important.
*My bag **was stolen**.* (= I don't know who stole it)
*A bomb **was left** in the station.* (= we don't know who left the bomb)

Language note: the passive is more frequent in formal speech and writing.

First conditional

if clause		Main clause
If	+ present simple	I/you, etc. *will / can / might* (not) + verb

Use the first conditional to talk about a possible future situation.
***If** it **is** bad weather, I'**ll** watch TV. But **if** it's sunny, I'**ll** go to the beach.*

Use *will*, *might* or *can* in the main clause:

- *will*: the speaker thinks it's likely that the situation will happen
- *might*: the speaker is not sure that the situation will happen
- *can*: the speaker is not sure if it will happen or not

The *if* clause can be the first or second clause in the sentence.
***If** we take the train, we'll enjoy the journey more.*
*We'll enjoy the journey more **if** we take the train.*

Second conditional

if clause		Main clause
If	+ past simple	I / you, etc. *would / could* (not) + verb

Use the second conditional to talk about an unreal future situation. It is unlikely or almost impossible that the situation will happen.

***If** I **didn't** have to work, I'**d go** to the beach today.*
(But I have to work so I won't go to the beach)
***If** I **had** lots of money, I **could travel** round the world.*
(I don't have lots of money and it's unlikely that I will have lots of money in the future)

Language note: we sometimes say *If I were* instead of *If I was*. Both verbs are correct. *Were* is especially common in the expression *If I were you …* when giving somebody advice.

Unit 8 Exercises

The passive voice

1 Write about eight modern buildings. Use the present or past passive. Sometimes you need *by*.

1 The Empire State Building in New York / use / in the *King Kong* film.
2 The two Emirates Towers in Dubai / connect to / a huge shopping centre.
3 30 St Mary Axe in London / call / 'the Gherkin' / Londoners.
4 Sydney Opera House / build / to look like a ship.
5 The Guggenheim Museum in Bilbao / often / compare / to a fish or water.
6 The Petronas Towers in Kuala Lumpur / occupy / international companies.
7 The new Jewish Museum in Berlin / design / the architect Daniel Libeskind.
8 The Pompidou Centre in Paris / name / after a French president.

2 Rewrite these sentences with the passive so they mean the same.

We sold our flat last week.
Our flat was sold last week.

1 Somebody built the flats in the 1980s.
2 They call the building *Huntingdon House*.
3 Restaurants and cafés surround the building.
4 They painted the walls in our flat white.
5 We put in a new kitchen last year.

First conditional

3 Complete the sentences with the correct form of the first conditional.

1 If I ____________ (*give*) you my email address, ____________ (*you / send*) me the details?
2 I ____________ (*call*) the police if I ____________ (*see*) him again.
3 If you ____________ (*not have*) a ticket you ____________ (*not / can / get*) on the bus.
4 He ____________ (*might / take*) you to the airport if he ____________ (*have*) time.
5 If the weather ____________ (*be*) nice, we ____________ (*can / go*) to the top of the tower.
6 If we ____________ (*go out*) for a meal, we ____________ (*not have to*) go food shopping.
7 She ____________ (*not listen*) to him if he ________ (*not tell*) her the truth.
8 If the internet ____________ (*not work*) again, I ____________ (*complain*) to the company.

Second conditional

4 Complete the conversation with the correct form of the second conditional.

A: What would you do (1) ____________ (*if / you / be*) me?
B: Well, if I were in your shoes, (2) ____________ (*I / go*) on a long trip.
C: Yes, I'd take a month's holiday tomorrow (3) ____________ (*if / my boss / give / me*) time off.
B: If I had the choice, I think (4) ____________ (*I / go / walking*) in New Zealand or Peru.
C: Yes, I'm sure I'd forget all my problems (5) ____________ (*if / I / do*) something like that.
B: Perhaps your boss would help (6) ____________ (*if / you / explain*) everything to her.

5 Match the conditional sentences.

1 If I went to America,
2 If we went on the bus,
3 If we take the credit card,
4 If I don't wear sandals,
5 If we go camping,
6 If I had a problem,

a we won't have to look for accommodation.
b I'd go to San Francisco.
c we won't have to take lots of cash.
d my feet will be too hot.
e we'd save lots of money.
f would you help me?

Unit 9

Modal verbs of advice

Use *should / shouldn't* (+ infinitive without *to*) to give advice and make suggestions.
You ***should*** *go to bed if you don't feel well.*
You ***shouldn't*** *read in poor light – it's bad for your eyes.*

We often use the structure *I (don't) think* with *should.*
I ***don't think you should*** *drink any more.*
Not: ~~*I think you shouldn't drink any more.*~~

Ought to can be used instead of *should* but it is more formal. *Should* is more common.
You ***ought to*** *take an aspirin.*
You ***ought not to*** *watch TV without your glasses.*

Must is similar to *should* but it is stronger and more definite (see Grammar focus 5 page 140 for more on *must*).
You ***must*** *take an aspirin.*

Could / couldn't, had to / didn't have to

(For modals of obligation and possibility in the present, see Grammar focus 5 page 140)

Use *had to / didn't have to* to talk about past obligation.
I ***had to*** *take tablets for a long time.*
I ***didn't have to*** *stay in hospital long.*

Use *could / couldn't* to talk about things that were possible or not possible in the past.
When I was in hospital, I ***couldn't*** *get out of bed.*
We ***could*** *have visitors in the afternoon.*

Past perfect

Affirmative	Negative	Question
I/You/He/She /It/We/They **had ('d) worked.**	I/You/He/She/It /We/They **had not (hadn't) worked.**	**Had** I/you/he /she/it/we/they **worked?**

Use the past perfect to talk about an event in the past that happened before another event or a specific time in the past.
He cried because they ***had lost*** *the match.*
I ***hadn't been*** *to a football match before last Saturday.*

With *before* and *after*, we can use the past simple instead of the past perfect as the order of events is clear.
Before *I started doing regular sport, I was overweight.*
Before *I started doing regular sport, I had been overweight.*
The players celebrated ***after*** *the match finished.*
The players celebrated ***after*** *the match had finished.*

Use the past participles *been* and *gone* in the same way as in the present perfect (see Grammar focus 5 page 140).

they had lost the match ↓   *he cried* ↓
Past |———————————————| *Present*

Reported statements

Use reported statements to say what another person said.
I'm not feeling well. → *He said that he wasn't feeling well.*
I'm going to the doctor's. → *He told me that he was going to go to the doctor's.*

In reported statements, the verb goes one tense *back*.

Direct statements	Reported statements
present simple 'I *like* your new hairstyle.'	**past simple** She said (that) she *liked* my new hairstyle.
present continuous 'I'*m getting* married.'	**past continuous** He said (that) he *was getting* married.
present perfect 'We'*ve bought* the tickets.'	**past perfect** She said (that) they *had bought* the tickets.
past simple 'I *missed* the bus.'	**past perfect** He said (that) he *had missed* the bus.
will 'I'*ll* see you later.'	***would*** She said (that) she *would* see me later.
am/is/are going to 'I'*m going to* join a gym.'	***was/were going to*** She said she *was going to* join a gym.

In reported statements other words can also change:

- pronouns: '***We****'re meeting at* ***my*** *flat.*' → ***He*** *said that* ***they*** *were meeting at* ***his*** *flat.*
- places: '*I got* ***here*** *by train.*' → *He said he had got* ***there*** *by train.*
- *this / that*: '*I've just bought* ***this*** *book.*' → *He said he had just bought* ***that*** *book.*
- times: '*I met her* ***last week.***' → *He said he had met her* ***the week before****.*

Be careful with *say and tell:*

- we say something (to somebody)
- we tell somebody (about something)

The doctor ***told*** *me I was stressed. I* ***said*** *I knew that.*

Unit 9 Exercises

Modal verbs of advice

1 Complete the second sentence so that it has a similar meaning to the first. Use *should* or *shouldn't*.

I think you need to stop smoking.
I think you should stop smoking.

1 Don't worry about it.
You ______________.

2 Go and see your doctor.
You ______________.

3 You don't drink enough water.
I think you ______________.

4 You drink too much coffee.
I don't think ______________.

5 Don't go to bed so late.
You ______________.

Could / couldn't, had to / didn't have to

2 Complete the text with *could, couldn't, had to* or *didn't have to*.

Yesterday, I broke my ankle while I was running. I (1) __________ walk so I (2) __________ phone my girlfriend and she (3) __________ take me to the hospital. Luckily I (4) __________ wait long for an X-ray. The doctor put a bandage on my foot and said I (5) __________ go home. Unfortunately I (6) __________ move for days and my girlfriend (7) __________ do everything for me. The only good thing was that I (8) __________ go to work.

Past perfect

3 Join the sentences. Use the past perfect.

1 She ran 20 km. She was tired.
She was tired because __________.

2 I finished playing tennis. I took a shower.
When __________.

3 The swimmer failed a drugs test. He lost his medal.
The swimmer lost his medal because __________.

4 She was optimistic. She won the race.
Before she won the race, __________.

5 The referee sent a player off. The team played with ten men.
After __________.

6 She hurt another player. She paid a fine.
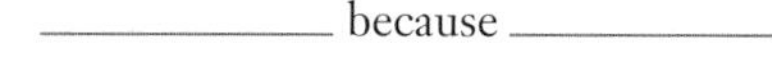
__________ because __________.

Reported statements

4 Read the dialogue and report back the conversation between a doctor and a patient.

D: Good morning. You're obviously having trouble with your back.
P: Yes, I woke up this morning and I had problems getting out of bed.
D: Have you had this problem before?
P: No, I've never experienced that before.
D: OK, I'm just going to take a look. You'll feel a pain …
P: Ow! That hurt! … But my back feels much better.

She said that I was obviously having trouble with my back.
I told her that (1) ____________________ and ____________________.
She asked me if (2) ____________________.
I said that (3) ____________________.
She said that (4) ____________________.
Then she told me that I (5) ____________________.
I said that it (6) ____________________ but that my back ____________________.

Unit 10

Defining relative clauses

Defining relative clauses give more information about a person or a thing. Relative clauses are formed with *that / which* to describe things, *who* with people and *where* with places.

Language note: we can use *that* instead of *who* and *which* but not instead of *where*.

He's the doctor ***who / that*** *saved my life.*
It's something ***which / that*** *I don't like talking about.*
I know a good Italian restaurant ***where*** *we often go for lunch.*
Not: ~~*I know a good Italian restaurant that we often go for lunch.*~~

Definite article (*the*)

Use *the* when a person or thing has been referred to before.
We've found a new flat so we were painting ***the*** *flat all last night.*

Use *the* when there is only one of this person or thing or it is clear which one it is.
My parents met ***the*** *Queen once.*

Language note: we use *a / an* (for singular nouns) or zero article (for plural nouns) when we talk about things in general.
New Zealand is ***a*** *country with many mountains, rivers and lakes.*

The can also be used:

- when it's part of a superlative phrase

You're ***the best thing*** *that has happened to me.*

- when it is part of a name (such as a river)

the *Mekong,* ***the*** *Black Sea,* ***the*** *Titanic,* ***the*** *Golden Gate Bridge*

- for nationalities and groups in society

the *British,* ***the*** *unemployed*

Verb form review

Present simple	I **work**.	See Grammar focus 1 page 132
Present continuous	I**'m** work**ing**.	See Grammar focus 1 page 132
Past simple	I work**ed**.	See Grammar focus 3 page 136
Past continuous	I **was** work**ing**.	See Grammar focus 3 page 136
Present perfect	I **have worked**.	See Grammar focus 5 page 140
Past perfect	I **had worked**.	See Grammar focus 9 page 148
will	I **will work**.	See Grammar focus 4 page 138
going to	I am **going to work**.	See Grammar focus 4 page 138

active	The company **makes** cars.	See Grammar focus 8 page 146
passive	The cars **are made** in Germany.	See Grammar focus 8 page 146
first conditional	**If** the bank **gives** me a loan, I**'ll** buy a small second-hand car.	See Grammar focus 8 page 146
second conditional	If I **had** the money, I**'d** buy a fast sports car.	See Grammar focus 8 page 146
modals: obligation & possibility (present)	**can / can't** **must** **have to / didn't have to**	See Grammar focus 5 page 140
modals: advice	**should / shouldn't, ought to / ought not to**	See Grammar focus 9 page 148
modals: obligation & possibility (past)	**could / couldn't** **had to / didn't have to**	See Grammar focus 9 page 148

Both, neither

Use *both* to talk about two things. *Both* is used with a plural noun and a plural verb.
Both *cars are quite old.*

Use *neither* to say something negative about each of two things. *Neither* is used with a singular noun and verb.
Neither *car is very reliable.*

Use *both of* and *neither of* with a plural noun or pronoun.
Neither of *the cars is economical. Let's sell* ***both of*** *them.*

Unit 10 Exercises

Defining relative clauses

1 Complete the dialogues with *who, which, that* or *where*.

1 A: Who's that?
B: He's a chef __________ has written lots of best-selling cookery books.

2 A: Can you recommend a hotel in New York?
B: Yes, there's a good hotel __________ we stayed last year.

3 A: Hi, what's new?
B: Well, I got the job __________ I told you about last time.

4 A: Where's the dictionary?
B: Over there. It's the big blue book __________ is on that shelf.

5 A: Who were the first Europeans there?
B: I think it was the Vikings __________ sailed there first.

6 A: What's that big building there?
B: Oh, that's the new supermarket __________ you can shop 24 hours.

Definite article (*the*)

2 Complete the sentences with *a / an, the* or nothing (-).

New South Wales is (1) ______ state in (2) ______ south-east of Australia. It is (3) ______ oldest and most populated state in Australia and its capital Sydney is home to famous sights such as (4) ______ Sydney Opera House. It has (5) ______ very diverse climate with hot summers and cold winters. (6) ______ state has great locations for visitors: (7) ______ beautiful beaches, national parks and snowy mountains.

Verb form review

3 Underline the correct verb.

1 The first plane that *had to / could* be controlled in the air *was invented / invented* in 1903.
2 The plane *flew / has flown* for 12 seconds.
3 The Wright brothers *were making / had made* bicycles when they *became / were becoming* interested in planes.
4 They *built / were building* the plane after they *have watched / had watched* how birds fly.
5 The biggest passenger plane, the Airbus A380 *made / is making* its first flight in 2005.
6 Since then, several airlines *have ordered / had ordered* A380s.
7 Airbus *is planning / is going to plan* to produce an even bigger plane in the near future.
8 If everything *went / goes* according to plan, the new plane *will be / is being* nearly 80 metres long.

Both, neither

4 Rewrite the sentences about two friends using *both / neither* or *both of / neither of*. Sometimes more than one answer is possible.

1 The two friends live in a big city.
2 They aren't married.
3 The friends don't have a car.
4 Each friend owns property.
5 The two friends enjoy playing chess.
6 They've written books but their books haven't been published.

Audioscript

Unit 1

1.02

1 Sorry, yes. My last name is Torrance. That's T–O–R–R–A–N–C–E.

2 I live on Janssen Street. I'll spell that for you: J–A–N double S–E–N

3 Write this down. The name of the state is K–E–N–T–U–C–K–Y. That's Kentucky.

1.03

1 **A:** Oh, when was this photo taken?
B: That one? Five years ago, I think.
A: Mmmm. It's quite a good photo of you.
B: I don't know. I don't think I looked good with that beard.
A: I think you look nice and, mmm, intelligent.

1.04

2 **A:** How's the baby?
B: Oh *great*. Great.
A: It's a 'she', right?
B: Yes, yes. I'll show you a photo. She looks like her father.
A: Oh, yeah, bald just like her dad! How old is she?
B: Six months now.
A: She looks really happy. She's got a great smile.

1.05

3 **A:** Who's this a photo of?
B: Don't you know? It's Bella!
A: Bella? Oh yes! She looks so different here. How long ago was this?
B: At the end of university.
A: Wow. Her hair was much *longer* then, and so *curly*.

1.06

4 **A:** What does the suspect look like?
A: I can't hear you. What does the suspect look like?
B: The suspect is a white, older man.
A: Anything else?
B: Just a second … yes. He's got grey hair and a moustache.
A: What kind of car does he drive?
B: An old white Volvo.
A: Thanks.

1.07

1 Pilar is my Spanish neighbour. She's on vacation in Mexico, and I've got her cat and her plants.

2 OK, Hans. Hans and I aren't really friends. He's more of an acquaintance. He's director of the German department.

3 Ken is a colleague of mine at the university. He teaches French, and I teach German.

4 I take a computer class in the evening. Sofia is my classmate.

1.09

The theory of Six Degrees of Separation works like this. Imagine you and John are colleagues. John is married to Mary, but you don't know her personally. So you and Mary have one degree of separation. Mary has a sister, Jane. Jane and you have two degrees of separation. Jane's neighbour, let's call him Robert, works for a big hotel in the city centre. You and Robert, Jane's neighbour, have three degrees of separation. Robert doesn't own the hotel. He works for Mr. Smith, the president. You and Mr Smith … four degrees of separation. Mr Smith, because he's an owner of a big expensive hotel, he's often in touch with important people. He's friends with the Ambassador for example. So you and the Ambassador have five degrees of separation. And well, the Ambassador goes to New York three times a year, and he knows the Secretary General of the United Nations. So, if you make all the right connections it means that you and the Secretary General of the United Nations have six degrees of separation.

1.10

A: What are you doing?
B: So, what do you do?
C: Excuse me, we're trying to work.
D: You're not listening!
E: How's it going?

1.11

1 **A:** Hello.
B: Hello.
A: First time here?
B: Sorry?
A: I said, is this your first time here? At the conference.
B: Yes. Yes.
A: Well, hello. My name's George.
B: Hi George. Nice to meet you.

1.12

2 **A:** Oh, look at the time. It's getting late.
B: What time is it?
A: Eleven o'clock. And I have a class tomorrow.
B: Oh. Well, OK then.
A: Yes. Thanks for everything.
B: No problem.
A: Goodnight.
B: Bye.

1.13

3 **A:** And this is from me.
B: Aww.
B: Oh my …
A: It's a dog! Isn't that great?
B: Er, yes. A dog. Thank you very much.
A: You're welcome. Happy birthday.

1.14

4 **A:** Hello? Oh hi, listen I'm on the train. It's not a good time right now…
B: Hey!
A: Wait a minute … Oh, I'm sorry. I didn't see you and …
B: That's all right.
A: Here, let me help you with your bag.
B: No, it's fine.

Unit 2

1.18

Zao Shen is the god of the kitchen. He is a figure in Chinese mythology. He watches families and tells the other gods if a family is good or bad. He has the power to make families rich or poor. Zao Shen also protects the home from evil spirits. Many homes in China, Taiwan and Southeast Asia have a picture of Zao Shen in the kitchen.

1.20

Human beings need water to live. A human being can live for weeks without food, but only a few days without water. We often hear that our body is two thirds water, but what exactly does water do to help the human body?

Water helps to protect important parts of the body, such as the eyes. The brain is 75% water. We also need water to breathe, and to keep our body temperature normal. Water carries nutrients and oxygen to all parts of the body. Blood is, in fact, 92% water. In addition, water helps to convert food into energy and removes waste from the body. It is also very good for a person's skin. Even the bones in our body are made up of 22% water.

The human body gets water not only from water itself but also from other drinks and food. Water is a major part of many foods, particularly fruit and vegetables, which may contain from 85 to 95% water. Because the amount of water we need may change with climate, level of activity, diet and other factors, there is no one recommendation for how much daily water you need to drink. However, adults typically need at least two litres (eight cups) of water a day, from all sources.

1.23

1 **A:** Good evening.
B: Hello. It's a table for two, please. We've got a reservation.
A: Name?
B: Moore, that's M – double O-R-E.
A: Ah, yes. Just this way.
A: Now, what would you like to order?
C: I'll have the fish.
B: Just a minute. I haven't seen everything on the menu yet.
C: Sorry, then can we have another minute to decide?
A: Of course.

1.24

2 **A:** Here you go. Anything to drink?
B: Sorry, I think there's a mistake here. I wanted a hamburger, not a hot dog.
A: OK, sorry. Just a minute. One hamburger, please.
B: Thanks.
A: Anything to drink?
B: Uh… A diet Coke, please.
A: Small, medium or large?
B: Small, please.

1.25

3 **A:** More coffee?
B: No thanks, I'm fine.
A: Did you enjoy your breakfast?
B: It was lovely, thanks.
A: Good.
B: Could I have the bill?
A: You have to pay over there for the buffet service.
B: Sorry, where?
A: Over there, next to the plants and the exit sign.
B: Oh, I see it. Thanks again.
A: You're welcome.

1.27

1 Mo, Iran
Typical traditional Persian food. It consists of rice and minced lamb, kebabs and chickens and dried fruit.

1.28

2 Gianfranco, Italy
Pizza. Of course not Pizza Hut but Napoli pizza. Yes, pizza, lasagne and pasta.

1.29

3 Elena, Russia
Borsch – it's very interesting – it's like a salad. But it's boiled in water, I don't know, with beetroot, with onion, potato, with meat, or maybe with chicken, or maybe with turkey. Yeah and it's very tasty really.

1.30

4 Marlies, Germany
A schnitzel dish. It's kind of a meat, it's fried and you most often have it with French fries and salad or potato salad which is rather typical of German food again.

1.31

5 Matt, US
Candy makes me think of home. There are certain candy brands that whenever I see them they remind me of my childhood and they remind me of growing up in the United States.

1.32

6 Sonia, Spain
Spanish tortilla makes me think of home and that's a very typical answer but I think it is a very simple dish which is made from eggs and potatoes and it's made like any other tortilla.

Unit 3

1.38

In 1877, Thomas Edison made one of the first ever sound recordings. Edison predicted that sound recordings would be used for office dictation, speaking books, education, talking clocks and music.

In 1903, the first records were released with recordings on both sides. People used to listen to these on record players called gramophones.

In the nineteen-twenties sound recording met film. The first films with sound were called 'talking pictures'.

In 1962 the company Philips introduced the audio cassette tape player. One year later the first discotheque in America opened in Los Angeles.

The seventies and eighties saw the introduction of VHS video, cassette Walkman and CD. The CD revolutionised the music industry.

It was in the early nineties that digital music and video appeared. In 1996 the first digital music player was sold in Japan. One year later the first MP3 player came out. But it wasn't until the beginning of the 21st century that digital music and MP3 players really began to become popular. In 2001 Apple released the first iPod, a portable MP3 player.

The history of sound recording has always been to make devices that are smaller, but contain more sound. The first record played for only six minutes and needed a large machine to play it on. The current generation of music players go in your pocket and can hold more than 15,000 songs, video and photographs.

1.42

Music has always been a very important part of film and television. A film can be completely transformed depending on the kind of music you use.

For example, if you want the audience to feel scared you want to use some kind of tension music. Here is an example of music that makes people feel tense or scared. It uses violins played on a very high note and very quickly.

Gentle music is good for making an audience feel calm and safe. I use guitar, violin or even piano. This kind of music is good with love scenes.

I sometimes use choral music for certain special scenes, or to make people feel sad. I use this for when a character dies in a film.

Finally, sometimes individual characters or ideas in a film have their own kind of music. I did the music for the British television programme *Robin Hood*, and every time the character of Robin appears you hear this kind of music. It uses trumpets, which are always good instruments for heroes.

In the past, to record the music for a film, the orchestra used to play in front of a large screen showing the movie, so the composer could get the timing just right. Now with computers, it isn't so necessary. Everything is much easier, and we do a lot of the work in the studio.

1.44

1 **A:** So, what did you think?
B: I don't know. Horror films, well, they should be thrilling, you know, be a bit scary.
A: I think so too.
B: And that film wasn't.
A: Oh come on, it was.
B: No, I don't agree. It was not scary.

1.45

2 **A:** Now, you believe that there are too many big budget action films in the cinema.
B: That's right.
A: And that there should be more space for films from around the world. More 'world cinema'.
B: Exactly. There are lots of great films from other countries, but we only see our own American films here. And I don't think that's right.
A: I agree with you there, John. So what films do you think we should see?
B: Well …

1.46

3 **A:** What about this one?
B: What, a musical?
A: I know you think that musicals are terrible.
B: Absolutely, you're absolutely right. They are awful!
A: Well, maybe but … I read this one was different. We always see the same films anyway.
B: Oh please. We see lots of different films. Last week we saw a French film.
A: Fine, you choose the DVD then.

Unit 4

1.48

A: …?
B: OK, well. My name's Josh Gross and this is Helle Hansen.
C: Hi.
B: And … well, we're aid workers with the Danish organisation Milene Nielsen Foundation. Helle, do you want to… say something about it?
C: It's starting a new project in Guatemala next month. We're going to be in a small village …
B: In the mountains.
C: In the mountains. It's a very poor place.
A: …?
C: We're going to work with the children there.
B: Basically, we're going to be responsible for the children during the day. Playing, cooking…
C: Cleaning …
A: …?
B: I'm a teacher originally, and Helle has a background in child psychology. We both wanted to help people.
C: I fell in love with Guatemala when I was there on a holiday two years ago. The people are friendly and the country is beautiful. I remember thinking: 'I'm coming back here one day.'
B: It's going to be my first time in Guatemala. I'm looking forward to going on this trip very much.
C: Yeah, me too.
A: …?
B: Good question. I guess I would say that hope is the most important thing. If you don't have hope, you don't have anything.
C: Yes, this is especially true when you're working with people who have, really, *lost* hope. If you have hope, well that helps you keep going.

A: ...?
B: Thanks. We'll let you know how it goes.
C: Thank you.

1.52

A: *An Inconvenient Truth?* Isn't that a documentary from a few years ago about global warming? No, I haven't seen it, no. I heard it was interesting.
B: Well, of course I knew about global warming a bit before I saw the film... but, well .... wow. I mean, it really makes me think about what I'm going to do. If we don't do something now, we'll have serious problems in the future.
C: All I want to say is that I saw this film. It was a great documentary, and it's very, very important.
D: Oh, yes I remember this film. I saw it after Al Gore won the Nobel Peace Prize. I learnt a lot. It was different from a usual Hollywood film.
E: I didn't like it. These kinds of documentary films are always frightening. And anyway, when this climate change happens, I'll be dead. So I don't want to worry about it now.
F: I haven't but my son saw this film at school, in his geography class. He was talking about it all evening. He said: "You'll think differently after you see it." I think it's good that he learns about this kind of thing at school.

1.53

1 **A:** Oh. Look at the time. My train's leaving soon.
B: Shall I pay for these?
A: That would be great.
B: OK. Wait. I don't have enough for both of them.
A: Hold on. How much is it?
B: £2.75.
A: I'll pay for it. Here's five. I really have to go now though.
B: Thanks again. Have a good trip, and see you next Monday!
A: Bye! See you Monday.

1.54

2 **A:** Hey! What time do you need to get to the airport?
B: I'm planning to be there two hours before the flight. Why?
A: Well, look at the time. The airport train leaves in five minutes.
B: Oh no.
A: I'm sorry, we were talking and I didn't see the time...
B: No, don't worry. I ... I won't take the train. I'll take a taxi.
A: A taxi? They're quite expensive. Let me drive you to the airport.
B: Really? That would be great. Thanks.
A: No problem. We can continue our conversation in the car.

1.55

3 **A:** Can I help you?
B: Yes, thanks. Erm, I ... I've missed my train. Can I use this ticket for the next train?
A: Yes, you can. The next train is the six o'clock fast train. You'll need to pay an extra ten euros for that. Or you can take the six fifty train and you don't have to pay anything extra.
B: OK, I'll take the six fifty train then. Thank you.
A: You're welcome.

1.56

1 **A:** Are you ready to order?
B: Yes. I'll have a salad.
2 **A:** I don't understand this.
B: That's all right. I'll help you.
3 **A:** The next train is in twenty minutes.
B: Shall we take it or wait?
4 **A:** Here, let me take those bags.
B: Thanks, but it's OK. I'll carry them.

1.57

1 Abdul, Libya
Actually I'm learning English because it will be helpful for my career.

1.58

2 Olga, Russia
I'm learning English because first of all I want to be a teacher of English in my country.

1.59

3 Mert, Turkey
I would like to work for some companies who work in Canada and USA and they need really good English skills and I have to speak English very well and to work for them.

1.60

4 Naif, Saudi Arabia
Well I believe that English is very important nowadays as you cannot continue studying without using English because it's the international language nowadays.

1.61

5 Arthur, France
I am learning English because I love it. I love the English culture, the American culture, its movie, its music.

1.62

6 Dain, South Korea
English is a world language so we need to study English. It's essential. And personally I want to be a politician or I want to be a diplomat, which my father wants. So I think English is the most important thing for a politician or a diplomat so that's why I am studying English in Britain now.

Unit 5

1.63

1 Oh, hello, good to see you. Listen, somebody has to work this Saturday morning. Susan has called in sick. Now, I know that you've worked every Saturday this month, but there isn't anyone else. That all right? You can take next Saturday off.

1.64

2 Excuse me? Yes, come here, please. Now, I don't know if anybody told you, but we have a dress code here. Employees mustn't wear jeans to work. It's not allowed. You don't have to wear a jacket and tie, but try to be a little bit more formal.

1.65

3 No, no, NO. How many times do I have to say this? You *can't* use the computer to send private emails and you *can't* send personal messages to each other on the computer. You are on company time, and you *must respect* that time. That means *working* everybody, and *not talking*.

1.66

4 It's *OK*, you know. Of course you can go on your lunch break now. You don't have to come in to my office and ask me every time. I like to keep things informal around here, and as long as everyone does their work then I don't see a problem. All right? By the way, I recommend the Italian restaurant on the corner if you don't know where to go. *Very* good pasta.

1.69

Good afternoon. My name is Robert Macarthur, and I'm here to talk to you about the serious leisure perspective.

The serious leisure perspective comes from the expert on leisure, Robert Stebbins, at the University of Calgary in Canada. He has been working on this theory since 1974. According to Stebbins, there are two main forms of leisure: casual leisure and serious leisure.

Casual leisure is just that, casual. Sitting about at home is casual leisure. Doing nothing is casual leisure. Watching television, reading a book. Maybe just going for a walk or chatting with friends over dinner. People enjoy doing these activities because they feel good, because they're relaxing, because they're fun.

For many of us here in America, leisure has a bad reputation because it's not work. We live in a society that says work is more important than leisure because leisure is lazy.

But there is another form of leisure, called serious leisure. Serious leisure activities are activities which lead to personal development.

Doing a sport regularly, like cycling, running, skiing, or swimming are examples of serious leisure.

Serious leisure activities can also include making things, or collecting things. Here, for example, is an image of a website for collectors of rubber ducks. This is funny, yes, but an example of serious leisure too.

Finally, serious leisure can mean volunteer work. By volunteer work, I mean unpaid work helping people other than your family. For example, volunteering in a local hospital. Or in a school. Or in a home for old people.

I believe serious leisure is important because it's fun, yes, but it also satisfies a need in us, it can change our lives.

And now, moving on to my own research …

1.73

1 **A:** Right. Hello and thanks again for coming. The purpose of today's meeting is to give you all the information about …
B: Excuse me. Could I just ask a question?
A: Yes, Mrs Davies.
B: My son doesn't have all the books yet. Is this a problem?
A: Not at all. We can talk about the books in just a moment.
C: Can I add that my daughter doesn't have the books either? They haven't arrived.
A: Thank you, Mr Brown. Please don't worry about it now …

1.74

2 **A:** And I think you will find that the starting salary is *very* good.
B: Yes. Thank you. May I ask about working hours again? I'm not sure that I understood. What time do you expect me to arrive in the morning?
A: Seven o'clock.
B: Fine. Seven o'clock. That's early.
A: We need people early in the morning to talk to our European offices.
B: Of course.
A: Is there a problem?
B: No, not at all. Not at all.

1.75

3 **A:** OK, so the next item on the agenda is …
B: Can I say something here?
A: Is it about wages?
B: No, it isn't.
A: All right then. Because we aren't talking about wages in this meeting.
B: Can I just say that the dress code we have now is terrible. Terrible.
A: Thank you, David.
B: I *hate* these ties.
A: I know … which is why we're talking about a change in the dress code.
B: Can I also mention that the trousers are so *uncomfortable*.

Unit 6

2.02

1 I did this last summer. It was an interesting part-time job – much more interesting than the other jobs I've had. There were 15 of us in total. The study was in Texas and the scientists were looking at the effects of no gravity on the human body. For the study we had to stay in bed for 15 days. Every day the scientists put us in a special machine that turned us around and around upside down for an hour really quickly. I felt like my brain was in my stomach after the first day. But … at the end of the project I got $6,000 – enough to get me to Los Angeles and to look for work as an actor.

2.03

2 Many people think my work is just disgusting, but I think it's interesting. I spend all day working in people's rubbish. It's not as bad as you think. Not always, anyway. I often work at a city landfill, you know, the place where they put all the rubbish. Sometimes I study specific kinds of rubbish. I'm finishing a project at the moment on office rubbish: paper, plastic, that kind of thing. Office rubbish is much less disgusting than restaurant rubbish. That was last year's project.

2.07

1 www.ebay.it, that's I-T for Italy.
2 j324@hotmail.com
3 www.facebook.com
4 www.itt.com/english
5 Jason_17@gmail.com
6 www.myspace.com
7 www.amazon.de, not com, D-E…
8 sean@yahoo.co.uk, that's S-E-A-N at Y-A-H-O-O dot C-O dot U-K

2.08

1 **A:** OK. Try now.
B: No. It's still not working.
A: Nothing? Can you see anything on the screen?
B: Yes. But when I click on the internet button nothing happens.
A: And now?
B: Yes! It's working now. Oh *thank you thank you.* What did you do?
A: The cable was old. I took a new cable and connected it up to the internet again.

2.09

2 **A:** So, tell me the problem again?
B: OK, when I try to print out a document the computer prints out a *different* document.
A: You mean, not the one you want to print?
B: That's right.
A: Have you tried …
B: I've tried everything!

2.10

3 **A:** No, no, it's OK, the computer person is here now. You're here.
B: Yes? What's the problem?
A: Well, I try to open my email … and … I get this.
B: Urg … yuk.
A: Yeah. Disgusting, huh?
B: Yeah. OK. Shut down the computer and leave it.
A: Is it a virus or something?
B: I'm afraid so.

2.11

4 **A:** Oh no. No!
B: What's wrong?
A: The laptop's gone down again!
B: Did you save your work?
A: No.
B: You should really back up all your work. I always do.
A: Great … Thanks for the advice.

2.12

5 **A:** OK, ready to do this?
B: Yep. Definitely.
A: First, click on this button here.
B: OK … done.
A: Now log on to the system.
B: What?
A: Log on. Type in your username and password.
B: Oh.
A: What?
B: I can't remember my password!

2.15

A: Hi, excuse me. I noticed your bag. Are you going to the Technology conference?
B: That's right.
A: Me too! Could we share a taxi?
B: Sure.
A: The conference centre, please.
C: OK.
A: Have you been to San Francisco before?
B: Er, no. No I haven't.
A: Neither have I. Nice weather.
B: Mm.
A: My name's Frank, by the way.
B: Nice to meet you. Claudia.
A: Hi Claudia. Where are you from, Claudia?
B: Frankfurt.
A: Wow. Frankfurt. You don't have a German accent at all.
B: I went to school in England.
A: So did I. Well, I'm English so … I guess that's normal.
B: Yes, I guess.
A: So … do you work for ABT Technology?
B: Yes. I work in the Frankfurt office. This is my first conference.
A: Oh, I've been to lots of conferences. They're very boring you know.
B: Really?
A: Oh yes. The worst part is listening to our president, Lance Thomas.
B: Really?
A: Gosh yes. His talks are so boring. But the evening party is quite good. Do you like parties?
B: No, not really.
A: Ah. Me neither. Not really.
B: Thanks, Frank.
A: You're welcome. Are you staying in the conference hotel?
B: No, I'm not.
A: Ha. Neither am I. It's horrible. Where's your hotel?
B: I er… I don't know. Oh look, here's my husband.

Audioscript

A: Oh. Oh.
B: Lance, this is Frank. Frank, this is my husband Lance.
A: Oh ...Er ...
D: Nice to meet you, Frank. Glad you could be here.
A: Hi.

2.16

1 Honor, England
I think that the most useful technical advance for me has been the internet, yes, because I can do things like booking tickets and so forth.

2.17

2 Arthur, France
Television is very important for the information and for entertainment.

2.18

3 Sara, Italy
The most important useful technological advance is, we could say now is a computer. It's very important. I think that nobody could really live or work without a computer.

2.19

4 Antonis, Greece
I think the plane. The aeroplanes, yeah.

2.20

5 Maxim, Russia
I think that most important technological advance for me it is SMS services, of course so mobile phone, but especially SMS services.

2.21

6 Starla, England
For me the most technological advance I'd say is the internet because it's convenient and quick and saves you a lot of time.

2.22

7 William, Ghana
Well, I think the internet is the most important, especially when you are looking for information.

Unit 7

2.25

The concept of time in the English language, and in western culture in general, is very much linked to money. Time can be seen as a form of currency. You can spend time and money, or save it. Time can be wasted. You can give someone your time, just like you can give them money. We have free time, extra time, spare time and overtime. We can convert time into money, and money into time. Time, money and work are intimately connected.

2.35

1 **A:** Do you speak English?
B: A little.
A: How much is the shirt?
B: This one?
A: No. The checked one.
B: Hundred and fifty.
A: A hundred and fifty? That's expensive.
B: You can have it for a hundred and twenty-five.
A: A hundred and ten?
B: Sorry, no. A hundred and twenty-five.
A: No thanks. I'll leave it.
B: OK! OK! A hundred and ten.

2.36

2 **A:** Hello. Can I help you?
B: Can I have some of these, please?
A: Which ones, love?
B: The red and white ones. They'll look nice in the living room.
A: Right. Here you are. Three pounds.
B: Thank you.
A: Would you like one of these small plants? They're lovely at this time of year.
B: Oh. All right. How much is it?
A: Only 75p.
B: I'll take it. Here you are.
A: Here's your change.
B: Goodbye now.
A: Bye.

2.37

3 **A:** ¿Puedo ayudarte?
B: Sorry, I don't speak Spanish.
A: Can I help you?
B: No, I'm just looking, thanks.
A: OK.
B: Sorry, yes. How much is this book?
A: Two euros.
B: Only two euros. That's cheap.
A: Yes. I put the price at ten euros. Nobody wants to buy it. At five euros. Nobody wants to buy it. So I made it cheap. Two euros. Do you want to buy it?
B: Oh.
A: What's wrong?
B: I'm the author.
A: The author?
B: Yes. I wrote it. I'll take it. For two euros.

Unit 8

2.41

1 The Tower of London was originally built in 1078. It was used as a home for the kings and queens of England for almost six hundred years, but also served as a prison. Two of the most famous prisoners in the Tower were the young princes Edward and Richard. In 1483, Richard the Third, their uncle and king of England, put them in the tower. They were never seen again. The princes were ten and thirteen years old. Today, people say the tower is haunted by their ghosts.

2.42

2 **A:** Look, look!
B: Oh, I recognise this place. It's from a film.
A: Yes, it's the house from some scary movie.
B: Right! It was used in the film *Psycho*.
A: Hold on, the guide says ... this is probably one of the most well-known film set houses in Hollywood history. The old house and motel next to it were built originally for the Hitchcock film *Psycho* in the 1960s.
B: Mmm.
A: Sometimes, at Halloween, the house and motel are opened for the public to come and stay.
B: Brrr. Staying at this place on Halloween? No thank you.

2.43

3 Well, welcome to Bran Castle, one of the most famous castles in Romania. The castle was occupied by the government in communist times, but was returned to its owners in 2006.
Of course, as many of you know, the castle is known as Dracula's castle. People believe that Vlad Tepes – the original Dracula – lived here. This isn't exactly true, however, but he *was* kept as a prisoner here for some time. The castle is now a famous tourist attraction, and it is visited every year by thousands of people.

2.46

1 **A:** Well, now is really the time to visit the United States.
B: Really?
A: Oh *yes*. The dollar is not very strong, so things are really cheap.
B: Oh. I wanted to go to France. But, cheap is good.
A: Listen, if you travel this month you'll get an extra twenty per cent discount.
B: This month isn't possible.
A: Next month?
B: Yes. I have a week's holiday next month. Are there any specials then?
A: I'll ask if you like.
B: Yes, please.

2.47

2 **A:** And here is the main square and the tower. The tower is more than five hundred years old, and is the tallest building in the city. The view from the top of the tower is truly amazing. Today, with this beautiful sunshine, if you go up the tower, you won't regret it.
B: Excuse me, does it cost anything to go up the tower?
A: I'm afraid so. It costs eight euros.

2.48

3 **A:** These are the carpets. I thought you were going to show me the food part. And have some lunch.
B: Yes, yes. The food is on the other end of the market. Do not worry, my friend. We'll go there later if you want. As your guide, though, I have to show you everything. Look, isn't this amazing?
A: Mmm.

B: Some of these carpets take more than two months to make. They are all made by hand.
A: I'm just hungry, that's all.
B: Are you sure? If you buy one of these carpets now, I can get a good price for you.
A: Oh. Well ...
B: She says if you buy two she will give you a *big* discount.
A: OK, then. How much ...?

2.51

1 **A:** Hello, Greenway Holidays.
B: Hi, my name's Pablo Alonso. I'm calling about the English learning holiday.
A: You need to speak to Mrs Knight. I'll put you through.
B: Thank you.
A: Just a moment, please.

2.52

2 **B:** Hello?
A: I'm sorry, but the line's busy. Do you want to hold?
B: OK, I'll hold.

2.53

3 **A:** Hello?
B: Hello, is that Mrs Knight?
A: No, I'm afraid she isn't here.
B: Can't you give me information about the English learning holiday?
A: I'm sorry, I can't. Can I take a message?
B: No, that's all right. I'll call back.

2.54

4 **A:** Hello, Greenway Holidays.
B: Hello, this is Pablo Alonso again. Can I speak to Mrs Knight?
A: I'll put you through.
C: Sandra Knight speaking. Sorry to keep you waiting.
B: Oh, hello. My name's Pablo Alonso. I'm calling about the English learning holiday.
C: What would you like to know?
B: Well, I've looked on your website and I have a few questions about the cost.
C: Right, of course, Mr Alonso. Our prices, I think you'll find, are very competitive …

2.56

1 David, Georgia
So homes in Georgia are very big – some big ones and so we have two kind of homes. There are block of flats – there are many of them and we also have houses. Houses usually are in the outside of the country – in the villages.

2.57

2 Elena, Russia
In my country we have different homes like in England, because in England many people live in cottages, yes, but in my country we have very big houses. Many flats, but not so big, but good, and mostly Russian families have a cottage – it's not a cottage, it's maybe a little house in the countryside where we can grow fruit and vegetables but we don't live in these cottages, but what I can say more. Maybe prices – if you buy – if you sell your flat in Moscow – little flat – you can buy three houses in Great Britain.

2.58

3 Valería, Bolivia
I would say homes in Bolivia are much more coloured. Here, above all in Oxford, all the homes looks very similar I would say but in Bolivia you can find a red house just besides a yellow house and it is a pretty nice combination of colours.

2.59

4 Katie, Northern Ireland
Where I live in Belfast homes are … they're quite varied. In inner city Belfast you have very small red brick terraced houses. Two up two down houses and they're – I think they date from the 1800s – they sort of typify whenever you think of the city you think of red brick terraced houses.

2.60

5 Bea, England
Homes where I live are quite large. In my street in particular the houses have four or five bedrooms. They are usually shared between lots of different house mates. I personally live with two people I didn't know before and now one of them is a very good friend. The houses have kitchens and separate living rooms and dining rooms and the best thing about my house is that it has a large garden.

Unit 9

2.61

The common cold can be caused by more than 200 different viruses.
An adult gets between two and five colds a year, while for children or babies the number is higher; between 6 and 10 colds a year.
From the moment you get a cold to the moment you feel the symptoms is between 24 and 48 hours.
The total time in your life that you will have a cold is two to three years.
The common cold is not a deadly disease, but it is expensive. In the US alone, experts estimate that it costs the economy 3.5 billion dollars in lost time at work and school.

2.65

1 You should eat hot chicken soup as soon as you feel ill.
2 Just drink water. Lots of water.
3 Drink orange juice and lots of vitamin C.
4 I think you should eat foods with vitamin A, like carrots.
5 Drink hot water with lemon and honey in it.
6 I think you should drink water with a spoonful of salt.
7 Breathing hot steam works. Go for a sauna.
8 You should eat garlic. It works, I promise!
9 Just take two aspirin and stay in bed.
10 Cold medicine. Take cold medicine.
11 You shouldn't do any exercise. You should stay in bed. Don't go out.
12 I don't think you should stay in bed. Be active. Go out.
13 What you should do, what you really *ought to* do, is to wash your hands regularly.
14 You should stay dry. Don't wash your hair or go out in the rain.

2.70

A: Harry, is that you?
B: Yes, yes… I'm home.
A: Well, what did the doctor say?
B: Er. Nothing much. She said I was healthy. No serious problems.
A: Oh, that's wonderful. Did she say anything about a diet?
B: A what?
A: A diet.
B: Oh, oh yes. She said, she said… I could eat *some* red meat. Just once a week.
A: That's good. You do eat a lot of meat. What about salt and sugar? Shouldn't you cut down on those?
B: Um. No, no she didn't say anything about salt or sugar.
A: Oh. That's strange. What about coffee?
B: Er, coffee, yes, coffee.
A: You drink five cups of coffee a day. Isn't that too much?
B: Oh yes. She told me that I could only drink … two cups a day.
A: OK. And can you go back to work?
B: Yes. I start tomorrow.

2.72

A: Hello, can I help?
B: Yes, I erm, need something for a sore throat. It really hurts.
A: Well, we have this syrup or these tablets.
B: Which is better?
A: They're both good. The syrup is more expensive.
B: Oh, well ... I'll take the tablets then. How many do I take?
A: Just one ...
B: Sorry. I'm sorry. And how often should I take it?
A: Just one every four to six hours. Take it before mealtimes. Are you allergic to any medicine?
B: No.
A: Then you'll be fine with this.
B: Can I get some antibiotics too?
A: I'm afraid you need a prescription for that.
B: Oh.
A: You know, you should really see a doctor if that cough continues.
B: I know. I know.
A: Anything else?
B: No thanks.
A: That'll be £4.50 then, please.

Audioscript

Unit 10

2.73

A: So, your book *Brave New Words* is all about new words in English. How do new words appear?

B: One of the most common ways of making new words is simply to combine two words which already exist. So for example in the past we had texts, and we had messages, now with mobile phones we have …

A: Text messages.

B: Yes. That's right. Another common way of making a new word is to combine parts of words. Consider brunch. Brunch is a meal that people can have at 11 o'clock in the morning, a combination of breakfast and lunch.

A: So combinations are how new words are made.

B: There are other ways too. Abbreviations, for example, are a common way of making new words. Do you know what a digital versatile disc is?

A: Er …

B: A DVD …?

A: Of course.

B: Yes, the abbreviation becomes the new word. Another way is to give a word a new meaning. We have new meanings for all kinds of words connected to computers – for example mouse and virus.

A: Or windows.

B: Yes. Finally, we can borrow words from other languages. An example of this would be a tsunami – a Japanese word which became very frequent in English after the natural disaster in Asia in 2004.

A: Will all these new words continue to exist?

B: Maybe not. Some will continue, others won't. But the way we create these new words … combination, abbreviation, giving old words new meanings or borrowing words … well these are going to be with us for a long time.

2.77

In 1929 many people in the United States suddenly lost their jobs. This was the beginning of what Americans call the Great Depression, and it lasted for about four years. During the Great Depression, two of the most famous board games in the world were invented: Monopoly and Scrabble. While the games are very different, the story behind each one is similar …

Alfred Butts, the inventor of Scrabble, and Charles Durrow, the inventor of Monopoly, were both American. Neither inventor had a job. Butts had lost his job as an architect in 1929, and Durrow was an unemployed sales representative in 1933.

At the beginning, the inventors made every edition of their game by hand. Neither game was accepted by toy companies at first.

They said that Monopoly was too complicated, and that nobody would be interested in Scrabble.

Both games are played on a board, and can be played by two or more people.

Both games have been extremely popular: according to its makers, more than 750 million people have played Monopoly, and two hundred million copies of Scrabble are sold every year.

Both of them are successful worldwide. They are published in over 25 languages today, and are available in more than 80 countries.

2.79

1 **A:** Oh, hello, there you are.
B: Hello.
A: Listen, I'm afraid there's some bad news.
B: Oh?
A: Yes. The thing is, the company is closing.
B: Really? When?
A: Tomorrow. The whole thing. It's been sold.
B: Sold?
A: Yep.
B: So… so, what's going to happen to everyone?
A: There'll be an official announcement. Oh, here's my floor.
B: Er … I'm still …
A: Anyway. Sorry to rush off. Talk later, OK?
B: OK. Bye.
A: Goodbye.

2.80

2 **A:** Phew. Isn't it hot?
B: Hmm. Sorry?
A: I said, isn't it hot?
B: Yes. Yes. Very hot.
A: I can't remember a summer like this since … since the nineteen seventies.
B: Yes. It is very hot.
A: Nineteen seventy-six it was.
B: I don't really remember, I was quite … young then.
A: I guess you were. Well, it was so hot that…
B: Really.
A: Yes. I was in love then …
B: Oh look. Here's my floor.
A: Oh.
B: Well, I have to go. Nice to talk to you.
A: Yes, yes.
B: Goodbye.

2.82

1 I know, I know. It *was* funny. Anyway … talk to you tomorrow OK? Yep.

2 …and so that's what we'll do. Right, that's it. We'll continue after the break, OK?

3 **A:** What time does the film start?
B: Nine o'clock.
A: Nine o'clock. OK, see you then.
B: OK, bye.

4 Well, I think that's it. Yes, I'll send the email. Bye.

5 **A:** Was there anything else?
B: No … I don't think so.
A: All right. You can pay over there.
B: Thanks. Bye.
A: Bye.

2.83

1 Arthur, France

My favourite expression in English is 'Oh my god'! That's it! Because we heard this expression very often in movie, in television and I think it's a cliché of the English people or American people. Oh my god.

2.84

2 Diego, Italy

There are a lot of very interesting words in English. My favourite word is for example love.

2.85

3 Kristina, Russia

My favourite words in English. I think when I came to England last year everybody said, oh he looks gorgeous and it's gorgeous, the weather is gorgeous and so it became my favourite word.

2.86

4 Elodie, Switzerland

My favourite words in English are – I really like the word perhaps. I don't know why – because of the sound, because of the pronunciation, I don't know. Perhaps. What else? Well I don't know.

2.87

5 Semih, Turkey

For me, my favourite words in English are awesome and legendary. I don't know why because when I say awesome or legendary it makes me feel happy.

2.88

6 Bea, England

OK my favourite words in English are 'you know' because they're very useful words. When you are not sure what to say you can use them to fill in a sentence and they're very good words to give you time so that you can think about, you can concentrate on what you are thinking and maybe think of different ideas, you know.

2.89

7 Guy, England

One of my favourite words in English is harmony. I think it's a nice word, it's got a nice sound to it. I like the structure of the word. I think the ideas that it represents are very positive, whether you are talking about musical harmony, or artistic harmony, or harmony when people work together well or understand each other well. And I think probably there's a similar word in many other languages, so it's a word that a lot of people understand quite easily.

Macmillan Education
4 Crinan Street
London N1 9XW
A division of Macmillan Publishers Limited
Companies and representatives throughout the world

ISBN 978-0-230-03309-2

Grammar Focus section by Rebecca Robb Benne

First published 2010

Original design by Barbara Mercer and Katie Stephens
Page layout by eMC Design Limited
Illustrated by Jonathan Burton, Peter Harper, Celia Hart, Robin Lawrie and eMC Design
Picture research by Sally Cole, Perseverance Works Limited
Cover design by Barbara Mercer
Cover photograph used by permission of the Museum of the History of Science, University of Oxford/Keiko Ikeuchi

Author's acknowledgements

First and foremost, I would like to thank Rafael Alarcon-Gaeta for his support and nurturing of this project from the very beginning. The team working on Global have all done an incredible job. My gratitude to Nick Sheard, Stephanie Parker, Stig Vatland and Barbara Mercer for constantly rising to the challenges this book presented and coming out on top every single time. Many thanks also to Selina Hansen for her comments and help on the manuscript.

A lot of the inspiration for this book came from the hundreds of teachers I've had the chance to meet around the world. This would not have been possible without the help of the tireless people at Macmillan who organised my trips and gave me insight into the countries I was visiting.

This book is dedicated to my children Lucas and Marcos, whose curiosity about life and everything has been very motivating to me as an author.

The author and publishers would like to thank all the teachers and consultants who have piloted and reviewed the material. Particular thanks go to the following people: Andrea Córdova, Susana Flores (Anglo Multimedia School of English, Haedo, Buenos Aires, Argentina); Ma. Cristina Maggi, Ma. Cristina Buero de Chinton (Friends' School of English, Adrogué, Buenos Aires, Argentina); Mirta Zampini, Aldana Anchorena, Elizabeth Rainieri, Ma. Soledad D. Mangiarotti, Pamela Sabrina Pecorelli (IECI, Haedo, Buenos Aires, Argentina); Alejandro Jorge Listrani (Cultural Inglesa de Palermo, Ciudad Autónoma de Buenos Aires, Argentina); Lilian Itzicovitch Leventhal (Potential/ Colegio I.L.Peretz, São Paulo, Brazil); Ana Maria Miranda (Cultura Inglesa Ribeirão Preto, Ribeirão Preto, Brazil); Magali de Moraes Menti (FACCAT - Escola Municipal Lauro Rodrigues, Porto Alegre, Brazil); Simone Sarmento (PUCRS, Porto Alegre, Brazil); Laura Lee Lehto (Cultura Inglesa, Fortaleza, Brazil); Viviane Cristine Silva Grossklauss, Analice Sandovetti (Cultura Inglesa Jundiaí, Jundiaí, Brazil); Celia Aguiar de Almeida Costa (Cultura Inglesa de Juiz de Fora, Brazil); Corina Celia Machado Correa (Associação Alumni - São Paulo, Brazil); Jane Godwin (The Four, São Carlos, Brazil); Caroline Toubia (The Holy Family School, Jesuite, Egypt); Amany Shawkey, Heidi Omara (Macmillan Publishers Ltd, Egypt) Caroline Franz , Dana Jelinkova (MVHS Muenchner Volkshochschule, Munich, Germany); Irene Rodriguez, Haydee Gutierrez Palafox, Antonio Morales de la Barrera, Javier Ramos de Hoyos (The Anglo Mexican Foundation, Mexico City, Mexico); Viviana Caruso de Curtius (freelance author and consultant, Mexico City, Mexico); Emma Dominguez (Academic Studies Manager, The Anglo Mexican Foundation, Mexico City, Mexico); Katarzyna Rogali ska-Gajewska (Archibald, Warsaw, Poland); Małgorzata Wo niak, Dorota Pachwicewicz, Agnieszka Kilanowska (Centrum J zykowe 'Euroclub', Gda sk, Poland); Fabiola Georgiana Hosu (Little London School and Nursery School, Dimitrie Cantemir University, Bucharest, Romania); Lydia B. Korzheva (Diplomatic Academy, Moscow, Russia); Ludmila A. Pokrovskaya (Russian Academy of Foreign Trade, Moscow, Russia); Olga S. Petrischeva (Moscow State University of International Relations, Moscow, Russia); Albina Valieva (The International Language School 'Denis School', Moscow, Russia); Karen Dyer, Cathy Harris, Frank Hodgkins (International House, Madrid, Spain); Carlos Trueba (E.O.I Villaverde, Madrid, Spain); Patricia Plaza Arregui (E.O.I. Malaga, Spain); Maria Esther Álvarez Rico (E.O.I. Sagunto, Valencia, Spain); Burcu Tezcan Ünal (Bilgi University, Istanbul, Turkey); Dr. F. Ilke Buyukduman (Ozyegin University, Istanbul, Turkey); Sarah Shaw (The British Council, Chiang Mai, Thailand); Aomboon Burutphakdee (Payap University, Chiang Mai, Thailand); thanks to: Nattinee Khueansri, (Payap University, Chiang Mai, Thailand); Claudia Edwards (London School of English, London, UK); Sally Jones (Regent Oxford, Oxford, UK); Katherine Griggs (Community English School Oxfordshire Adult Learning, Oxford, UK).

A special thank you to Jackie Halsall, Sarah Paterson and all the staff and students at Eckersley, Oxford and Regent, Oxford for all their help with Global voices.

The authors and publishers would like to thank the following for permission to reproduce their photographs:

Cover Credit: By permission of the Museum of the History of Science, University of Oxford/Keiko Ikeuchi.

Alamy/John Arnold Images pp14(r), 48(tmr), Alamy/N.Boyd p99(tr), Alamy/P.Dazeley p85(b), Alamy/Mary Evans p81(t), Alamy/P.Gibbs p121(t), Alamy/S&R Greenhill p124, Alamy/P.Horree p30(bl), Alamy/Imagebroker pp24(d), 50(l), Alamy/Imagestate pp82, 122(bl), Alamy/isifa Image Service s.r.o p100, Alamy/Lordprice Collection p21(br), Alamy/Iain Mas p11, Alamy/J.Marshall/Tribaleye Images p94(b), Alamy/Nagelstock p96(bm), Alamy/North Wind Picture Archive p45, Alamy/C.Pearsall p98(mr), Alamy/C.Pefley p21(tr), Alamy/C.Richardson p24(e), Alamy/Vario Images GmbH & Co K.G pp26(ml), 37(l), Alamy/N.Vereker p50(ml), Alamy/C&M Werner p79(mr), Alamy/J.West p62(r), Alamy/H.Westheim Photography p106(t); Bananastock pp17(b), 59(tl), 59(tm), 59(bm), 137; Brand X pp103(7), 110(bl), 133, 143; Comstock p110(bm); Corbis/K.C.Armstrong p46(br), Corbis/Atlantide Phototravel p96(ml), Corbis/C.Barria/Reuters p48(t), Corbis/BBC p56, Corbis/J.Beeden p95(m), Corbis/ Bettmann Archive pp6(br), 23(bl), 38(ml), 46(bl), 145, Corbis/T.Bognar p147(bl), Corbis/W.Bossen/Stock this Way p73, Corbis/Bursein Collection p30(br), Corbis/F.Cevallos p91(b), Corbis/J.Cooke p72, Corbis/R.Eshel p106(bmr), Corbis/Envision p126(b), Corbis/R.Faris p74(ml), Corbis/R.Galbraith p84(b), Corbis/G.Hall p71(b), Corbis/P.Hardy p131, Corbis/D.Houser p86(br), Corbis/Hulton Deutsch pp31(b), 81(br), 91(t), Corbis/Jagadeesh/Reuters p55(l), Corbis/L.Lefkowitz p96(br), Corbis/T.Levine/Zefa p83(t), Corbis/P.Lissac/Godong p84(t), Corbis/T.McGuire p67(t), Corbis/M.Nicholson p23(br), Corbis/S.Oskar/Zefar p86(tl), Corbis/A.Peisi/Zefa p74(mr), Corbis/O'Brien Productions p14(ml), Corbis/L.Psihoyos p68(m), Corbis/A.Redpath p122(tr), Corbis/N.Sarony p33(b), Corbis/D.Scott p24(f), Corbis/J.Sohm,Visions of America p31(t), Corbis/P.Souders pp30(tl), 48(b), Corbis/Stock Photos p20; Corbis RF pp16,24(c), 103(9), 106(tm), 106(bl), 106(bml), 106(lm), 149, 151(t); Digital Stock p92(tl); Digital Vision p112; Fotolibra/D.Breed p35(h), Fotolibra/G.Headley p94(m), Fotolibra/F.Kay p135(m), Fotolibra/J.Rich p120(t); Guardian News & Media Ltd 2006/C.Johnston p55(r); Getty Images/AFP p96(t), Getty/Aurora p10(l), Getty/Car Culture p119(t), Getty/DK Images p28, Getty Images Entertainment p47(l), Getty/Gallo Images pp42(tl), 99(tm), Getty/T.Gipstein p78(t), Getty/

Getty/N.Emmerson p86(bl), Getty/Iconica pp6(m), 26(r), 108(b), 122(tl), Getty/M.Lannen p128(t), Getty/S.McAllister p58, Getty Images News p13, Getty/Photographers Choice pp50(mr), 60(l),78(b), Getty/Photonica pp7, 12,34(l), 48(tml), Getty/Reportage p50(r), Getty/Retrofile/FPG p35(b), Getty/W.Smith p21(tl), Getty/Stone pp6(tl), 34(m), 68(b), 71(t), 81(bl), 88, 102, Getty/Taxi pp6(bl), 59(ml), 74(l), 74(r), 79(l), 86(tr), 121(b), Getty/The Image Bank pp22(b), 36(t), 70, 98(ml), 109, 122(br), Getty/ Time & Life Pictures p106(tml); Image Source pp17(t), 25, 52, 64, 83(mr), 85(t), 98(r), 103(3), 103(8), 135(b), 151(b); Joshua Tree Photography pp 9, 10(r), 19(portraits), 42(b,r), 43, 44, 60(b), 83(tl); Kobal Collection/ Anglo Enterprise/Vineyard p47(r); Lonely Planet Images/R.L'Anson p90(t), Lonely Planet/C.Polich p48(bmr); Macmillan Publishers Ltd/P. Bricknell p103(6); Mary Evans pp23(ml), 118(b), 118(h), Mary Evans/ Imagno p23(tr); Masterfile/N.Hendricksen p62(l), Masterfile/Jerzyworks p62(mr), Masterfile/M.Roman p62(ml), Moodboard p106(br); Motoring Picture Library pp 118(a), 118(g), 118(f), 119(b); Naturepl/A.Sands p92(ml), Naturepl/J.Freund p95(b); Panos Pictures/G.Akash p59(r), Panos Pictures/T.Derven p120(l), Panos/G.Pirozzi p22(l); Reproduced by permission of Penguin Books Ltd cover of The Beach by Alex Garland (First published by Viking 1996, Penguin Books 1997) copyright © Alex Garland, 1996, p95; cover of High Fidelity by Nick Hornby (Penguin Books Ltd, 2000) copyright © Nick Hornby, 2000, p37; Photoalto pp 59(m), 103(4), 103(5); Photodisc pp83(m), 92(tm), 92(tml), 92(br), 92(tr), 92(tmr), 92(bm), 92(bl); Photolibrary Group/age fotostock pp48-49(b), 84(m), 92(bl), 105(l), 147(r), Photolibrary/Arcangel Images pp35(f), 147(tl), Photolibrary/M.Bail p33(t), Photolibrary/IFA-Bilderteam p25, Photolibrary/Productions Burke/Triolo p24(b), Photolibrary/ Digital Vision p98(l), Photolibrary/F1 Online p107(l), Photolibrary/ Flirt Collection p60(t), Photolibrary/B.Foubert p21(m), Photolibrary/ Fresh Food Images pp103(2), 128(b), Photolibrary/D.Hurst p35(b), Photolibrary/Imagestate p57, Photolibrary/JTB photo pp19(m), 35(e), Photolibrary/G.Kirk p19(t), Photolibrary/R.Llewellyn p34(tm), Photolibrary/T.de Ling/Time Out p26(mr), Photolibrary/Nonstock Jupiter Images p83(b), Photolibrary/Oxford Scientific pp99(tl),105(m), Photolibrary/Photocuisine p103(1), Photolibrary/Phototake Science pp127, 129, Photolibrary/A & G Reporter p48(bml), Photolibrary/H. Rice p24(a), Photolibrary/B.Robert p32(m), Photolibrary/SGM p35(c); Photoshot p26(l), Photoshot/bilderlounge p135(t), Photoshot/J.Blackler p61, Photoshot/P.Seheult p35(d), Photoshot/Tetra Images p32(t), Photshot/WpN p14(mr), Photoshot/World Pictures p96(bl); Plainpicture/ Briljans p59(br), Plainpicture/Johner p93(tr), Plainpicture/G.Lenz p54, Plainpicture/O.Boe p14(l); Press Association/AP Photo/K.Kasahara p106(mbl); Prestwick House Literary Touchstone Classics: The Picture of Dorian Gray by Oscar Wilde, Cover Design by Larry Knox, copyright © 2005 by Prestwick House, Inc. revised 2007. Reprinted by permission. All rights reserved.p33(tr); Rex Features pp120(m), 126(t), Rex/M.L.Antonelli p40, Rex/M.Bjorkman p35(g), Rex/C.S.U Archive/Everett pp46(t), 69(t), Rex/Everett Collection pp36(bl), 38(l), 90(bl), Rex/S.Meddle p35(a), Rex/Miramax/Everett p38(mr), Rex/Paramount/Everett p49(t), Rex/J. Pepler p121(m), Rex/Sony Pictures/Everett p38(r); Robert Harding/ Occidor p90(br); Rubberball p83(mb); Sally Mais Photography p36(br); Science Photo Library p116, Science Photo Library/J.Daugherty p105(t), Science Photo Library/Gusto Images p110(t), Science Photo Library/G. Kidd p110(br), Science Photo Library/M.Kulyk p24(l), Science Photo Library/P.Psaila p68(t); The Art Archive/Musée du Louvre Paris/Gianni Dagli Orti p93(tl), Art Archive/Musée d'Orsay Paris/Alfredo Dagli Orti p31(tm), The Art Archive/Egyptian Museum Cairo/Gianni Dagli Orti p32(b), The Art Archive/Museo del Templo Mayor Mexico/Gianni Dagli Orti p30(bm), The Art Archive/National Gallery London/Eileen Tweedy p31(bm); Dr L. J. Reed, The Centre for Neuroimaging Sciences, Institute of Psychiatry, London p67(b); Topfoto/The Granger Collection pp118(e), 118(c), Topfoto/R.Voillet p107(r); Wellcome Library London p104; www.eggling.com, made in Japan by Seishin Togei Inc,distributed by Noted p114(t), Macmillan Reader, Frankenstein Corbis/Bettmann p69(b). Commissioned photography by Joshua Tree Photography pp 27, 51, 75, 99 (portraits),123; Roger Scruton p115 (portrait)

The author and publishers are grateful for permission to reprint the following copyright material: Extract from 'Six Degrees of Separation' by John Guare, copyright © John Guare 1999, reprinted by permission of Methuen Drama, an imprint of A&C Black Publishers Ltd. Extract from 'The Beach' by Alex Garland, copyright © Alex Garland 1997, reprinted by permission of Riverhead Books, an imprint of Penguin Group (USA) Inc. for website and printed World rights, excluding EEC & UK territories. Audio and printed rights for territories EEC & UK acquired from Andrew Nurnberg Agency. Adapted material from 'The Book Of Lists' by Amy Wallace and David Wallechinsky, copyright © Amy Wallace and David Wallechinsky, first published in Great Britain by Canongate Books Ltd., 14 High Street, Edinburgh, EH1 1TE, reprinted by permission of the publisher. Poem – 'Routine' by Stuart Doggett, reprinted by permission of the author. Extracted material from 'Exploring Comfort Food Preferences Across Age and Gender' copyright © Elsevier Science 2003, reprinted by permission of the publisher. Extract from 'This much I know: Rajeshwari Singh: Call-centre operator, 20, Delhi' by Amelia Gentleman, copyright © Amelia Gentleman 2006, first published in The Guardian 26.11.06, reprinted by permission of the publisher. Extract from 'Six Degrees of Separation' by John Guare, copyright © John Guare 1990, reprinted by permission of International Creative Management, Inc. USA. Extract from retold version of 'Frankenstein' by Margaret Tarner for Macmillan Readers, copyright © Margaret Tarner 2005, reprinted by permission of the publisher. Extract from retold version of 'The Picture of Dorian Gray' by F.H.Cornish for Macmillan Readers, copyright © F.H.Cornish 2005, reprinted by permission of the publisher. Material from 'Brave New Words' by Kerry Maxwell, copyright © Kerry Maxwell 2007, reprinted by permission of the author. Adapted material from 'Trade Secrets: Food & Drink' by Alexandra Fraser, copyright © Alexandra Fraser 1999, reprinted by permission of Orion Non-fiction, an imprint of Orion Publishing Group, London. Extract from 'High Fidelity' by Nick Hornby, copyright © Nick Hornby 1995, reprinted by permission of Penguin Group UK. Material from article 'The Worst Jobs in Science 2007' by Jason Daley. Screenplay Excerpt from 'Bram Stoker's Dracula' copyright © 1992 Columbia Pictures Industries, Inc. All Rights Reserved, courtesy of Columbia Pictures. Material from article 'Concerned Citizens' published in Education Citizenship and Social Justice by Associate Professor Cathie Holden at University of Exeter, copyright © Cathie Holden 2006, reprinted by permission of the author. Fitter Happier – Words and Music by Thomas Edward Yorke, Jonathan Richard, Guy Greenwood and Dan Rickwood. Warner/Chappell Music Limited (PRS). All Rights Reserved.
We are very grateful to Andy Price for generously allowing us to interview him and include extracts of his music.

Printed and bound in Thailand

2018 2017 2016 2015
20 19 18 17 16 15